Gravity's Arrow

Gravity's Arrow

Jack Mann

First Published 2019 by Fantastic Books Publishing

Cover design by Ramon Marett

ISBN (ebook): 978-1-912053-07-0
ISBN (paperback): 978-1-912053-06-3

To Farhana, my wonderful, amazing wife

ACKNOWLEDGEMENTS

All the people that read and fed back on this book, including, but I am sure not limited to, my siblings Mike, Dunc and Ro, Mum and Dad, Claire Litherand, Adnan Haque, Rozana Haque, M.A.T. Mellor, Tom Thornley, KP, Trevor Grams, Tom Brothers, Sean Giblin, John Allen, Dolly Garland, David Gullen, Gaie Sebold, Lorella McDonald, Rene Mann, Craig Pay, Eric Steele, Katya Fawl, Una Manapat and Lynne Martin. Thanks also to Ryan, Zara and Adam for behaving so well, and letting me get on with this.

PROLOGUE

The base of the giant monolith fell into shadow as the sky went dark over the plains. Worshippers, of all species of the galaxy, called out towards the towering rock in a hundred different tongues.

Struggling through the bustle and clamour, two stooped figures drew the attention of those they passed.

'Priest! Bless this blade. It has taken the lives of a hundred and eight unbelievers.'

'Let my master travel in peace,' said the acolyte, sweat trickling down his straining face. With thick arms he supported the cowl-shrouded figure beside him forward another step. 'He has more important business here than your bloodied knife.'

The worshipper bowed, and cowered back among the watching earthmen, scale-skinned yeal, and feather-faced hegel.

'Not much further,' the acolyte whispered into his master's ear.

Cries went up about them.

'Make way, a holy arbiter has come!'

'The prophet, Avithen, shall be recognised!'

'Praise be to Aten!'

Bodies moved aside, fell to their knees and prostrated themselves. As the priest and his disciple passed, the path filled in behind them. At its end they paused, confronted by a row of obelisks embedded with skulls. Crude warnings had been chiselled into the bone of some, above where eyes had long since rotted away. An open space stretched out beyond

to where the stony shoulder of the monolith jutted up through the earth.

'Master Uthrius, can you continue?' asked the acolyte.

Uthrius, bent double over his disciple's elbow, coughed into his free hand. He wiped the blood of his lungs on to his robes and gazed up at the looming rock. He steadied himself and took a stride forward. 'Wait here, brother. By the will of Aten, the rest of this journey I must make alone.'

One of the prophet's guards, standing before a barricade of spikes and traps, called out to Uthrius as he neared. 'Who approaches the sacred enclosure?'

Uthrius reached into his cloak and brought out a scroll.

Upon reading it, the fire that had burned in the guard's eyes went out. 'The prophet has been expecting you. I would be honoured to be your guide.'

Uthrius assented. He was taken to where a passage had been dug into the monolith itself. By flaming torchlight the guard led him upwards through labyrinthine caves, passing watchful bands of armed men at every turn. Just when Uthrius felt his old legs were ready to give up, the tunnels opened into expansive chambers, and light shone upon him from a bright crystal high above. More stairs waited ahead, but among these airy and well-lit rooms, overcoming them seemed less arduous. At a high place, filled with wide columns of mote-filled light, Uthrius was left standing before a table made of thick, wooden beams. Its dark, wax-stained surface was covered in worn-edged books and rolls of cracking parchment. At its far side sat a man with a long-feathered quill in his hand. There was a moment of silence as Uthrius locked eyes with him. Then the other man stood and called, 'Bring him a chair.' In a kinder voice he said to Uthrius, 'Please, sit.'

Uthrius shuddered as he lowered himself into the seat. He

accepted the bowl of tea he was offered, but did not remove his cowl.

'Dear priest,' said the man, when the servants had made themselves scarce, 'you look in pain. May I bring you something? We have many remedies in this place. The meadows south of here grow herbs for all manner of ailments.'

'Your offer is kind,' said Uthrius, 'but I wish not to numb my wits.'

The man watched the old priest drink. He sat down. 'I am Avithen. I hope, having found me, your journey has come to an end.'

'Call me Brother Uthrius,' answered the priest. 'And my journey will not be complete until I report to the Church of Elders.'

'If there is any assistance I can offer with your travels, you only have to name it.'

'My request is that you make this quick. The sooner I am on my way, the safer. There are many that would use unholy methods to accomplish what they believe are righteous ends. Many that fear I will accept your prophecy.'

'It is a sign of these dark times,' said Avithen. 'Now, praise be to our Lord, Aten, our prayers have been answered.'

The priest sipped his tea, the sound of his wheezing drowned out by the chanting outside.

'How does this work?' asked Avithen.

'I ask questions, and you answer them,' replied Uthrius.

Avithen's brow furrowed as he resettled himself into his chair. 'How will I know the outcome of their decision?'

'You are uncertain that you are a prophet.'

'I did not say this, brother!'

'I sense your fear,' said Uthrius, without looking up from his tea.

'I believe Aten has chosen me to be his voice. In him I trust.'

'But you do not trust the ageing beings of the flesh that claim a divine right to appoint his prophets.' Uthrius laughed.

Avithen bowed his head. 'I have faith in the Church of Elders, and I recognise their divine mandate.'

'Of course you do. Tell me, how did you find yourself in communication with Aten?'

'I would not say I communicate with him,' answered Avithen. 'He communicates through me. I pray, and in my prayers I find divine answers to our troubles.'

'Very interesting,' said Uthrius after several, drawn out moments. 'And what troubles are these?'

'You know of what I speak,' said Avithen, his eyes ablaze. 'Our religion is dying. Those who stay true to The Calling fill mass graves across the Near Quadrant of the galaxy. Billions more perish from hunger and disease as they flee their would-be killers. Our leaders, meanwhile, are burned alive, cast from high towers, or are torn apart so that their bones may be used to build false idols.'

'All Followers who die in Aten's name are blessed.'

'But against such evil, dying without fighting achieves nothing,' said Avithen. 'We cannot preach our truth to the galaxy if we no longer exist! How are the sheep to shepherd themselves without Aten's word to guide them?'

'Have faith,' said Uthrius. 'Trust in Aten, our Lord.'

'I do so absolutely, and now our Lord has spoken.' Avithen pointed to himself. 'There is no price too high to pay for the salvation of the galaxy. In this age that price is the blood of those who would destroy us.'

Uthrius bowed his head. 'And we will soon become all that we abhor in our enemies.' He took another sip of his tea. 'Among the planets and continents laid to waste by your armies were the lands where I was raised. My family, and all those I knew in my youth, are dead.'

Avithen stared at the priest for a while. 'I am so sorry. I did not know I had caused you such loss.'

'They belonged to a misguided people,' said Uthrius, 'but what they needed was our help. You, however, have sent them to their maker unready. I only pray that Aten had mercy on their souls.'

'I will pray to Aten. Our Lord will show them leniency.'

'Do you pray for all your victims?' asked Uthrius. 'You must be busy.'

'My warriors are Aten's tool against the tyranny that would wipe his Followers from the galaxy. My hold over them grows. Such atrocities can be prevented and controlled.'

'You are no general,' muttered Uthrius.

'If Aten wishes it, I will be.'

The priest said nothing, but his eyes burned with contempt.

'Why did they send you?' asked Avithen. 'You have nothing but hatred for me.'

'Your place is not to question our methods,' said Uthrius. 'How many of your Followers, might I ask, know that you have had no visions, heard no voices and experienced no unexpected command to preach as you have done?'

'Very few, though I have not claimed otherwise.'

'Interesting.' Uthrius' voice resonated with contempt. 'It would seem that reason, rather than revelation, has guided you to your conclusions. Reason is a tool for mortals – unfit for the divining of Aten's intentions.'

'A tool given us by Aten, however imperfect it may be, so that we can know his wishes,' said Avithen.

'Know you nothing of ancient history?' asked the priest. 'Long ago, when the Ancients ruled the galaxy in the golden age, people followed their reasoning, even when it led them further and further from the teachings of Aten, our Lord. And so it was that their punishment was terrible, and the galaxy was wiped near clean of life.'

'The Ancients you speak of dared to think they understood Aten,' said Avithen. 'It was their arrogance that Aten punished with the Great Dying.'

'That is your interpretation,' said Uthrius. 'It is not mine. Beware reason and where it takes you.'

'So be it,' said Avithen, 'but I shall not entertain you with stories of visions I never saw, or voices I never heard.'

Uthrius nodded. 'And without such confirmation, what, then, will you conclude when you are branded a liar? How, then, will you justify all you have done, and the suffering and death you have brought upon his creation?'

'I shall conclude that Aten had spoken, but the galaxy was not listening.'

'And upon ignoring our Lord's message, all the galaxy would be damned to the swamps of hell?'

'If we had been guaranteed our salvation,' said Avithen, 'then we need not have concerned ourselves with finding it.'

Uthrius gave no response to this, but continued to watch Avithen.

Avithen's breathing slowed, his gaze darting across the priest's face, desperate now to guess the older man's thoughts.

'Master!' A female acolyte appeared at the door, hesitating when she saw Uthrius sitting opposite Avithen. 'They are calling for you again. They ask for you to lead them in prayer.'

Avithen looked past her to the large chamber beyond. Cool air came from there, carrying the calls of the horde outside. 'My followers await.'

Uthrius seemed to shrink in size. 'Go to them,' he said, his voice feeble. He watched the prophet stand, adjust his robes and walk past the messenger. The chants outside became jubilant shouts, eclipsed by rising song. Uthrius listened in silence, and then he prayed.

PART 1

CHAPTER 1

Fhiro kept his eyes open, gazing over his father's shoulder, as they plummeted into a sinking column of air over the Thylan Ridge. A surge of terror charged through him as his stomach rode up into his chest. Despite the aching bones in his fingers, he gripped harder on the chains connecting him to Siwular, the giant bird they rode, while his father, Oljon, grappled with the reins to hold them steady.

Beneath them a river snaked along the bottom of the chasm, buried in shadow. Siwular beat her wings to maintain altitude as she passed high above it, but when they neared the steep mountains rising up on its far side, the eddies and currents blasted skywards. Siwular spread her wings, surfing over them. Higher they went, until Fhiro felt his back exposed to the warmth of the morning sun.

The ocean came into view as they soared past the steep crags at the far side of the ridge. Underneath them, rocky terrain dropped away towards the grassy foothills guarding the shore. Oljon adjusted the reins. Seeing his father do this, Fhiro felt the fear within him mingling with growing excitement. He bared his teeth against the wind and grinned. His father's wrists twitched, and then they were in a dive, plunging into the expanse of air below.

Fhiro's head jolted against the inside of his helmet. Rushing air beat his face.

Oljon pulled the reins taut. Siwular unfurled herself into a glide, only a short height above the sloping hilltops. The air roared. The tall grass between the bushes was so close that

Fhiro could see the individual blades blasted aside in their wake. Then the grass gave way to sand dunes racing under them.

Fhiro wanted it to last forever.

'Slow now!' called Oljon, pulling on the reins again.

The bird tilted her wings, caught the air and slowed, forcing Fhiro into her back. She floated down to the landing area, slowing further before her feet touched the sand and brought them to a halt. Then she lowered her body.

Fhiro removed his goggles and slid to the ground. Two other saddled, feathered beasts stood proud and stern before him. Beyond them the laboratory entrance, air vents poking through its downward-sloping roof, cut the horizon like a giant knife in the sand. Wording on the door warned *Keep out, authorised staff only*. Etched into the frame above was 'ISNAS', declaring the premises property of the Institute for the Study of Native Andelic Species.

Fhiro helped Oljon secure Siwular to one of the posts, pausing when he caught sight of a shadow on the mountains they had just crossed. He squinted into the sky, his heart pounding, as he searched for its source amid the clouds. Then, as he discerned the narrow shape of a windeater, he relaxed. What detail he could not confirm with his eyes he imagined; rows of long, thin, fin-like wings that stretched the length of its body, and a muzzle-shaped mouth with broad, sharp teeth. He observed its progress along the range of peaks, its body rippling as it weaved through the racing winds. Devouring the airplankton in its path, its eyes watched for unwary birds struggling in the currents.

'You've seen windeaters before,' remarked Oljon.

'I thought it was the wregg.' Fhiro finished wrapping chain about the hooks on the post.

'The wregg,' muttered Oljon, shaking his head. 'Those

deluded crones have better things to do than trouble my twelve-year-old son with such nonsense.'

'I bet you'd look twice too,' said Fhiro.

'The God of The Calling does not send rare pestilence-ridden birds to warn his people,' said Oljon. 'Nor does he save us by revealing ancient powerful artefacts on distant planets. He speaks through prophets. If he so wishes, another will appear.'

'We'll need more than another prophet to save us now.'

'Forget the Creedate,' said Oljon. 'Concern that overactive mind of yours with matters closer to home.' He gathered some feed into his palm and opened it before the bird's face. Siwular reached forward and buried her beak into his glove. 'This business with your old friend Hubbort, for instance.' His palm empty, Oljon strode towards the laboratory entrance.

'What business?'

'I know what you're thinking.' As Oljon opened the door, he turned to look into his son's eyes. 'If he gets up to any mischief, you tell us, or one of the other parents, understand? There's to be no fighting.'

Fhiro frowned but said nothing.

'I didn't teach you those skills so that you could police the other children.' Oljon descended the steps into the dark laboratory interior.

'Hubbort doesn't listen.' Fhiro closed the door behind them. He took his activator out of his pocket and swiped the crystal beside him. Tiny lumia-crystals along the walls lit up. 'You taught him too, once.'

'All the more reason to avoid getting into a fight,' said Oljon. 'He's a fair bit taller than you are, too. Don't underestimate the importance of weight and reach.'

'I've got Dorrick to remind me of that.'

Oljon laughed. 'You'll miss your brother when he leaves.'

Fhiro followed in silence. He resented the assumption that he would weep and mourn like the rest of them when Dorrick finally left home. As he imagined the responsibility that day would bring him, he tapped his chest to check the book he was returning to Professor Millorn was still in his pocket. Then he hurried down the stairs to catch up.

Thirty steps down, beneath the surface of the beach, Oljon pushed open a door. He ruffled Fhiro's hair. 'Pay attention, all right? A lot of work to be done today.'

'Yes, Pa,' said Fhiro.

Oljon smiled, then entered his office.

Fhiro continued his descent to the bottom of the stairs. There he turned into the ocean-view chamber, and stared out through the glass. The visibility was excellent today. Three-legged snakes and aqua frogs flurried to and fro but, as always, Fhiro's attention was stolen away from such creatures by the bright-coloured coral bed, which stretched out far before him, as clear as a flower-filled field under the noon sun. The contrast between the diversity and beauty beneath the sea, and the bland appearance of the beach above, returned him to his recurrent fantasy of turning into a strafer-fish, or even better, one of the sentient pichi; the native aquatic creatures that the laboratory had been built to study.

'Beautiful day, isn't it?'

Fhiro recognised Ereput's voice from beside him. As with all yeal that spoke Galactic, it was indistinguishable from that of an earthman. 'I just wish I could be out there in it,' Fhiro replied.

'Well we're too busy for any of that today,' said Ereput. Then he blinked, his inner eyelids closing into vertical slits, and the outer lids shutting and opening like those of an earthman, creasing the surrounding skin so that the tiny, grain-sized scales became visible. 'Yetco dropped off scrolls two minutes

ago.' Ereput pulled Fhiro's sleeve and led him towards the centre of the large chamber.

'Already?' Fhiro shook free his arm as he followed Ereput. 'I've got to tend the hapgees and oliks in the mills. We won't get much work done without air and water.'

'They'll be running a while yet,' said Ereput. 'Prof wants translating to take priority. She's expecting to hear from headquarters at any moment.'

They reached the workspace in the centre of the chamber. A long scroll, dripping with seawater, was draped over it. Characters, in black ink, worked their way from the bottom to the top of the page.

Fhiro helped Ereput to cut the scroll into sections. 'He must have been working on this all night.'

'Poor guy,' said Ereput. 'How different he wrote when we first brought him here.'

Fhiro considered that Yetco's writings had only changed in the last few days. The pichis from the Eastern shores of the continent had come here several years ago, with the assistance of ISNAS, to explore this western ocean. There was jubilation and excitement when, last month, Yetco and his colleagues made contact with their evolutionary cousins, but something had gone wrong. The natives had attacked, and only Yetco and a few guards survived.

The scroll now divided and labelled, Ereput handed Fhiro a section. 'Tell me when you've finished.'

Fhiro went to his desk and set to work translating the pichi script. Yetco had written it to his friends, relatives and colleagues back home in the East. It started the same as all the recent messages Fhiro had translated. Half way through, though, there was a noticeable change in its tone.

Fhiro decided to show Ereput, but on his way to the screen caught sight of Yetco. Two and a half metres tall, the leader of

the pichi expedition to the West withdrew from the base of the screen, amidst a shower of rising bubbles. Reflected sunrays danced off his shell-encased limbs, and glimmered through his translucent fins. Behind him two more pichis carried spears and ligament-bound contraptions of coral-bone.

Ereput pulled a lever within the ocean-view chamber. Fhiro put down the scroll he had been working on and ran to assist Ereput pulling the drawer through, causing water to spill all over the floor. Ereput pulled out the scroll and unravelled it while Fhiro forced the drawer shut again.

'Another one?' asked Fhiro.

'Good to see you're keeping up.'

'I keep having to look up the words like "guilt" and "despair",' said Fhiro.

'He thinks he should have been captured too,' said Ereput. 'Isn't his behaviour amazing?' The yeal's inner eyelids were retracted to each side further than usual.

Fhiro wondered how Ereput, who always seemed like a very thoughtful individual, could look past the gravity of Yetco's misery and replace it with scientific zeal. Yeals were known to be at least as sensitive as earthmen in these matters.

'We're witnessing him process a significant event for him, and his species,' Ereput continued. 'This response of writing in such volume is not one I'd ever expected. Especially given that he doesn't seem to be talking to his guards about this.'

'If our conclusions about their hierarchies and interclass religious practices are correct,' interjected Professor Millorn, who appeared beside them, 'the warriors do not grieve in the same way.' She shook her head. 'I believe he is recording this so that others of the Depths caste, to which he belongs, might read it and mourn with him later.'

'He also wants to kill them all,' said Fhiro. 'Says his

evolutionary cousins are not his brothers. That they only understand threat and conflict.'

Ereput paused, glanced at Millorn, and then looked at Fhiro again. 'It really says that?'

Fhiro showed them the section of scroll, and Ereput took it from him.

'If only we could build a haven for this laboratory, with which to spy out the depths of this ocean,' said Millorn, peering through the screen.

'As you never stop telling us,' said Ereput, without looking up from the scroll he was reading. 'I doubt this planet was ever blessed with the presence of sorcery.'

'It would cost far too much to maintain, of course,' continued Millorn, as though Ereput had not spoken. 'Have you ever seen the powers of sorcery, Fhiro?'

'No,' grumbled Fhiro.

'Of course not,' continued Millorn, 'but I have.' She turned away, searching the sea, just as Fhiro's eyes rolled in their sockets. 'Sight with such clarity, knowledge of such breadth, life eternal!' She stroked her chin. 'You know, there was once an ocean planet with a haven hidden deep underwater. A primitive one, mind you, considering its inhabitants would have to rebuild its sorcery-circuits every time a crystal came near. I wonder if it still exists. Such a fragile thing, I suspect not.'

'Dear me,' said Ereput, now finished reading. 'I hope this isn't some gross, cross-culture driven misunderstanding.'

Fhiro saw Yetco through the screen, drifting close to its upper edge, watching them. 'Well if Yetco wants war,' he said, 'the Creedate will probably bring it here long before the oceans reunite the western pichis with the eastern ones.'

'Let's please not talk about the Creedate,' said Ereput.

Yetco retreated a little, then turned and propelled himself away with a thrust of his finned legs.

'Professor,' said Fhiro, suddenly remembering something, 'I've got that book you lent me.' He took it out of his pocket.

'*Meditations on Representation*?' she asked. 'Finished it?'

'I liked the beginning of it,' said Fhiro, handing it to her.

Millorn laughed. 'You liked the questions, but not the answers, then?'

'The author is renowned for his insight into where philosophy meets spirituality,' said Ereput. 'Perhaps give it another read when you're older.'

Fhiro frowned, wondering how different his way of thinking would be when he grew up. 'The answers he gave all seemed …'

'Baseless.' Millorn finished his sentence.

Fhiro noticed Ereput's scales flutter, something that yeal did when their emotions were heightened. Fhiro had not wanted to embarrass Ereput.

'I agree with you,' said Millorn. 'The questions at the beginning were not original either. They have been asked by many over the ages, but that does not make them any less important.' She smiled and patted his head. 'Keep your mind open. Keep asking questions. And if you find any answers, be sure to come tell them to me.' She winked.

Fhiro smiled back, but doubted he would be able to think of anything to help someone as wise as Professor Millorn. He noticed Ereput was making his way towards the other end of the ocean-view chamber. 'Professor,' he asked, 'what do you think about the discovery in the old Smugglers' Union?'

Millorn sighed. 'Fhiro, it's all right to be afraid. I mean, who isn't? But rumours like these, about fanciful powerful artefacts, are typical of times like ours. Nothing kills reason faster than fear does.'

Fhiro felt foolish for asking.

Ereput returned from the far side of the chamber. 'I am sure I just saw something move out there.'

'A Gruthor-eel?' asked Fhiro.

'I don't think it was that big.'

'It's probably about time we ordered some deterrence pheromones for this place,' said Millorn. 'I'll have to ask–'

A loud noise, like the grinding of heavy stones, rocked the laboratory.

Fhiro stared as a boulder tumbled back to the ocean bed from the upper-left corner of the screen. Where it had been struck, great cracks appeared in the glass. Expanding, like slow forks of lightning, they crossed the expanse of the screen, some thin, some deep. Jets of water spurted through into the chamber.

Fhiro was frozen to the spot.

'The pressure will cave it in,' cried Ereput. 'Run!'

Fhiro turned on his heels and sprinted. His insides felt cold and twisted, as though his intestines were filling with ice and tying themselves in knots. He could feel the weight of the sea outside, trying to force its way through the screen.

Ereput raced past him.

His father was upstairs. Did he know? Could he be warned?

The rush of water jetting into the room rose to a roar. Fhiro glanced back and saw Millorn slip and land on her elbows. He hesitated. More horizontal fountains erupted into the chamber.

The professor struggled to get to her feet.

'Get up!' Fhiro cried.

The bursting of water through the cracks multiplied into a screeching torrent.

Fhiro felt a strong hand grip his collar. Then the material was choking his neck as he accelerated towards the stairs. The hand let go, and he travelled a few feet before his feet made contact with the floor again. When they did he half stumbled, half ran to the first step.

A deep, shrieking blast pulsed into the room. It shook Fhiro down to his bones as it passed through him, shredding the air around him.

The ocean was coming.

His mind snapped into focus, and he leapt straight to the third step. He could sense the unstoppable weight of the water bearing down towards him. He would outrun it. He had to. He cleared two steps more with his second jump. The assault on his ears increased, its violence relentless. He leapt forwards again.

Ice cold wetness slammed in and enveloped him. Like a rag doll, he was dragged upwards and forwards.

He reached out, trying to clutch or grip or steer himself, but his efforts were wasted against nature's might. Tossed and scraped against the walls he battled the urge to scream out what precious air his lungs still carried.

Then, as he twisted and spun, pain exploded in his head as it slammed against metal.

CHAPTER 2

'Fhiro!'

'Ma?' Fhiro opened his eyes. He saw his father, his mother Hanu, his older brother Dorrick and his little sister Chinda, leaning over him with a mix of terror and relief on their faces. Above them the dark sky was filled with stars. He felt sand against the skin of his hands. 'What happened?'

Hanu gripped him so tight Fhiro thought he would die. 'Thank Aten,' she whispered.

Oljon clasped his shoulder and smiled. Then he turned and shouted, 'Doctor Lutwi, he's awake!'

A hegel, her facial feathers dyed green, bustled over Fhiro. 'Fhiro, my boy, glad to see you up.'

'What time is it?' Fhiro asked, conscious of how dark it was.

'You must be examined,' flustered Lutwi. 'Can you stand?'

'Go on, son,' said Oljon, letting go of him.

His mother was much slower to release him.

Fhiro struggled up, brushing damp sand out of his clothes. He was on the beach, but the sight of so many fires, people shouting orders to each other, and huge objects being dragged towards the sea, astonished him. Dr Lutwi obstructed the view by shining an activated lumia-crystal into his eyes. As he forced himself to look at the light, he noticed his parents whispering, and tried to eavesdrop.

'He requested you,' said Oljon.

'He'll wait until we know Fhiro's all right,' said Hanu.

The doctor's instructions grew increasingly complex and

strange. 'All right, now push against my hands. Good. Now pull. Now keep your wrists straight.'

Fhiro was relieved she had filed down her talons. When the parade of bizarre exercises and questions were complete, he expected to see his older brother in fits of laughter, but Dorrick's face was solemn. Even Chinda, his little sister, looked subdued as she paced about on her heels, making dents in the sand.

Relief flooded Lutwi's face. 'Excellent,' she said. She peered over Fhiro's head. 'That is quite a bruise on your crown.'

'Ow!'

'Sorry, I had to check it.'

'Is he all right?' asked Hanu.

'Yes, Reverend sister,' said Lutwi. 'Without a visit to the shrouded havens there is nothing more I can test for. Just keep a close eye on him.'

Hanu rushed to embrace her son again, but with twice as much force as the first time. Soon Oljon and Dorrick joined her. Then Fhiro felt Chinda's arms grab his waist.

'Don't do that to us again,' said Hanu into his ear.

'That's a tough head you've inherited,' said Oljon.

'Shame there's nothing in it,' said Dorrick.

Fhiro gave his brother a shove, sending him backwards on to the sand. However, his sister also tumbled over.

'Enough messing about.' Hanu let go and bent down to pick Chinda up.

'Idiots,' said Chinda.

A hooded man appeared, bowed to Hanu, and spoke in hushed tones.

Witnessing this, Dorrick, who had been poised to leap on to Fhiro, lowered his arms.

Hanu brushed grains of sand from her daughter's hair. 'Very well.' She hugged Fhiro one more time. 'Don't ever scare me

like that again, all right?' She was smiling, but Fhiro could see there were tears in her eyes. She kissed his forehead, then turned and strode down the beach.

Fhiro saw a great fire, pouring light into the sky, in the direction his mother was heading. Men and women, in postures of prayer, were silhouetted against it. Fhiro looked past the flames and across the sea. Above, its rays reflected off the waves, Andelic's second moon glowed with pride. 'Where's Ma going?'

'To lead the ascension rites for Millorn,' said Oljon.

Fhiro bowed his head. Part of him had already known.

'Are you all right, son?'

Fhiro nodded, though he felt his own tears brewing. He thought about Millorn's husband. 'How's uncle Rorb? Is Ereput all right?'

'Ereput is fine,' said Oljon, forcing a smile. 'Rorb is coping as well as he might. Would you like to pay your respects to your old master?'

'I'd talk to Rorb,' Fhiro said, 'if he'd want me to.'

'He's by the fire.'

Seeing that Dorrick was distracted by a conversation with Chinda, Fhiro seized the moment to wipe his eyes without his brother noticing. 'I remember being underwater,' he said. 'How'd I get here?' He turned and saw the laboratory entrance, its straight-edged frame jutting out of the sand above the high tide mark. Silent, stirring shadows surrounded it. He blinked. Siwular, his family's bird, rustled her blue and golden wings near the doorway close to the birds owned by Millorn and Ereput. However, an array of larger beasts with carriages strapped to their backs surrounded them. Two were six-eyed gully-hawks; their bellies islands of faded red within coats of grey. Another three were the familiar, earth-coloured transport marcrows. Towering over them all, though, were

four beakless creatures with giant wings covered in feather-like scales, curled under their breasts. 'Where did everyone fly here from?'

'To answer your first question,' said Oljon, 'Ereput and I dragged you from the water before you'd a chance to breathe it in. As for the second, the four woada voyaged here across the continent from ISNAS headquarters in Talucia. The other birds were sent by the mayor after he heard what had happened.'

'One of the marcrows stopped by Chimahess to pick us up,' said Dorrick.

'Woada,' said Fhiro. 'They're huge!'

Dorrick nodded. 'But they don't seem very bird-like.'

'They aren't birds,' said Fhiro.

'They have big wings, though,' said Chinda. 'They stirred up a proper sandstorm when they got here.'

'Most creatures the sorcerers conjured were made from the essence of something similar,' said Dorrick. 'The baxten look like oversized armoured hegelian oxen; oliks look like flattened earthen rhinos; and garglethiders resemble a demonised form of something on the recci evolutionary tree. Woada don't look like anything.'

'Why would sorcerers have made the garglethiders?' asked Fhiro.

'Warfare?' suggested Dorrick, shrugging.

'Millorn might have known,' said Fhiro. 'She was from a haven.' He blinked hard.

'It's all right, son.' Oljon put his hand on Fhiro's shoulder and pulled him nearer.

'Was Millorn a sorcerer?' asked Fhiro.

'I never really thought about it,' said Oljon. 'I don't think her works ever concerned the application of sorcery to any great extent.'

Fhiro had known, and not known, the professor for years.

He saw in his mind the old woman sitting on her chair and stirring her tea, gazing into the ocean just as Fhiro loved to do. Approachable in all matters of knowledge, Millorn's soul was ever somewhere else, distant. 'What happened in the ocean-view chamber?'

'Western pichis,' said Oljon. 'We don't understand why they're so hostile. They launched that boulder and shattered the screen.'

'Is Yetco all right?' Fhiro's voice was hopeful.

'He is now,' said Oljon. 'Those woada carried water-filled containers full of pichi warriors from the East. They've secured the shallows around here.'

'So much for the peaceful ambassadorial mission,' said Dorrick. 'I never expected any of us to get hurt.' He paused and pointed. 'Someone's coming.'

Against the backdrop of the beach, drenched in darkness but for the scattered camp fires over which fish roasted and water boiled, a shadowy form grew in size as it approached. Fhiro started to discern the limbs and faces of its individual constituents as it came near. At the front of the crowd was a crooked figure, her hair matted and grey, her skin weathered and worn. The flames from Millorn's ascension ritual illuminated her face with a flickering orange light.

'The child has survived,' said the Crone. Those behind her murmured to one another and stared at Fhiro, his siblings and his father.

Fhiro did not like the way the crone looked at him.

'Leave us,' said Oljon. 'Our survival is no sign from Aten.'

'Aten!' the crone cackled. 'Those that come to destroy us call their God by that name. If Aten exists, he has long abandoned us. Only the ancient ways are left now, and the signs are clear. Only by flight might our lives be saved from the Creedate.'

'Many of us are here after fleeing the Creedate already.'

Oljon drew himself up. 'Perhaps you have not realised, but there is nowhere left to fly to. Your preaching undermines the resolve of our people, and thus only serves the enemy.'

'Hah!' The crone pointed at Oljon. 'You misguided fool. Your stubbornness will be your death. Your head shall join those of all that resist them, piled up into the towering mountains of rotting skulls they build wherever they go. There, if you are fortunate, your lifeless eyes might gaze upon this precious home of yours, until carrion visit you with their sharp beaks.'

'Stubbornness in the face of lunacy has always been a virtue of mine,' said Oljon.

Some of those that had accompanied the crone looked affronted by this, and Fhiro wondered if there was any risk that they might become violent. His father, though, seemed unconcerned.

'Ignore the warnings at your peril,' said the crone. 'Marallel's armies are invincible. We must pray to the Hill-spirits for deliverance. Even now there are signs of things to come. Powerful weapons are being unearthed far from here, that might draw away his eye.'

'Fear clouds your thinking,' said Oljon. 'Do not entrust your destiny to wild hopes outside your control.'

'Excuse me,' said a familiar voice.

Fhiro turned to see Ereput walking towards the crone. By his side was a broad-shouldered earthman wearing an embroidered cloak.

'Please leave these people alone,' said Ereput. 'Oljon's had a rough day. The last thing he needs are your nightmarish visions of the future.'

The crone's eyes narrowed. 'May the Hill-spirits forgive your arrogance.' She disappeared into the crowd that had followed her, as it shuffled away into the darkness.

'Thanks, Ereput,' said Oljon.

'No problem old friend,' said the yeal, grinning. He turned to the other earthman. 'This is Oljon himself, and these are his children: Dorrick, Fhiro, and little Chinda.'

'I'm not little,' said Chinda, giving her brothers a stern look. 'And I'm smarter than these morons. I can't even see how we're related sometimes.'

The broad-shouldered earthman looked somewhat startled. Then he smiled and offered his hand to Oljon. 'Lirai Loskin, head of security for the Institute for the Study of Native Andelic Species. Ereput here has been telling me what you did for our clients. Most brave of you!'

'Merely doing my duty,' said Oljon.

'A terrible shame it's come to this,' said Ereput.

'And a tragic loss in Millorn,' said Lirai. 'I gather we recruited her from a haven.'

'Where she might have lived forever, if she so chose to,' said Ereput.

'She made her choices,' said Oljon. 'She was not one to have regrets.'

'Indeed.' Lirai's eyes met with Oljon's. 'I've not heard how we recruited you, though. Fortune finds unusual times to smile upon us; I would not have expected such heroism from the director of logistics and security at the western lab.'

'Ereput was at least as heroic,' said Oljon, slapping the yeal on the back.

'After your inspirational words, who wouldn't be?' Ereput laughed.

'A great speaker, too?' Lirai looked impressed. 'Perhaps the two of you have talents that might be better put to use elsewhere? We have plenty of positions suited to those with leadership qualities at headquarters in Talucia.'

Ereput's eyes lit up, but Oljon betrayed no sign of elation.

'This place has become my home,' said Oljon. He rested his hand on Dorrick's shoulder. 'Maybe when all my children have come of age I'd consider it.'

Lirai forced a smile. 'Well perhaps regular visits, then, to remind those colleagues of yours you rarely see, of the great people counted among their numbers?'

'Pa,' said Fhiro, tugging at Oljon's sleeve. 'What did you do?'

Instead of answering, Oljon's eyes glazed over a little. Fhiro could not read minds, but he realised his father was choosing his words. There were details his father did not want him to know.

'Following the attack that cost Millorn her life,' said Lirai, 'your father persuaded Ereput, here, to dive back into the sea with him, grab the biosuits and rifles, and fight off the western pichis before they could harm Yetco. That's enough selfless bravery and skill to warrant the highest of accolades ISNAS can offer.'

Fhiro was speechless. He was banned from taking action against Hubbort at school, but his father was allowed to risk his life to save Yetco? No wonder his father seemed irked, all of a sudden.

'What if the pichis grow envious of our military capabilities?' asked Dorrick. 'None of their guards survived.'

'Really,' said Oljon to Lirai, 'we were merely helping a friend in need.'

'Say what you will,' said Lirai. 'However, I do have a report to write for my superiors. Ereput informed me of his own underwater combat training, far from here, during his national service as a youth in the Sublepi republic. Was it a similar story for you? I gather you also immigrated here, years ago.'

'Yes,' said Oljon. 'A similar story. I was born coreward.'

'Where, might I ask?'

'It was actually one of the Creedate heartworlds,' said Oljon, with a lowered voice, 'but I'd rather that were not widely known.'

'Do you think Marallel will show any discrimination if the fanatical horde he rules ever conquers this place?' asked Lirai. 'You are a more optimistic man than I.'

'Marallel,' said Oljon, shaking his head. 'Who can predict what he'll do. I'd still rather not heighten his hatred of me and mine.'

Ereput nodded, his smile fading.

'Well, the story of today will soon be common knowledge around here,' said Lirai. 'Let us seize from it what opportunity we can. A few more details for my report, to sate the curiosity of my superiors, if you will. Tell me, at least, the planet you came from.'

'For the sake of your report only,' said Oljon. 'It was Essera.'

'Essera!' Lirai's eyes lit up. 'I heard it is very beautiful.'

'It is, and I don't deny that I miss it dearly.'

'So how long ago was that?' Lirai took a step back and studied Oljon. 'I would have guessed your age to be somewhere between forty and forty-five.'

A slight smile crossed Oljon's face at this, but he said nothing.

'Your children were raised here, I gather, so you must have left Essera at least fifteen years ago.' Lirai's voice lost a little of its cheer. 'That would place you within the Creedate in Thurgon's time. Before the death of the prophet.'

Fhiro found Lirai's probing questions annoying. Could this idiot not take a hint? At the same time, he wanted to hear the answers probably even more than Lirai did.

Oljon blinked. 'Correct. We could not have timed our departure any better. I gather it became impossible to escape after those events.'

Lirai nodded. 'An evil time, though a respite for the enemies of the Creedate, as its armies fell upon one another, until Marallel established his leadership.'

'Indeed,' said Oljon. 'Are you an exile yourself? How is it you came to live on Andelic?'

'I was from elsewhere in the Luwol Federation,' said Lirai, looking away, 'from Gewrat. I had studied xeno-zoology and was good with alien languages …'

Fhiro had heard enough. He was starting to boil with anger at his father's hypocrisy, his temper stoked by Lirai's persistent questions. Fury built within him like a supernova in a pressure cooker.

Before he exploded, he turned and marched away, hearing Lirai break off mid sentence to say, 'Oljon, where is your son going?'

'Fhiro!'

Ignoring his father's shout, Fhiro stomped on without turning. He did not slow down until he was certain no one had followed him. He was furious at his father. Furious at Lirai. He was even angry at the professor; she had no right to die. There was too much she had yet to teach him.

He stood among the giant boulders and deep rock pools that bordered the ocean near the laboratory. A school of tiny glow fish swam close to the surface for an instant. Then, like a collection of lumia-crystals scattered in the water, their brightness dimmed as they returned to the depths.

The professor. He could not be angry at her. She had always been good to him. Taught him and Dorrick when Andelic's state-funded education system would not. Memories of her swarmed his mind. She had been alive just moments ago, and now she was lost to the galaxy forever.

No longer afraid that his brother might see him, Fhiro wept.

He cried for Millorn and her husband. The small creatures

that circulated air and water into the laboratory from outside were also forgotten victims of this tragedy, and he shed tears for them as well.

He retraced his steps to the sandy shore and walked until the sounds from the camp were just audible over the soft song of the sea. He took off his shoes and lay down, his feet splashed by the occasional surge of surf. Already damp and dirty, he did not care about the sand sticking to his hair and clothes.

Eventually his tears slowed, and then dried. Time passed as he lay on the sand, and his anger started to grow again. He welcomed it to the forefront of his mind. It was a relief from sadness. It energised him. Unlike before, it was now focused. One person stood out as the primary source of his frustration.

His father's decision to rescue Yetco had been a huge unnecessary risk. Millorn's demise caused a fraction of the grief he felt when he imagined losing his father.

His fury threatened to incinerate every fibre of his soul.

Lying a distance away from the fires and lamps, the stars shining in the sky above him were clear to see. He beheld the galaxy, its bright arms stretching outwards from the glowing mass of light at its centre, turning with imperceptible slowness. Andelic was far from its core, so all but its outermost periphery was within his field of view. Heroic, mysterious and evil legends were brought alive in his mind as he imagined the worlds they were born in: The Empire of Kartna, the Jashpuri Republic, the Kingdom of the Old Man, and the realms of the lizardmen, the recci and the hoppers. He longed to see them for himself, but that could never happen. All routes went through space controlled by the Creedate, the unstoppable religious empire, founded on the teachings of the false prophet, Avithen.

'Fhiro?' Dorrick's footsteps came closer, discernible over the noise of the waves.

Fhiro did not answer.

'Father sent me to look for you.' Dorrick took his shoe off and sampled the wet sand with his foot before deciding to sit down. 'What are you doing?'

Fhiro shrugged.

'I ran into Uncle Rorb,' Dorrick continued.

'He's not our uncle,' said Fhiro.

'His wife just died,' said Dorrick, venom in his voice. 'I know you're angry, Fhiro, but that's worse than just rude.'

'Sorry,' said Fhiro. 'Didn't mean that. Not … not thinking straight.' No excuse, he thought.

'You really don't deserve this,' said Dorrick.

'Deserve what?'

Dorrick took from his pocket a palm-sized device, made of four crystals bound by thick, metal wire. He took out his activator and tapped it. The crystals released a faint glow, and the device moved, by itself, in his hand.

'Your gravi-trap?' Fhiro sat up and stared.

'Rorb promised to give me another if I gave you mine.' Dorrick lowered his hand and the gravi-trap bounced, then hovered, then bounced again, but in a way Fhiro had not expected. 'He thought it might cheer you up.' Dorrick placed it into Fhiro's outstretched palm. 'Millorn gave it to me when she said there was nothing left for her to teach me, though I doubt that was true.'

'Thank you … I mean, thank him.'

'Thank him yourself, you ungrateful slug.'

'I'm sorry,' said Fhiro. 'Didn't mean to sound like such a … ' He felt devastated about Millorn, but that was not something he could talk to his brother about. Not now.

Dorrick gazed out at the ocean, and then up to the stars. 'ISNAS are going to throw an event in Kadgel.' He picked up a clump of sand and threw it far into the sea.

'About today?' asked Fhiro.

'Yes,' said Dorrick.

'I'd like to pay my respects to Millorn,' said Fhiro, 'but I'm leaving if they start praising Pa.'

Dorrick sighed. 'Ungrateful and self-obsessed. That's you, basically.'

'I can't let it go,' said Fhiro. 'Tells us one thing, does another.'

'So you'll what ...? Walk out on to the streets of Kadgel, half-way through, at night?'

Fhiro deactivated the gravi-trap; its glow melted away and the crystals collapsed closer to one another. 'After he saved me he should have stayed on the beach.'

'And looked after you while Yetco got killed?' asked Dorrick.

'Pa could have got killed,' said Fhiro. 'He had no idea that the western pichis were as primitive as the eastern ones. No idea they'd be sending spears and arrows at him while he gunned them down with a rifle. Assuming that's what happened.'

'That's what it sounds like,' said Dorrick. 'That Lirai fellow thinks it will be great for the relationship between the starfaring species of Andelic and its native water-dwellers.'

'That Lirai's too nosy for his own good,' grumbled Fhiro.

'Arrogant too,' muttered Dorrick.

'I always liked Yetco,' said Fhiro, 'but even if the pichis were people, only Yetco was still alive by the time Pa and Ereput decided to risk both their lives.'

'Wasn't it this sort of behaviour that had Pa strike out across the countryside, searching for you and your friends, after you were kidnapped?'

'I was his son. He was rescuing his son.' Fhiro hammered a crater into the sand. 'He's supposed to be there for us. You've come of age now, so maybe it doesn't matter to you.'

Dorrick lay down on the wet sand, his arms stretched out

behind his head. 'Well I'm glad they saved Yetco. Wish I could have been there to help, but I was miles away. I was miles away, and useless.'

'If you don't want to feel useless,' said Fhiro, 'stop dithering about which force you want to join, and sign up with any of them.'

'It's not that simple!' Dorrick sat up and glared at him. 'Which would you join, then? You're coming of age in two years. Got it all worked out, have you?'

'Calm down!' said Fhiro. 'Don't blame you for being scared. I hate the idea of rushing out to–'

Dorrick had one hand to Fhiro's throat, and the other balled into a fist. 'Don't *dare* call me that again.'

'Get off me!' Fhiro stuttered as he tried to free his neck. 'I only… said I… understand!'

Dorrick released Fhiro and slumped down next to him. 'You don't understand anything.'

Fhiro rubbed his throat. 'Pa thinks we could drive the Creedate off, with a bit of luck.'

'We could, or we *could* get obliterated within the first hour of space-battle,' said Dorrick. 'Just wish the Federation was stronger. Strong enough to *really* hurt them.'

Fhiro wondered if he would be brave enough to sign up, when he came of age. Dying fighting had to be better than waiting to get butchered when the Creedate did win.

'I'll sign up,' Dorrick muttered. 'I swear it. Got to do something. Gotta try to make a difference.'

Fhiro did not respond. The sounds of the sea crashing against rocks further north mingled with the gentle breaking of the waves nearby. He watched the crater he had dug soak into itself, leaving a mere ripple in the surface of the sand. Soon the tide would come in again, and all evidence of his having lain here would be gone forever.

CHAPTER 3

'Hey Fhiro,' said a thin boy with a tail of uncut hair at the back of his scalp. He halted his wood-filled wheelbarrow so Fhiro could pass.

'Hi Pijan.' Fhiro tried to smile.

'Are you watching the sky?'

'Watching the sky?'

'The wregg,' said Pijan. 'It's been seen flying over Kalepo village. Everyone's trying to catch a glimpse of it.'

Fhiro had almost forgotten about the wregg. 'Hasn't it moved on from here yet?'

Pijan shook his head.

Fhiro looked to the north. The shadows and animals had been scared away by the baking sun, and the dusty surface of the West Valley road glared a harsh yellow. 'I was thinking of heading to Kalepo anyway,' he said. 'It'd be good to see the wregg, though my pa doesn't seem that impressed. He thinks it's all just climate change and coincidence.'

'I think it means we're all going to die.' Pijan twiddled his fingers and looked at his feet.

'You would say that,' said Fhiro.

'If the Creedate asked you to save yourself by saying you believed in Avithen, would you do it?' asked Pijan.

'I'd fight first,' said Fhiro. 'I hate the Creedate.'

'You're twelve,' said Pijan. 'You can't sign up.'

Fhiro shrugged. 'All right, I'll hide in the forest and attack Creedate soldiers at night-time.'

'What if they just burn down the forest?'

'I'll run into the mountains.'

'What if they're guarding all the mountain passes?'

Fhiro frowned at the sky in exasperation. 'Let's just hope the Federation stops them first.' He started walking again.

'Don't go too fast,' Pijan pleaded as he struggled to get the wheelbarrow moving again. 'I'll drop this off and catch up with you.'

Fhiro slowed his pace a little, uncertain if he wanted Pijan's company. Millorn, his and his father's brush with death, and everything else from the day before was still churning his mind into gristle-riddled mincemeat. He looked up, searching for the wregg, but without the excitement he had felt before. The sky was a cloudless blue and the mountains rising up to his left were free of mist. There was no sign of the rumoured giant scavenger.

'Fhiro!'

Fhiro looked ahead again. It was his neighbour. 'Hello Mr Uwun.'

'Heading out to Kalepo?' Mr Uwun slowed down and wiped his brow.

'Trying to spot the wregg,' said Fhiro.

'Pah,' said Uwun. 'If I saw the thing, I'd probably blow it out of the sky, lest it bother me hens.' He tapped the shotgun hanging from his shoulder. 'Heard you had trouble at the lab yesterday.'

'Yes,' said Fhiro quietly.

Uwun patted the top of Fhiro's hat, which made Fhiro wince – the bruise on his scalp had not got any smaller. 'Thank Aten you and your pa are all right.'

'Thanks.'

'See ya at the Congress.' Uwun set off the way Fhiro had come from.

Fhiro started walking too, testing his scalp with his fingers

to see just how sore it really was. Then his gaze chanced upon a tree with crooked branches, standing out by itself in a clearing between two orchards. He recognised the sweet Chulop fruits hanging under its wave-shaped leaves, and walked over to pluck a ripened one from a lower branch. He returned to the road and bit into its juicy flesh as he made his way north again.

In his twelve years the surroundings had changed little. To his right there were fields of crops and grass, separated by hedgerows. The eastern side of the valley rose up further on, and sloped into the mountainsides of the snow-capped peaks and crags of the Larris heights. Somewhere there, hidden behind a grassy ridge further north, was the house he had stayed in with his family two summers before.

He finished the Chulop fruit and was left with a polished clean thumb-sized stone. He imagined its contents. It was no piece of rock, but a source of tree life and, potentially, more sweet Chulop fruits.

The streams that ran under the road became infrequent, and soon the hedgerows were no more. The grass faded into dry, sandy soil. This was the patch of land between the villages of Chimahess where he lived, and Kalepo where he once went to school. Wild trees and roots were as rare and thin as the bodies of water they thirsted from. Fhiro imagined the strong roots of a Chulop tree would be good for the soil here.

He picked up a stick and dug a hole. He was about to plant the stone, when he was struck by a sudden thought. No one would appreciate him for doing this. Not until he was much older would the land here reap any benefits from the presence of a Chulop tree. He may well have moved away, or even died; few if any people from Andelic ever gained immortality in the shrouded havens.

If there was no appreciation or other benefit to be won,

planting the stone seemed pointless. He sat down deflated. For a few minutes he had felt good about himself, and now he felt like an idiot. He wondered how far he could throw the stone.

He stared across the valley again. What would his mother, father or Professor Millorn have thought? He wondered if it was the appreciation of others that had motivated his intentions. Or was there something more at work? He rarely agreed with the teachings at the Worship Congress, but he did believe that there was a purpose to his existence. He believed he could do something good with his life. He believed there was such a thing as a 'good' thing to do. He could never decide whether or to what degree, it was tied up with Aten, alleged creator of the Universe. All the same, he hoped Aten was watching him, if Aten did indeed exist.

'Fhiro,' said Pijan, catching his breath as he slowed to a halt.

Fhiro was too busy smoothing the soil over where he had planted the stone to look up.

'What are you doing on Farmer Urog's land?'

'He never uses it.' Fhiro stood up. 'Maybe we should just go back to Chimahess now.'

'I just came all the way out here!'

'Sorry, Pijan. We can go to Kalepo if you want. I just needed to calm down.'

'That's all right. We can go back. What were you angry about?'

'Doesn't matter.'

They strolled southward, the sun warming their faces. Soon the road was winding through the orchards again.

'Is it something to do with the laboratory?' asked Pijan.

'What?'

'Why you're angry.'

'Oh,' said Fhiro. 'Sort of. Don't worry about it.'

'I heard about your tutor.'

'Did you know Millorn?' asked Fhiro.

'No,' said Pijan. 'But she was lucky your mother was there. I hope when I die, a revered holy person can perform my ascension rites.'

'I guess.'

'Your mother invited us to the party in town,' said Pijan. 'Are you excited?'

Fhiro did not answer. He stopped and stared ahead of them.

'What's wrong?' Pijan returned his attention to the road and then he, too, froze where he stood.

Beneath the long branches of a Wick-willow tree, almost entirely in shadow, was a blue-grey feathery rippling mass. Its beak was buried in the carcass of another bird upon which its four-fingered talons were hard at work gripping ripping and tearing. The wregg pulled its head upwards, the tension in its neck mounting as it sought to wrench away a sliver of flesh. As the meat tore free and the huge beast opened its beak to swallow its prize, its beady eyes took stock of the boys.

Fhiro felt the challenge in its gaze. He looked down for a moment to study the features of the dead creature it was feasting on.

'Whe–' Pijan stammered. 'That's the wregg.'

Fhiro nodded.

'What's it eating?'

'A phryialla,' said Fhiro. 'But it doesn't look long dead. How did it bring the carcass here?'

'Wreggs are scavengers, right?' asked Pijan.

Neither of them could take their eyes away from the monstrous bird as it fed.

'They're supposed to be,' said Fhiro.

'Let's get out of here.'

'In a minute.' Fhiro took a tentative step forward.

'What are you doing?' Pijan backed away.

'Looks like there are markings above its beak.' Fhiro continued to approach the wregg.

'It's not the sort of creature you'd keep as a pet,' said Pijan. 'It smells terrible, even from here. Why'd anyone mark it?'

Fhiro remained where he was until he had committed the pattern to memory: three thick coloured lines above its beak: one red, one blue and one olive. 'Let's keep our distance by going through the trees,' he said.

Checking over their shoulders, they left the road and dodged deeper into the orchard, walking a hundred paces parallel to the road before making their way back to it.

'I guess we've got to tell everyone.' Fhiro wiped the sweat off his hands when the pounding of his heart subsided.

'Absolutely,' said Pijan.

Soon they reached the junction where a dirt road branched towards Chimahess, the grass of its near corner worn into mud by the passing of countless hooves and wheels. Every few steps they exchanged thoughts on how different friends and relatives might receive the tale they were about to tell.

Upon rounding a bend in the road they were surprised to see a great crowd of village children blocking the way. Fhiro was glad the most important audience in his life was all in one place, to hear about the encounter with the wregg from him personally. However, he became suspicious when some of those who saw him started muttering to one another: 'It's Fhiro!'

'What's going on?' he asked.

'No idea,' said Pijan. 'They seem excited to see you, though.'

'Then why aren't they greeting me?' Having slowed to a walk, Fhiro braced himself and marched forward. Bodies moved aside to allow him through. Some fell in behind him. Fhiro smelled trouble. Reaching the centre of the crowd he saw Teret, an old school friend of his, struggling to shield his

bleeding face. Holding Teret's hair in a tight grip was Hubbort, a stocky boy, tall for his age.

'Fhiro,' Hubbort sneered. 'I was hoping you'd find Teret after I'd finished with him.'

'Stop it.' Fhiro's eyes narrowed.

'He doesn't know his place. He doesn't know when to shut his mouth.'

'He's allowed to talk,' said Fhiro. 'You can't do this any more.'

'You and I are different,' said Hubbort. 'We should be respected.'

'Put him down now,' said Fhiro.

Hubbort laughed. 'Come on Fhiro. Stop being such a softy. You've been hanging around Pijan too much. That'll turn you into a dithering coward, if anything will.'

In the corner of his eye Fhiro caught sight of Pijan's shoulders slumping.

Hubbort turned back to Teret who, holding his breath in anticipation of the next strike, was watching the exchange. 'I won't be laughed at by this whelp again.'

Fhiro took a step forward. One of Hubbort's friends made to stand in his path but Fhiro looked at him, and the boy backed away. Fhiro took two more steps towards Hubbort. 'Don't hit him again.'

'Don't be stupid, Fhiro. Your father taught me to fight too.'

'It seems there is only one way to resolve this.' Fhiro threw his hat to the floor.

Teret, dropped by Hubbort, thudded on to the dirt before grasping his nose and crawling into the crowd.

Fhiro did not wait to be attacked. He feinted at Hubbort's face before kicking his nearest leg as hard as he could. Hubbort wailed and lunged at Fhiro. The two wrestled and fell to the floor, but Fhiro twisted with Hubbort's momentum, enabling him to gain a dominant position. He rained several blows upon Hubbort's head before strong arms pulled him upwards.

'Stop,' shouted Dorrick, holding him back.

'He can't get away with it again.' Fhiro's struggles were ineffectual.

'What do you want to do? Kill him?' Dorrick threw Fhiro on to the grass by the road.

Blood poured from Hubbort's nose as he struggled up and sat down heavily on the ground. His friends wavered, uncertain of whom they were more afraid. Then they ran. Hubbort stumbled after them. The rest of the crowd, including Teret, dispersed.

Only a tall looming figure remained. 'Fighting?' asked Oljon.

'Yes,' said Dorrick.

'I had to do it.' Fhiro glared at the earth. Then he looked up. 'At least I knew what I was up against.'

'You're coming home,' ordered Oljon. 'Now!'

* * *

Waiting on the couch in the living room, Fhiro tried to prepare for his parents' questions, but this only served to further tie his thoughts up in knots. He tried meditating, the way his mother taught him, but that did not help either. His parents were smart. Too smart. It was thanks to all their training and teaching that he could run circles around the children from the village in any argument. Whatever he possessed in knowledge and wits, his parents had more of it. Much more.

Hanu and Oljon entered. Hanu gave Fhiro a tight hug, rubbing his shoulder. 'Thanks for waiting, Fhiro.'

Fhiro shrugged.

Oljon sat down on the couch opposite Fhiro and placed their tea on the small table between them.

'I'm so glad you weren't hurt just now,' Hanu continued,

joining her husband. 'You've put us through too much in the last twenty-four hours!' She smiled again, but Fhiro could read the sadness in her. He had not wanted to make her suffer. He looked at his father, sitting silent and expressionless, staring straight back at him. His father was not his usual self either.

'Fhiro,' said Hanu, 'we have to talk about this. You agreed not to get into fights. What your father taught you makes you dangerous. It's for emergencies only.'

'Wasn't this an emergency?' asked Fhiro. 'If I'd done nothing, Teret would've been beaten up much worse.'

'We only talked about this yesterday,' said Oljon.

'Yesterday, when you led by example, and shot however-many western pichis saving Yetco.'

'That was not the same. You promised you'd talk to us instead of fighting.'

'Why do I have to discuss things when you don't?' asked Fhiro. 'I thought there was a reason I spent my last birthday running through a river, then climbing a mountain with soaking boots, only to get grilled on maths and philosophy at the top. After all that I'm supposed to just let my friend get hurt?'

'I thought you liked your birthday.'

Fhiro had, but admitting it now would not be helpful.

'A violent action is, at best, merely a lesser of evils,' said Oljon. 'It's never a good thing. When you're older, and your judgement's matured, and if you're unlucky enough to have to make such a choice, then perhaps it will be the right thing to do. One day, *far in the future*. At your age, it's out of the question.'

'Your father's right, Fhiro.' Hanu reached out and took his hand, her eyes softening. 'We want what's best for you.'

'Being young doesn't make me wrong,' said Fhiro.

'I know,' said Hanu. 'But please try to see everything at once. Think of the wider effects, like on the community, and the

afterlife.'

'Religious talk, again, Ma?' asked Fhiro.

'Your mother is one of the most respected authorities–' Oljon began.

'Of – What – Religion?' interrupted Fhiro. 'You make more sense, Ma, than any priest or even any prophet I've heard of. But we aren't "Followers of The Calling". The Church of Elders say Avithen was a prophet. If we disagree, that makes us heretics! We should call ourselves "The Heretics of Luwol".'

'Fhiro!' Oljon shouted, standing up.

Fhiro's heart thumped hard in his chest. Had he gone too far?

Then Hanu rose to her feet, her hand taking her husband's arm.

Oljon's stare held Fhiro for a long second. His father exhaled, and turned round to stare out of the window. As he did so he seemed to shrink, as though his outburst had cost him what little energy he had left after the previous day's exertions.

'Fhiro,' said Hanu. 'We've been over this many times. The Church of Elders has been corrupted. Aten chooses prophets, not those misguided fools in the High Tower.'

'No wonder everyone in the village is turning to witchcraft, thinking the wregg is a sign, or praying that some discovery in the Smugglers' Union will make a difference,' said Fhiro. 'They'll take up any crazy idea. Same way those murderous Creedate fanatics blindly do what their priests tell them.' Fhiro thought for a moment. 'You know I saw the wregg today, up close. If I started preaching, would people listen to me?'

Hanu's smile vanished, and her eyes hardened. 'You saw the wregg?'

'Pijan and I almost walked into it,' said Fhiro. 'It was eating a phryialla, which can't have been dead for long.'

Hanu turned to Oljon.

'How close did you get to it?' asked Oljon.

'Quite close.' Fhiro frowned. They both looked as though they had seen a ghost. 'What aren't you telling me?'

'Not right now,' said Oljon. 'Listen Fhiro. This is important. You noticed something about the wregg.'

Fhiro's frown deepened, but he replied, 'Well ... yes. There were colours above its beak.'

Oljon closed his eyes and placed his arm across Hanu's shoulders. 'Tell us.'

Fhiro described what he had seen and then watched his parents as they sat and thought. Both of them looked troubled in a way he had never seen before. 'Can I go now?' he asked after they had not spoken in a while.

'Yes,' said Hanu. 'Yes, all right, Fhiro.'

Confused, Fhiro left and headed upstairs, his mood growing fouler with every step. His parents kept too many secrets. It might not be so maddening if they acted like the other families that fled here from the Creedate. Over the years Oljon and Hanu had taken roles of increasing prestige in the community. His mother now chaired the Green River Valley council meetings. Then there was all the survival and combat training, and the after-school teaching that helped Dorrick and Fhiro graduate school six years early. Yet this strangeness was accompanied by no sound unifying explanation.

On the landing Fhiro brought down the ladder and made his way through the trapdoor in the ceiling. As expected, he found Dorrick staring out over the low wall at the roof's southeastern edge. Assembled about his brother were pots of paint, sets of brushes and clusters of paper. Fhiro studied the incomplete painting that rested on Dorrick's lap. 'That's very Dorrick of you, Dorrick.'

'This?' asked Dorrick.

'I've never seen colours like those in the sky.'

'It's called imagination, Fhiro. Stop embarrassing yourself by constantly reminding people you don't have any.'

Fhiro ignored him and examined the transparent boxes fixed to the roof wall. Within each, a crystal glittered as it absorbed the sunlight. One was unlocked and he removed its stone. Patterns danced on his palm as he turned it in his hand.

'I'm sure life without imagination is hard,' said Dorrick, without looking up, 'but if a blaster-crystal goes off in your hand and blows your fingers off, it will be harder.'

'Shut up, Dorrick.' Fhiro put the crystal back and closed the box. 'Any idea why Ma and Pa are acting so strange today?'

'Do we ever know what they're really thinking?'

Fhiro picked up some painting materials with a view to proving Dorrick's assertions about his imagination wrong. However, before long a brush stroke went amiss. He found a way to transform the mistake into a depiction of the wregg, its wings spread out and its eyes ravenous, its shadow a growing menace in the sky.

'Ten different children came over wanting to ask you about the wregg,' said Dorrick, looking at Fhiro's painting, 'but you were busy downstairs. Pijan thinks you're both lucky to be alive.'

'Pijan thinks we're lucky a super-volcano didn't drown the planet surface in lava yesterday, and the day before, and the day before that,' said Fhiro. 'That phryialla it was eating, though, looked fresh. It didn't look scavenged.'

'That's a bit weird. Most the villagers seem to think it means Chimahess is doomed for especially vicious punishment by the Creedate. Some are even planning mass suicides if the Federation surrenders.'

'What?' asked Fhiro. 'That's stupid.' He folded his arms. 'If they want to die, they can die fighting. If they're scared of capture, rig

the defences to blow up. Last one alive lights the fuse.'

'That's how I'd want to go,' said Dorrick, 'if I've not been killed in battle.'

'So you really are signing up?'

'I've got to,' said Dorrick.

Fhiro put the painting materials down and rubbed his head. He wondered when it would stop hurting so much. Then he took out the gravi-trap and activated it. He spun it around on the floor, watching it bounce and float. 'There was a suggestion in the sitting room just now that what I did earlier might get me sent to hell.'

'As in beating up Hubbort? I don't imagine Aten intended us to go around beating each other up, no.'

'But if bad deeds were prevented by well-timed moments of violence, like mine, then the galaxy would be a better place.'

'And we have these people called police,' said Dorrick, 'who are trained to use force for that reason.'

'Are they allowed to hit children?'

'I don't know, actually,' said Dorrick. 'Could ask Chinda to provoke them next time we go to Kadgel. See what happens.'

'But you've made my point,' said Fhiro. 'The law allows soldiers and police to use violence, so it must think some violence is morally all right. But the law does not invent the morals. It must be assuming the morals are already there, like they came from a higher place, right?'

'What the hell are you going on about now?' Dorrick started painting again.

'Never mind.' Fhiro wished his parents would talk about such things with him without referring to the scriptures all the time. Millorn would have been good for such a conversation. Realising he was thinking of his professor in the past tense made his eyes water. He turned away to make sure Dorrick did not see.

Just then Chinda came up through the trapdoor, banging it

closed behind her. 'What are you doing up here?'

Fhiro wiped his eyes quickly.

'Don't knock me, Chins,' Dorrick warned her.

'Why,' said Chinda, 'in case you slip and make that rubbish painting any worse?'

'What's wrong with it?' asked Dorrick.

She took a closer look. 'Actually it's quite nice, but where did the weird colours come from?'

'I think he's been experimenting with shrubs from Medley Forest,' said Fhiro.

'Yeah,' said Chinda. 'We aren't in the Smugglers' Union, Dorrick.'

'That you two can't recognise creative genius is not my problem.'

Chinda sat down on the wall. 'I've got a message.'

'You're putting the boxes in the shade.' Fhiro pointed to where her shadow covered several crystal-boxes along the wall. 'The crystals need to charge.'

Chinda ignored him, and from her higher position stared over their heads at the trees and village rooftops around them. 'Pa's fed up with all these rumours about the wregg.'

'Nothing new,' said Fhiro.

She grinned. 'But this is: he's not sure it is a wregg any more. He wants to capture it, and he thinks he knows how to.'

'He what?' cried both brothers at once.

'We're packing for an expedition tonight and setting off first thing in the morning.'

'Are we bringing it back alive?' asked Fhiro. 'Some of the villagers think it's a divine message from Aten, or an incarnation of a local spirit. I'm not sure they'll be that thrilled if Pa brings it back with its head blown off, and lights up a barbecue.'

'Pa thinks there might even be a reward,' said Chinda. 'He

thinks people will stop worrying so much when we've got it.'

'Do you think it's dangerous?' Dorrick looked at Fhiro. 'What did Pa say about it to you?'

'He didn't say much,' said Fhiro. 'What are we supposed to pack?'

'Usual camping stuff, I guess,' said Chinda.

Fhiro rested back against the wall. He picked up the gravi-trap and threw it in the air. It hovered, wobbled and veered on its way back to his palm. 'What a horrible, weird week.'

'Really weird.' Chinda's eyes were fixed on the gravi-trap. 'Why did it do that?'

'I don't mean this.' Fhiro tossed the gravi-trap in the air again.

'I used to keep that hidden from her,' said Dorrick. 'I was worried she'd eat it.'

'Eat it?' cried Chinda.

'Or lose it,' said Dorrick.

'I don't lose things,' said Chinda. 'What is it?'

'Gravity-crystals,' said Fhiro, 'connected by crystal-cables to reverse their effect – sort of.'

'You mean it can fly?'

'No, but it's the nearest anyone's ever got to making crystals levitate.'

'Anything more complex just gets sucked to the ground quicker,' said Dorrick. 'Haven't you learned about them yet?'

Chinda was on her knees, peering into the gravi-trap.

Fhiro threw it again and just as it was about to land on Chinda's nose, it spun and swerved, falling into his waiting hand.

'I know I call this place boring,' said Dorrick, 'but I wish it'd stayed that way.'

'I wish yesterday was just a bad dream.' Fhiro clutched his fingers tight around the gravi-trap. 'Nightmare, more like.'

'I didn't really know the prof,' said Chinda.

'She was … She was great.'

Fhiro threw the gravi-trap into the air again, but this time Chinda snatched it. She threw it to herself before remarking, 'The sun's setting. Now your colours are even more wrong, Dorrick.'

'Now, that's a sky I want to paint.' Fhiro picked up his brush again, but slower than before. His mind struggled to disentangle his thoughts about Millorn from everything else.

'Can I have this?' Chinda asked him.

'Until tomorrow, Sis,' Fhiro replied. 'Don't lose it, or eat it.'

CHAPTER 4

'Fhiro, wake up!'

Fhiro felt someone prodding his shoulder. He rolled over and pulled his blanket over his head. 'Go away.'

'Wake up!'

It was his mother's voice, but it was loaded with too much tension. Too much urgency. But his half-woken brain was failing to engage properly, and could make no sense of this. Fhiro opened his eyes. It was still very dark. 'What time is it?'

'Time to go,' said Hanu. 'We've got to go now.'

'Right now?' asked Fhiro. 'Why?'

'We'll explain,' said Hanu. 'Just get changed and see you downstairs in five minutes.'

He half stumbled into his clothes, then grabbed his bag, but it was wrong. Something was wrong. The bag was too heavy. Had someone loaded it with extra water while he slept?

Downstairs Dorrick and Chinda looked at him with bleary eyes. Hanu was moving about, but soon enough she went to the back door. 'Come on,' she said, motioning them to be silent.

Outside the sky was still purple, and the sun nowhere to be seen. The birds were silent, and the trees cast dark shadows across the earth.

Oljon appeared from the bushes at the edge of the garden. 'Thanks for waking quickly,' he whispered. 'Follow me.'

They had done many early-start camping trips, and secrecy, communicating in silence, and avoiding detection were all part of the skillset his parents had been at pains to drum into

them over the years. Never before, however, had he wondered if it might not be a drill.

Oljon led them over the garden fence, and across the property of several of their neighbours, before sneaking into the forest. Dense branches above shrouded them in blackness. Fhiro's eyes strained to see the way through the dimness until they struck the path to the mountains.

Higher they climbed. Fhiro's thighs began to burn. Every time they neared a clearing, or a fallen tree, his stomach grumbled. He prayed to Aten that his parents might drop their rucksacks and stop for a snack. As such places receded into the distance behind him, his stomach groaned all the louder. Several times he opened his mouth to complain, but one look at his parents, and their grim, silent faces, left any thought of doing to so dead before it could bear fruit.

After a few hours the trees thinned out. The sun was emerging from across the other side of the valley, lighting up the trails of mist over the river. Beyond and above, where it was not obscured by the murky grey clouds, shades of red stretched across the sky.

Then Fhiro caught sight of movement. Barely discernible against the greyness of the countryside beneath them, dark shapes passed over the trees. He stopped to watch them slow down, one by one, above Chimahess, and settle upon the landing field. 'Who are they?' he asked.

'Get to higher ground,' said Oljon.

Fhiro frowned. This could not be a coincidence. He saw Dorrick and Chinda throwing worried glances the way they had come.

'Keep looking ahead,' said Hanu.

Fhiro did not sense any sincere reassurance in his mother's voice. He shared a suspicious look with Dorrick. His brother looked as miserable and worried as Fhiro felt.

Oljon went up ahead faster than the rest of them. When Fhiro caught up, where the ground levelled off, a picnic mat had been opened up, and sandwiches were arrayed across it.

'Eat,' said Oljon.

Fhiro looked down at the food, and then watched his father walk away, a pair of binoculars in his hand. Hungry, Fhiro stopped to pick up a sandwich. It appeared to be full of almost every filling they had at home, including a few boshberkins. He paused to pick these out; he never understood why everyone else in his family loved them so much. Then he followed his father.

Oljon reached an outcrop of rock, lay down, and placed the binoculars to his eyes.

Fhiro lay down next to him, making as little sound as he could, and took a bite from his sandwich. He peered down and could tell, even with his naked eyes, that the dark shapes in the landing field were transport birds. He could also make out figures walking the street. It was far too early for anyone to be moving goods or trading.

Hanu lay down on the other side of Oljon, and took out her own pair of binoculars.

'What're we doing here?' whispered Fhiro. 'Why'd we get up so early?' Then he heard a series of loud cracks from the village. They came again, twice more, but this time he glimpsed the flashes of light that preceded them.

He sensed his parents tense.

'What's happening?' When they did not respond, he raised his voice a little. 'Let me look!'

'This is no drill,' said Oljon from behind the binoculars.

'We know,' said Dorrick. 'So show us what we've just run away from. If our village is in danger, I want to know why we're out here hiding, and not running back to help.'

Oljon grimaced, then handed Dorrick the binoculars.

'We're so sorry,' said Hanu. 'None of you deserved to be deceived.'

Dorrick took a sharp intake of breath.

'Then tell us what's happening,' said Fhiro.

'We aren't hunting the wregg?' asked Chinda.

'No,' said Oljon. 'Our enemies are invading our home.'

'What?' Fhiro felt incredulous, enraged and terrified, all at once. 'Who are our enemies?'

'Lirai Loskin,' said Dorrick as he handed Fhiro the binoculars.

It took Fhiro a moment to find their home. Several strange men stood there, all armed. Two had their weapons drawn. Lying at their feet, in the middle of a dark stain in the earth, was a body, a shotgun close to its outstretched arm.

A tongue of fire arced through the open door of Mr Uwun's house. Moments later flame licked the doorframe and smoke billowed from the windows. A woman and two children stood some metres away, cowering before another armed stranger.

He adjusted the binoculars back to his house. The garden was full of figures, pushing through the bushes, crouching close to the ground, searching. One man stood upright directing the others.

Lirai Loskin.

His grip on the binoculars tightened.

'She can see if she wants to,' said Oljon. 'But Chinda, you won't like it. There are people in our house, and Mr Uwun has been murdered.'

'Let me see.' Chinda snatched the binoculars from Fhiro.

'Why is he doing this?' asked Fhiro. 'I thought he liked you.'

'He's a Creedate agent,' said Oljon.

'How d'you know?' asked Dorrick.

'Did we bring rifles?' asked Fhiro. 'We can lure them out into the narrow pass towards–'

'It's too dangerous,' said Oljon. 'We might win an engagement, but the odds are not good enough to merit risking it. I'm not risking any of you.'

Chinda put down the binoculars, tears running down her cheeks.

Hanu cuddled her. 'I'm so sorry, Chins.'

'We're just a family of cowards,' said Dorrick.

'They hunt us,' said Oljon. 'If we do not get far enough away, fast enough, they will find us. They have seen through the false trails I left.'

'Dorrick,' said Hanu. 'I know it doesn't sound valiant, but please trust us.'

'This is crazy.' Chinda sniffed.

'If you realised Lirai was a spy,' said Dorrick, 'why didn't we run away yesterday?'

'Because only yesterday did I become sure of it.'

'You saw him yesterday too?' asked Fhiro.

'No,' said Oljon, 'but yesterday you brought me a message.'

'No I didn't …' As he spoke, Fhiro realised what his father meant. 'But you don't believe in signs. You said the God of The Calling would not send pestilence-ridden birds as a warning.'

'The God of The Calling does not,' said Oljon, 'but there are other gods.'

'What?' asked Dorrick.

'There will be time for explanations later.' Oljon urged them all to keep low as they retreated from their vantage point. 'I hope I don't need to impress upon you any further the urgency of our situation.'

'I don't want to go,' said Chinda. She followed her father away from the outcropping, the binoculars still in her hand, her little cloak fluttering in the wind. 'Can't we stay here and wait for them to go? Please?'

'They won't go, darling.' Oljon took the binoculars off her

and pulled her close. He half hauled her forward the next few steps before letting her down, keeping hold of her hand.

Fhiro watched his mother take his sister's other hand. Hanu did not look her normal self. Her teeth were clenched shut, but her eyes were sharp, her face grim, wrought of sadness and determination. As she set off Fhiro realised he was being left behind.

'Keep moving,' Oljon said to him.

'We can't let them get away with this. Not after what they've done to Mr Uwun.'

'If you want to do anything useful with your lives while you still have them, stop wasting time and follow us now.'

'Hypocrites,' Fhiro grumbled as he stomped after them. 'Lie to us. Still expect our trust.'

'We're pathetic deserters,' mumbled Dorrick.

'How much time do we have?' Hanu asked Oljon.

'Either Lirai has hired a skilled huntsman, or he is one himself,' answered Oljon. 'Our window for escape is shorter than I'd hoped.'

'Are we going to lose them in the mountains?' asked Dorrick.

Fhiro looked up at the narrow passes and steep slopes ahead, wondering where they might hide.

But Oljon did not answer. He led them round a corner along the westward pass until they reached a large mound jutting out by the ascent to Gauleye's Ridge. Oljon assembled a shovel from components within his pack. He marked a spot on the mound and started digging. Soon he hit something hard. 'All right everyone,' he said. 'You've all got one of these in your bags. Lend us a hand.'

Hanu opened Chinda's bag and removed the components of her daughter's shovel.

'This is why our bags were so heavy?' asked Dorrick.

Fhiro assembled his own without thinking, but as he watched his parents tearing a crater into the earth, his anger got the better of him. The clamour they were making rendered all the hiking in silence a total waste of time. He hurled his shovel at the mound, where it embedded itself in the grass. 'No,' he said.

'What do you mean, no?' asked Oljon, turning to stare at him.

'You owe us an explanation,' said Fhiro. 'What have you been keeping from us for all these years? Why are we abandoning our friends?'

'We're doing the very opposite of what you told everyone, me and my friends included, to do,' said Dorrick, his voice so tarnished with regret his words were more croaked than spoken.

Oljon placed his own shovel against the mud he had been digging into.

'I mean, what are we even doing?' cried Fhiro. 'One minute we're walking in silence, now we're smashing up a mountain as though we want to draw attention to ourselves. Is this random environmental sabotage? The Creedate aren't coming here to convert the grass.'

Oljon took a step towards Fhiro. There was a fierceness in him Fhiro had never seen before.

'You don't know,' said Dorrick, 'they're religious lunatics.' Then Dorrick saw their father's face, and he took a step backwards.

Fhiro too found himself retreating before the fire in his father's eyes.

But he was right. His parents had wronged him.

He steeled himself. 'Is the plan to make this area look so rubbish that the Creedate will decide it's not worth invading Andelic?'

Oljon's glower only intensified. 'Of all days, do not test me today. Never once have I raised my hand against any of you in anger, but your insolence is going to get us all slaughtered.'

Fhiro felt the blood drain out of his face.

Oljon took a deep breath. He pointed to where Fhiro's shovel was buried into the grass. 'Dig.'

Fhiro nodded. His defiance was gone. He pulled the shovel from the earth, and without saying a word, plunged it into the hillside. The joints in his arm jarred as the blade impacted. Then, as he forced it deeper, he felt the metal scrape against roots and stones in the soil. He levered and pulled the tool back towards him, and flung debris over his shoulder. On his third thrust he felt a jolt through his palm and his elbow. There was something hard inside the mound that could not be pushed aside. He turned and saw Dorrick frowning.

Then the mound shuddered. Fhiro leapt backwards. His siblings were scrambling away, horrified looks on their faces, but his parents stepped back as though they had expected this. Black mud, riddled with green grass, crumbled and fell at their feet. Beneath, where Fhiro had assumed there was rock, a shiny surface sparkled. Dorrick, Fhiro and Chinda watched, unable to speak, while their father searched the edges of it. He clasped something and moved his arm. A door opened, revealing an entrance into a dark passageway.

'What is this place?' Fhiro breathed.

'Go inside,' said Hanu. 'Quickly.'

Oljon led the way and with his activator turned on a row of lumia-crystals. Hanu closed two doors behind them. There was a sucking sound as the materials lining the door sealed shut.

As Fhiro's eyes adjusted to the gloom he could see much of the walls and ceiling were covered in gleaming, fabric-covered cushioning. The rest was sculpted from a bronze-coloured

glossy material with fine details etched into every surface, as though every particle had been engineered with a specific purpose in mind. 'It's like the cave of glass,' he said, almost to himself. 'The cave of glass I found when I was five.'

Dorrick paused and looked at Hanu.

Hanu put her arm around Fhiro's shoulders. Her voice was full of sadness when she asked, 'Was it really like this?'

'Everything looked so neat, but instead of this stuff ...' he pressed his fingers against the cushioned fabric. 'There was glass, or something like it.'

Hanu shook her head. 'For that to be true ...' She sucked in a deep breath. 'The reason this place looks this way is because it was built with sorcery.'

Dorrick had been watching her too as she spoke to Fhiro. 'We're in a ship,' he said. It was a statement not a question.

'We're in a ship?' Fhiro turned, his eyes wide, and he stared at his mother in disbelief.

'You might feel lost right now, Fhiro,' said Hanu, caressing his arm, 'but you don't need to. I know this is all a shock, but we're here with you, protecting you. There are no Garglethiders in this place.'

'We're going into space ... today?' asked Chinda. 'I don't want to leave Chimahess.'

Fhiro watched his sister break down and cry. He wanted to say something. Something to support her. Get their parents to change their minds and stop this madness, but he was speechless. His voice was gone.

'Come on, Chins,' Hanu said, releasing Fhiro and rubbing Chinda's shoulders. 'Join father on the bridge.' She tugged her daughter along, and she smiled, but Fhiro could see her eyes were sorrowful.

Dorrick and Fhiro followed after their mother and sister, both of them in a daze. Fhiro's befuddled brain struggled to

process the details of everything they passed, and each new feature they saw was stranger than the last. Cables and pipes, as thick as his arm, ran across the floor. Thick tomes, piled on top of one another, littered a circular table. Inside that table, and towering upwards from its centre, was a huge crystal, fashioned more in the shape of unrefined ore, than the symmetrical, polygonal structures he was familiar with. Blue light shimmered from within it, but every few moments it turned violet, white or green just for an instant.

Beyond where the crystal stood was a room walled by transparent screens, through which the earth and stones of the mound that encased them were visible. Hanu had left Chinda by the entrance and was helping Oljon check various levers and devices embedded in the floor, walls and ceiling.

'By Aten's grace,' said Dorrick, 'I wondered if I'd ever see something like this.'

Fhiro stumbled in, and then sat down, staring about himself in bewilderment.

Oljon and Hanu continued their work, both fully absorbed in their tasks.

'Please,' said Dorrick, 'someone explain this.'

'Those men are still coming for us,' said Oljon without looking up.

The thought of Lirai and his men, finding them here, cooped up inside a stranded ship, took shape in Fhiro's mind. 'We have to get out of here.'

'Agreed,' said Oljon.

'But where are we going?' asked Dorrick. 'The Creedate control all the worlds coreward of here!'

'Some passages remain open,' said Oljon. 'With the right ship and the right knowledge, we might make it.'

'With better odds than we'd have going back out there and killing Lirai and his posse?' asked Dorrick.

'Killing them would not change the need for us to leave Andelic,' said Oljon, 'and like I said, not all of us may make it back from that.'

Chinda began to sob.

'Come here, Chins.' Dorrick pulled her into his arms.

Fhiro glanced at the huge crystal he had passed earlier. A navigation-crystal. 'How long has this craft been here?'

'When we arrived here, the Creedate were experiencing a crisis of leadership,' said Oljon, moving back to the navigation-crystal and turning the pages of one of the heavy books. 'Its Generals fell upon one another until Marallel eliminated or pacified them all. During that period their power diminished.'

'It was brought here back then?' asked Dorrick. 'By who?'

'The Kartnan Empire,' said Hanu.

'Kartna?' cried Dorrick.

'The Kartnan gods sent the wregg?' asked Fhiro.

'I know not if the gods themselves were directly involved in the decision,' said Oljon.

'Too much too fast,' murmured Dorrick. 'An immortal god, in the Kartnan Empire, sent a ship, here, for our pa?'

Fhiro gaped at his parents. 'Is that supposed to be no big deal?'

'We'll explain it all soon,' said Oljon.

'Who the hell are you?' demanded Dorrick.

'Who are we?' asked Fhiro.

'What we all will be is dead,' said Hanu, 'if we don't stay focussed. Get to the fall room and strap yourselves in. Now!' She came over and ushered them into the seats that surrounded the navigation-crystal. Fhiro was still not himself. As his mother strapped him to his seat, he just wanted to be approaching the village, armed, and ready to avenge Mr Uwun.

'How long 'til we jump?' Dorrick asked.

They were going to jump. Of course they were going to jump. The idea of leaving the planet, and floating in space, inside the tin can they had found wedged into a mountain, did not feel like a good idea at all.

Oljon did not look up from the charts. 'Could be an instant after I have input my instructions.' He turned to another book. 'Could be in several hours. Depends how fast our navigation-crystal synchronises with the other crystal-auras in the vicinity.'

'And if these Creedate agents catch up with us before we leave?'

'Positive thinking, please, Dorrick,' said Oljon.

'If it's taking too long,' said Hanu, 'we'll have to put this on hold and take care of Lirai's hunting party.'

Fhiro felt a strange stirring in his stomach. He wanted, more than anything, to measure out justice against Lirai and his men. But now his mother was suggesting going through with such a plan, the enormity of it weighed upon him like a vest of solid iron. Was he ready? He had trained, again and again, to exhaustion, in the art of long-range and close-quarter combat. His family knew the land better than Lirai could possibly hope to. But when he imagined watching a living person down the sites of a weapon, and pulling a trigger, snuffing out a life, or being shot at or killed by his opponents, explosions, fires, watching his family dying around him, being captured and tortured …

'Thinking about it won't stop it happening,' said Dorrick.

Fhiro snapped back to reality. 'Just wondering if I could actually go through with it.'

'They killed Mr Uwun,' said Dorrick. 'You could go through with it.'

Somewhere in Fhiro's mind, though, he recalled the Worship Congress meetings about violence and vengeance.

They always counselled against action in the heat of anger, and he had always agreed. But would Aten not approve of them defending themselves and the village?

Did Aten exist?

The Creedate thought Aten was on their side.

'What's that?' asked Chinda, strapped in beside them, pointing at a creature adhering to one corner of the screen. It had a bright pink and orange sharp-toothed sucking orifice.

'Insects have been making the outside of this ship their home,' said Hanu.

Fhiro saw a few other such creatures, but also many worms and small, dark, multi-legged insects crawling between the stones and dirt that covered the screens in the ship's walls.

'This ship is airtight, right?' asked Dorrick. 'I don't want to find one of those things in the room I'm sleeping in.'

The teeth on the creature were terrifying. 'It's a ship,' Fhiro said, more to reassure himself than for his brother. 'It flies in space. If it's not airtight, bedbugs are the least of our problems.'

Oljon brushed and scratched the navigator-crystal with a smaller set of crystals encased in a dark, shiny material. The brightness and hue of the light coming from within the navigation-crystal varied with each stroke Oljon made. Then, like a living heart, its centre started to pulse yellow and green, while its edges darkened. Oljon scampered to his seat and strapped himself in.

'Well maybe, when it's on a planet surface, and the pressure outside is higher than it is in space, it isn't airtight,' said Dorrick, his voice strained.

Fhiro really wanted to think about the giant bed bugs outside, but his attempts to put his mind on to anything other than their immediate departure, into the vacuum of space, were all hopeless.

'And I'd hardly call that a bed bug,' Dorrick continued, his voice monotone. 'It could take your finger off.'

'Get ready everyone,' said Oljon. 'This might happen very–'

There was no warning.

The soil and insects that covered the windows about them drifted off. Fhiro thought he saw one of the gelatinous looking creatures explode. Beyond the debris, as it disappeared, was the blackness of space awash with clusters of pinpoint-lights. 'We … we got out,' said Fhiro.

'Thank Aten,' said Hanu.

'Amen to that,' said Oljon.

'So many … It's beautiful,' said Dorrick.

The absence of an atmosphere made billions of stars twinkle brighter than Fhiro had ever seen before. Besides the sudden change of view through the screens, the only other evidence Fhiro could detect of the instant teleportation was the strange absence of gravity. He felt a weak pulling to his side that seemed to drag around him until it forced him forwards against the straps of the chair. At the same time the bright white round-edged planet surface came into view. Transparencies and divisions in the clouds revealed azure oceans, green plains, dark forests, yellow deserts and grey-brown peaks.

'We lost Lirai, then?' asked Dorrick.

'For now,' said Oljon. 'He will learn of our departure soon, though, and in two days every Creedate Agent within five hundred light-years will be looking for us.' Oljon used his activator on the gravity-crystal hidden below them, and Fhiro felt his weight return. 'It's safe to unstrap,' he said. He and Hanu were soon at the controls of the ship, steering the gas propulsion system to bring them to a safe orbiting speed.

The children released themselves and walked to the screen.

'We'll be jumping again soon,' said Oljon.

'Where?' asked Chinda.

'Tsia,' said Oljon. 'A star port near here.' He left Hanu and returned to the navigation-crystal. 'I need to consult the charts again first, though.'

Fhiro reached the screen itself and pressed his hand against it. It felt cold, but he knew it was warmer than the freezing temperatures of space outside.

Dorrick, standing next to him, seemed to change his demeanour. It was as though his brother was slowly waking up.

Fhiro pressed his forehead against the screen and closed his eyes. Space was only inches away from his brain. Space.

'We abandoned them,' said Dorrick.

'I'm sorry,' said Hanu, joining him. 'So sorry it had to be like this.'

'When are we coming back?' asked Chinda.

'If everything settles down one day, Chins,' said Hanu, 'it might be safe to come back.'

Fhiro opened his eyes. 'I'm going to destroy the Creedate.'

'We'll all destroy them,' said Chinda.

Fhiro stepped back to be closer to his mother and siblings. A light wispy haze laced across the planet surface below, like discarded fabric. He wondered where their home was, amidst the tiny mountains and seas so far beneath them.

Then Fhiro felt a wave of sadness surging through him. Everything he knew – his entire world – was about to disappear before his eyes. Tears were coming, and it was a bitter fight holding them back.

He turned away and took two steps. Before him was his father, hard at work at the glowing navigation-crystal, its radiance now red melting into yellow. He could not look at it, for he hated its power to transport him far from where he wanted to be. He went to the small part of the bridge dedicated

to cooking and dining. Here there was some resemblance to the life he was familiar with, but the surfaces were too polished and the materials looked unnatural; there was no wood or rusted metal. He put his hand on a chair and it spun, slowly, rotating over the supporting pillar that joined it to the floor. He sat on it. He rested his head on his arms and closed his eyes to shut out the absence of a world around him.

CHAPTER 5

A dark, expanding shape obscured the light from Tsia's star.

'That's Tsia's port?' The tears had dried, and Fhiro's mind was starting to put itself back together.

'Yes,' said Hanu.

'Are those Washlights?' asked Chinda.

Fhiro followed his sister's gaze. Shimmering shards of light rippled and vanished in the distance, only to reform and disappear again somewhere else.

'It's a *lot* of Washlight,' said Hanu.

Washlights were a poorly understood phenomenon. Fhiro's favourite legend attributed them to the actions of spirit-ghosts that travelled in the dimension that ships, such as the one Fhiro was in, teleported through when they jumped. These spirits loved to bathe in the massive crystal-auras around star ports and planets. On arrival they shed the magical garments that allowed them to teleport, causing the myriad of colours seen at crystal-aura boundaries. 'I didn't think they would be so beautiful,' Fhiro said.

'Can we talk now?' asked Dorrick. 'You can't avoid it forever.'

'Yes, Dorrick,' said Hanu, her eyes downcast. 'You can have your answers now.'

'They'd better be good.'

'I'm sorry, Dorrick,' said Oljon, sitting down next to Hanu. 'If we had attacked Lirai's men, we might have got killed, and at the very least we would have been slowed down. They may have been reinforced, and more villagers could have wound

up dead. The risks were far too great, and the gains too uncertain.'

'Who will bring Mr Uwun's murderers to justice?' asked Dorrick.

'We'll have to leave that to the local police,' said Oljon.

'Unbelievable,' said Dorrick. 'You know friends of mine are signing up, some of them inspired by the talks you gave. You always said we should stick together and fight. That the Luwol Federation could repel the Creedate.'

'And I maintain that that's the right thing for them to do,' said Oljon.

Dorrick glared at him. 'So it's all right for us to run away, simply because we can, and trick everyone else into dying needlessly? This is cowardice! It's hypocrisy!' He ran a hand through his hair as he paced the room. 'I almost signed up myself. Would you have left me to die on a tour somewhere with the Federation fleet? You don't think the Luwol Federation stands a chance, do you!'

'They do,' said Oljon. 'Fighting is the best chance they have. If you had signed up you'd probably be safer than you are now. As a civilian, however, staying was not an option. We've all heard the stories. Every few years an individual, or even a family, is found murdered. The Creedate has a long memory for those it has marked for death, and its agents are always searching.'

'Why do the Creedate want to get us so badly?' asked Fhiro. 'Loads of families came to Andelic because they disagreed with Avithen, or to avoid conscription into Marallel's religious wars. The Creedate don't go after all of them, surely.'

'Marallel plans to reach them one day,' said Hanu, 'but we have been convicted of treason against the Church of Elders. We are *real* fugitives.'

Dorrick slowed his pace. 'What did you do?'

Fhiro felt Chinda come and stand beside him. Though he sensed her distress, he knew that she too yearned to hear what his parents were about to say.

Hanu looked at her sons. Her eyes were red. She was not smiling. 'How far back do you want us to go?'

'We may as well start at the beginning,' said Oljon, 'and that means we start with me.'

Fhiro could feel his heart pounding in his chest.

'I am older than I look,' said Oljon.

'To be honest I've forgotten how old you are,' said Chinda, 'I just know you're old.'

'Thanks, Chinda,' said Oljon. 'But I'm not forty-eight. Prior to meeting your mother I was rejuvenated in a shrouded haven.'

Fhiro felt his jaw drop. 'A shrouded haven?'

'You've been rejuvenated?' asked Dorrick.

'Wow,' said Chinda.

'I was born in the Kartnan Empire,' said Oljon as they gawped at him, 'where I lived until I was eighty-seven.'

'Aten's tits,' said Dorrick.

'Dorrick!' cried Hanu.

'Aten *might* have tits,' said Fhiro. 'Might not be male. Might not be female either.'

'Shut up, Fhiro,' said Chinda.

'I was eighty-five when I converted to The Calling,' said Oljon, 'the religion you have all been raised in.'

Actually they had been raised to believe in The Heresy of Luwol, Fhiro thought, but said nothing.

'Though my peers were unhappy with this decision of mine,' Oljon continued, 'I had achieved much in the service of the Empire, and sought to achieve more still by building the relationship between Kartna and the Creedate. As a genuine convert I offered to work for Thurgon.'

'No!' cried Fhiro. 'You did not!'

Oljon raised a hand to silence his son. 'Indeed, Thurgon's forces were guilty of terrible war crimes, but back then their viciousness was not endorsed by the Creedate leadership like it is now. Thurgon wanted power. He wanted victories. But it was the complexity and enormity of what he was trying to achieve that resulted in so much bloodshed and suffering. It was my wish, and Kartna's intention, that he might be steered away from the path he had taken. That the youthful, expanding Creedate Empire might transform into a peaceful society that truly reflected the noble teachings of the prophets.'

'They didn't think you were a spy?' asked Dorrick.

'The details of how I won Thurgon's trust and respect are a conversation for another day,' said Oljon. He stared at his own hand, opening it and then clenching it into a fist. 'My goal was noble, but I regret much of what I did back then.' He went silent.

Fhiro did not know what to say. That his father, who he loved regardless of their recent conflicts, had worked with Thurgon, past leader of the hated Creedate, stifled Fhiro's emotions like a clot of mud in his lungs.

'But earn his trust I did,' said Oljon. 'My accomplishments for Kartna were not lost on him. He had much to learn from me, and learn he did, as did his other commanders. It seems, unfortunately, that among them it was Marallel that learned the most.'

Fhiro felt guilt constrict his heart. He fell to his knees.

'Fhiro?' Hanu came and knelt beside him.

'Pa!' said Dorrick. 'Billions of people had been put to the sword, or burned in their homes, and had their heads stacked into blood-soaked, rotting mountains that cast shadows across cities. You can't have helped with that!'

'He's not my father,' said Fhiro. He looked up at Oljon. 'You … you're one of them!'

'I … I did what I thought was right,' said Oljon.

'We were trying to stop it,' said Hanu. 'Sometimes even the best intentions go awry.'

'So go on, then,' said Dorrick. 'After you gave our enemy the tools to destroy us all, what did you do next?'

Oljon shrunk a little in his chair.

'Darling,' Hanu whispered to Oljon, 'you knew this'd happen.'

Oljon looked at his children. 'This is just one of the reasons we never spoke to you about our past.'

'Well get it over with,' said Dorrick. 'Don't like where this is going.'

'As you know,' said Oljon, 'I did not successfully redirect Thurgon's energy into a force for good. Paranoia, and a perverse sense of revenge and justice, came to govern his decisions. The violence worsened, and the atrocities mounted. Your mother and I decided the High Priests and Thurgon had to be stopped.'

'So how were you involved, Ma?' asked Dorrick.

'I was born in Essera,' said Hanu.

'So we really are from there?' asked Fhiro.

'I had excelled in my study of the *Scriptures of the Prophets*, and could recite the entire text by heart when I was six,' she said. 'Because of this I was invited to live among the Poet Nuns, in their convent, in the shadow of the Tower of the Church of Elders on Indin, the holy planet.'

'Marallel's tower,' gasped Fhiro.

'Since declaring himself Holy Protector of The Faith,' said Hanu, 'Marallel often resides there now, but when I first visited, its political significance was nothing compared to its religious and spiritual importance.'

'How did you meet Pa if you were in a convent?' asked Chinda.

'When I came of age I asked to leave,' she said. 'Our order was more a right-of-passage, than a life-long calling. I became a scholar in the tower itself.'

'Amazing,' whispered Chinda.

'There I would debate scripture, philosophy and politics with the High Priests and the prophet,' said Hanu.

'Avithen!' Dorrick tilted his head, as though trying to get a better look at her face.

'I'm sorry we've kept so much from you,' said Hanu.

'We've talked about the guy a million times,' said Dorrick. 'You never ever hinted you'd seen him, let alone spoken with him.'

'Many long conversations,' said Hanu. 'I tried to talk him into seeing sense. Tried to persuade him to speak out against Thurgon and the Generals, and their plans to turn the great many planets they controlled into an engine of war.'

Fhiro frowned and bit his lip. 'You, my ma, you personally tried to persuade Avithen, the prophet himself ...' Fhiro paused. '... false prophet or whatever he was, but the same Avithen whose name is known by most of the galaxy right now, to speak out against Thurgon and the High Priests?'

'Yes, but my attempts were no more successful than those of others before me,' said Hanu.

'How long after you tried was he murdered?' asked Fhiro.

'Not long,' she answered.

'They feared that others would try as Hanu had,' said Oljon. 'Were Avithen ever to have been persuaded, the ambitions of the High Priests and the Church of Elders might have been undone.'

'But I always thought Avithen was evil,' said Fhiro.

'He wasn't evil,' said Hanu. 'He thought he was doing the right thing, but however misguided he was to begin with, his message was twisted by others. Twisted into something foul

and cruel. He provided the High Priests what they had been looking for; a mandate upon which to establish an empire. They called him their saviour, and he preached their ideas as his own to the people. One day he learned how he'd been manipulated.'

'Avithen's an idiot,' said Chinda.

'Careful, Chins,' said Hanu. 'The Creedate have ears everywhere.'

'We're not in a public place,' Chinda replied. 'In fact it's the opposite. We're prisoners on this tiny space-canoe.'

'Pa worked for the Creedate,' muttered Dorrick.

'It's not what it sounds like,' said Oljon. 'I was trying to stop the bloodshed.'

Fhiro cut in by asking, 'So why didn't Avithen turn against them when he knew how he was being manipulated?'

'Sometimes the truth can be too much, even for the strongest of minds,' said Hanu. 'I believe all of us, to some extent, commit acts of self-deception. And the more important the issue, the greater the inclination to do so. Avithen's prophecy was his life's work. He hoped to save trillions of souls and change the face of the galaxy. He was no fool, though. He eventually recognised the reality of what he had done. But rather than accept his mistakes, he tried to negotiate with his conscience. It was easier to convince himself that all would be for the best in the end, than to admit the error of his ways to the multitudes that worshipped him. In his struggle to reconcile his misdeeds he fled in despair to the Monastery of Lamentation on the Swamp-cave planet of Wrurleth.'

Fhiro shot his mother a troubled look. 'There's a planet known for its swamps-caves, and someone built a monastery there?'

Chinda gave a short chuckle. Hanu glanced at her. No one else smiled.

'There are still stranger things in the history of The Calling,' said Oljon.

'Kartna's no better,' muttered Hanu. 'Walking, talking gods? Honestly.'

'So, Pa,' said Dorrick, 'as both of you failed to change Thurgon's heart, and Ma failed to show the prophet the error of his ways, what did you do?'

'We were both involved in the great rebellion against Thurgon,' said Hanu.

'Were it not for the treachery of Marallel,' said Oljon, 'we might have succeeded.'

'And you went to Andelic,' said Fhiro, 'and lived there for years. And had us.' He took a deep breath. 'And now the Senate, or the gods, or someone from Kartna has summoned you again.'

'The wregg was also a warning,' said Oljon. 'The Kartnan agents in Talucia were aware that the Creedate were getting closer. They could not, however, have predicted our coincidental encounter with Lirai.'

'You think that was a coincidence?' asked Hanu.

'Yes,' said Oljon. 'The Creedate might be powerful, but they couldn't persuade the western pichis to act up in a way that would justify one of their spies visiting our laboratory. It would have been far simpler to send someone to the area under another guise if they suspected us. I believe Lirai was as surprised as I was when we met each other.'

'Surely he knows who Ma is, then, too?' asked Fhiro.

'I don't know that the Creedate ever connected her with the conspiracy around the rebellion,' said Oljon. 'We will, of course, all be careful, but I suspect she is in less danger than I am.'

'Surely if she disappeared right after the rebellion,' said Fhiro, 'that looks suspicious.'

'But so many died then,' said Hanu, 'including many close friends of ours.'

'Oh,' said Fhiro. 'Sorry.'

'Don't worry.' She smiled and started straightening his hair. 'We've been very lucky, and we celebrate our luck every day. Now we just need a lot more of it if we're going to get through this, right?' She glanced at Oljon.

'Quite,' said Oljon, as Fhiro tried pushing his mother's hands away. 'It will take a few weeks to reach the rendezvous point. I hope there aren't any complications on the way. Kartna has a plan for us, I'm sure, but we'll only know of it when we link up with them. As previous insiders of the Creedate governing organisation, we are valuable assets.'

Fhiro's mind journeyed many light years to Kartna, just as it did with every mention of the Empire's name. Like the galaxy of the Ancients, it was a place he had always dreamed of going to, but while the Ancients had vanished with the Great Dying, Kartna was real – and he was heading there. 'What kind of plan might they have?' he asked.

'They will meet us close to the Smugglers' Union,' said Oljon. 'I have an uneasy feeling they have taken an interest in that discovery you obsess about. Time will tell if that's the case.'

Fhiro's eyes widened. 'The ancient discovery in the Smugglers' Union?'

'It's not called the Smugglers' Union any more,' said Chinda.

Dorrick, who had been silent for a while, asked, 'What happened to the port?'

'We can see stars again,' said Chinda.

Fhiro looked outside. The darkness that had blotted out Tsia's star had expanded beyond the limits of what could be seen through the forward screens. Ahead, a million sparkling lights glittered in a pattern of interweaving lines, all leading to a central point.

'They're lumia-crystals,' said Oljon, 'guiding us to the docking stations of Tsia's port.'

'How far away is Andelic?' asked Chinda.

'A hundred light years,' said Oljon. He exchanged a look with Hanu, and then the two of them took their seats at the piloting controls. 'You'll all be more comfortable if you strap yourselves in.'

Fhiro took hold of Chinda's wrists but she wriggled them loose. 'Got to get something.'

'Pa said we need to get strapped in,' said Fhiro. He chased her into her room, where she opened her bag and pulled out a book. 'Come on, Chins!'

The two of them rushed back to the fall room. Dorrick had already strapped himself in. Chinda grasped the strap of the nearest seat, so Fhiro had to scramble around her for the next one.

'What did you pick that one for!' he cried. 'So selfish. Always thinking of–'

The ship lurched. Fhiro and Chinda fell on top of each other, next to the navigation-crystal.

'Stop laughing,' Fhiro said to his sister. 'We could've got hurt, or broken the navigation-crystal!' He had to admit, though, that he envied her ability to smile right now, after everything that had happened.

'Chinda,' called Hanu. 'Do that again and we'll confiscate whatever you're reading.'

Chinda grinned and helped Fhiro to his feet, but then the ship lurched again. This time Chinda bumped her head on the table. 'Ouch.'

'You deserved that,' scowled Fhiro.

Chinda looked away from him and hid her face.

He realised that, despite her laughter, she was at least as deeply affected as he was about running from home. He

crawled over to her and put his arm around her shoulders. She shrugged him off. 'Chins, I'm sorry. Can I check it?'

'You're no doctor,' said Chinda.

'We should try to strap in now,' he said. He looked up and saw his parents adjust the propulsions on the ship, guiding it into a new trajectory. The sway of their environment pulled at his stomach. 'Maybe we're safer staying here on the floor, actually.'

Chinda followed his gaze out the screen beyond their parents. The two of them crawled a little nearer to it to get a better look.

'Can I get out of my seat now?' asked Dorrick. 'Those two are on the floor.' When neither parent answered him, he unbuckled his straps and joined his siblings.

Now they were rounding in towards the centre of the port-panel, where the clustering of lights was most dense.

'How dangerous is this place?' asked Hanu.

'It's not the safest,' said Oljon, 'but we've no reason to enter the port itself. We can purchase all the energy, gas, water and food we need from the docking station.'

'I wanted to go inside,' said Chinda.

'Sorry Chins,' said Hanu. 'Another port, later on, when we're far from danger.'

'Spaceship-prison life is boring,' mumbled Chinda.

'I thought it was a space-canoe,' said Fhiro.

'Tell me about it,' said Dorrick.

'We're really sorry,' said Hanu. 'All I ever wished for was for you three to live out your days in peace, away from the war and the murder.'

'It's all right, Ma,' said Fhiro, crawling over and putting his hand on her shoulder.

'I'm sorry,' she said, turning to kiss his hand. 'I'm so sorry.'

Fhiro took another look outside. Some of the port's

structures were now enormous. Smaller details within them expanded, as they neared, into giant interlocking frameworks of metal. He remembered that at school he had often joked with his friends, calling each other names like 'ant on a port-panel' or 'too blind to find a port-panel in the garden'. He knew none of them had ever imagined what he now beheld. 'How did they build this?'

'It was built during the Golden age,' said Hanu, 'when sorcerers roamed freely across the galaxy. That was when most of the star ports and terraforming around here was done.'

'Then this port must be ancient.' He imagined the great machines of the sorcerers, binding the giant components of the star port together. Dragging planets into new orbits. Grinding rocks into soil. Converting atmospheres and sowing countless seeds. 'The Poshokans made it.'

'Almost certainly,' Hanu replied. 'It is older than history remembers.' She focussed on the controls, making a rapid series of adjustments to the ship's angle and velocity.

The Poshokans. The Ancients. The great creators. They had tamed and designed the galaxy, before the Great Dying had wiped them out of existence. Fhiro's fascination with them was unparalleled, but what knowledge of them, and their ways, that had survived from those times was scarce and fragmented at best.

The view changed as the nose of the ship turned away from the panel. They continued to drift in close, but now real stars could be seen over the horizon of the panel surface as they flew parallel to it. A rounded shape rose up ahead like a giant orb of diamond-encrusted jewellery towering over a wide shadowy basin. It was covered in shining crystals and was lit from within. Fhiro recognised symbols of the Luwol Federation and emblems of many other local nations painted on its surface.

Around them, huge projecting columns jutted from the

panel floor. Most stopped abruptly but attached to others were spacecraft, some smaller and some larger than their own. Not far off was a ship at least a hundred metres long. Fhiro knew these projections were the charge docks where one could connect one's craft to the panel with crystal-cables. It was a far more efficient method of recharging than star basking – orbiting a star until the crystals on the ship's surface soaked up enough starlight directly.

Oljon slowed them down while Hanu assisted with the fine-tuning of their alignment with one of the charge docks. There was a sucking clunk as their outer airlock slotted into it. Oljon turned down the heaters by flicking some switches on the terminal in front of him. 'The charge up should take about seven hours. I'll be nipping out for a few minutes to make the arrangements and get everything else we need.'

'Can I sneak out for a bit too?' asked Chinda. 'I promise no one'll see me.'

'What about this, Chins,' answered Oljon. 'We need to give this ship a name so I can tell it to the people working in the port. Why don't you choose one?'

'She's nine, Pa,' said Dorrick, 'not four.'

'Can't I think of one?' pleaded Fhiro.

Dorrick clasped his own face with his hands. 'I despair of this family.'

'Call it *Siwular*,' said Chinda.

Oljon hesitated. 'I think naming it after our bird back home is a bit risky, given that we're trying to stay in disguise.'

'What about *The Spear of Truth*?' suggested Dorrick.

'*The Destroyer of Civilisations*,' said Fhiro, nodding to himself.

'Er …' Oljon scratched his head. 'Perhaps a bit grand and …' He looked at Fhiro, 'Intimidating. Try thinking of a name suitable for a ship like this.'

'Something small?' asked Dorrick.

'*Siwob*,' said Chinda, 'to remind us of Siwular and spiders.'

'Why don't you call it *Siweb*, then,' said Fhiro, 'or *Swider*?'

'Why do we want to remember spiders?' asked Dorrick.

'The Siwob,' Oljon announced in a loud voice.

'A lovely name for a ship.' Hanu smiled.

'The youngest child just gets what they want,' huffed Fhiro.

'You were the youngest for a while,' said Dorrick.

'But you always get to be oldest,' said Fhiro. 'The middle child always gets the worst deal.'

'Not this again,' sighed Hanu.

CHAPTER 6

The space-canoe really was prison, and Fhiro doubted his sanity could survive another minute locked inside it.

Every book had been read at least once and every board game played to exhaustion. As for the view through the ship's windows, stars against dark backdrops no longer inspired excitement when there was no countryside to contrast them with. In fact everything he looked at just made him miss home.

Their umpteenth game of 'Sky Lord' degenerated into the three of them throwing cushions at each other. Then Fhiro and Dorrick were wrestling, and Fhiro wound up knocking his head against the wall, lacerating his scalp, and bleeding everywhere.

'Ma! Pa! They're fighting again!'

Through the pain in his head Fhiro heard Chinda rushing off to tell tales. Then his parents burst in.

What did they think they were doing? Had they lost their minds, fighting again at a time like this?

'But Pa, we're so bored,' moaned Fhiro, his hand on his wound.

Dorrick nodded agreement.

Hanu's incredulous stare swung from one to the other. 'Aten's breath!' she cried. 'Bored? Is that all–'

'Ma!' gasped Chinda. 'You took the Lord's name in vain.'

Hanu's mouth gaped open, and then she bowed her head and began chanting forgiveness prayers.

'It's just his breath, Ma,' said Fhiro, trying to sound as positive as he could. 'Aten won't mind.'

'Shut up, Fhiro,' said Dorrick.

Oljon put his arm around his wife and caressed her shoulder. 'Can't you see what's happening to us? We're losing ourselves.'

'But what can we do?' asked Hanu.

'Please let us go to a space port, Ma,' begged Chinda.

Fhiro was desperate to see a port too, but his mother's evident anxiety about such a plan worried him.

'How about this,' said Oljon. 'At the next star port, while we charge up and resupply, I'll go and check the port for signs of Creedate presence. If there isn't any, we'll go into the port-city and have a meal together. Stretch our legs.'

'This is the Near Quadrant of the galaxy. Avithen's followers are everywhere,' said Hanu.

'Trust me. I'm good at this. We need a break.'

'It's Port Calagan, isn't it?' asked Dorrick. '*The Devil's Throat* by Ulip Cashar was set there.'

Fhiro nodded. 'And that guy drowned in the port canal.'

'That bit was messed up,' mumbled Dorrick.

'It can't be that safe if Ulip Cashar set a novel there,' said Hanu.

'It should be fine,' said Fhiro. 'The Loriti-Thilodoth conflict ended a hundred and fifty years ago.'

'Any sign of the Creedate and we won't venture out,' repeated Oljon. 'That's the rule.'

Hanu buried her head in her hands. Then she looked up, grimaced, and met her husband's eyes. 'Fine, but I've had just as much experience dodging Creedate agents as you. I'll check first.'

* * *

From the outside Calagan was one of the largest ports Fhiro had seen. His imagination took fire, as it had at the sight of every other port they had visited over the last two weeks, creating a world full of mystery and wonder he longed to explore.

Except this time they were going aboard, and now the moment was upon him, the dangers he might face started to stack up in his mind.

After they docked it was a long four hours before the news came that there was no sign of danger. Hanu removed the dressing from Fhiro's head and gave it another gentle clean, and a moment later he was in a small passageway outside the Siwob. Despite his fears he felt exhilarated. He would have jumped in the air if it were not for the yeal in uniform a few metres away, studying pipes and vents in the wall.

'Is it a long way to the port-city?' Fhiro asked as they turned into a long, wide corridor.

'It's a bit of a walk,' admitted Oljon.

This turned out to be a significant understatement, but the spacefarers in all their different clothes, shapes and sizes, the translucent airlock-gates draped around the walls, and the views of the ships outside, kept his excitement alive.

After a while he saw the corridor opening out in the distance. 'Can we go ahead?'

'As far as the balcony,' said Oljon. 'I don't want to lose sight of you.'

Fhiro ran, weaving between the travellers and tradesmen, followed by Dorrick, who soon caught up, and then Chinda, only moments behind them. Then he was outside, sprinting across an open space, a warm light shining on his face. He grasped the balcony as he slammed into it, and looked over its edge at the enclosed world that was Calagan's port.

Tiny people meandered the streets far below like insects, or pulled rickshaws to and fro. Towering structures, connected

to each other on multiple levels by suspended walkways, were separated by bright, landscaped gardens. Cutting zigzag through the blocks were murky canals, full of litter, along which boats and barges carried mountains of cargo, dodging round each other and sneaking under bridges. Fhiro watched as an immense ship was dragged into a harbour by a team of men straining at cables thicker than his arm. High above the centre of the colossal cavern hung a lumia-crystal so powerful it stung Fhiro's eyes. 'Does that crystal provide enough energy to feed the grass and the trees here?'

'"*A sun, within a cave, by a star*",' said Oljon, joining them.

'That's poetry of the Yellow Wordsmith, isn't it?' asked Dorrick.

'It is,' said Oljon. 'He recorded the most ancient Kartnan poems.'

'Is the water full of sewage?' asked Chinda. 'It doesn't look clean.'

'There are far worse things than sewage in that water,' said Oljon.

'Like what?' asked Fhiro.

'Just don't fall in,' his father replied.

'Would you like to buy a fish, little ones?'

Fhiro jumped.

A hegel, whose beak had been divided into ten pointed triangles, pulled a trolley with long, silver-grey fish hanging from hooks.

Chinda stared at the hegel until Hanu pulled her away.

Fhiro watched the crowds passing by around them. Among the earthmen, yeal, and the hegel he was used to seeing, there were also small groups of hegel with thinner limbs and prominent wings. 'Flyers?' he asked Dorrick.

'Must be.'

'Wow.' He had only ever seen Toolers before, the dominant

subspecies of hegel who were incapable of flight. But his fascination subsided under the weighty feeling he was being watched. Looking about he caught eyes with various passers by. They stared back at him long enough to make him feel uncomfortable. He sensed he was being scruitinised and measured up.

A yeal, with a scarred face and a lopsided smile, dragged his rickshaw over to them. 'A lift to the city for the family? Five Galactic Credits, ten Creedate Trade Tokens, forty-two Kartnan Minas or seven Cadriotan Schillings.'

'We'll walk, thank you,' said Oljon.

'How does he remember what it costs in all those currencies?' asked Fhiro.

'He only needs a rough idea,' said Oljon. 'He then adds about four hundred percent when he sees us, and won't settle for less than double what he should.'

'Is everyone corrupt here?' asked Fhiro, as he watched a group of nervous looking men in long coats, casting glances over their shoulders, board the rickshaw Oljon had rejected.

'Just stay close while we're in these crowds,' said Oljon, 'and be watchful.'

'That applies to you two, too,' Hanu called out to Dorrick and Chinda, who had fallen behind, distracted by the touts and colourful stalls nearby.

A knee-bruising number of steps later they had descended to the level of the port-city.

'So many people.' Fhiro had no sooner finished uttering these words when a short, hooded hegel, with one eye covered by a crude patch, bumped into him, almost knocking him over. Fhiro scowled, but then he was filled with dread. A Creedate assassin! A poisoned needle! He jumped back, franticly patting himself down, looking for injuries.

'Makes Kadgel seem tiny,' said Dorrick.

Fhiro tried to calm himself down. If he had been poisoned, he would probably know by now.

Suddenly thin fingers gripped tight around his arm and pulled him towards the edge of the road.

'You look like a special child,' croaked the old earthman who held him, his rancid breath blowing into Fhiro's face from an inch away. 'Come with me and I'll tell your fortune.'

'Very kind of you,' said Hanu with a confident smile, prising the man's fingers from Fhiro's arm, 'but we're quite busy. Maybe some other time.'

The old man nodded his near-hairless head as Fhiro let his mother take him away.

'Thanks Ma,' he gasped.

'Stay very close now,' she said.

'I'm a bit scared,' said Chinda, biting her thumb.

But Oljon and Hanu appeared anything but worried. His mother, in particular, he found himself marvelling at. He knew she had grave concerns about being out here, but she showed no sign of them. Both his parents looked as though nothing could touch them.

They crossed the murky canal over a bridge, and a turn or two later they found a roofless restaurant with a blackboard at the entrance declaring a 'special' of mutton on the bone. Fhiro liked the sound of this, though before they ordered Oljon had to make some enquiries about which animal 'mutton' came from in this region of space. It was glorious to eat a traditionally cooked fresh meal again, with the scents filling Fhiro's nostrils as fine spices soaked his tongue.

'Can Dorrick and I have a look at the shops?' he asked.

'When we've all finished,' said Hanu. 'Chinda's still eating her dessert.'

'That's because she spent ages chasing the wobble shrimp around her plate,' said Fhiro.

'It's not our fault she picked a main course that was still alive,' said Dorrick.

'Interesting people eat interesting food,' said Chinda.

'Relax, everyone,' said Oljon. 'Be glad you're getting family time outside the ship. Let's enjoy being together.'

'You can't *make* us relax,' said Chinda.

But not much later, his stomach full, Fhiro was feeling quite at ease as they crossed the grass to the shopping district. 'Let's visit a bookstore,' he piped as an idea struck him. Dorrick and Chinda did not share his enthusiasm, though, and stayed with Hanu to investigate the pet shops and crystal dealers.

'Was there something in particular you wanted?' asked Oljon. 'Another novel series? There are a number of good authors like Ulip Cashar you might like.'

'No,' said Fhiro. 'I'm tired of only knowing about one religion. I want to know what else is out there.'

'Oh.' Oljon went silent for a moment. 'Is that necessary?'

'Yes,' Fhiro replied. He recalled *Meditations on Representation* that Millorn had lent him. For all the things he had agreed with in its pages, he was surprised it did not recommend studying other belief systems as a way to develop his understanding about the questions that bothered him: Why was he here? What was his purpose? What would happen when he died? 'You knew about Kartna's religion, but then learned about The Calling. I need to know what the other religions say too, or how can I ever be sure of what I believe?'

Oljon exhaled. 'Guess I can't argue with that.'

Once they were in the right part of the market Fhiro led Oljon from vendor to vendor and stall to stall, but nothing took his fancy. After a while, in the old quarter of the book market, they entered a store with a bizarre creature behind the counter. Numerous, black, tentacular arms grew from its body. Some had hands, others eyes, mouths, suckers or spikes. Some

appeared devoid of purpose or were very short. Its skin was dry and cracked. A mouth and two eyes, upon their own short tentacles, protruded close to its body. Fhiro hesitated at the sight of it. He felt his father's hand upon his shoulder. 'Go on son. Have a look around.'

The recci, for Fhiro knew what it was, watched him with both of its eyes. He saw only one tentacle move. It went a distance away from its main body, and then turned towards him. Fhiro saw, at its end, a third eye looking at him. He tried to ignore this as he walked about the stall. He searched the categories, hoping to find what he wanted here so that he could tell Dorrick about the creature he had bought it from. After a while he found a large book titled *Mythologies of the Galaxy*. It was old and worn, but the pages within were detailed and full of pictures, diagrams and symbols. He hurried along to the recci with the book under his arm, but then he hesitated, for he had not yet heard it speak. 'How much is this, please?'

The recci withdrew its eyes and tentacles so that it was entirely in front of Fhiro, as though this amounted to polite behaviour. With a guttural voice it spoke; 'Fifty Glacs.'

'It's quite expensive considering how old it is,' said Oljon, 'but I don't think the subject has changed that much in recent years. Are you sure you want it?'

Fhiro nodded.

'I see your heart's set on this one,' said Oljon. He took the book and placed some coins on to an outstretched tentacle.

The recci seemed to smile.

'Thank you.' Fhiro smiled back.

'This is a hobby of yours?' croaked the recci.

'Sort of,' said Fhiro. 'How do I know I'm believing the right thing if I haven't considered anything else?'

The recci bobbed some of its tentacles up and down. 'I

know not whether to envy or pity you, for asking yourself such questions. You choose a path few can bear to walk for long.' Its eyes glanced at Oljon. 'Be thankful to your master, earthboy. Many a wise inquiring mind has been stifled by the stubborn ignorance of others.'

Oljon nodded. 'Farewell, ancient one.'

The recci made a strange noise that sounded like laughter to Fhiro. 'Go in peace.'

'That's the first recci I've ever seen!' Fhiro blurted out once they were outside.

'There are few recci in the Near Quadrant,' said Oljon. 'The dread of the earthmen-recci wars remains a stain upon the Galactic consciousness even now.'

'But the last of those was over a thousand years ago,' said Fhiro.

'True, but as conflicts go, they were particularly terrible.' Oljon peered about to check his bearings. 'It's a shame. They're very intelligent, and most are of warm character.'

'Thanks for the book, Pa.'

Oljon smiled. 'You're welcome.' But as they neared Hanu and the others, Fhiro noticed his father growing agitated.

'Get something good?' asked Dorrick. 'I got a manual on piloting. Ma and Pa said they might train me on the controls.'

'Is everything all right?' Hanu asked. 'I promised Chinda I'd take her to one more place.'

'That's fine,' said Oljon. 'There's just something I've got to check, though. Why don't you two boys go to the park to read what you've picked up?'

'Sure,' said Dorrick.

When they were out of earshot of their parents Dorrick muttered, 'Sorry about earlier.'

Fhiro had been trying to read and walk at the same time. 'What? Oh, don't worry.' He patted his head wound. 'I'm all

right.' In truth he was still quite annoyed, but the apology did feel sincere.

They walked until they reached the canal and sat on a bench facing it. Dorrick opened up his piloting manual while Fhiro took bites from a grain bar as he turned the pages of *Mythologies of the Galaxy*. He had just finished a graphic description of how the Zelebites sacrificed one another to appease the god of black holes, when his brother interrupted him.

'What are you planning to find in that, anyway?'

'Not sure,' said Fhiro.

'What's wrong with our religion?'

'Too much of it doesn't make sense.'

'Like what?' Dorrick looked hurt.

Fhiro closed the book, checked over his shoulder, and then waved his arm in the air. 'Like why hell exists.'

'That's obvious,' said Dorrick. 'Aten wanted his people to be good so that they could serve him in heaven … enjoy heaven. Those that reject him are sent to hell, to protect heaven, and to encourage others to do the right thing.'

'But if Aten is all powerful, why not simply make everyone good, and get rid of the need for hell at all?'

'I guess that's something only Aten understands. We'll probably never know.' Dorrick nodded to himself. 'It's beyond our mortal comprehension.'

'In fact,' said Fhiro, 'if Aten's all powerful, why are people even necessary? Aten could use unlimited powers to just stop needing us. He could just stop needing *anything*.'

'I really think it's pointless to try to understand Aten's reasons. He is Aten, after all.'

'And if Aten is all loving and all powerful, and sends people to hell, then that's sick.'

Dorrick opened his bag and took out a hefty book with

tattered corners. 'Well if we're going to get an answer, it will be in the *Scriptures of the Prophets*.'

'You carry around a copy of the *SOP*?' Fhiro raised his eyebrows.

Dorrick turned the pages, which were made from the thinnest paper Fhiro had ever seen, and isolated one. 'The prophet Gedo describes Aten as all powerful and of unlimited compassion. She also talks about hell.' He handed it, open, to Fhiro.

Fhiro read quickly. 'In my opinion, the prophet Gedo contradicts herself.' He looked up. 'Now what do we do?'

'Ask Ma?'

Fhiro frowned. 'She promised me a conversation, but I've been dreading it.'

'She knows a lot,' said Dorrick.

'I just–' Fhiro stopped. 'I'm worried we'll get into an argument.'

'Ma's good at those.' Dorrick relaxed and picked up his book. 'You'll learn something, I'm sure.'

Fhiro spent a short while trying to work out what was worrying him. He took another bite from the grain bar to help him concentrate, but concluded it was not to his taste. He threw what was left of it over the fence, into the canal.

The water erupted. A swirling mass of thick, scaled bodies with dull fins, thrashed over one another where the crumbs had landed. Then the swarm died down, descending out of sight.

Dorrick picked his beast-care manual back up, off the floor. 'Do you reckon there's a law against feeding the canal's monster fish?'

They grabbed their books and walked away, Fhiro's head downcast. 'It was brilliant though, wasn't it?'

Dorrick gave him a gentle thump in the arm.

'We could go somewhere else and do it again!'

'No!' Dorrick hit him again. 'If Ma or Pa saw that we'd be dead.'

'Good day, young men,' said a woman.

Dorrick and Fhiro both started.

'You almost look guilty!' The man with the woman laughed. 'Look, the *Scriptures of the Prophets*! I admit I am very pleased to see the young reading the sacred texts.' He reached out and took it from Fhiro's hand.

Fhiro saw a Creedate insignia on the shoulders of the couple before them. Was this a coincidence? Where were his parents? He tried to smile.

'We were just debating the prophet Gedo,' chirped Dorrick.

'Excellent,' said the man.

'And what is that other book you are carrying?' asked the woman.

'Oh.' Dorrick slapped the *Mythologies of the Galaxy* book that Fhiro still held, causing Fhiro to wobble on his feet under the weight of it. 'We keep bumping into people who want to argue with us about our beliefs. Thought it would be a good idea to know more about theirs – if only for the sake of arguing.'

Fhiro nodded, but then stood helpless as the Creedate woman picked the book from his grasp and leafed through it.

'Be careful reading about such things,' she said. 'Don't let their heathen messages damage the purity of your souls.'

'Yes,' said the man. 'If people won't hear the message of The Calling, and Aten's latest prophet, Avithen, I would not concern myself with saving them at your age. Though, I must add, it is commendable that you have tried. You will both make splendid missionaries when you're older, I'm sure.' He smiled, and placed the *Scriptures of the Prophets* into Fhiro's outstretched arms.

'Thank you.' Dorrick beamed.

'Have a good day.' The woman dropped *Mythologies of the Galaxy* on top of the *Scriptures of the Prophets* and Fhiro stumbled. 'Do not waste too much of it learning about false paths. Keep to the truth.'

The couple left.

Dorrick's shoulders slumped.

'How come Ma and Pa didn't spot them?' asked Fhiro.

'They didn't exactly fine-tooth comb the entire port,' said Dorrick. 'This place is huge.'

'But I thought they'd be keeping a look out.' Fhiro watched the couple approaching other people in the park.

'I suppose I shouldn't hate Creedate Evangelicals,' said Dorrick. 'At least they aren't forcing people to think like them.'

'Is that what they are?'

'What else are they doing here? Look, they're handing out papers to people.'

'Why didn't they hand them to us?' asked Fhiro.

'Because we're already Followers.' Dorrick shook his head. 'Such avid Followers, in fact, that we're wandering around with a copy of the *Scriptures of the Prophets* in our hands! Perhaps we ought to hide your silly book for now, though.'

Fhiro juggled the books in his hands until he could pass Dorrick *Mythologies of the Galaxy*.

'Now where are we? Or more importantly, where are our parents?'

While Dorrick peered back the way they had come, Fhiro watched the evangelicals. The Creedate couple walked to an isolated stall that stood on the path back to the shops. They handed the storekeeper a piece of paper and moved on. Fhiro squinted. 'Does that stall sell waffle-wafers?'

'What?' asked Dorrick.

'That stall there,' said Fhiro. 'The sign above it. I'm sure those are waffle-wafers.'

'Whatever,' said Dorrick. 'It's on the way back. Do you have any money on you?'

They plodded over.

'Fancy something?' The earthwoman manning the store looked up from the document the Creedate couple had handed her.

'Just looking, thanks,' said Dorrick. 'We'll be back with our parents soon.'

'Do you make your waffle-wafers with wheat or cerudge-meal?' asked Fhiro.

'Since when were you a connoisseur of waffle-wafers?' asked Dorrick.

'Only whole-meal wheat, we do,' answered the vendor.

'Ah,' said Fhiro.

The woman returned her attention to the document. '5000 Tokens,' she muttered. 'If I had that much money I wouldn't need to sell another Asika-sap waffle ever again!' She pinned the paper on to the board behind her. 'Shame. Quite a handsome fellow.'

But handsome was not the word that came to Fhiro's mind. 'Father,' he said.

'Sorry?'

'He means he has to go and get his father,' said Dorrick. 'Our father, I mean, to buy one of your ... waffle ... things. Father's got our money.'

'Go along and get your parents before I'm sold out.' She smiled.

Fhiro felt the blood draining from his head. His brother had to pinch his shoulder to draw his eyes away from the poster with Oljon's face on it.

Once they were out of earshot Dorrick scoured the crowds. 'Look, there's Ma and Chinda.'

'That Creedate couple are heading straight towards them!' said Fhiro, rubbing the bruises on his shoulder.

'But they only have a picture of Pa,' said Dorrick.

'But they might have a description of who he's travelling with,' said Fhiro, setting off.

'They've changed direction,' said Dorrick as the Creedate agents swerved towards the right.

Fhiro followed their trajectory and saw Oljon facing the other way. 'They've seen Pa!'

'Quick!' said Dorrick.

As they broke into a jog they saw Oljon meander into a souvenir shop.

'He hasn't seen them,' said Fhiro.

The Creedate agents pushing through a crowd. They had almost reached where Oljon had disappeared from sight.

The two brothers broke into a run.

The Creedate agents strode into the souvenir shop. By the time Fhiro and Dorrick caught up they could see no sign of life inside the store. Fhiro entered, and Dorrick went after him, whispering as loud as he could, 'What are we going to do if we find them?'

Fhiro was frantic. 'Where did he go?'

Dorrick peered over the counter. 'No one manning this place, either.'

Fhiro walked around it. He could not think straight. Were their orders to capture or kill? Was his father still alive?

'What are we doing here?' asked Dorrick.

Fhiro saw a door beyond the counter. He pushed it open and found himself in an alleyway.

'Fhiro,' whispered Dorrick, as loud as he dared.

Fhiro ran forwards.

Muted cracking-sounds echoed in the confined space of the alley ahead.

Fhiro stopped dead. The noise was familiar to him. He knew that sound. He had heard that sound in training. It was the sound of ...

Dorrick collided with him, and they collapsed in a tangled heap. Fhiro pushed himself up to his knees, and looked forward, suddenly desperate to escape.

A figure staggered into view from one of the alleys ahead. It was the male Creedate evangelical. His chest stuttered as he tried to breathe, and blood bubbled through his fingers where he clutched it, and burst from his mouth with every cough.

The muted cracking sound came again. The man's head jerked forwards, and a burst of red gushed forth from his forehead. He fell to the floor and lay still.

A figure emerged from the alley where the evangelical had come from. Fhiro saw the pistol, its barrel connected to a silencer. He covered his face in terror. He felt Dorrick climb off him, and then a firm grip on his wrist pull him to his feet.

'They won't be alone,' said his father.

CHAPTER 7

'Strap yourselves in, all of you,' gasped Oljon as he sealed the door behind them.

'They followed us?' asked Hanu, pausing to catch her breath.

'I thought they hadn't,' Fhiro cried out in spite of his burning lungs. They had just run the entire length of the corridor from the city. 'You said … no tail.'

Oljon shoved him towards the fall room. 'Ships leaving this place all the time.' He made his way to the controls. 'They won't notice us.'

'They probably know which corridor we've been sprinting down, though,' said Dorrick as he fastened his belts.

They detached from the charge dock. Fhiro could see through the screen, a larger sleeker ship detach at the same time. It had multiple gun barrels protruding from its surface. Flashes of light burst from beneath it and sped across the viewports of the Siwob.

'They know it's us!' cried Hanu.

'Pilot for me Hanu,' said Oljon. 'Get away from that cruiser.' He pounced upon the leather-bound charts around the navigation-crystal.

Fhiro could see sweat trickling down his mother's forehead as she worked at the controls. Her arm made an abrupt movement, and then the floor swept away under his feet, and Fhiro tumbled, helpless, trying to shield his head.

'Get strapped in!' called Dorrick.

Outside the screen, docked ships and charging structures raced

towards them, until Hanu turned the controls again, banking out of harm's way, but sending Fhiro spiralling in another direction. He wildly flailed for something to grab, but there was nothing in reach before he slammed into Dorrick and Chinda.

'Gerroff!' mumbled Dorrick from under Fhiro's armpit, pushing him off.

'Sorry!' Fhiro used one of the handles by the seating area to extricate himself.

'I'll try to help Ma with the piloting,' said Dorrick. He dragged himself to Oljon's empty piloting seat.

'Are we going to die?' Chinda asked Fhiro as he strapped her in.

'Don't worry,' he breathed, forcing himself to smile at her. She looked terrified though, so he rubbed her shoulder with his free hand.

At that moment the ground lurched under him, and gravity flipped, lifting him off his feet and pulling him towards the front of the ship. Fhiro somersaulted, lost his grip on the handle, and tumbled into the navigation-crystal.

'Be careful!' Oljon, nudged by Fhiro's flailing leg, dropped an instronavia-crystal. It bounced on the navigation-crystal twice before landing on the floor. The room started to pulse blue and white.

'Sorry,' cried Fhiro.

'Now what's going on?' Oljon's eyes begged the glowing stone for answers.

Fhiro hauled himself to the seat next to Chinda and belted himself in as fast as he could. Beyond Oljon he could see the pilot's mirrors Hanu was using. He assumed the images of an approaching ship, firing bolts of crystal-energy, came from those that faced to the rear.

Fhiro watched her take them hurtling around a giant support structure. He could pick out the individual rivulets

and joinings of the vast metal components it was made of. They were getting too close. As the bulk of the structure swung into full view, their ship only now trying to pull away, Fhiro closed his eyes and prepared for impact.

He opened them a moment later, and the side of the Siwob was still intact, not ripped to pieces, exposing them to the silent, freezing death that awaited outside the hull. But then the view ahead changed again, the horizon of the port's panel rising up and up and out of view. He felt his stomach jump into his chest as they dove right down towards the panel's surface below them. What was his mother thinking?

'That'll do,' shouted Oljon, turning away from the navigation-crystal and pocketing the instronavia-crystals. Somehow he flung himself from one set of handles towards Dorrick's seat, and strapped himself to the back of it. 'Move aside, Dor.'

'What d'you mean?' asked Hanu, panic in her voice.

'Fhiro bashed my arm,' said Oljon, swapping places with Dorrick. 'Will be an inaccurate jump.'

'*How* inaccurate?' cried Hanu.

'About half-a-percent chance of finding ourselves in dead space.'

Dorrick glanced at Fhiro.

Dead space was anywhere incompatable with survival, whether it be too far from anywhere to resupply, or unavoidably close to a massive object.

But it was all irrelevant if his mother did not take them out of this plunge soon enough. Hot energy blasts turned the surface of the port in front of them glowing red. Fhiro realised their pursuers were directly behind and above them, following them in the crazy dive his mother had embarked on. The surface of the panel was rushing up to the screen ahead of him. He made himself watch.

At the last moment they swerved, and darted through a small gap that led to a short tunnel running under the surface of the panel. Hanu brought them out of it and over surface again.

'They're still following,' said Oljon.

'We'd better jump soon,' said Hanu, her eyes fixed on the screen and mirrors.

'Ports are easier to jump from than planets,' said Oljon. 'There are fewer crystal-auras to adapt to. The further we get from the main port hub the faster we'll be out of here.'

'The further we get from the other ships the less cover we'll have to hide behind!' cried Hanu.

The port-panel absorbed a blast that had passed under them. Fragments of glowing metal burst from its point of impact and bounced against the screen.

'Too close,' said Hanu. 'That was too close!'

Their surroundings changed. They were in open space.

'We jumped!' cried Dorrick.

'Thank Aten,' said Hanu, releasing the controls and collapsing into her chair. She turned around to check on the rest of them. 'Is everyone all right?'

'I don't see any nearby stars,' said Fhiro, his voice feeble.

Oljon set up a telescope and coordinate plotting equipment. He wrote down some notes. 'Hanu, I'm making a short jump to triangulate the readings.'

'Ready when you are,' said Hanu, wiping her hands and gripping the controls again.

Oljon returned to the navigation-crystal. In a few seconds he stood back, and a few seconds later Fhiro felt the jump.

'That was fast,' said Chinda.

'Because we're nowhere near anything,' said Dorrick.

'How nowhere-near-anything?' asked Fhiro.

Oljon returned to his plotting, altering the angles of the telescopes a minute fraction to assess how the alignment of

the stars outside had changed. 'We are light years from anywhere so, according to some definitions, we are in dead space. But the other thing to take into account is how far we have travelled just now.' He checked the navigation-crystal.

Dorrick glanced at Fhiro, but then looked away.

'I'm– I'm really sorry,' Fhiro whispered.

Dorrick unstrapped and walked over to the screen.

Fhiro's heart shrivelled.

'Oh,' muttered Oljon. 'I didn't mean to go that far.'

Fhiro's heart started to rot.

Oljon turned the telescope again, mapped out a star and consulted the charts. He smiled.

'Naked star?' asked Hanu.

'No, no. There's a port not far away.' He grinned, walked over to ruffle his second son's hair.

Fhiro winced. Why did everyone always forget about his bruises?

'This particular attempt to kill us all has failed, you little rascal!'

* * *

Twenty-four days after they had abandoned their home, Fhiro and his family waited aboard the Siwob, hidden among the shadows of an asteroid. The navigation and lumia-crystals within the craft were dimmed and covered.

Oljon had guided them here after a rendezvous with Kartnan agents in the star port of the Nyfua system.

Despite his desires to see the interior of Nyfua's port, as with every destination after Calagan, Fhiro had kept such thoughts to himself. His parents had told him about the system, though. Nyfua was a Kartnan protectorate in all but name. Two hundred years ago its populace overthrew the tyrannical dynasty that had

ruled and oppressed them for generations. Kartna had lent a helping hand on the condition that the Kartnan Minas became their sole currency upon liberation. The new nation found itself surrounded by hostile neighbours, and dependent upon a distant empire for trade and survival. Were war to erupt from the fragile balance, the Senate would consider this justification to intervene and expand Kartnan influence. As yet, the Empire's hopes were still to be realised.

The Kartnan Empire. Fhiro's heart skipped a beat at the thought he might actually see it.

After what felt like forever, waiting in darkness and playing imaginary noughts-and-crosses with Dorrick and Chinda, Fhiro saw a black shadow pass across the stars. It circled the asteroid and then approached, stopping several hundred metres in front of them.

Oljon took Hanu's hand. She turned around and said, 'Children, please come and be with us.'

They came forward and stood with their parents. Hanu made sure she had her arms around all of them. She had the anxious look about her that Fhiro was still getting used to.

'Ma,' he said, 'it'll be all right.'

Hanu closed her eyes and smiled. 'We took you to Andelic to keep you all out of danger,' she said. 'So that you wouldn't have to run around, frightened for your lives. We wanted peaceful lives we could live out, according to how Aten wanted us to be.'

'You did really well, then,' said Fhiro.

'He's right, Ma,' said Dorrick. 'You did it for us. It's not your fault that danger came and found us.'

Oljon kissed Hanu's forehead. 'It was a good thing that we had.'

'Aren't you both used to dangerous things like this?' asked Chinda.

'But this is far more terrifying than anything either of us

have done before.' Oljon pulled Chinda closer to him. 'We've got you three to look after now.'

'I don't need looking after,' said Dorrick.

'Sorry Dorrick,' said Oljon. 'Of course you don't.'

A pod detached from the ship and came towards them. There was the familiar sound of airlock seals connecting to one another, followed by a knocking on their outer doors. Silently Oljon led them to greet their visitors.

Two men of solid build entered. Oljon looked relieved.

'Ishthen,' said the first, saluting him, 'to see you alive warms my heart! I am Vawal, a Lieutenant at the port embassy. My father fought under you at Ospa and forever spoke highly of your captaincy.'

'My Lord,' saluted the soldier beside him, 'please forgive me for taking a more senior officer's place on this trip, but I begged to be one of the first to greet you. My grandfather and uncle were surrounded at Thico when you relieved the siege there. Pral is my name.'

Oljon shook hands with them both and relaxed. 'I am but a humble civilian now. I don't seek glory or power. I have served the Empire and wish only for peace in my second life.'

'Lord Valachrad is the ambassador here,' said Vawal. 'He knows you well from times of war and politics. Your fate lies in his hands.'

'Senator Valachrad?'

'The same,' Vawal answered. 'He has been frequently engaged in foreign affairs since his rejuvenation, speaking with clout and authority when he holds the sceptre of the Imperium.'

'I commanded him, through General Marsh, at Haveth, and now he has authority over me?' Oljon shook his head. 'Indeed, fate plays strange games.'

'Come aboard our shuttle,' said Vawal. 'Take everything you care for with you. We will not be returning to this place.'

As the two Kartnans led the way Hanu gripped Oljon's wrist. 'Our *fate* is in someone's hands?'

'Relax,' said Oljon, 'they always talk like this.'

'What kind of *fates* are available?' asked Hanu.

Oljon motioned for her to be silent.

Hanu glared back at him.

'Aren't you coming?' asked Vawal, grinning.

Oljon beamed. 'Of course. Just checking we hadn't forgotten anything.'

Soon they were speeding away aboard the shuttle. Chinda wept as she waved goodbye to the Siwob. Fhiro was quite annoyed at himself for the powerful pang of sadness he felt as their small, short-lived home, was lost from sight.

'How well did you know this ambassador?' asked Hanu as they approached Nyfua's port.

'A little,' said Oljon. 'I had a number of meetings and conversations with him during the Haveth campaign. But later we were senators. He was renowned for his great oratory skill. He and I had a few disagreements over policy, but he shouldn't have taken any of it personally.'

'And now our fate is in his hands,' said Hanu, her voice mocking that of Vawal.

Their shuttle, rather than connecting with a charge-dock, slowed down over an enormous vessel that was, itself, connected to the port.

'Welcome to the Blind Vizier,' said Vawal, 'Lord Valachrad's ship.'

Fhiro was speechless as the shuttle entered a small hangar inside the Blind Vizier. He saw the hangar shut above them, and then there was a rush of air outside, after which their shuttle's pilot checked some devices at the air lock, before opening it.

Upon exiting the shuttle Vawal and Pral led them through

another airlock into a corridor. Statues of figures that appeared to be fusions of familiar creatures, rose from the floor or reached out from the sides of the corridor at intervals. Fhiro assumed these were representations of Kartna's gods. In general, they were portrayed in a manner that communicated holiness, wisdom and power. In plenty, however, there were hints of cunning, cruelty or menace. Fhiro felt at once in awe, but also afraid of these gods, of whom he knew very little. That he was entering their realm, and becoming subject to their will, unsettled him.

Between the statues, framed and fastened to the walls, were paintings both abstract and figurative. The themes depicted included hard work, achievement, conflict, conquest, bravery and dominance. The floor under Fhiro's feet was covered in soft, patterned fabrics.

Fhiro considered that this ship's interior was more decorated and polished than any house or building he had seen in his life. Their journey through it lasted as long as it would take to walk from one end of Chimahess to the other. He could not imagine how large the ship must have looked from the outside.

They reached a gold-plated door. It was so polished and shiny, Fhiro could see his reflection in it. Two soldiers and a woman in plain robes stood beside it.

Vawal spoke to the woman. She smiled and nodded to him before turning to the family. 'If you want to straighten your clothes out a little, we shall enter when you are ready.'

They all made some effort to neaten their appearance, except Oljon who appeared lost in thought. Hanu checked his clothes for him. 'How you look does matter, dear.'

Oljon murmured in agreement, his mind still somewhere else.

Hanu nodded to Pral who, with a stiff back and a swollen

chest, pushed the golden door and led the way in. The room beyond was covered in soft material from floor to ceiling. There were couches everywhere with servants weaving between them, carrying trays of food and drink. On their right-hand side three musicians stood on a platform. One played small, leather drums, the furthest blew notes upon a mussette, and the nearest plucked and strummed a long-necked, square-shaped lute. The style of music was not one Fhiro was accustomed to, but he did not mind it.

'Valachrad,' Oljon said softly to himself, as he stared across the room at a large man surrounded by a troop of young officers. The large man laughed a rich laugh as one of them finished recounting a tale. Oljon walked straight towards the ambassador and Vawal struggled to keep up. Hanu then followed, holding Chinda by the hand. Dorrick and Fhiro trailed after. He saw Vawal starting to make introductions.

But the ambassador stood up. 'Ishthen!' He smiled, showing his teeth and placing a half-eaten, pastry-wrapped parcel of food on to a tray. He wiped the crumbs off his hands and put his arms out to embrace Oljon. 'How great to see you!' He slapped Oljon's back. 'You still keep in shape, don't you!'

'I see we both follow our old habits,' said Oljon.

Valachrad paused, his eyes wide. The officers and servants nearby, including Vawal, went silent and tried to look away. Then Valachrad burst into loud laughter. He grabbed his stomach where it swelled above his waist. 'Yes, yes of course! But we earned our rejuvenated bodies. I don't even have to feel guilty to my mother for abusing this one.' He continued to chuckle. 'Sit! Sit!'

'This is my wife, Hanu.'

'A pleasure to meet you.' Valachrad kissed her hand.

'The honour is mine.' Hanu did her best to smile.

'No, really, it is so good to have Ishthen back among us. And

these are your children? You really have changed, haven't you man!' Valachrad looked back at Hanu. 'Now here is a woman who knows her husband really did spend an entire life-time searching for her!' He laughed so loud Fhiro thought he was shouting.

Hanu grinned and shot a knowing glance at Oljon.

The atmosphere relaxed with the ambassador's visible happiness.

'So what are your names?' asked Valachrad.

'This is Chinda,' said Hanu.

'That's a lovely name. I don't think I've heard it before. Is it a name from Essera? That is where you met, isn't it?'

'It's quite common on Andelic,' said Oljon, 'the planet we've called home for many years.'

'Of course.' Valachrad touched his nose. 'I've kept good friends in the Ministry of Shadows and, running one of the closest outposts to your hiding place, I wondered if this day might come during my stint here.' He looked around, and his eyes fastened on the boys. 'And what're your names?'

Dorrick and Fhiro told him.

'Have you two come of age?'

'Dorrick is recently fourteen,' said Oljon, 'and is considering a career as a pilot.'

'A pilot? A very interesting and worthwhile profession.' Valachrad nodded.

'I'm thinking about it,' said Dorrick.

'Good idea. Definitely keep your options open. Why, your father and I have had lots of careers! Perhaps you will join one of the academies in Kartna. That would set you up for all kinds of possibilities. Come, sit!'

Oljon sat between Hanu and the ambassador. She had Chinda on her lap while Fhiro and Dorrick found cushions to sit on in front of them. The officers and civilians in their fine clothes slid away, while servants gathered nearby.

'So Fhiro, how old are you?' asked Valachrad.

'Twelve.'

'That is the same age as my boy!' said Valachrad. 'He has been getting rather fed up, being stuck out on this port for so long. We've been stranded here, preparing to embark on a journey. In the meantime I can hardly permit him to leave here for long; we might be leaving any day now.'

'Where are you going?' asked Oljon.

'All to be discussed in good time,' laughed Valachrad. 'Well, actually, why not? Between us, we are heading deep into the Smugglers' Union. You've heard about the recent discovery?'

Fhiro had to stifle a gasp of amazement. He had hoped so hard that the discovery would be important. Hoped that, from the ashes of the Great Dying, the Ancient Poshokans may have sent a dagger forward through time right at Marallel's heart.

'Of an ancient Poshokan artefact, alleged to be a weapon?' asked Oljon. 'I have, but to be honest I didn't take it seriously. Evidently Kartna thinks there is substance to this rumour?'

'The Senate does not want to be caught off guard if it is anything,' said Valachrad. 'So off we go.' He winked.

Fhiro felt smug. He wondered if he should ask for an apology from his father. Then again, if it turned out to be nothing, he would look doubly foolish himself. He realised Valachrad was looking at him.

'As for my son, he hopes to enrol in an academy in two years, but I thought the upcoming trip would be useful to him,' said the ambassador. 'Good experience and all. Something to write on the application papers or talk about at interview. Fhiro, if your brother has already come of age he can stay here, but it might be an idea for you to spend some time with my son. He's going to meet with our special guests for lunch in the port-city.'

Fhiro looked at Dorrick. His older brother was smiling, but looked uncertain and troubled at the same time. Fhiro imagined his own face might be coming across the same way: which, of the two of them, was getting the better deal? Fhiro faced Valachrad and, with a slight bow of his head, said, 'All right – I mean, thank you, my Lord.'

Valachrad burst out laughing.

'Who are these guests they are meeting?' asked Hanu. 'Should we go too?'

'Oh, don't worry,' said Valachrad. 'Ghorad, Imial's guard, will be with them, and I have met these guests myself. A very pleasant group. They're archaeologists from the Greater Magellan. Their expertise in Poshokan artefacts and ruins is second to none. We are negotiating a deal whereby we escort them to this discovery.'

'To curry favour with the local rulers,' said Oljon, 'or will these archaeologists be reporting to you?'

Valachrad laughed again. 'In the details, Ishthen. In the details. But come, now it is time to eat and relax. You must pay attention to the lute player, here. Enchanting melodies effortlessly flow from her fingers.'

Fhiro had to agree the lute player was talented.

'Yelba,' Valachrad called over the woman who had met them outside the room. 'This is Yelba, my chief and most trusted servant. Yelba, take this boy to Imial, and get Ghorad to escort them out for lunch.'

'We have until now been followed by Creedate spies,' said Oljon. 'Is there not a risk they will recognise Fhiro on the port?'

'We herded them all out of here an hour ago,' said Valachrad. 'We have ways of keeping tabs on those who keep tabs on us.' He smiled.

Fhiro looked at his parents, as Yelba gestured for him to

follow her. His mother looked at Valachrad, then at Oljon and then turned and nodded to Fhiro. 'You'd better go then, but be careful.'

'You'll be fine,' said Oljon. 'See you soon.' His calm smile did a lot to reassure Fhiro.

'Bye, then,' said Fhiro, standing up. He tried to smile too. His sister looked most concerned about his departure, but none of his family looked at ease, except perhaps his father. Still, he considered, if they were to survive the pursuing Creedate agents, they needed protection, and there was no better protection he could hope to find in the galaxy besides that of Kartna. He should count his blessings – if blessings were actually a real thing with any tangible meaning.

Sometimes he wished he had never asked himself whether Aten was real or not.

Fhiro followed Yelba away from his family, glancing from time to time at the musicians as they changed key and tempo in a winding medley that made him think of racing round and round a mountain towards its summit. Then, passing back through the golden door they had arrived from, the music almost vanished, so effective was the soundproofing of the chamber he had just left. Yelba led him down long corridors, further and further away, until Fhiro wondered if he would be able to trace his way back. He felt very alone in this unknown ship of an alien culture. Yet he considered that this was the very culture he might have inherited had his parents made their way to Kartna, and not Andelic, all those years ago when they fled from the Creedate. His father seemed comfortable here, like he belonged. Did Fhiro, and the rest of the family, have a right to feel the same?

Yelba took Fhiro to a sparsely decorated room with white walls. A boy of his age sat on the floor, near the door, reading a book.

'Imial,' said Yelba, 'your father wishes this boy to accompany you to lunch.'

Imial looked surprised and then, with an intense look on his face, studied Fhiro. Fhiro was aware that his clothes were rather dirty and travelled in, while everything about Imial looked impeccable and clean. When Imial did not speak Fhiro decided to break the silence. 'I'm Fhiro.'

Imial did not extend a hand to him. 'I see. Yelba, where is Ghorad?'

'I will bring him.' She left.

Fhiro looked for somewhere to sit down. He found a neglected cushion on the floor.

'Did I say you could sit?' Imial's voice was cold.

Fhiro, adjusting the cushion, was surprised to have his intentions questioned. He resolved to deny Imial any chances to make claims of superiority. He kept his voice calm and polite. 'Does that matter?'

CHAPTER 8

'I am the ambassador's son,' said Imial, 'and I would judge from your dress that you are some kind of street urchin, or one of those port performers that demands money for tricks.'

'I've been travelling for a long time,' said Fhiro.

'Sorry?'

'We've been in quite a rush,' Fhiro flustered. 'I'm not–'

'Do you have a home?'

'At the moment I don't.' He noticed the beginnings of a snarl on Imial's face. He knew the smart thing to do was to tell Imial that Valachrad had sent him here, but his curiosity had got the better of him. He wanted, now, to find out just how far Imial would go towards forming an opinion of Fhiro while knowing almost nothing about him. Fhiro sat down and watched for Imial's reaction.

Imial's eyes widened. 'What is someone with no home doing in my presence?'

'Why do people normally come here?' asked Fhiro.

'This is no place for common people.'

'What does that even mean?'

'Where are you from?'

'Andelic,' said Fhiro. 'The Green River Valley in Andelic.'

Imial laughed. 'Where in the galaxy is that?!'

'The periphery.'

'So nowhere!' Imial continued laughing. 'Look, just go. Get out of here.' He turned his attention back to his book.

Fhiro studied Imial and considered his response. Without good reason he knew he would find submission to this

arrogant rudeness intolerable. He was also, probably, quite safe; Imial did not act, or carry himself, in a fashion of one with with training in violent confrontation. Fhiro's training, on the other hand, was extensive.

Imial looked up at him. 'Have you not gone yet? I said go!'

Fhiro tried to force a smile, but he did not move.

Imial looked out of the door, as though he might see someone he could order to remove Fhiro.

'Why should I leave?' asked Fhiro.

'Because you do not belong here.'

'Why?'

'You want me to explain it to you?' Imial's chuckle was high-pitched. 'I'm terribly sorry, but I don't have time to waste on stupid peripheral beggers like you. Just do as you're told.'

Fhiro wondered if he was missing something. Imial seemed so confident. Perhaps there was something cultural he did not understand, and that his father had not warned him about. A rule he had broken, that would have bad consequences obvious to anyone raised in Kartna.

But whatever complicated explanation Fhiro could use to justify Imial's behaviour, they all relied upon him knowing something he did not know. Therefore he failed to see how it could be his fault, so he resolved to sit it out.

Imial scowled at him, and made towards the door.

Just then a tall, thick-bodied man walked in. He wore formal clothes rather than a uniform, but Fhiro could see a handgun strapped to his belt.

'Ghorad,' Imial commanded, 'who is this boy?'

Ghorad stopped in his tracks. He looked at Fhiro. 'Fhiro? Son of Ishthen?'

'My father's name is Oljon, not Ishthen,' said Fhiro.

'Imial, in accordance with your father's wishes, we've

arranged for you to dine with the archaeologists this lunch, and your father has requested that Fhiro come along too.'

Imial's eyes narrowed as he stared at Fhiro. Then he turned to Ghorad. 'Very well. We shall honour our planned engagements.'

'Thank you.' Ghorad led them into the corridor. Outside, other men dressed in a similar manner to Ghorad fell in behind them.

'So, who is this *Fhiro*?' Imial asked Ghorad.

'You can ask him yourself.' Ghorad stopped to fix Imial's collar and tuck his shirt in.

'I want to know why my father sent him to be with me.'

'He is the son of Ishthen,' said Ghorad.

'Who's that?'

'Supreme commander during the Martial Uprising,' said Ghorad.

This was new information to Fhiro. The Kartnan Martial Uprising had been an existential crisis for the Kartnan Empire, famous enough he had been taught about it on Andelic.

'His father was a Tetrarch-legate?' asked Imial.

Fhiro was still holding his breath. He hoped his shock at learning the scope of his father's previous power did not show on his face.

'For security reasons,' said Ghorad, 'it is better we refer to his father as Oljon, the name he has adopted since converting to The Calling.'

'You're a Follower of The Calling?!' The awe in Imial's face melted into one of assured confidence and disdain.

'My parents are.' Fhiro decided against challenging Ghorad's view on his father's name; he already had one influential and hostile person too many to contend with in this new world of Kartnan ambassadors and Creedate spies.

'Pitiful fool,' said Imial. 'One God? I should be more

forgiving of your stupidity, for you have never seen the gods. They are very real, you know. Far more real than the nonsense you believe.'

'And how d'you know that?' asked Fhiro.

'I have seen our gods,' said Imial. 'They command and all of our empire obeys.'

'I've heard the Kartnan gods can appear in different forms.' Fhiro remembered the chapter from *Mythologies of the Galaxy.*

'Yes,' said Imial. 'Sumrubbikut is my favourite. The head of a dragon and the mane of a lion, he is the god of war and harvest.' Imial's nose wrinkled as he examined the inferior materials of Fhiro's clothes. 'Perhaps you will be drawn to Ulret, the Snake god. You have a crafty look about you.'

Fhiro could not decide what to make of this last comment. 'Could your gods not have been made with sorcery?'

'Blasphemy!' cried Imial.

Ghorad also turned to glare at Fhiro.

'Forgive me!' Fhiro, wide-eyed, made every effort to look as apologetic as he could. 'I've never seen them. I just know sorcery can do amazing things.'

'Your imagination could never capture the glory of the gods,' said Ghorad. 'I too have been blessed enough to witness their magnificence. However, it is probably best we do not debate religion. Enough blood is being spilled across the galaxy on that account already.'

Imial smiled at Ghorad, though the guard took no notice.

Ghorad brought them through the outer airlock of the Blind Vizier and into the port interior. Soldiers, carrying assault rifles and submachine guns, stood aside to let them pass.

Fhiro felt his breath escape him again; this was only the second port he had seen from inside. They stepped on to a walkway suspended in the air that led out over the stalls and parks and roads beneath, all the way to a platform on the far

wall. Fhiro became transfixed by a collection of creatures sitting around a table below them, taking turns to inhale the fumes from a machine full of bubbling liquid. 'Are those hoppers?'

Ghorad looked over his shoulder. 'Not seen them before?'

'Never,' said Fhiro. 'Andelic is mostly full of earthmen and yeal, with quite a large hegel population too. There are no recci or hoppers.'

'Few hoppers in this part of the galaxy, I would say,' said Ghorad. 'The deep Near Quadrant is mostly made up of earthmen, for this is where we came from. Now stick together on this platform, boys. Don't wander off.'

'Where did we arrange to meet the archaeologists?' Imial asked, not once looking at Fhiro, as though he was pretending the other boy did not exist. 'I'm in the mood for Hecklish cuisine.'

Ghorad paused. 'This morning you requested the archaeologists meet you at a Roastfire restaurant. We've booked the *Drak-Dragon's Heart*.'

Imial frowned, but then smiled. 'All right.'

'Your father told us about the archaeologists,' said Fhiro. 'Apparently they're experts in Poshokan artefacts.'

'We're offering to escort them into the old Smugglers' Union,' said Imial, his voice full of heartfelt superiority.

'I hope the discovery turns out to be a weapon of some kind,' said Fhiro.

'That is what some people think,' said Imial. Then he laughed. 'Were you wanting to use it to catch animals for food? What else would a street urchin like you want a weapon for? You'd probably end up just blowing your own face off with it.'

Fhiro steadied his breathing. 'I was hoping it might be used against the Creedate.' Then he remembered where he was, and looked over his shoulder, scouring people nearby for signs they might be Creedate agents.

Ghorad noticed this. 'You're safe now. This port has been cleared of Creedate spies.'

Fhiro's shoulders relaxed. 'That's what the ambassador said.'

'He spoke the truth.' Ghorad grinned. 'You too, now, are under our protection. Kartna might be feared for her military accomplishments, but her success is as much a credit to diplomacy and good spycraft.'

However, Fhiro could not help pausing to cast an eye over his shoulder every now and then. 'Is the ambassador not joining us?'

'Not today,' said Ghorad. 'He has already met with the archaeologists. He thought it would be good for Imial to get to know them before we set off.'

'Have you met them Ghorad?' asked Imial.

'Yes,' said Ghorad. 'Their leader, Cerilina, seems impressive and capable. They are grateful guests, eager to inform and educate about their work and intentions. Meeting them would be good for both of you.'

'How many are there?' asked Fhiro.

'Ten,' said Ghorad. 'The only other one I've spoken to, though, is Borlin. He is the one Kartnan archaeologist in their group.'

'Good to hear that one of our own is among them,' said Imial.

'Don't be too excited,' said Ghorad. 'Good archaeologists study the origins of the Empire. There's probably a reason Borlin wound up studying the Poshokans.'

'The others are all from the outer Magellan,' said Imial. 'Have you ever met a clouder before, Fhiro?'

'No,' said Fhiro. He had met very few people from outside the Luwol Federation until a few weeks ago. He had heard about the civilisations of Magellan's cloud, but it was a long way away from the Near Quadrant.

After crossing over the port-city, and reaching the far platform, they made a short journey through a labyrinth of stairs and narrower walkways to the restaurant itself. Most of the tables were outside, if the interior of a port-city could be called 'outside'. There was a roofed building, made of Serowood; the heat-mouldable material built of complex hydrocarbon polymers, grown by trees that had been altered by sorcerers millennia ago.

Fhiro considered the value of the roof, and figured it must be a security feature, rather than one to protect the contents of the building from the weather, there being no weather in a port-city. Unsavoury characters were rumoured to gather in port-cities, somewhere they could easily be stranded and have no means of escaping.

Kartnan guards greeted them under the hanging sign that read *The Drak-Dragon's Heart.* Fhiro and Imial were shown to a long table where a number of people were already seated. On seeing Imial and Ghorad arrive, they stood up. Fhiro saw that, besides a few yeal, they were all earthpeople, and they wore similar clothes; white, loose fitting garments with coloured segments and patterns.

'Imial and Fhiro,' said Ghorad, 'may I introduce Cerilina, the leader of the archaeologists from Irenzel.'

'A pleasure to make your acquaintances,' said Cerilina. She had a pleasant smile, and thick, auburn hair rested on her shoulders.

'The pleasure is mine,' Imial replied.

'And mine,' said Fhiro, really not sure what he was doing here.

Imial looked annoyed that Fhiro had spoken. 'You have come a long way, I hear,' he said to Cerilina.

'Thanks to generosity of your Senate, we were protected by a military escort for much of the journey,' said Cerilina.

'And this,' said Ghorad, with a little less reverence in his voice, 'is Borlin. An archaeologist from Kartna.'

A bleary-eyed man, who had been sitting opposite Cerilina, grinned as he gazed at them. 'Hello.'

'Allow me to introduce my other colleagues,' said Cerilina. She pointed to the dark-haired woman next to her. 'This is Vuwek, and beside her …'

Fhiro did his best to keep track, but was distracted by a dark shape flying overhead. A large bird swerved above them, symbols dyed into the feathers under its wings. It changed direction a few times, and atop it Fhiro could make out an armed, uniformed man, looking this way and that as he led his steed on a patrol across the enclosed sky.

'If the gods are willing,' said Imial, 'I shall get to know all of you better in time.'

'And Fhiro,' said Cerilina, 'are you a friend of Imial's?'

Fhiro snapped to attention. He prayed none of the archaeologists expected him to remember their names.

'I'm not sure what he is,' said Imial.

'His family are working with us,' said Ghorad. 'We'll explain in detail back aboard the ship.'

Fhiro decided not to add anything to this. He assumed Ghorad knew better how to manage such a situation.

'Can we eat now?' asked Imial. 'I'm hungry.'

They all sat, and the staff soon brought them drinks and small dishes.

'Borlin, how is it you came to be on this expedition?' asked Imial.

'Borlin has been a very good friend to us,' said Cerilina. 'His contacts in the Empire helped get us this far.'

'Are you in a big research department?' asked Fhiro.

'If my tiny office, and some storage space round the corner counts,' said Borlin, 'I think the answer would still be no.'

'Studying the Ancients is a bit taboo in the Empire,' sniffed Imial.

Borlin took a slurp of his wine. 'I've never been much good at avoiding taboos.'

'Did I hear correctly that we cleared the port of Creedate spies?' Cerilina asked.

'Really?' Borlin's eyes lit up.

Ghorad nodded, but looked a little troubled as he spoke. 'It's true.'

'Well that really is something to drink to.' Borlin stood up. 'Did you hear that, everyone? There aren't any Creedate spies in the port today!'

There were a few uncertain cheers as the other archaeologists and guards checked their surroundings.

'To the death of the Creedate!' cried Borlin. 'And if this ancient Poshokan installation we're looking for turns out to be a weapon, may it forever elude Marallel's filthy claws!'

'Borlin!' cried Ghorad over the din of cheers and laughter. 'The port may have been emptied of spies, but anybody might overhear your shouting.' He pointed over the balcony wall to the path that ran underneath the restaurant. It was filled with people, all walking in the same direction. 'Just metres below us the Followers of The Calling are heading to their Worship congress.'

Borlin laughed. 'Such a spoilsport, Ghorad.' He sat down.

Ghorad shook his head. 'We should have left you back home.'

'Ah,' said Borlin, patting Cerilina's arm, 'Ceri's always been like a mother to me. She could never have done that.'

'I tutored you,' said Cerilina. 'You could say I shaped your career, but I didn't raise you.'

Fhiro thought Cerilina looked much younger than Borlin. He recalled his own father, and the wonders that could be achieved in a shrouded haven. Surely, then, Cerilina had been rejuvenated at some point in her life. How many times,

though? He considered asking her, but imagined that might be a rude thing to do.

'Do you have an apprentice to run errands for you while you're gone?' asked Imial.

'My last apprentice tried to get me arrested,' said Borlin, staring into his goblet.

'Shall we talk about something else?' Cerilina suggested.

Fhiro's mind was bubbling with questions. 'What makes you think this discovery is a weapon? I heard it was buried underground.'

'So we've been led to believe,' said Cerilina. 'I, also, can't imagine what a kind of weapon gets buried in such a fashion. There's an entire mountain on top of it, apparently. Local havens have tried to scan it from a distance, but are having limited success.'

'Sneaky Poshokans,' said Borlin, 'hiding what they were doing.' He refilled his goblet, spilling some wine on the table, and then took another gulp. 'Sneaky.'

'But the documents that led the local populace towards this discovery did imply it carried great military significance,' said Cerilina.

Fhiro recalled Professor Millorn's disinterest in the discovery again. His mind began to drift, recalling his conversations with his departed teacher. Her face. Her sayings. Her wise, calm ways. He blinked. What had Cerilina just said? 'Documents?'

'Shall I assume neither of you know the details of the discovery so far?' asked Cerilina.

'I didn't think there was much to know, yet,' said Imial, 'and I'd be amazed if Fhiro, from the periphery, knew any more than I did.'

Fhiro would have given away his gravi-trap if it meant he could know more about this subject than Imial right now.

Cerilina looked at Ghorad. 'May I tell them?'

'Tell them what?' asked Ghorad.

'About the documents aboard a Sufferer ship?' she asked.

Ghorad's eyes widened a fraction, before relaxing again. 'You probably have to, now.'

'Sufferers?' asked Imial.

'I read a bit about them once,' said Fhiro, recalling a few snippets of information in *Mythologies of The Galaxy*.

'What's a Sufferer?' Imial asked Borlin.

'Nothing you'd be interested in,' said Borlin, yawning. 'Ancient history. You know, from the ancient times, and we know Kartna's got no time for that. Seriously.'

'Don't throw me off,' said Imial. 'Tell me!'

'They were not the most popular of people,' said Cerilina. 'They were exterminated after the Great Dying.'

'The good old days,' sighed Borlin. 'Coordinated, cross-cultural exterminations. Don't see those any more.'

'You are a strange man,' said Ghorad.

'A Sufferer ship drifted out of an asteroid field near Pelorn, the planet we're heading to,' said Cerilina. 'It had been there for two thousand years.'

'Wow' said Fhiro.

'Inside were documents describing what the occupants had been up to. They were interrogating a Poshokan, who told them there was a weapon hidden on Pelorn.'

'So why didn't these Sufferers find the weapon themselves?' asked Fhiro.

'That crafty Poshokan found a way to kill them,' said Borlin. 'Like I said, they were sneaky. Clever, crafty and sneaky. Gotta love 'em.'

'I dread to think what she went through before she managed that, though,' said Cerilina.

'Did she escape?' asked Fhiro.

'Oh no,' said Cerilina, 'but death is a good outcome for any

captive of the Sufferers. They were an evil people, devoted to the mastery of torture and pain.'

'All right,' said Ghorad, raising his hand, 'enough details about the Sufferers. Stick to what's relevant.'

'Sorry,' said Cerilina. 'Any scholar of the Poshokans inevitably ends up studying the Sufferers as well. They're a bit of a guilty pleasure. Fascinating but terrifying. You know the sort of thing.'

'And thankfully all dead,' said Ghorad.

'See now why they were wiped out?' Borlin asked Imial and Fhiro. 'Must say, galaxy's probably a lot more boring without those guys around.'

'Borlin,' said Ghorad, 'enough.'

'Sorry.' Borlin smiled.

'I suspect most of the galaxy will breathe a sigh of relief if this discovery turns out to be nothing at all,' said Ghorad.

'There are quite a few Followers of The Calling living on Pelorn and on the planets nearby,' said Borlin. 'If this find is anything worth fighting for, Marallel will invent some justification to conquer the whole region.'

'Not all Followers support the Creedate,' said Fhiro.

'Yeah, I know,' said Borlin, nodding, 'but plenty of them do. Fanatical lunatics.'

A scream ripped through the din of dining and merrymaking. Some of the guards rushed to the balcony running along the edge of the restaurant. Fhiro, unable to resist finding out what had captured everyone's attention, jumped up and followed them.

'I've been cleared!' cried a man's voice.

Fhiro stood on tiptoe and craned forward to see the floor below. Not far away stood a man with his back to them. His grey cloak was covered in embroidered, overlapping, scarlet symbols of different sizes.

'A greycloak,' muttered Ghorad.

'A plague-bearer?' Imial joined them, but had to keep jumping to catch a glimpse over Fhiro's shoulder. 'I can't see!'

Fhiro's attention was fixed to the scene below. In front of the greycloak stood a group of men with beams of wood or metal pipes in their hands. The foremost of them carried a bat, the likes of which Fhiro used to play the game Rack-ball with at school. This man, a wildness in his eyes, adjusted his grip on the bat as he spoke. 'The plague isn't welcome on Nyfua.'

'I've been cleared,' shouted the greycloak again. 'I wouldn't have been allowed into the port if my papers weren't in order.'

'Papers can be changed,' said the wild-eyed man.

Ghorad cupped his hands to his mouth. 'I order you to leave that man alone!' He turned to the restaurant staff. 'Signal the port security, now!'

The wild-eyed man returned his gaze to the greycloak. 'Your friends are a little far away, I'm afraid, and there's nowhere left to run.'

'Please,' said the greycloak, 'let me see my daughter again.'

'And give her the plague too?' The wild-eyed man grinned. Some of those behind him laughed.

'You three,' Ghorad ordered some of his men, 'make your way down there and stop this. Use lethal force only in defence. We'll have you covered from here.'

Three of the Kartnan guards ran from the restaurant.

Fhiro felt rage well up inside him. 'Let him show you his papers!' he shouted.

'And catch his plague from those?' cried another one of the gang. They all moved towards the greycloak, raising their weapons.

'Go for the body,' said the wild-eyed leader. 'I don't want any disease spraying in my eyes.'

'I bring you no harm,' pleaded the greycloak. 'Please believe me!'

There was a torrent of rushing, whistling air, followed by thudding and crunching as the blunt instruments came down upon the greycloak. First it was his arms, raised up over his head, that cracked and gave way. Then his ribs were smashed and his legs beaten until he collapsed. Fhiro turned away, wincing at the sound of each impact.

A dark shadow passed over the restaurant and then over the gang below. Fhiro looked up and saw the same bird he had noticed earlier.

'Port security,' muttered the wild-eyed man. He kicked the greycloak one last time and then, along with the rest of the gang, fled into the alleys leading off the road. One of the gang members ran in a different direction, but was kicked off his feet by the guards Ghorad had sent down to help. The Kartnan guards then split up; one secured the gang member, another sprinted after the attackers and the last saw to the injured greycloak.

The bird touched down on the path and its rider ran over to join the Kartnan beside the greycloak. Together they turned the injured man on to his back.

'Braver men than me,' muttered Borlin. 'I wouldn't touch that greycloak.'

'Cowardice is not a luxury for a soldier of the Empire,' said Ghorad, turning away and heading towards the table. Gradually the rest of those that had been watching from the balcony, including Fhiro, joined him there. Fhiro's appetite was gone. All he could think about was how painful the beating must have felt for the greycloak.

The waiters that brought the food apologised on behalf of the local community for what their guests had just witnessed. Fhiro and the other guests said little back, and less still to each other, as they began to eat.

'It was good of you to shout, Fhiro,' said Ghorad. 'Sadly some animals can't be reasoned with.'

'Thanks,' said Fhiro. He wanted to be sick. He looked around and saw that even Borlin looked subdued, his nose wrinkling as he sniffed his wine without drinking it, a gravy dripping joint of meat untouched on his plate.

The men that Ghorad had sent downstairs returned. 'The greycloak lives,' one of them informed him, 'but there's no telling whether he will survive the next few days.'

Ghorad nodded. 'And the culprits?'

'Being pursued by the port security forces,' answered the guard. 'The one we caught is being interrogated.'

'What kind of an interrogation?' asked Ghorad.

The guard looked at the boys, and then back at Ghorad. 'I think they've already broken his arms, sir.'

'That kind of an interrogation,' muttered Ghorad.

'I think the port authorities are very upset that our meal was disturbed,' continued the guard.

'They're grateful for our continued custom,' said Ghorad, 'and the favour Kartna shows their nation. Had we not been eating here they probably wouldn't have done anything. Oh well. Do sit down and eat.'

'If Kartna were fully in charge there'd be order in this place,' said Imial.

'I thought we were in charge,' said Borlin.

'It's not our law,' said Ghorad. 'I think we should avoid this area in future, regardless of how good the food is.'

Borlin raised his arms. 'That's not the fault of the restaurant. This place is brilliant!' He looked at Imial. 'It's a harsh Universe. It's probably good for the boys to see things like this.'

'Such decisions are not yours to make,' said Ghorad.

'How dangerous is the Smugglers' Union?' asked Fhiro,

hoping to take his mind off the greycloak. He wondered if he would ever want to eat again.

'It isn't the Smugglers' Union any more,' said Imial.

'I know.' That the smugglers had all begun to style themselves as kings did not change the history of the place as far as Fhiro was concerned.

'Compared to the interior of the Kartnan Empire, it's very dangerous,' Ghorad answered. 'After the Union collapsed the entire region was afire with war. That said, some nations are better than others. I've been led to believe that Pelorn is relatively safe.'

'I heard they were a cultured people,' said Cerilina. 'I'm looking forward to seeing their festivals.'

'Ah yes,' said Borlin. 'They worship their Beast Gods, don't they?'

'Beast gods?' asked Fhiro.

'I think we'll find out more when we arrive,' said Ghorad. 'Their culture centres around the native creatures that evolved on the planet.'

'It can't be that bad out there,' said Fhiro, watching Imial eat. 'The ambassador must think it's safe or he wouldn't have brought his son.'

Imial sat bolt upright. 'As a servant of the Empire, I do not back away from danger.'

When Imial had returned to his food Borlin winked at Fhiro and mouthed, 'It will be fine.'

Fhiro noticed Ghorad give Borlin another stern look. He then became aware of distant voices singing and chanting. He looked out of the other side of the restaurant. Across a chasm of space, traversed by suspended bridges, a tall pointed building stood out from the smaller structures around it.

'The Worship Congress for Followers of The Calling is in progress,' said Ghorad.

First Fhiro felt fear, but then he remembered the guards they had with them. As he recognised the melodies that carried over the air, he remembered sitting, kneeling and standing in the Worship Congress back home on Andelic. In recent years all he ever did, while everyone around him had been praying, was analyse the statements in the scriptures, and the words spoken from the pulpit. He would pick them apart in his head, finding them rife with contradictions and disagreeable implications. Now, however, the terrible cost of this cleverness weighed on him. He longed for guidance. He longed for a sense of belonging.

Why could he not just be like everyone else?

CHAPTER 9

Hanu showed no sign she had noticed Oljon placing his hand on to hers, as she stared at the wall across the table.

They were all sitting in the breakfast room within their small living quarters inside the Blind Vizier.

Fhiro and Dorrick placed cups of tea before them both and sat down with Chinda.

'So,' said Oljon, 'we aren't quite out of this yet.'

'How d'you mean?' asked Fhiro.

'He means,' said Hanu, 'that despite dedicating an entire lifetime-and-a-half to serving the Kartnan Empire, including putting himself in grave danger far from home, they don't trust him.' She sighed. 'They don't trust us.'

Oljon sighed too. 'It's not quite like that. They do appreciate what we've done for them, but they've asked us to help them with something.'

'Something dangerous,' added Hanu.

'It might *not* be dangerous,' said Oljon.

'They want us to go with Valachrad,' said Hanu, 'all the way into the Smugglers' Union.'

Fhiro felt a rush of excitement.

'It's not called that any more,' said Chinda.

'Yes, I know,' said Hanu, 'but it's still a dangerous place.'

'They want us to go to the discovery,' burst Fhiro. Now, though, his excitement was being contaminated with powerful doses of anxiety and fear. 'The Poshokan weapon, under the mountain.'

'Whatever it is,' said Oljon, 'yes. Valachrad is bringing his

own son, so it can't be that bad. They want our help because of all of our knowledge of The Calling and the Creedate.'

'We're going to be experts?' asked Dorrick.

'Your ma and I will,' said Oljon. 'The Creedate have already sent agents to Pelorn, and are negotiating with its ruler. We need to ensure they do not gain an advantage from this.'

'I thought you thought this discovery was a load of rubbish.' I told you so, Fhiro thought.

'I still do, if I'm honest,' said Oljon, 'but Kartna does not want to take a chance on the matter.'

'Maybe they know something we don't,' said Dorrick.

'Perhaps,' said Oljon. 'Perhaps not.'

'The place will be crawling with Creedate spies,' said Hanu. 'If they spot us, we'll be hauled off to the Grafters and tortured to death.'

'Can't we say no?' asked Chinda.

'Not really,' said Oljon. 'Not unless we break all ties with Kartna.'

'Let's do that, then,' said Chinda. 'Can't we find a nice place to live?'

'If we leave they'll keep tabs on us,' said Oljon, 'but not in a good way. We'll lose any loyalty Kartna has towards us now. We could even be turned over to the Creedate as part of an unofficial trade.'

'Valachrad'd do that?' asked Fhiro.

'It wouldn't be his decision,' said Oljon. 'He would just be following orders.'

They all sat in silence.

'I've always wanted to know more about the Poshokans,' said Fhiro. 'I'd love to go and see this discovery, even if it doesn't do anything.'

'If we go,' said Dorrick, 'will we be safe after that?'

'We will be welcomed back to Kartna,' said Oljon. 'That is the safest play for us, in the long run.'

'We are refugees,' said Hanu. 'Again.' She left one hand under her husband's, but the other she took to her mouth and bit gently on her knuckles.

'It'll be all right, Ma,' said Fhiro.

She smiled at him. 'Thanks Fhiro.'

'It *will* be fine,' said Oljon, 'but we'll all need to work hard at this if we're going to see it through. Understand?'

Oljon outlined the plan. He was to disguise himself as an Aculei warrior-priest and attach himself to Valachrad as a bodyguard, see what the ambassador saw, and advise him. Dorrick, having come of age, would become an apprentice to Valachrad's pilot aboard the Blind Vizier.

'When we reach our destination, you might even get a chance to do some beast flying,' said Oljon. 'It's essential training for atmospheric re-entry.'

'That would be amazing,' said Dorrick.

Hanu would be one of Valachrad's advisors. Chinda was disappointed to hear she would simply remain her mother's daughter, brought along on this long journey as children sometimes were, under such circumstances. They were the only members of the family who were to remain related to each other, when in public.

'What does Fhiro have to do, then?' Chinda asked, shooting her brother a cold stare.

'You, Fhiro, would be better off not pretending to be your mother's son,' said Oljon. 'However, you haven't come of age. I don't want you out of our sight, either.'

'Can I be an apprentice spy?' asked Fhiro.

'Apprentice spy?' asked Dorrick. 'Who sends an apprentice spy, with no training, off on dangerous missions into the Smugglers' Union?'

'What I had in mind is a little like that, though not quite,' said Oljon, 'but you'd have to promise to do exactly as you're told.'

* * *

They joined Imial and Valachrad for the evening meal, earlier than they would have eaten aboard the Siwob, but they were living according to Blind Vizier time now. Fhiro and Dorrick's appetites were unaffected. Valachrad nodded approval as they tucked in. Chinda, however, only picked at her food.

Valachrad leant across and said, 'Try some Muchtak sauce with that,' as he poured a spoonful of thick burgundy-coloured paste on to her plate. Chinda eyed it with deep suspicion, but with the ambassador watching her, she dipped in a morsel of food and brought it tentatively to her mouth. Her eyes lit up as she chewed with enthusiasm and dipped in again. 'Goes with everything,' murmured Valachrad with a smile.

'What are you going to be doing on Pelorn?' Imial asked Fhiro. 'I'm going to be my father's apprentice. He'll take me to all the meetings he can.'

'I'm like you then,' said Fhiro. 'I'll be my father's apprentice, but I've got to pretend I'm not his son.'

'Will you manage?' asked Imial. 'Do they have good acting schools out in the galactic periphery?'

'Probably,' said Fhiro, 'but I haven't been to any. I was in a play once.'

'Was it a big part? Did you get a lot of coaching?'

'I was a talking tree,' said Fhiro. 'In another play I was a pirate that got killed by the hero. I don't think I got any special coaching.'

'Hmmm.' Imial rested his chin on his fist. 'I wish you the best of luck. Remind me what your father will be doing?'

'Protecting your father,' said Fhiro, 'and advising him too. He'll be disguised as an Aculei priest.'

'Of course.' Imial nodded to himself quickly. 'I'd heard.'

Fhiro was pretty sure Imial was finding this out for the first time.

'The Aculei are very rare, you know.'

'In my book it says they're mask-wearing warrior priests from the Dusty Mountains.'

'Yes,' said Imial, 'on Nurej. They are heretics that worship the first Kartnan Emperor. For some reason the Senate allows them to live on holy ground. I think they should all be put to death.'

'Oh,' said Fhiro.

'I hope you don't ruin his disguise,' said Imial. 'If the Creedate are looking for him, you could put all of us in danger.'

Fhiro turned his spoon over and over in his pudding, wondering whether he was up to the job.

'Fhiro is it?' asked a man in a flowing glittering coat. 'And are you Chinda? I am Yogric, Imial's tutor. I understand you'll be joining us for lessons? I'm looking forward to teaching you both.'

'What lessons?' Fhiro turned to his mother.

'You two aren't getting to slack off while you're here,' said Hanu.

'What about Dorrick?' asked Fhiro.

'Three words,' said Dorrick.

Fhiro screwed up his face. '*Is-too-stupid*? Fair enough.'

'*Come-of-age*,' said Dorrick. 'I'll join you for the training, though.'

'Training?' asked Fhiro.

Dorrick grinned. 'There's a practice room here, and a weapons range. Pa's got all kinds of ideas already.'

'Wow,' said Fhiro, flexing his arms. 'I wondered if I'd go soft, cramped up in spaceships for such a long time.' He looked at Imial. 'Want to join us?'

'Why would I need to learn anything from you?' snorted Imial.

* * *

During tuition the next day Fhiro was the first to finish the assignments Yogric had set them. This drew the tutor's attention, but there was nothing Yogric could ask him that Fhiro could not answer.

As they considered an equation to determine crystal-energy expenditure while travelling through space, Fhiro said, 'The energy isn't always directly proportional to the distance light would travel.'

'Where would you get an idea like that?' exclaimed Yogric. 'When isn't that the case?'

'At the extremes of a crystal's capacity, and in areas of severe wash interference,' said Fhiro. 'There were experiments in the Shard zone that showed–'

'No one lives in the Shard zone,' scoffed Yogric, 'and I haven't heard of such experiments.'

'What's the Shard zone?' whispered Chinda as Yogric turned away.

'Professor Millorn would've told you,' Fhiro whispered back, his shoulders slumping as he mentioned his old master.

When the teaching was finished Yogric clapped his hands. 'Class dismissed.'

'Aren't you coming to the recreation suite?' asked Imial as Fhiro and his siblings left in a different direction.

'Training,' said Fhiro.

Imial scoffed at this. 'I'd like to see what's so great about this training you find so important.'

After two hours of obstacle courses, striking and grappling, both with and without weapons, and target practice, the four of them collapsed on the floor.

'I'm coming for you Dorrick,' said Fhiro, giving his brother a shove.

'You're not as close as you like to think.' His brother shoved him back.

Fhiro grinned, then turned his attention to Imial. 'You did well.'

Imial lifted and turned his head, panting with every inch of movement. Struggling to open his eyes, he gasped, 'I'll overtake you sooner than …' He collapsed again, his lips moving in silence. Apart from the words 'Street boy' the rest of his sentence was inaudible.

'That's the spirit.' Fhiro shook Imial's shoulder and laughed.

'He's got to beat Chinda first,' said Dorrick, getting to his feet.

'He's got to get up before that.' Chinda stood and went to where she'd left her water bottle.

'Let's grab some food,' said Fhiro.

'After Imial drinks some water,' said Dorrick.

Imial drank noisily, almost draining the bottle. Dorrick offered his arm. Imial hesitated, then accepted Dorrick's help and rose to his feet. 'I can show you round the ship,' he said unexpectedly. 'If you're allowed.'

The siblings exchanged glances.

'Pa?' asked Fhiro.

'It'll be late when you've finished eating,' said Oljon.

'It's perfectly safe in here,' said Imial. 'Every member of this crew has been hand picked–'

'Yes, yes, I'm sure it's the safest place in the galaxy,' Oljon interrupted. 'But get back soon. You'll need your sleep.'

Fhiro watched Imial over dinner and during the tour. He was curious to see how the arrogant ambassador's son reacted to being beaten both at academic and physical pursuits. The response was rather underwhelming; Imial seemed neither angry, nor appreciative, but though not physically cowed, he directed fewer insults towards Fhiro's street urchin status.

Imial's tour first took them to the bridge. Dorrick, having already been there, was greeted by the pilot, the co-pilot, the captain and the navigator. After some persuasion the navigator agreed to show them the ship's navigation-crystal. Several airlocks deeper into the ship's interior, they entered a room twice the size of the Siwob. The crystal, which from a distance resembled a tilting, bright, blue and white, glowing egg, was so large it almost reached from the floor to the ceiling. It rested on a small platform, sealed into which were pipes and cables, some thicker than Fhiro's chest. Standing by its side were a set of ladders held together with a wide, wood-frame contraption. The navigator demonstrated how he could move this around the crystal, by pulling on certain cords and chains, to reach any part of its surface.

'And,' he said, tugging a thick chain over his head, which sent him, and the system of ladders, hurtling towards the outer wall of the chamber, 'I can easily get to the bookshelves from here, too.'

Fhiro then saw the volumes of charts, like those he had noticed littered around the floor on the Siwob, filling bookshelves across every wall of the room. 'How many charts are there?' he asked.

'This is what they call the "essential collection",' said the navigator, laughing. 'These charts cover every major star system in the galaxy. There are, of course, more detailed libraries for explorers and those wanting to travel to regions further out, but for the purpose of our mission ...' He exhaled '... this is definitely overkill.'

Imial then led them to the library with its high ceiling and its own elaborate ladder system. Fhiro saw Cerilina and some of her colleagues reading in a booth. Fhiro introduced his siblings to her.

'Well it's nice to meet you all,' said Cerilina.

'Where's Borlin?' asked Fhiro, sliding along the long, leather covered cushion opposite her.

'Drinking?' she shrugged, and shared a glance with one of her female friends, the first clouder she had introduced at the restaurant. Fhiro struggled to remember her name. 'I'm glad to hear you're coming along, though. We didn't put you off?'

Fhiro rested his hands on the dark, wooden table between them. 'Did you always want to study the Poshokans?'

'Yes,' said Cerilina. 'It's a well-respected field of study where we're from, unlike in Kartna. We send experts across the galaxy from time to time when discoveries are made, but this find sounds more interesting than most.'

'The Poshokans were heretics that angered the gods,' said Imial, 'and their passing gave Kartna its chance to take power in the galaxy.'

'Yes, we know,' said Fhiro. 'And the Kartnan gods caused the Great Dying, and created the Universe, and painted it black, with paint.'

'Do not mock our gods,' said Imial, his face turning sour.

Dorrick gave Fhiro a gentle elbow in the ribs.

'Sorry,' said Fhiro, 'didn't mean to cause offence. But do the Kartnan gods say *how* they killed all the Poshokans?'

'The gods do not offer details about this,' said Imial. 'It was before they took form. In those times their energies were still powerful, but complex and different. They did not see the galaxy in the way we do, so they cannot describe how their actions in the spirit realm translated into physical events.'

'That sounds interesting on a philosophical level,' said Cerilina.

Fhiro wanted to say it sounded like a good way to avoid answering a direct question, but instead said, 'It sounds complicated.'

'I wouldn't expect you to understand,' said Imial, now

seeming more interested in one of the dark portraits hanging at the far end of the library.

'According to those who follow The Calling,' said Dorrick, 'the Ancients thought they understood Aten, and stopped trying to be of service to him. Their arrogance angered the Lord, and thus his vengeance was unleashed upon them.'

'Any of the gods from the mythologies I've read about in my book might have done it for the same reason,' said Fhiro.

'Maybe a flying spaghetti monster did it,' said Chinda, bursting out laughing.

There was a, 'Shush!' from somewhere else in the room.

'This *is* a library, Chins,' said Dorrick.

Fhiro looked around. At the far end of the room a few people sat at long tables covered in thick, leather-bound tomes. 'But whichever divine power did away with them,' he said a bit quieter, 'it could have done things differently, right?'

'We aren't second guessing divine powers again are we, Fhiro?' asked Dorrick.

'Seriously,' said Fhiro. 'Even if it wasn't an all-powerful divine power, it must have been *very* powerful. Why not just use its power to reveal this undeniable truth to some influential Poshokans?'

Imial looked like he was about to mock Fhiro for this statement when Cerilina said, 'The Poshokans would have considered that a very valid question, Fhiro.'

Relieved someone thought he was not mad, Fhiro added, 'They could have put up a big sign telling people what to believe. Now everything remains ambiguous. The whole galaxy might make the same mistake the Poshokans made, and end up exterminated again.'

'Exactly,' said Cerilina. 'I'm not inclined to agree with Imial, or those who think like him, but I respect that those are his beliefs.'

'Would you respect his beliefs if you were a hundred percent sure he was wrong?' asked Fhiro. 'Or do you respect them because of the tiny chance he might be right?'

Dorrick elbowed Fhiro again.

Imial glared at Fhiro.

'Sorry,' mumbled Fhiro. 'You don't have to answer that.'

Cerilina laughed. 'Are you trying to get Imial to throw me off this ship?'

'I'll have Fhiro thrown off first.' Imial's eyes narrowed.

'You can't do that,' said Fhiro.

'Yes I can.'

Dorrick elbowed Fhiro again, while asking Cerilina, 'How do you think the Great Dying happened then?'

'An elaborate, coordinated attack, perhaps,' said Cerilina. 'Or maybe the Poshokans decided to wipe themselves out.'

'That's stupid,' said Chinda.

'If you surrender yourself to any guiding force,' said Cerilina, 'whether it be a person, a book, or the reasoning of your mortal mind, you no longer control your own destiny. Who can tell where you'll end up?'

* * *

A week into the voyage Fhiro went aboard the port-city of the Hanjan system with Imial and Ghorad. The gravity field here was weaker than he was used to, and he found walking a constant struggle. Imial, perhaps having visited a similar low-gravity port before, took to it far easier, and made a point of laughing at Fhiro's difficulties.

They reached a balcony, similar to the one Fhiro had looked out from at Calagan's port. Hanjan's port-city was smaller but cleaner, and intricate colours snaked across every surface. As they made their way towards the centre, though, the sense of

an overall coherent pattern lessened. By the time they sat down to eat all Fhiro could make out were jumbled clusters of bright-coloured tiles across the walls.

'This is one of the older ports in the region,' said Ghorad. 'Built by the Gedrillan Republic of old, it has changed hands many times over the ages as the tides of power moved back and forth across the Near Quadrant.'

'Weren't most ports built by the Poshokans?' asked Fhiro.

'In this region of space,' said Ghorad, 'most of the ancient ports were destroyed during the wars with the recci after the Great Dying. Those built more recently have not fared much better, as the Near Quadrant has seen centuries of continuous conflict. Only four hundred years ago the Smugglers' Union was consumed in a revolution.'

'Ghorad is very knowledgeable,' said Imial between mouthfuls. 'He's of the First Legion of Kartna.'

'I don't really know about Kartna's legions,' said Fhiro.

'In the First we are chosen for intelligence and cultural awareness, and groomed for roles in diplomatic security,' said Ghorad as he wiped the table where Imial had spilt some of the broth he was drinking.

After they had finished Imial leaned back, patting his tummy. 'I can't wait to reach Pelorn,' he said. 'I haven't seen sunlight in so long, I feel like a Thirster.'

'Do not speak of such evil things!' said Ghorad.

A strange shadow loomed over the table. Fhiro spun around. A man in a dark cloak stood watching them. Covering his face was a pointed, elliptical mask. Fhiro felt his heart beat faster. Why was Ghorad doing nothing? Had the Kartnans sold him out to the Creedate?

Ghorad kept his voice low. 'Your disguise is – intimidating!' He laughed.

When the strange figure spoke, though, Fhiro felt himself relax.

'Allow me to introduce myself. Priest Veltir of the Aculei.'

'That's the mask of an Aculei priest?' whispered Fhiro.

Oljon nodded, sitting down with them.

'It's scary. Can't I have one?'

'No,' Oljon replied. 'Only a fully trained disciple who has passed the vigorous and dangerous tests in the Dusty Mountains may wear one of these.'

'But you haven't completed the tests,' said Imial, frowning but also talking quietly.

'Imial makes a good point,' said Ghorad. 'They already earn their right to live on holy land by volunteering to fight for the Empire, willing to accept the most dangerous assignments. If they ever hear of it, they may consider your disguise an insult.'

'If the Aculei are unhappy with this they should take it up with the Senate,' said Oljon. 'I am willing to prove my worth to them, if they wish me to do so. However, I would remind them that I was once in the Second Legion.'

'Would they kill you for disguising yourself as one of them?' asked Fhiro.

'They could try,' said Oljon.

CHAPTER 10

Fhiro, Dorrick and Imial were playing the card game *Sky Lord* again when Ghorad interrupted them.

'To the fall rooms.' He grinned.

The moment Fhiro had dreaded for weeks was finally upon him.

Ghorad threw them a small container that rattled as it flew across the room.

Imial caught it.

'See you all soon.' Then Ghorad left.

Imial smiled at Fhiro. 'Never landed on a planet before?'

Fhiro shook his head. He knew Imial was enjoying knowing something he did not; a rarity in the lessons they had shared. But the technicalities of designing a sorcery-circuit were somewhat less terrifying than plummeting through an atmosphere.

'It's normal for first timers to feel afraid,' said Imial. 'It can be painful, and if the counter-gravity-crystal malfunctions, it can be nauseating too.' He held up the container he had caught. 'That's even with the landing pills.'

Fhiro glowered at Imial. 'I'm not afraid.'

'Hey, Fhiro,' said Dorrick, 'it's our first jump!'

'You sure?' Imial was still talking to Fhiro. 'I dare you not to take one.' He turned the container and the pills rattled from one end of it to the other.

An hour later Fhiro struggled to open his eyes as the Blind Vizier decelerated through Pelorn's atmosphere. The floor, walls and ceiling were covered in vomitus – once one crew member

had started the smell had started a chain reaction among the others. From the cries of disbelief Fhiro had also deduced that the gravity fluctuations they were experiencing were far stronger and more frequent than was normal. He considered it a miracle he had not vomited himself, despite not taking the pills.

He turned to get a look at Imial. The boy was still retching, with Ghorad trying to comfort him. Fhiro turned in the other direction. Dorrick and Chinda were laughing. Fhiro grinned at them and shook his head. Then he closed his eyes tight shut. The pressure on his body from the deceleration was an extreme form of unpleasantness the specially designed fall room chairs were doing little to alleviate. He just had to hold on a few minutes longer.

Soon enough the noise and pain subsided, and the gravity fluctuations stopped. Fhiro imagined the blue oceans they were gliding over at this very moment – the Supra Atmospheric Bombardment Accord obliged all planetary arrivals to take place over an ocean to limit the potential devastation of a high momentum impact.

He saw Imial had passed out, and asked Ghorad. 'What happened?'

'It was Imial, I'm sure of it,' said Ghorad.

'What?'

'He finds deceleration very unpleasant,' said Ghorad, 'so he tampered with the counter-gravity-crystal.'

'How d'you know it was him?'

'He said he'd been talking to the navigator about it.' Ghorad shook his head. 'I told him not to try, but I should have known he might.' The bodyguard's eyes shone with concern.

With a bump and a jolt the craft touched down. Fhiro felt it rolling across the ground until it slowed to a halt. After he unstrapped he and Dorrick helped Ghorad take Imial out of his chair. Then Dorrick wiped some of the foul-smelling

splatter off his robes, and studied the underside of his shoe. 'I guess we didn't need the pill, but I wish I'd taken it.'

After they were cleaned and changed they waited in the ship's wide entrance bay with everyone else. By now the Blind Vizier was already on the move again, hooked up to giant beasts that were dragging her to an allocated bay in the space port. Fhiro wished he see these animals; his imagination took flight as he tried to picture the enormity of an organism capable of moving an entire spaceship.

Nearby Borlin and Cerilina were deep in conversation. Oljon was standing close to Valachrad's guards, his pointed mask making him easily visible. Hanu, on the other hand, was with Valachrad's officials and advisors, dressed in similar flowing garb to her new colleagues.

Fhiro stumbled as they turned and ground to a halt. A breeze fluttered across his face as the entrance bay airlock opened and a ramp was lowered. Some officers descended and then a few marched back up again.

Imial, led by Ghorad, appeared next to Fhiro.

'Are you all right?' asked Fhiro.

'I had to drink tons of water, and eat disgusting salt snacks.' Imial shuddered. 'Almost made me vomit all over again.'

Then Valachrad was among them with his Imperial secret service guard, his aides and Captain Jard, the chief military officer on board.

Jard nodded at the officers nearer the ramp. They led the party out on to the landing field, though why it was called a field puzzled Fhiro; he saw very few blades of grass. However, it felt glorious to place his feet upon Pelorn's earth, regardless of how cracked and dry it was. He was on a planet, one with a near-identical gravity profile to Andelic. Compared to every port and ship he had boarded since fleeing Chimahess, this was by far the most he had felt like being back home.

Greeting the Kartnan delegation were a man and a woman with soldiers and officials from Pelorn. Beyond them were rows of craft, separated by wide tracks. Their vast sizes, far more appreciable on the ground than connected to the outside of a star port, almost overwhelmed Fhiro. They were vast, unnatural assemblies of dark, sharp shapes against the bright sky and dusty, yellow earth. At their feet, like tiny creatures scavenging for sheddings of skin, engineers and groundsmen scurried to and fro. Fhiro looked over his shoulder at the Blind Vizier, and stumbled into Dorrick.

'Watch where you're going!'

'Did you know how big our ship was?' asked Fhiro.

Dorrick looked round.

The spikes had started to extend from its surface, cutting lines through the blue sky and white clouds beyond it. The crystals, at their tips, twinkled in the sun. Fhiro tried to imagine how each of these was connected to the enormous navigation-crystal he had seen near the start of the journey from Nyfua.

'The pilot taught me her dimensions,' said Dorrick, 'but I never quite saw it in my mind.'

'How much of her weren't we allowed in?' asked Fhiro.

'Be quiet!' Imial's voice had regained some of its former strength.

One of the officers from Pelorn stepped towards Valachrad, his arms behind his back and his uniform fluttering in the breeze. 'Welcome to Pelorn. I am Palis, of the Royal Guard. May I introduce Countess Jebberel.'

'I pray your journey,' said the countess, 'and in particular your landing, was not too uncomfortable, Ambassador Valachrad. King Suloa sends his most heartfelt welcome to you and your party.'

CHAPTER 11

'That's the temple?' asked Fhiro.

'Must be,' said Imial.

They were two-thirds the way up a mountain, among hundreds of officials and foreign delegates, on a flat, grassy plain. Fhiro had asked whether this part of the mountain was so flat by design, or by nature, but no one seemed to know. Behind them and the rows of transants they had ridden here, the ground dropped away through the lower cloud canopy. Ahead, between Fhiro and where the mountain resumed its steep climb, a giant, cube-shaped structure glinted in the sun. 'It looks like it was just dropped there,' he whispered.

'According to Palis,' said Ghorad, 'it's eight hundred years old.'

'The Senate buildings in Kartna are at least as ancient,' said Imial.

'No,' said Ghorad. 'The old Senate chamber was destroyed in a fire five-hundred years ago. Many of our temples, though, do date much further back.'

'Will we be allowed to eat when the King comes out?' asked Fhiro, feeling his stomach grumbling again. The religious dispositions of the inhabitants of Pelorn had found yet another way to discomfort him. He was already struggling to understand how individuals here felt comfortable belonging to multiple different, and as far as Fhiro could tell, contradicting faiths. People from this planet, and the worlds nearby, called themselves Niquani. They worshipped the balance of life and its manifestation in the native fauna that

had evolved on Pelorn. But many also worshipped the Elements, a religion imported by a previous ruling dynasty. The temple he now glared at was dedicated to the 'Matter' Element. There were even Niquani who considered themselves Followers of The Calling.

'Don't hold your breath,' said Borlin. 'Kings like people waiting on them.'

'We had brought some extra snacks,' said Cerilina, 'but I'm afraid they're all gone now.'

Not a helpful or useful comment, thought Fhiro. 'Couldn't the King have chosen a temple closer to the city?'

'If you ever have the fortune to be granted an audience with the gods of Kartna,' said Imial, 'you may be expected to travel to the Havens in the Ziomellia star cluster.'

'Presumably you don't have to walk there,' mumbled Fhiro.

'You didn't walk here!' Imial gestured to the transants behind them. Antennae wafting before their many-eyed heads, the giant, cuboidal creatures ambled about, grazing from troughs by the road.

'And presumably you aren't forced to starve on the way,' said Fhiro.

'Just be patient,' said Yelba, Valachrad's chief servant.

Fhiro looked around. Beyond the steep mountainside that rose up at the far side of the plain, only the barren, pyramid-shaped peak was visible, far in the distance. Fhiro guessed it would be a good two-day's climb to the top from where he stood. Looking at it inspired him to turn around and eye the palace keep in Pelorn's capital, Riletta. Its curved roof bulged through the sea of clouds in the distance, and its spire pierced the sky. Even Imial and Ghorad had been impressed by its size on their arrival. It was the largest architectural structure Fhiro had ever seen, excluding the star ports.

Two of the King's honour guard trudged past him and the

horned, four-legged creature motif embroidered on their cloaks caught his eye. Dorrick would have had something to say about that, he thought. Then again, he might be too busy scheming to climb higher up the mountain, but his brother had the enviable excuse of training with Pelorn's air force. Fhiro clenched his fists and gritted his teeth again, the way he did every time he remembered this gross unfairness.

The air rang with a sudden blare of trumpets. A piece of the temple wall opened inwards, revealing a hidden door. Several guards in shining semi-transparent armour came out. Then a large man, wearing only simple robes, stepped backwards as he retreated from the temple, bowing and hailing the structure with every step. From the reaction of those nearby, and the way the guards stood aside for this individual, Fhiro guessed he was Pelorn's King.

After some time the temple sealed itself and the King turned to be introduced to Valachrad, Oljon and other senior members of the Kartnan delegation. Fhiro noted that the King and the Kartnan ambassador resembled each other in both size and style.

Chairs and tables were erected for the King and Valachrad. More servants appeared and, with a rapidity that stunned Fhiro, they covered the stretch of the plain between the standing guests and the temple with carpets.

'I hope they've stuck to the plan,' said Ghorad. He took out an embroidered piece of red fabric. Fhiro thought the black, yellow and white images on it resembled horned animal heads.

'Don't get lost,' said Yelba.

'Thanks for the vote of confidence,' said Ghorad. 'You're taking the archaeologists?'

'We're sitting separately from Fhiro and Imial?' Borlin looked surprised, but then he pretended to square up to the boys. 'Think you're too important for us, then?'

'We're the ones being honoured,' said Cerilina. 'We have places close to the King himself.'

'It means you can't get drunk,' said Ghorad.

'It's breakfast, Ghorad,' said Borlin. 'I have got some manners.'

'Where are we sitting, then?' asked Imial, as Ghorad led them off.

Fhiro knew they would be in the same area as his mother and sister, even if he did not know exactly where that was. He wondered if she would be much good at pretending to be unrelated to him if they did run into each other. Now he was finally in public, despite all the training from Ghorad and his father, he worried he was not up to the job of pretending to be something he was not.

Ghorad took them to a guarded section of the carpet-covered plain.

'Can I offer you a drink, young sirs?'

'Would you be interested in a snack?'

Servants surrounded them. Once their hands were filled with delicious smelling treats, Ghorad found the boys a place to sit. Fhiro noticed that the material covering the ground was decorated with the same pattern as the small piece Ghorad had been holding in his hand earlier.

Fhiro looked around to see where his sister was. She and Hanu were about ten metres away. Chinda was trying to entertain a few small children who had been brought by other members of the Kartnan delegation. She saw Fhiro watching her and smiled.

Imial was eying everyone with suspicion, from the couple sharing cocktails in front of them to the elderly group of female yeal and earthwomen reclining on a cluster of large cushions in the corner. 'Where's Ghorad?'

'He's gone to talk to Palis and the countess.' Fhiro pointed

out the three of them to Imial. He wondered if Ghorad liked talking to countess Jeberrel, because they seemed to have done a lot of talking since they had first met on the landing field the day before. At that moment, however, Fhiro noticed a tall earthwoman looking straight at him, and his heart froze. She was surrounded by earthpeople, yeal and hegel in the long flowing robes of Creedate priests. One of these was an ancient earthman wearing the pointed hat of a prelate elder, a disdainful look in his eyes as he surveyed those around him. At the woman's side stood a grim-faced earthman, his face almost as scarred as his shoulders were broad.

'I'll go and find out who's who around here,' said Imial, nodding to himself. 'Best not to talk to anyone in the meantime, all right?'

Fhiro looked at Imial, unsure what to say, or how to quietly alert him. He opened his mouth, but before he could speak Imial had stomped away.

Fhiro looked again to check that the woman was no longer watching him, and was relieved to see her entourage of priests were blocking her line of sight.

'Would you like another drink, young master?'

'Do you have any redberry juice?'

'Certainly!' the servant replied.

Fhiro was glad. Yellow bean-berry nectar was a local delicacy they were being encouraged to drink, but it tasted disgusting. Still, despite how pleasant the redberry juice was, it could not wash away the icy chill running through him. Who was the Creedate woman? Had his disguise been seen through? From time to time Fhiro cast another glance in her direction, but the thickening crowds between them made her harder and harder to see. He looked for Chinda, or his mother, wondering if he could somehow warn them.

'Hello!'

Fhiro turned to see a girl about his age with curly hair and a smiling face, standing in front of him. 'Oh, hi,' he said, recalling Imial's warning. He wondered if he should just ignore her.

'You must be new here,' she said, offering her hand. 'I'm Chenessa.'

'I'm Fhiro.' He shook her hand. 'Are you the daughter of an ambassador?'

'Don't I look like one?' She giggled. 'No, I suppose I must look more like a princess.'

'I didn't– What?'

'I'm the daughter of Reshna, ambassador of the Creedate,' she said.

Fhiro felt the blood drain from his face. 'My … my master accompanies the embassy from Kartna,' he stammered.

'Is your master an ambassador too?'

'He's an Aculei priest,' said Fhiro.

'What's that?' asked Chenessa.

'Holy priests of the God-Emperor of Kartna.' Fhiro did his best to puff out his chest and look proud. 'He chose me as his apprentice. Only the most intelligent and gifted children are so selected.'

'Sounds very exciting,' she said. 'We have lots of priests. My mother can't seem to get away from them. What do Aculei priests do?'

'Er …' Fhiro hesitated. 'We worship the God-Emperor, and kill the enemies of Kartna. That's the general gist of it.'

She mulled this over for a moment. 'Fair enough. May I join you?'

Fhiro dared not object while she sat down. He glanced about whenever she faced away from him, hoping to catch sight of Imial, Ghorad, or anyone.

'I hope we don't have to wait too much longer before breakfast,' said Chenessa.

'Me too,' said Fhiro. 'My stomach's going to eat me inside out if I don't fill it soon.'

She laughed. 'The King likes greeting new guests out here. Once they got so swept up in their diplomatic banter, out on this lovely mountain lawn, they forgot how long they'd been chatting for. The weather changed and it started raining.' She shook her head. 'Silly customs.'

'Seems like all cultures have silly weirdnesses,' said Fhiro.

'Too right,' said Chenessa, sighing. 'Though, now we're on the subject, I could do with learning more Kartna, its culture and religion.'

'Of course,' said Fhiro, nodding. He caught sight of Imial talking to Ghorad, not too far away. 'My friend over there, Imial, is the son of the Kartnan ambassador. He's better suited to tell you about Kartna.'

'Well you're considerably nearer,' said Chenessa.

'True,' said Fhiro. 'Good. Yes. All right. So Kartna is a large empire near the Galactic core.'

'I think everyone that hasn't spent their whole life in a cave knows *that* about Kartna,' said Chenessa.

'Fhiro!' Imial stormed over, his face horrified. He turned to Chenessa. 'I'm Imial, son of Valachrad, the Kartnan ambassador.'

Fhiro tried not to look too relieved at Imial's arrival.

'Chenessa,' she responded, and bowed. 'Daughter of Reshna, the Creedate ambassador. A pleasure to make your acquaintance.'

'Right.' Imial scratched his head. He saw the redberry juice in Fhiro's hand. 'I need another one of those.'

Chenessa looked behind her and within an instant a servant had brought them all fresh glasses.

'Fhiro, here, has spent most of his life living out the frugal existence of an Aculei apprentice, far from the heartworlds of the Empire,' said Imial. 'I, however, have lived among the elite of Kartnan society my entire life.'

'So which of you knows more about Kartna?' asked Chenessa.

Imial frowned, but then just carried on. After what sounded to Fhiro like a very embellished account of Kartna's recent achievements, Imial asked Chenessa if her parents were nearby.

'My mother, Reshna, is just over there, talking with Ambassador Winle from Hithostun.' Chenessa pointed out the woman who had been watching Fhiro before. The grim-faced man, and a hegel in a blue cloak, stood within a metre of her. They appeared to be the woman's guards.

Fhiro took a deep breath. He tried to pretend that he was not reeling in terror, knowing the most powerful Creedate representative on Pelorn had been staring at him.

'That woman your mother's talking to,' said Imial, 'she looks quite fierce. She's the Hithostun ambassador?'

'She is.'

'All the people surrounding your mother look quite fierce,' said Fhiro. 'Are those two men your mother's guards?'

'Yes,' said Chenessa. 'There's Hussuf in the blue cloak. He's nice enough.'

Fhiro tried to commit the name to memory. 'The other one looks like he smashes boulders with his face for exercise every morning.'

Imial shot Fhiro a horrified look from behind Chenessa.

But Chenessa had burst out laughing. 'That's Tubrin. He probably looks that way because he's spent his whole life … well … fighting things. My mother feels safer when he's around, though. He's got an impressive battle record.'

Fhiro was relieved he had not just caused gross offence to the Creedate delegation. Or perhaps he had. Perhaps she would tell that guard and … Fhiro did not want to follow the train of thought much further.

Imial identified his own father, Ghorad and Priest Veltir.

'Who's that lady sitting with your father, Imial?' asked Chenessa. 'She's talking with the King.'

'That's Cerilina,' said Imial, 'our chief archaeologist, from Irenzel in the Greater Magellan. She's offered her services to Pelorn on behalf of the Kartnan Empire.'

'Really?' Chenessa's eyes lit up. 'I knew she was important.'

'She seems nice,' said Fhiro.

'We don't talk to her that much,' said Imial.

'No,' admitted Fhiro.

'And all those other people sitting around her,' asked Chenessa, 'do they work for her?'

'They're her team,' said Imial, nodding.

'This place is full of archaeologists,' said Chenessa. 'They're all clamouring to study the dig site or the Sufferer ship.'

'I keep meaning to ask someone more about the Sufferers,' said Fhiro.

'You don't know about them?' Chenessa shuddered. 'Took me a while to extract all the details from my tutors.'

'Tell us what you know, then,' said Fhiro.

'Not now,' said Chenessa. 'It's a bit early in the day. We haven't had breakfast.'

As the conversation drifted back to the topic of life in the Kartnan Empire, Fhiro felt compelled to answer the occasional question before Imial could, if only to maintain his authenticity. He was glad he had spent so much time with Imial, and for his book, *Mythologies of the Galaxy*. Eventually they remembered to ask Chenessa about her home as well.

'Well my father is from Locon, which is quite far from Qanex and Indin. But my mother is from Essera.'

Fhiro realised both of their mothers had grown up on the same planet. Could they have known each other?

'Are you all right?' asked Chenessa.

He badly needed more practice not displaying his thoughts

on his face. 'I was just surprised you called it Qanex,' he blurted, to cover for himself. 'I would have thought you would refer to the capital by its planet's name, not the city.'

'Oh,' said Chenessa. 'Everyone always talks about Qanex because Qanex is where Marallel retires to between campaigns. The rest of Jashan is just boring and bland. It's all military installations and everyone's a soldier. Qanex is nice, though. We go there a lot.'

Fhiro had known this, but at least the suspicious look on her face was gone.

'Waiter!' barked a loud voice from behind Chenessa.

All three children turned to see Ambassador Winle glaring at one of the servants.

'Do you wish to return home in chains?' cried Winle. 'I do not have the time or patience to seek your attention.'

The man in front of her fell to his knees and bowed until his head touched the floor.

Behind him another man appeared, looking flustered. 'How can I help, madam?'

'Relieve this wretch of the bottle he carries before he allows it to touch the ground,' said Winle. 'It's worth more than his life is. See to it he does not work for me again.'

'As you wish,' said the senior servant, grasping the wine bottle, pouring some out for the ambassador, and then dragging his cowering subordinate away.

Winle soon moved on.

Fhiro turned to Chenessa. 'How are servants treated in the Creedate worlds?'

'Depends on who they work for,' said Chenessa. 'You can't kill them, though. A senior priest was recently imprisoned for throwing a servant off the High Tower.'

'I don't think my father would ever talk to Yelba like that,' said Imial.

Fhiro noticed Reshna, Winle and some of the other ambassadors had started walking away from them. 'What's happening now?'

'They're going to pay their respects to the King,' said Chenessa.

As the different ambassadors paid their respects Chenessa explained who they were. 'Well, you know Winle, now. It's a shame her daughter had to leave. Apparently I was distracting her from her studies. That can't have been the real reason, though. How could you blame me for anything?'

Fhiro tried to force a smile.

'There's Zakil with his tall hair, the ambassador from Iap,' continued Chenessa, 'and this one is Olita. That's got to be a wig she's wearing. She's the Baworl ambassador. I think Shali, the Vinaran ambassador, is very pretty.'

Fhiro's mind boggled. He hoped he was not supposed to remember all these people. Presumably he could just greet them with 'my lord' or 'my lady' if he ever needed to.

'There's Larif, the Timale ambassador,' Chenessa continued, 'and this last one is Evix from Norio. That left arm of his is actually prosthetic.'

Fhiro wondered if Imial could recite all their names. He thought he could remember Zakil, with the hair, and Larif with the arm … No, wait, that was wrong.

'Don't ambassadors get such injuries repaired at a haven?' asked Imial.

'There are few havens in these parts,' said Chenessa. 'I think Hithostun has a good relationship with one of them.'

'These nations don't directly rule any havens?' Imial looked shocked. 'They share them?'

'They're small,' said Chenessa. 'There aren't enough havens to go around. Welcome to what used to be the Smugglers' Union!'

Imial looked stunned.

'So where's your father?' asked Fhiro.

'He runs the affairs of our house,' said Chenessa. 'Our family has lots of property and land across the converted territories.'

'Oh, really?' Fhiro did his best to sound impressed, but wondered how many innocent people might have been dispossessed or put to death to free up the properties that Chenessa's family now owned.

Servants brought them their breakfast. It took all of Fhiro's willpower not to gobble it up as fast as he could. He noticed Imial also struggled not to bolt down his food.

'So what happens after this?' asked Imial. 'Is there anything to do?'

'There's tuition,' said Chenessa. 'Do you have a tutor? I used to share tutors with the Hithostun girl.'

'Oh no,' said Fhiro, his shoulders slumping at the thought of more hours spent with Yogric.

'Don't get too upset,' said Chenessa. 'We do get to go out.'

'Where do you go?' asked Fhiro.

'Into town, to the games, to the gardens. I hope you two can come too.' Chenessa looked at Priest Veltir's mask and then back at Fhiro. 'Will your master allow it?'

'Er, of course,' answered Fhiro.

'I suppose you'd better check,' said Imial.

'Yes, I'd better check.' Fhiro nodded.

'Hi guys,' said Chinda.

Fhiro almost choked. What was she doing here?

'Ah,' said Imial. 'Hello, Chinda.'

'Hello,' said Fhiro, trying his best to sound as though this was no big deal. 'This is Chenessa, the daughter of the Creedate ambassador.'

Chinda's eyebrows rose. 'Nice to meet you! I'm Chinda. My ma works for the Kartnan ambassador.'

'Nice to meet you too,' said Chenessa.

Please don't say anything stupid, Fhiro prayed. He was sure she was supposed to stay with their mother.

'I got bored over there,' said Chinda. 'There were some cute babies, but they don't talk much.'

'You've found the best this party has to offer right here,' said Chenessa.

'You were telling us what there is to do on Pelorn,' said Imial.

'Of course,' said Chenessa. 'There'll be lots to do, especially now. The yala beast festival began today.'

'The festival looks exciting,' said Chinda.

Fhiro had seen flags fluttering and processions through the street when they had travelled from the space port to their Embassy. He knew the yala beast festival was especially important to the Niquani, but did not really understand why. However, they had also seen signs of trouble during the trip. 'Our antcade had to stop a few times so that the guards could clear the way ahead,' he whispered. 'I think they even hurt some people. Are these festivals dangerous?'

Chenessa checked that no one else was in earshot. 'I'm sure your officials will learn this soon enough, but the discovery in Fawast has stirred up a lot of unrest.'

'Fawast?' asked Imial.

'How long have you been here?' asked Chenessa.

'Since yesterday,' said Fhiro.

'Oh.' She smiled. 'Fawast is the wild continent where they're trying to excavate this ancient Poshokan installation.' She looked them each in the eye. 'You do know about that, don't you?'

'Oh yes,' they all said, nodding.

Fhiro hated this game.

'When we arrived it was terrible,' said Chenessa, shaking her head. 'Our antcade was attacked with explosive missiles.'

'That's awful!' said Chinda.

Fhiro had to stop himself wincing every time a word came out of his sister, so certain was he that she would somehow drop them all into terrible danger.

'The tension between the Niquani and the Followers of The Calling on this planet was already close to boiling point before the discovery,' said Chenessa.

'At least you're all right,' said Fhiro.

'Thank goodness,' said Chinda, nodding with enthusiasm.

'We were fine,' Chenessa replied, 'but the soldiers guarding us opened fire into a crowd nearby. It was horrible.'

'I don't get it though,' said Fhiro. 'I thought everyone here considered themselves Niquani, even the Followers of The Calling.'

'It's all very complicated,' said Chenessa. 'Most Niquani, from what I can gather, exclusively worship these beast gods. Some of them, though, have other beliefs but still call themselves Niquani.'

'Like the King then?' asked Imial. 'He worships the Elements.'

'I read about the Elements religion,' said Fhiro. 'This temple here is the Matter temple.'

'Aren't they the same Elements as in the five-suit pack of cards?' asked Chinda.

'I think the religion came before the playing cards,' said Chenessa. 'The ruling elite of Pelorn have a thing for the Elements, so King Suloa seeks guidance here from time to time. When we arrived he was in there for two whole days!'

'He only spent one day inside before calling us after we got here,' said Imial, looking annoyed. 'Why was that?'

'I don't' think the amount of days matters,' said Chenessa. She looked away and frowned at no one in particular. 'Anyway, even the King would consider himself Niquani too, as would

many that converted to The Calling over the last five hundred years.'

'Can you be Niquani and a Follower of The Calling?' asked Chinda.

Fhiro bit his lip. Did she have to ask a question like that?

'For those of us that heeded the message of Avithen, our great prophet, no,' answered Chenessa. 'But there are many here that do not hear the truth, or understand it, and continue to live misguided lives.'

Fhiro glanced at Chinda to see how she had reacted to this, but his sister's face remained keen and attentive.

'There are even Niquani atheists,' said Chenessa. 'It's all quite complicated.'

'That's ridiculous,' said Imial. 'They worship beasts and they don't believe in them? Atheists in Kartna might be shunned, but at least they don't contradict themselves.'

'Why are they shunned?' Chenessa frowned.

'Because,' said Imial, thinking for a moment, 'they're atheists.'

Chenessa rolled her eyes. 'I don't know how the Niquani thing works. Maybe it's like money: it makes sense so long as people think it does.'

Fhiro scratched his head. 'I don't know about that, but if the Niquani don't like the Creedate, or us for that matter, because we aren't Niquani, is that religious hatred or racism?'

'Not all Niquani are bad,' said Chenessa. 'All the ones I've met personally are perfectly nice!'

There was a moment of silence. Fhiro wondered how the conversation could be carried forward without anyone offending each other.

'How many festivals do they have a year?' asked Chinda after a while.

'All of the herbivores of Fawast are celebrated,' said

Chenessa, 'although not all are recognised with national holidays. It seems that the more food a species provided to Pelorn's early settlers, the greater the divine power it represents.'

'What of the carnivores?' asked Fhiro.

'I haven't heard that much about them,' said Chenessa. 'I believe there are some, roaming the forests of Fawast. They can't have been very popular with the early settlers; none of them are worshipped.'

'Strange,' said Fhiro. 'Most cultures admire carnivores.' He cast another glance at Chinda, but she appeared to be listening to him, without making strange faces, as a well behaved, unrelated girl her age might.

'Well I can't wait to see the dig site,' said Imial. 'Perhaps, while we're there, they'll take us on a tour to see the animals.'

Chenessa shook her head. 'The animals in Fawast have strict migration paths, and don't go anywhere near the excavation.'

'Oh.' Imial looked glum.

'We were scheduled to travel to the dig site in the next few days,' said Chenessa. 'Now the Kartnan delegation has arrived, they'll probably want to have another round of talks before we go. On the bright side, perhaps we'll get to go in the same aircade.'

Fhiro considered asking what an aircade was, but decided not to draw more attention to his ignorance about life in high-level politics. Luckily Chinda showed the same level of sense and limited her contributions to the conversation to small talk.

Fhiro kept wondering whether Chenessa's parents had personally killed any unbelievers. Then his thoughts turned to his own father, and what he might have done for Thurgon and the Creedate. Were all Creedate people this charming? Had his parents told him the truth? Maybe Thurgon, Marallel

and the High Priests were very amicable when you got to know them.

Then Fhiro remembered the pyramids of severed heads the Creedate left on the worlds they conquered. No. The Creedate were evil. Chenessa must be the anomaly.

'What are your plans for this afternoon?' asked Chenessa.

'I will have to confirm them with Ghorad,' said Imial.

'I didn't think we had any,' said Fhiro.

'Good,' said Chenssa, 'because if the last few meetings up here are anything to go by, the King will invite everyone to a show at the Grand Arena.'

CHAPTER 12

'They cannot go,' said Hanu, 'surely!'

'I understand your anxieties, Hanu,' said Valachrad, 'but they must go.'

'What reasons are so important they justify risking the lives of children?' asked Hanu. 'My children!'

Valachrad frowned. 'How do I say this.'

'It's not a choice, is it,' said Oljon. 'This is an order.'

'What?' cried Hanu.

'Maybe your children do not have to be here,' said Valachrad. 'Let us discuss this in private.'

'It certainly concerns them,' said Hanu. 'They have a right to know.'

'Fhiro, Chinda, Imial,' said Valachrad, 'please wait outside.'

The three of them went out of the small meeting room, but Fhiro and Chinda immediately turned once the door closed, and pressed their ears against it.

'My father said we should leave the room,' said Imial.

'And we left,' said Fhiro.

'I will tell!'

'Then I will beat you!' said Chinda.

Imial looked shocked, but then worried. Chinda still outclassed him in their match ups, though he was starting to catch up.

'Don't threaten violence Chins,' said Fhiro. 'Apologise.'

'Sorry,' muttered Chinda, 'but you'd better not tell. You'll just embarrass your pa.'

Imial frowned, then paced the room in silence.

Fhiro concentrated on what he could hear.

His mother's voice: 'If the Creedate realise who they are they'll kidnap and torture them. They're children!'

'Ghorad will be with them.' It was Valachrad. 'We will have agents close by at all times.'

'Torture children!' Hanu again. 'These two words should never be in the same sentence. We shouldn't do anything that puts them within three sentences of each other, let alone together. My children at that. I outright refuse!'

'I am sorry Hanu.' Valachrad's voice had softened. Fhiro pressed his ear more firmly to the door. 'I was sent here for a number of reasons, but my chief objective is to establish a line of communication with Marallel ... a secret line of communication ... to find senior individuals within the Creedate we can work with to preserve peace. Ambassador Reshna's an unusual choice. Our intelligence suggests she's close to Marallel, and her family is less well entrenched with the more bloodthirsty Creedate generals. She may have been sent here for a reason.'

Fhiro felt someone shoving him to the side. Imial had come and pressed his ear to the door too.

'Or she was sent here to tempt peaceful overtures from you, to use as a sign of weakness ... justify going to war with Kartna.'

'Marallel knows how costly war would be.' Valachrad's voice hardened. 'He knows he might lose. War might be inevitable, but Marallel is no fool.'

Fhiro took in a deep breath. Kartna and the Creedate were that close to war?

'There is probably nothing we can do to avert it,' Valachrad continued, 'but we cannot neglect this opportunity. Lives are at stake, Hanu. Trillions of lives. You know what the Creedate do to the planets they conquer. You know how bitterly we will resist

them. The galaxy has not had a war like this for a thousand years. The entire Near Quadrant will be soaked in blood.'

Oljon's voice cut in: 'If Marallel wished to negotiate with you, he could just send an emissary.'

'If only things were that simple. Marallel has the loyalty of the military, but they are accustomed to victory, and enjoying the spoils of war. His generals boast that all the great powers of the galaxy put together are no match for them. They would be humiliated if their leader attempted to negotiate a peace, especially one that we might accept. They would usurp him and take power, in order to realise their destiny as rulers of the stars.'

Hanu again: 'Has Kartna tried to set up such a secret channel?'

'Tried, yes.' There was a pause. Fhiro felt himself tense involuntarily. Was Valachrad suspicious he was being listened to? But then Valachrad's voice went on, 'No opportunity has presented itself like the one we have now.'

'You really think Reshna is trying to communicate through our children?'

'You know what Imial told me … what her daughter said. Through her, Reshna has complained about her priests. She wants to share information with us when the priests are not present.'

'Chenessa is a little girl moaning about things that annoy her while in the company of children her own age.'

'You might be right. What if you are wrong?'

A silence, then Fhiro heard someone moving. Another sound; was it his mother sobbing? A whisper that might have been his father. No words were distinguishable.

Then Valachrad spoke again. 'All three children will spend as much time as they can with Chenessa. They will get to know her, and report back to me daily.'

If his mother was really crying, Valachrad's behaviour felt callous.

'Someone's coming,' whispered Chinda.

The three of them slunk away from the door and sat on the sofas by the window.

Ghorad opened the door. Fhiro could make out his mother sitting on her chair, looking distraught. His father's arm was around her.

'You're to all get changed. You're going to the Grand Arena,' Ghorad said.

Fhiro wanted to smile back, but could not.

Ghorad frowned. 'I thought you wanted to go.'

Imial stood up and walked to Ghorad. 'Come on.'

Chinda slid off her seat next, and Fhiro followed after her.

Did the fate of the galaxy really weigh on them? On him? Fhiro prayed his parents could cope with the risks he was being made to take. But did he, himself really understand the risks he was taking? What had they gotten themselves into? Should they have made a go of it hiding in the forests back on Andelic after all?

He looked at Chinda. She seemed to have lost some of her cheer, but this was not the time to discuss it. Imial had a concerned look on his face, but his mind was unfathomable to Fhiro at the best of times.

As they were about to leave the embassy his parents caught up with them.

'I'm sorry, Ma,' said Fhiro. 'We'll be careful.'

'You've nothing to be sorry about,' said Hanu, clasping her son and daughter to her.

Fhiro looked up and smiled at his father. It was nice to see his face, uncovered by the sinister mask of the Aculei, while they were within the embassy walls.

'We should never have come here,' said Hanu. 'Should have

left Valachrad when we had the chance. Or found some other place to go when we left.'

'There was nowhere good to go to, Ma,' said Chinda.

'You're right, Chins,' said Oljon. 'It was always going to be difficult for us.'

Hanu wiped her eyes. 'At least, living on Andelic, we had those cherished years of happiness. Never forget them, you hear?'

Fhiro nodded.

'You will be careful. You must be. Don't give away who you are.'

Shortly after, along with Chinda, Imial, Ghorad, Cerilina, Borlin and the other archaeologists, Fhiro reached the transant that was to take them to the city. He was still trying to dispel the dread he felt, and his fear that he might ruin everything by saying the wrong thing at the wrong time.

The door-panel in the transant's body opened. 'Welcome,' said Palis, the royal guard who had greeted them on their arrival on Pelorn. Beyond him were a group of Creedate priests. From the shadows of one of their cowls, Fhiro could just see the glint of eyes watching him. He felt a shiver run down his spine. As he entered the living vehicle he exchanged glances with the fearsome looking Creedate guard, Tubrin. The scar-faced man's eyes seemed to burn with a constant, hateful fire. Surely Chenessa would not have told him how Fhiro had described his face. Perhaps he should say he felt sick, and ask to retire back to the Kartnan embassy.

Then he saw Chenessa. She was beaming as she walked up to them. 'So great to see you all!' she said.

Fhiro felt himself start to relax. Then he wondered if this was the Creedate plan – make him feel at ease enough to start slipping them information. What was he do? He should say something. He had to look calm.

'Great to see you too,' said Chinda.

A thousand curses! How was it his sister was such a natural at this? He did his best to settle in. He reminded himself he was supposed to be having fun. That he was excited about going to the arena.

The transant started moving once they were seated, its numerous legs keeping the floor beneath them smooth and stable, regardless of the terrain. They talked about life in their respective homes. At one point Fhiro suggested they play cards, but Tubrin, Chenessa's guard, scowled at him, making Fhiro flinch. If suggesting a game got such a hostile reaction, Fhiro shivered at the thought of what might happen if he ever accidentally trod on Tubrin's toes.

'Don't mind him,' said Chenessa.

'He looks like he murders children for breakfast,' whispered Fhiro, 'while chewing on steel nuts and bolts, and testing the endurance of his feet to molten lava.'

'He only looks that way,' said Chenessa. 'He's a big softy, really.'

Fhiro gave her a disbelieving look.

Chenessa chuckled.

'The vine-like projections that connect the buildings in Riletta are purely cosmetic,' said Palis, giving the same tour, it seemed, as when they had first arrived on Pelorn.

Fhiro looked outside to avoid meeting eyes with Tubrin again. The driver had taken a shortcut through a narrow street. Bright coloured washing hung above them, and pedestrians walked to and fro alongside, chattering in a sing-song manner that showed their excitement. Many carried or wore yala beast festival flags, symbols and banners.

Fhiro wondered if seeing all these heretical displays would make the Creedate priests even more angry. Perhaps Tubrin would need to vent his anger in some cruel, despicable way. It probably involved knives and lots of pain.

They rounded a corner on to a wider road where chanting crowds waved yala beast flags. A giant statue of a thick-legged animal with rows of short horns between its eyes stood before a wide, cone-shaped building.

'This is one of the principle yala beast temples of the city,' Palis informed them. 'The furniture has been fashioned entirely out of yala beast hide.'

'Your gods are very tolerant,' said Imial. 'If the Kartnan gods so much as overheard a joke about being turned into furniture, they'd send their holy assassins.'

'Many find the ways of the Niquani difficult to grasp,' said Palis. 'Perhaps you'd consider staying here for a while longer, after all this diplomacy has died down, to understand us better?'

Fhiro wondered if the Niquani had a view on foreign delegations torturing and murdering each other. As he considered this he noticed a flat-topped structure rising above the roof-tops ahead. Winding pillars snaked their way up its surface, thinning out as they reached into the sky.

'That's the arena,' said Chenessa.

'How big is it?' asked Chinda.

Other buildings obscured it as they came closer. Earthmen, hegel and yeal rode in the saddles of smaller animals, some of which pulled wagons, across their path. Another transant came into view ahead. The insignia of Pelorn's law enforcement was emblazoned on its armoured exterior, and several stern looking earthmen carrying rifles rode on its back.

'Is all this security normal?' Fhiro asked, raising his voice to be heard over the hubbub outside.

'Don't worry,' said Palis. 'There has been trouble in the city, but no visitors have been harmed.'

Police officers were erecting a barrier across the entrance to a road, much to the dismay of a group of yeal standing around them.

The transant slowed down. Fhiro saw the road ahead was clogged with beasts and wagons.

'What's the hold up?' Palis asked the driver.

'The police,' said the driver. 'They're always setting up road checks these days, looking for weapons and troublemakers.'

'They'll find plenty of weapons in here,' said Ghorad.

'They'll let us through,' insisted Palis.

'Have they been like this since the discovery in Fawast?' asked Imial.

'It was getting bad even before that ship came down,' said the driver, manipulating the transant's orientation nerve-organs.

'The Sufferer ship?' asked Fhiro.

'That's right,' said the driver. 'Everyone gets so excited about that cursed ship. Nobody cares how evil the Sufferers were, or that the ship wiped out a ranch full of soft-meat buffalo when it landed.' He shook his head. 'It'll take years for that village to replace 'em.'

Fhiro watched the dancing, masked yala worshippers, singing as they ran around the transant, waving their orange and black flags. 'What'll happen to that village, then?'

'Well, they're probably fine for now,' said the driver. 'Plenty of weirdos, not to mention archaeologists, looking for rooms to stay in so they can see that ship.'

'We're archaeologists!' said Borlin.

'And we're visiting the ship tomorrow,' said Cerilina, 'but for purely professional reasons.'

'Well I suppose if you've got to, you've got to,' said the driver. 'Rather you than me. Sufferers give me the creeps.'

'Forget the Sufferers,' said Borlin. 'They're ancient history. The Creedate are more than enough to be afraid of.'

The two Creedate priests with Chenessa looked round at Borlin, who smiled back at them, coughed and turned away. Fhiro, however, caught sight of Tubrin's hateful glare, directed

square at the back of Borlin's head. He hoped Borlin learned to watch his step before it was too late.

A long column of four-legged creatures, with thick necks and large heads, plodded towards them. They looked identical to the statue Fhiro had seen outside the yala beast temple moments ago, though they were not as big. Each drew a wagon full of people, wearing strange masks, who threw souvenirs into the gathering crowds.

Palis pointed at the feet of the passing creatures. 'See their strange front hooves? And thick limbs? In flight the yala beasts can be very dangerous, easily levelling the thrivilen trees that fill the forests of Fawast.'

'If they tried to trample us,' asked Chinda, 'would the transant roof be all right?'

'I think these ones are all domesticated,' said Chenessa. 'They don't do much trampling in the city. Imagine the mess that would make!'

Chinda laughed.

'Can I ride one?' asked Imial.

'No,' said Palis quickly. Then he hesitated. 'One needs proper training.'

'Chenessa says there won't be any animals near the excavation site,' said Fhiro.

'It's very unlikely,' said Palis. 'The migration patterns across Fawast are rigid, and do not pass close to the Old Harvester Fort, where the delegations stay during their visits. Though groups of animals can stray from the main herds, the activity at the excavation site will probably scare them far away.'

The next junction was before the arena itself. Fhiro's gaze followed one of the winding stone structures that adhered to its vast outer walls. Thicker at its base than his old house in Chimahess, it wove its way up and almost out of view above. 'Do these winding pillars help it stay up?'

Palis was still busy talking to Imial, Chenessa and Chinda about yala beasts.

'Perhaps,' said Ghorad.

'You must have lots of buildings this big in Kartna,' whispered Fhiro.

'Oh, we do,' Ghorad replied, 'but one is not easily numbed to such sights.' He turned around and pointed out of the transparent section of the transant's rear. 'In particular, a palace keep that towers over its city like that is not easily overlooked. This might be the middle of nowhere to us, but these Niquani are not to be underestimated. They certainly know how to build.'

'They must place a lot of faith in the Supra Atmospheric Bombardment Accord,' said Fhiro. 'An impact from space would level the keep, however strong it is.'

'Kartna will always enforce the accord,' said Ghorad.

Fhiro decided not to challenge this view. Commitments to enforcing the accord were a badge of pride for powerful nations, but also a means to gain influence and power in war torn regions when, by choice or accident, objects from space landed on planets faster than they were supposed to.

Ahead a group of beggars gathered before the arena's entrance. Some were clamouring against it while others approached the transant. As before, when they had encountered such a crowd on leaving the space port, soldiers and guards moved towards it. Soon the clatter of blunt weapons against heads and faces, and the cries of pain and anger from the straggly-dressed, thin-limbed men and women retreating from the onslaught, drowned out all the voices inside the transant. Only when they were through the arena's tall entrance did conversation pick up again.

The transants opened, and their passengers gathered before being escorted to the Royal enclosure. Fhiro caught sight of a

pointed shape spiking up from a crowd, and smiled knowing it was his father – until it came into better view and he realised he was smiling at the sour-eyed Creedate prelate elder. There were so many priests and officials from the Creedate, Fhiro wondered if some of them were kidnap specialists in disguise, ready to whisk him and Chinda away. He shuddered at the thought, and could not relax until he had picked out the pointy shape of his father's mask. He hoped that Ghorad, his father, and Valachrad's other agents were up to the task of keeping them all safe.

They were taken to a balcony that overlooked the arena floor. He took the first glass a servant offered him, then the second, and then asked for a third.

'What are you doing?' Imial hissed in his ear.

'Thirsty,' spluttered Fhiro.

'You're in high society now. Stop acting like the worthless street urchin you really are!' Imial shook his head.

'Better that than end up a pompous horse like you.'

'Are you *trying* to blow your cover and start a galactic war?'

Fhiro glowered back at him, but decided to slow his consumption of beverages, at least in public, and maybe just accept Chinda was better than him at this.

No, he would never accept that.

Chenessa ordered one of the Creedate priests to get out of the way so that they could sit at the front together. Fhiro squeezed between the archaeologists and Chenessa, but then felt further unnerved when he realised that her guard, Tubrin, would be standing behind him. Palis and Ghorad were behind them too, and Fhiro found himself hoping the Kartnan was a match for the Creedate guard in a fight.

Hundreds of performers danced on the sand below them. A huge group had linked limbs to form a vast dome-shaped structure, atop which a yeal was juggling flaming torches. A

female hegel tooler used a catapult to fling herself somersaulting over him. She missed the flying torches by inches, and then landed in a net on the other side. Fhiro was about to applaud when the air above the torch-throwing yeal became full of his teammates, spiralling about over his head in rapid succession, yet avoiding collision with him, his torches, each other, or flaming fireballs jettisoned by other colleagues of theirs, before reaching the safety of the nets.

'They're good aren't they!' said Chinda.

Fhiro felt a moment of dread. They were amazing, but perhaps this was routine entertainment for high society diplomats of Kartna and the Creedate.

'I think they're absolutely amazing.' Chenessa beamed at them.

Fhiro felt relief flood through him.

'Don't you like them Fhiro?' asked Chenessa.

'Yes, yes,' he replied, flustered. 'Very impressive.'

A loud voice echoed through the air. 'Please thank Riletta's Magical Air Circus for their display!'

Fhiro noticed that the lower stalls, many of which had been empty before, were now packed with cheering spectators. The performers collected their items, bowed, and made their way out of the arena. Fhiro looked around for the source of the voice that had made the announcement. To his right, and a few metres below, there was a female yeal wearing a blond and purple wig, made out of both earthman hair and hegel feathers. 'The opening acts will now commence,' she cried. 'Enter the Birdsingers of Chiaspen!'

Fhiro craned his neck to get a better view. Earthmen, yeal and hegel entered the arena, walking with confidence and swagger. Underneath their glinting, dark armour, half of them wore white and the other half blood red. Fhiro caught his breath as trapdoors about the ground plunged open, and giant

pillars rose up through the openings until they towered high above the audience. 'Where is Chiaspen?' he asked.

'A distant continent,' said Palis, 'beyond Fawast.'

Once the pillars had reached their full height, Fhiro heard a tremendous rush of air above him. He gasped and ducked along with all the other children, but saw that Chinda remained standing and giggling. A bird, with a wingspan the length of six earthmen lying head to toe, flew over him. Its underbelly was just over an arms-length away, and Fhiro could smell its animal odour. In its claws it carried a small wooden cube. The rider of the bird directed it over one of the pillars, on to which it placed the cube with a precision Fhiro thought impossible for a flying beast of that size. Then it flew back the way it had come. He noticed the beast's crooked-shaped beak, which curved upward at its origin, as though the creature was smiling. Upon its return it did not fly quite so close to him, and Fhiro made himself stay standing, but Chinda still managed to draw even further attention to herself by trying to jump up in the air and touch it as it passed. He wanted to scold her right now. He hoped Ghorad had seen her and would ban her from coming out with them again.

From all around the arena roof similar birds dropped through the air and deposited cubes on the pillars before returning to their roosts. He was surprised he hadn't seen them take their places earlier.

'This is the bird taming,' Chenessa gasped.

'Correct,' said Palis.

Opposite the Royal enclosure a large grill rose up to reveal an opening in the arena wall between the two groups of bird tamers.

'In red, we have the reigning champions from last year's tournament,' continued the yeal woman with her colourful wig, 'the Tortham Forest Sky-dwellers.'

There were cheers from around the arena.

'And in the white, from the Salt plains of Vinthor, are this year's favourites, the Cleth-Dragon Bone Stealers!'

Fhiro managed to catch Palis's attention despite all the wild cheering. 'Why are some bird tamers calling themselves Bone Stealers?'

'They used to be called "The Salters",' answered Palis. 'I think they've come under new management.'

'Good management, clearly,' said Borlin, 'if they're now the favourites.'

'Sounds like it's the match of the season,' said Cerilina. 'Lucky us.'

'And up on the arena rooftops,' the announcement continued, 'are Riletta's Urban Airborne Rescue Squadron on sky-capture duty. They've had a ninety-nine game run without any fatalities. Let this be their hundredth!'

The cheering was less enthusiastic, and Fhiro noticed a tall earthman in the stalls below them collecting handfuls of money from those around him, peering over his shoulder from time to time at the guards by the doors. 'Someone died a hundred games ago?'

'It's a dangerous sport,' said Palis.

'Death in every hundred games?' said Borlin. 'Sounds boring.'

'Where in Kartna do you come from, exactly?' asked Ghorad. 'The Ejshak system?'

Borlin laughed.

Fhiro felt his stomach ripple as the blast of a deep horn shook the arena.

'Let the taming commence!' cried the wigged yeal.

From under the grill appeared two birds. To Fhiro's left, one of the White-clad Bone Stealers brought forward a writhing, jumping, pale-feathered creature.

'A waste-wraith,' said Palis. 'I'm surprised they got one of those in here.'

'It doesn't look like the most dignified of creatures,' said Chenessa.

'It's called a waste-wraith,' said Imial. 'What did you expect?'

Chinda threw Imial a scowl.

Imial whispered in Fhiro's ear, 'Your sister needs to consider where her loyalties lie.'

'Its beak is lined with inward facing hooks, some of which are a few centimetres in length,' said Palis. 'I can't remember if the regulations for this game require them to be filed down.'

'Surely that's animal cruelty,' said Chenessa.

'Outside of a dedicated protection zone it's perfectly legal to shoot waste-wraiths on sight,' said Palis. 'This one's getting quite a good deal, by comparison.'

One of the red-clad Sky-dwellers appeared to the right of the waste-wraith. He dragged the reins of a larger animal covered in a dark grey coat of square-shaped feathers. Its neck was long and its eyes were bloodshot.

'That one looks drunk,' said Fhiro.

'It is,' said Palis. 'Certain levels of intoxication are acceptable, especially for the more dangerous animals. That's a blorach; it would eat its rider if it had the chance.'

'So can't these riders just drug up the animals so that they're easy to tame?' asked Imial. 'How are they challenging themselves?'

'That's just the point,' Palis answered, 'they aren't challenging themselves.'

Just as he spoke a whistle was blown. The two tamers swapped control of the beasts they had brought with them, and took a monstrous bird back to their teammates. A Sky-dweller leapt on to the back of the waste-wraith, and a Bone Stealer tried the same on the bleary-eyed blorach.

Fhiro watched riders from both sides struggle for control of the respective creatures. Their teammates shouted encouragements from nearby. The drunk-looking beast turned its head around and snapped at the Bone Stealer on its back. 'What if it hasn't been drugged enough?' he asked. 'If they're switching the animals, can't they rig the game by choosing really violent ones?'

'Before this contest each team must demonstrate to the adjudicator that the animals can be tamed,' said Palis.

A hegel that had been leading the Sky-dwellers in their attempts to gain control of the waste-wraith abandoned her efforts. A male earthman took over from her.

'Don't hegel have an advantage in this game?' asked Fhiro.

'Most hegel in these parts are Toolers, like the captain of the Sky-dwellers,' said Palis, 'so not really. There are only a few flyer hegel in the league.'

The Sky-dweller made yet another attempt to mount the wraith, managing to stay on its back for several seconds.

'He's whipping it!' said Chenessa.

'Let's whip him and see if he likes it,' said Chinda.

The Bone Stealer who had been trying to tame the blorach also stepped aside for one of his comrades to take over. With three quick steps, a yeal mounted the beast and the gripped the reins tight around its neck. Then, after some quick kicks into its sides, it took to the air.

'He's off!' cried Borlin.

'Did he just suffocate it?' asked Fhiro.

'It's a legal move,' said Palis.

'Wonderful,' grumbled Chenessa.

'Where is he taking it, then?' asked Imial.

'I don't think he's taking it anywhere,' said Ghorad. 'It's taking him into space.'

Palis nodded. 'Taming is a continual process. It's rarely

completed on the arena floor, I'm afraid. He'll have to make his way back here after he gets control of it.' He pointed to the roof of the arena to their right. 'See, the rescue bird taking off to follow him?'

'The rescue birds look sinister,' said Fhiro. The creature's grinning beak was all the more troubling to him in the context of it chasing after the yeal riding the blorach.

Back on the Sky-dwellers' side of the arena the waste-wraith had been taken into the sky as well.

'How have the waste-wraiths survived for so long if anyone's allowed to shoot them?' asked Chenessa.

'There are enclosures where their existence is encouraged,' said Palis. 'The Guardians of the Environment and Culture of Pelorn is a powerful political lobby group. They ensure the preservation of all our native species.'

'Will there be any waste-wraiths near the dig site?' asked Fhiro.

'A creature like that wouldn't survive long in the forests and plains of Fawast,' said Palis.

After five more creatures had been taken into the air, and the number of teammates waiting below had diminished to a few on each side, the yeal Bone Stealer riding the drunk-looking blorach drifted down from above, exercising complete control of its movements. He lowered it to one of the pillars nearer his own side and attempted to catch the small wooden cube on it with a net. However, instead he knocked the cube off the pillar. As it hit the ground below, the other Bone Stealers lunged forward and snatched it. The rider, meanwhile, had begun to ascend into the sky again.

'Why doesn't he just get the rest?' asked Chinda.

'He has to ascend to do a circuit around the arena every time he knocks off a square,' said Palis. 'If he'd caught it in his net, he could have continued.'

'You mean a cube,' said Chinda.

'Well, in the game they're called squares,' said Palis.

'Where's the waste-wraith?' asked Fhiro.

'Touring the city?' suggested Imial.

'I wish I could fly a bird,' said Chenessa. She started and pointed upwards, 'Someone's falling!'

From high above, a dark shape plummeted through the sky. Above it one of the rescue squadron birds dived in pursuit, its wings folded back as it sped towards the ground. Fhiro could see the white uniform of a Bone Stealer. However, before the bird could pull out of its swoop and stretch out its claws, a parachute unfolded from the Bone Stealer's back and caught the air. The rescue bird darted out of the way before it collided with the ballooning material. The parachute turned with the wind and the Bone Stealer set down on the arena roof.

There were cheers from the crowds.

'That was close,' said Fhiro.

'Is that good for the Sky-dwellers?' asked Imial.

Palis nodded. 'A little, but victory in this game usually rests on only a few riders getting control of their steeds.'

Fhiro checked on Chinda to ensure she was behaving herself, but realised with a jolt that Chenessa's seat was empty. Where was she? Looking back, he saw her walking away from the balcony, towards the entrance to their enclosure, where there stood an elderly man in worn, tattered clothes.

Fhiro looked to see who else in their enclosure had taken notice of Chenessa leaving. Imial and Chinda remained engrossed in the game, as were Ghorad, Cerilina and Palis. The Creedate priests and Tubrin, however, were oblivious to the birds and their tamers darting through the air above. All of them were now facing Chenessa.

'Where's she going?' Fhiro asked Ghorad, but even as he

asked he realised that it was not Chenessa, but the white-haired man she walked towards that had drawn the attention of the Creedate.

'Let's go find out,' said Ghorad.

Fhiro managed to get near enough, fast enough, to hear Chenessa greet the visitor. 'Master Saflua, what an honour to see you here.' She curtsied.

She was answered by a tuneful laugh that danced atop the roars of the arena. 'Chenessa,' Saflua replied, 'a pleasure to see you too. I'd dearly love to continue our conversation.'

Fhiro stopped a few feet behind Chenessa. There was something about how Master Saflua carried himself. Something traversing rooted unshakable permanence and floating ethereal extension, as though he connected the stars to one another, channelling energy between them.

'Perhaps now isn't the time,' said Chenessa, 'but if you're staying in the city, I'd be very happy to do so.'

'Excellent,' said Saflua. 'I look forward to it.'

Fhiro noticed the prelate elder approaching. In fear of the high-ranking clergyman's cold observant gaze, Fhiro shrank away to stay out of his sight.

'I had heard you'd gone travelling after you left the Holy Court,' the prelate said, with a smile that, to Fhiro, looked devoid of any sincerity. 'What brings you here, great sage?'

'It is partly by chance that I came this way. I was among the worlds of Baworl when I picked up the news of this ancient find. I sought to be where empires might meet; it is the unconverted and influential I wish to preach to.'

'I'm surprised they allowed you through,' said Chenessa. 'Pelorn's King is just over there.'

'One of our guards recognised and vouched for me,' said Saflua, 'but I would not want to trouble his majesty just now. Is your mother here?'

'Yes,' said Chenessa. She showed him where Reshna was sitting with her other priests.

'She looks busy,' said Saflua. 'I'll talk to her after the show.'

'She'd love to talk to you any time,' said Chenessa. 'If you want to join us more often, work your magic on Palis there. He knows our social timetable better than I do.'

Saflua laughed again. 'Sounds very conspiratorial.'

Under the direction of the priests, servants brought some chairs. Master Saflua took Chenessa's hand and they sat down together. 'And who are these young people?' he asked, looking at Fhiro.

'This is Fhiro,' said Chenessa. 'He's from Kartna, and is on the path to becoming an Aculei priest. Over there, watching the games, are Imial, the Kartnan ambassador's son, and Chinda, daughter to one of the Kartnan diplomats.'

'Well I would not want to distract them from the excitement taking place in the sky up there,' said Saflua, smiling at Fhiro. 'Don't mind us, young man. Chenessa and I are old friends.'

Chenessa smiled. 'Master Saflua is one of the few sages that doesn't mind me arguing with him. Do you?'

'Well when the arguments are so eloquently put,' Saflua replied, 'how could any self-respecting scholar fail to enjoy them?'

There was an eruption of deafening roars from behind him, but Fhiro had lost interest in the aerial theatrics. He recognised the name. Master Saflua was one of the great sages of The Calling, though Fhiro struggled to recall any other details. He realised he was in the presence of a recognised, true authority, and a source of wisdom on matters relating to The Calling.

He had a burning desire for answers. Answers his mother never gave him. Answers no one seemed to know. He summoned his courage, fighting through every feeling of

shyness, embarrassment, anxiety and fear. He made himself speak. 'May I ask you a question?'

Master Saflua looked at him.

Fhiro wondered if his mysterious but calming countenance was a consequence of great wisdom, numerous rejuvenations in the havens, or possibly even a genuine, spiritual connection to Aten and the heavens.

'By all means, young man,' said Saflua. 'You wish to become an Aculei priest?'

'If I am worthy of the honour.'

'Spoken like an Aculei also!' Saflua laughed. 'I have only ever met two of them, truth-be-told. What a rare pleasure to encounter a third! What knowledge do you seek from me?'

Fhiro started to feel the gaze of Tubrin, Ghorad, and the priests. Chenessa's expression was part puzzlement, part suspicion. Those servants in the enclosure not gripped by the bird taming had stopped moving. Meanwhile his own mind became a swarm of ideas struggling for supremacy, barraging into and tunnelling through each other, wreaking havoc with his thoughts. The safest thing to do now, he knew, was to apologise and be silent. Why had he opened his mouth?

But he knew why. The questions boiling up within him hurt. They were like a creature he could not dislodge that clawed at his soul. He needed to understand. He needed explanations that did not make things seem more complicated than they had at first. Perhaps Master Saflua could help to wash away all of Fhiro's doubts about The Calling, and let him be one with his family and the trillions of Followers across the Near Quadrant.

'I … I've seen some of your scriptures,' said Fhiro. There was a sudden awareness within him that this seemed like a bizarre thing for the apprentice of an Aculei priest to say. 'When I was young I was introduced to The Calling, and I

studied it before I committed my soul to the Aculei.' He tried to read Master Saflua's expression, but failed.

'Go on,' said Saflua, still smiling.

'I wanted to ask about the prophet Gedo,' said Fhiro.

'Ah yes,' Saflua nodded. 'What do you wish to know?'

'Gedo said a number of things,' said Fhiro, 'but three of them I cannot see all being true. Namely; that God, or Aten as you call him, is all powerful, that he loves people, and that he sends bad people – who he also loves – to hell, where they suffer for eternity.'

Out in the arena the cheers resumed again, but they came from far away, across an ocean of space and time. The wigged yeal made an announcement, but Fhiro did not hear her words.

'You, Fhiro, are both wise and brave,' said Saflua. 'To us mere mortals, imprisoned in our physical bodies and constrained by our simple minds, truths such as those told by Gedo are insoluble. As you say, this problem does not make sense to us. How could Aten, who loves his children so dearly, and wields such great power, ever allow any of them to suffer at all, let alone spend an eternity in hell? I myself defend your argument. I ask anyone to try to convince me that our reasoning can make sense of these ideas!' He looked about him, and his small audience stood listening and silent. Even Tubrin's face was placid and keen.

'None of you speak out against what this boy has said because this boy is right,' Saflua continued, 'but at the same time, what is impossible to us is not impossible to Aten. What we cannot understand is not beyond the comprehension of Our Lord, in his infinite wisdom.' Saflua returned his attention to Fhiro. 'All the same, though we might not understand such matters through reason, we can through realisation. There is an ingredient you miss, young Fhiro. An ingredient through

which you could bridge this gap. You are an Aculei apprentice, as you have told me, and so I know that you believe there is more to our existence than life, death, and then nothingness. It brings me joy to see your heart is not troubled by these doubts, at least. I am sure, however, that even in your religion, there are aspects of it that make you question yourself and your decision to follow the path you chose. Why, that is only natural, especially at your age.'

The cheering of the crowds reached a crescendo. Fhiro could sense the heightened tension, excitement and fear from those nearby, engrossed in the events above. He felt his clothes flutter and billow as a rescue bird flew overhead towards the arena.

'Fhiro,' Master Saflua continued, 'what you seek is not to break down this mystery so that you can put it back together and make sense of it. That cannot happen, for we are not great enough to put back together what only Aten could have made. What you need, Fhiro, is faith.

'Consider it a step into the unknown. A step taken in complete trust. If done correctly, you will find a clarity that I could never describe nor explain. Only then does the way become clear, and do the clouds part, and does the sun shine. Faith, Fhiro. Believe though your mind is in doubt, and it will learn a happiness you never believed you could enjoy.'

There was a peaceful stillness. Fhiro no longer felt people were watching him. All of them gazed upon Master Saflua, absorbing his enchanting presence. Fhiro felt he was, indeed, before a man of great spiritual wisdom and understanding, but somewhere, in the back of his mind, he felt cogs turning and a response brewing. He hated knowing that, whatever his next question was going to be, he would not have thought of it until long after Master Saflua had gone.

CHAPTER 13

'What were you thinking?!' Oljon slammed his mask on the table.

'I– I'm sorry,' mumbled Fhiro, fidgeting with the arm of his chair. They were in the family's quarters within the Kartnan Embassy.

Oljon had managed to improvise an explanation for why his apprentice knew the writings of the prophet Gedo, which the Creedate prelate appeared to have accepted as truth. But had he really? The prelate looked as evil as Chenessa's guard Tubrin was frightening. And what would Reshna conclude? Fhiro had not been looking forward to his return home.

'An Aculei apprentice,' said Oljon, shaking his head, 'knowing the *Scriptures of the Prophets* in such detail?'

'I know I always encouraged you to ask questions,' cried Hanu, 'but I meant for you to ask me or your father. Not to blow our cover talking to a Creedate sage!'

Fhiro screwed his eyes tight shut. 'Whenever I talk to you, I always end up feeling more confused.'

'Well I hope you feel better now, then,' said Oljon. 'I'd say everyone should seek answers to the big questions in life, but not if it means a lifetime of pain at the hands of Marallel's Grafters …' He stopped and stood still for a while.

'So was it worth it?' asked Hanu.

'What?' asked Fhiro.

'Did he dispel your confusion?' she asked.

Fhiro felt his gut turning. 'I wish.'

'Great,' said Oljon. 'All you were supposed to do was be nice

to this girl and keep your ears open. Do you want the galaxy to burn in the fires of war?'

'You do realise what's at stake, don't you?' asked Hanu.

Fhiro felt sick. His mind churned over all that was upsetting him; how angry his parents were, how much danger he had put them all in, that he might have triggered a war, or that he might be made to stay at the embassy from now on. What if Chinda was allowed to continue going on excursions and meeting with Chenessa and he was not?

'So,' said Hanu, 'you've nothing more to say?'

'I'm really sorry!' said Fhiro. He was. 'I won't do it again.'

The door opened and Valachrad, Imial, Chinda and Ghorad entered.

'Ambassador,' said Hanu, 'we're so sorry about this. We think it's only best if we keep Fhiro and Chinda here for the duration of our time on Pelorn.'

'No,' said Valachrad.

'What?' asked Oljon. 'We cannot trust these children not to give away our identity. If you're trying to prevent a war, Marallel realising I am under your protection will guarantee it. He would come here himself if he knew.'

'It is a risk we have to take,' said Valachrad. He gave Fhiro a distasteful look. 'Fhiro was an idiot. He almost got himself and his sister killed. We managed to cover for it, thanks to your quick thinking, Ishthen, but I'd be lying if I said the children are in no danger.'

Fhiro cringed.

'But this is bigger than Fhiro,' said Valachrad. 'Bigger than any of us, and everyone Kartna sent here aboard the Blind Vizier. We are, all of us, even my son, acceptable sacrifices in the pursuit of the Empire's goals.'

Fhiro caught sight of Imial's expression change to one of suppressed alarm.

'Even if the hope is slim,' Valachrad continued, 'Fhiro and Chinda's contributions are essential to it.'

'When we agreed to help,' said Oljon, 'I expected myself and Hanu might be putting ourselves at some risk. Please spare our children. Spare your own son!'

'Imial knows his duty,' said Valachrad.

Imial stood up straight, but his anxiety was obvious.

'My husband has worked tirelessly for your empire,' said Hanu, standing and glaring at the ambassador. 'He deserves to have the safety of his family protected.'

'A war with the Creedate would put your family in danger *wherever* they go,' Valachrad replied. 'While here, our agents will watch them with vigilance.'

Hanu slumped in her chair, her face drained.

'Ghorad will spend every free moment training them from now,' said Valachrad. 'He has managed assets in many environments and conflicts across the galaxy. Ishthen has vast experience in such matters too.'

Hanu said nothing. She wiped her eyes, and turned her head away.

Oljon put his arm around his wife. 'If it is the Senate's wish,' he said, his voice a little broken, 'then so be it. But honour your promises of protection. If their cover is blown, war is certain. I don't care how many Creedate need to die if our children are to be extracted safely, and you shouldn't either.'

Valachrad nodded. 'So be it.'

* * *

The next morning Oljon led his children, and Imial, through some training exercises in one of the courtyards.

'What's beast flying like?' Fhiro asked Dorrick, as his older

brother prepared to leave for the flying lessons with the Pelorn air force.

'Excellent,' Dorrick replied. 'I'm learning from Captain Tokun. He's brilliant. Really experienced.' He glanced about to check no one was listening, and whispered, 'I know we used to practice on Siwular sometimes, but these combat birds are so nippy.' He paused. 'It's an amazing feeling, even if I keep worrying I might fall off at any moment, or that my chute might fail.'

'Wow,' said Fhiro.

'Makes you appreciate being on the ground. Makes you appreciate being alive.' He looked at Fhiro. 'But at least I'm training for something when I'm putting myself in danger. You invite trouble for absolutely no reason! What is it with you?'

Fhiro, who had briefly been captured up in the fantasy of flying a combat bird, hung his head in shame.

'Just don't do it again, all right?' Dorrick gave Fhiro a rough pat on the shoulder, and strode off.

'Bye,' moaned Chinda, reluctantly being led back to the Embassy.

'Is flying part of Aculei training?' Fhiro asked his father.

'Yes,' Oljon replied, 'but you're not doing any. You'll accompany me to our councils with the King's advisors, apprentice!'

He had known about this, of course, but his father's mentioning of it made Fhiro's insides fill with fear again. He would be in full view of the Creedate, and all their spies in all their guises, once more. Ghorad's training had been thorough, and he felt better at putting on a confident, calm exterior, despite what fears might be rampaging across his mind, but doing so felt very unnatural to him. He was pretty sure he would forget his instructions, sooner or later.

Aboard the transant he watched the adults converse, and

strained his ears to listen in. His mother was speaking, capturing the attention of everyone around her, including Valachrad. Despite how sad she must have felt, she took to her new role with ease. His pa too, the eccentric fitness, combat, philosophy and maths-obsessed security worker at a laboratory, who had raised him, also fitted right in among these high-ranking officials. The two of them discussed matters of great consequence for the entire galaxy like they were born to it. Had he really ever truly known them?

It was all still so strange and alien. Throughout his life Fhiro had disliked the fact that his parents were so different, but right now, despite his fears, he could not help but be proud of them.

They rounded the bulging flank of the palace keep, heading to its entrance. Sensing the change of scenery had distracted the adults, Fhiro chose this moment to move a few seats nearer to them.

'Police blockades and weapon checks,' said Oljon. 'They're expecting trouble in the city.'

'To say nothing of the murders,' said Valachrad. 'Hanu, are you sure they're the result of fighting between extremist Niquani groups?'

'Perhaps it's always like this around the festival,' said Captain Jard.

'To an extent, it *has* always been this way,' said Hanu, 'but our sources suggest this is exceptionally bad. I think there has been trouble on the horizon, but this discovery has pushed the intensity to another level.'

'Find out what they are fighting for,' said Valachrad.

'We have people gathering facts in the city as we speak,' said Hanu, 'though if possible I should like to go myself.'

Valachrad nodded. 'I'd appreciate that.'

Oljon noticed Fhiro was listening in. 'This conversation isn't for you.'

Fhiro smiled, hoping that behind the mask his father was smiling too, but Oljon simply tilted his head in the manner Fhiro recognised as the order for him to make himself scarce. He joined Imial at the front of the transant.

'Anything to report?'

'Niquani extremists are killing each other,' said Fhiro.

'Well that's extremists for you,' said Imial. 'They're too busy fighting each other to threaten those in power.'

'I'm sure that's not always true,' said Fhiro.

Imial grunted and ignored him.

They disembarked within the keep itself. The Chamber of Resolutions was a short walk further, through the keep's looming, vaulted interior. It was a round, bowl-shaped room, with the speaking platform at its centre, in view of the rows of seats circling above it. 'It's like being back in the arena,' Fhiro whispered to Imial when they sat down together, close to Oljon and Valachrad. 'Do you think there are rescue bird squadrons hiding somewhere above us, in case–'

'Shut up!' Imial whispered harshly.

Fhiro glared at him, but subsided into silence all the same. He looked back and above them, and imagined Riletta's Urban Airborne Rescue Squadron hiding behind hidden doors in the walls or ceiling. He noticed his mother was towards the rear of the Kartnan delegation. Following the rows of seats around the chamber, he saw Chenessa sitting across from him, with her grizzle-faced guard Tubrin. He was about to wave when Imial grabbed his wrist. 'Not in here!'

Chenessa saw this, laughed a little, and then smiled at them.

Fhiro smiled back. Imial was probably right, though.

He saw the Creedate ambassador Reshna, and her other hegel guard, Hussuf, several rows in front of Chenessa, and surrounded by wizened priests, including the cruel-faced prelate elder in his distinctive, pointed hat. Fhiro noticed that

Master Saflua was not with them. This was mostly a relief, but part of him wished he could continue their conversation. He imagined he would never get the chance to do that now.

A middle-aged earthman approached the platform and drummed a tall wooden sceptre into the floor. 'This council is now in session. Welcome all.'

Formal introductions then began, followed by matters arising from previous meetings. As these dragged on for the best part of an hour, Fhiro felt his eyelids grow heavy.

'Don't fall asleep!' Imial nudged him.

'I really don't care about Iap's grievance over Pelorn's competition laws.'

'All things are important.'

'When will they start talking about technological treasures hidden under the mountain?' asked Fhiro.

Imial frowned at him, then turned his attention back to the proceedings. But as the routine business dragged on, Fhiro saw that even Imial's head was nodding.

Fhiro came out of his own daydreaming when Winle, the Hithostun ambassador who had scolded the servants the day before, descended to the platform.

'In response to Ambassador Zakil's statement, I would like to raise the issue of real importance here.' Her voice endured in the air between her sentences. 'Concerns about our intentions up until several months ago are now irrelevant. The scene has changed. Kartna and the Creedate have graced us with their attention, and courted Pelorn with such persistence she seems to have forgotten her place as the spiritual centre of the Niquani people.'

There were cheers from all around the chamber. The loudest were the provincial representatives sitting further from the platform.

'Of little interest to the rest of the galaxy was this planet or

any of our nations, before that cursed ship drew attention to Fawast's hidden secret,' Winle continued. 'The Sufferers thought it contained a great weapon. Possibly a crystal technology with which to defy gravity. But none have seen inside it yet. It might be nothing at all. This is a moment of great uncertainty for Pelorn; not the time to forget her sisters and brothers.'

There were echoes of approval. Fhiro took out his Gravi-trap and stared at it. Scientists and sorcerers had been trying to achieve levitation using crystals for millennia. Gravity-crystals, which could generate gravitational pull within a specified spatial field, were an obvious starting point for any such work, but despite the efforts of so many, the small unpredictable device in Fhiro's hand remained the best any civilisation had managed.

'Countess Jeberrel,' announced the speaker.

Fhiro watched the countess who, along with Palis, had greeted them upon their arrival on Pelorn. Jeberrel stood opposite Winle on the platform. 'You talk as though we owe our loyalty to Hithostun, in preference to the distant powers that now offer us help, enrichment and expertise. The Niquani may be one culture, but our history is no rosy tale of shared glory and achievements. For generations we and our neighbours have diverted nearly all our energies into war and strife. In particular, I might add, we've made terrible sacrifices to contain the ambitions of the rulers of Hithostun. You would rule all the Niquani if you could, and you are enraged that Pelorn, the planet from where our culture originated, has avoided your clutches so long.'

Winle laughed. 'Your entire Royal house is nothing but an offshoot of Baworl's! Your rulers cannot pretend to speak for the people you govern. Why, even now, popular dissent is overboiling. A nobleman, a city mayor, and thirty-two police

who were protecting them were killed fifty miles from here, yesterday.'

'The people of Pelorn remember who murdered the Royal line that reigned here before,' replied Jeberrel. 'Perhaps one day you will have your way, but Pelorn will always resist you. If our far-off friends can help bring us strength, then that is an offer we cannot overlook.'

'You would take help from the likes of the Creedate to protect yourselves from us?' Winle cried.

'There are other powers growing in strength, not so far from here,' said Jeberrel, 'and much closer than either the Creedate or Kartna. If the Niquani ever unite, and I hope that one day, peacefully, we will, our troubles will be far from over.'

'The powers you talk of might challenge us, but Kartna and the Creedate would sweep them aside like driftwood.' Winle pointed to where the Kartnan and Creedate delegations were seated. 'If anyone is going to harm your people, take away their dignity, and force them to swear allegiance to gods they do not believe in, it is these giants that you suddenly find at your door. You dare to call us ambitious! We only want to protect our culture. Peaceful unification has always been our intention. We cannot be held to blame for every ill that has befallen this region, just because we happen to be its most powerful nation.'

'Both Kartna and the Creedate have offered to sign treaties of alliance that prohibit them from attacking us or any of our neighbours,' said Jeberrel. 'The fears you speak of are unfounded. You dread a Niquani alliance under any banner other than your own.'

Fhiro could see the provincial representatives shuffle in their seats, some leaning to confer with one another.

'Ambassador Zakil,' said the speaker.

'We of Iap also live in fear of Hithostun,' said Zakil, his face dwarfed by his tall, finely crafted head of hair. 'We

welcome these foreign powers and their offers of alliance with our ally, Pelorn, and any advantage against Hithostun that comes with this.' He shot a glare at Winle, and there were murmurs of agreement from the benches nearer the platform. 'However,' he turned to Jeberrel, 'what assurance do we have that we are not substituting one dominant neighbour for another?'

Imial leaned nearer to Fhiro. 'Pathetic little countries, bickering over crumbs.'

'And what will become of this technology?' Zakil continued. 'If it does exist, why share it with those who will one day return and use it to devour us?' He turned to the rows of benches behind him. 'This is a blessing from the spirits! A sign that we, the Niquani, are destined for greatness! We must understand this powerful gift and use it for ourselves. Let us form an alliance together, and hold off all outside aggressors, lest they attempt to impose their will upon us.'

The shouting and applause was deafening.

'I don't think we're all that popular,' Fhiro muttered to Imial.

'Provincial people are stupid,' said Imial. 'I'm sure the King knows how to bring them under control.'

'Does Iap wish to form a federation?' sneered someone from close to the platform.

'What greater threat is there than the Creedate?' cried a voice from the back of the room.

'Or Kartna?'

'Silence!' boomed the speaker, crashing his sceptre upon the floor. 'Ambassador Winle, if you please.'

'Our past, like that of any successful power, may be chequered with grievances and accusations of transgressions against our neighbours,' said Winle, speaking fast, 'and as always, we are willing to discuss all such matters, and make amends where possible and appropriate.'

A woman in the audience laughed until the Speaker silenced her with a cold stare.

Winle took no notice. 'Our nations are all tied through blood, religion and culture. It is time to embrace our fate and face our future, strong and united.' She looked at Jeberrel. 'We shall not betray you. An alliance formed between us will be written in terms most favourable to Pelorn. Do not let our past be the cause of our mutual destruction! Let it be something that lives on as long as the Niquani grow and prosper.'

At this Valachrad stood up to be called, as did Ambassador Reshna of the Creedate. Fhiro did not notice either of them react when the speaker chose, instead, to hear from Countess Jeberrel once more.

'Shall not betray us, you say? Our relationship isn't chequered, it's a long list of cruel acts and war-mongering, sponsored or initiated by Hithostun. If unifying the Niquani was so important, why is it only now that, threatened by what strength these foreign powers might bring us, you think of offering us terms we might find favourable?'

'Ambassador Reshna,' the speaker spoke with less certainty as he eyed the tall, thin Creedate woman, and the rows of sombre priests beside her.

'The Creedate have done many things to inspire fear,' said Chenessa's mother, 'and we regret that this has sown seeds of distrust among those far from our heartworlds. Where we come from, cruelty has reigned long, infesting entire systems with deep-rooted evil. Against such a menace terrible acts have been necessary, and so our reputation has been tainted. I can assure you, an alliance between the Creedate and Pelorn is offered with the strongest of peaceful assurances.'

'How is the Creedate to convince us that they do not wish to convert us all to their religion?' asked Zakil.

'We have made treaties with such promises to other nations

in the past, and we have kept them,' answered Reshna. 'We offer one here also. Avithen's teachings have not altered our attitude towards those who follow The Calling already; his words just empowered us to protect our own. The Calling remains, and always will be, a religion of peace.'

Cackling and joking simmered among the benches further from the centre.

'The Creedate are liars!' muttered a voice.

The speaker glowered in its direction and slammed his sceptre into the floor again.

'Yet when your missionaries have made a nuisance of themselves,' said Winle, 'and brought about their own mistreatment, will Marallel not seek to *protect* them? Then the shock dragons will come, and our lands will be ripped and ruined, and all mouths that still have tongues will declare their belief in your God, Aten, or face death.'

'Enough!' cried the speaker.

'This is actually better than I was expecting!' Imial grinned.

'Ambassador Valachrad of Kartna.'

Fhiro felt very self-conscious as heads turned in his direction. He tried to remind himself that the last person they would pay attention to was a small boy, in the middle of the group, when the ambassador himself was speaking.

'Pelorn's choice is not so bleak as it sounds,' said Valachrad, his voice even louder and clearer than the ear-destroying boom he used in day-to-day conversations. 'It need not submit to the Creedate, who seem set upon forcing their beliefs on all they behold, nor must it sacrifice its culture. We admit interest in whatever lies beneath the mountain being excavated in Fawast. We also offer our expertise in maximising its value to Pelorn.' He looked at Zakil and Winle. 'To those representatives of the other Niquani nations, who fear what our alliance with Pelorn will bring, your concerns are valid.

Pelorn will become far more powerful. You will do better to unite under her flag, for as you have discussed already, your true enemies are not each other, but the threats that lurk further afield.'

'I would offer the same,' said Reshna. 'Kartna is no empire of saints. Our heartworlds are nearer here, and tales of our misdeeds are easier to come by. We have done much good also.'

'Have you really?' a voice from the other side of the chamber interjected, sparking more laughter.

'Do not think that you will be any safer living under the shadow of the Kartnan gods,' continued Reshna, 'you will not! There are many Followers in these parts. We have the interests of your people at heart.'

'All the more reason to be wary,' said Valachrad, 'for it is on behalf of such Followers that the Creedate may go back on their word and conquer all of you.'

'Do not doubt our word!' cried Reshna.

'See how these two bicker as though we do not matter?' Winle raised her arms in alarm. 'They only see each other in this. We are nothing but spoils to be divided by them!'

'Will you all please calm down?' begged Countess Jeberrel.

The voices in the debate continued to grow louder in volume and darker in tone. Fhiro felt he was watching peace give up its last gasps. He looked towards Chenessa and gave a worried expression. The girl, whose allegiance made her his opponent in this heated confrontation, seemed unconcerned. She saw Fhiro, grinned, and then hid her face.

Oljon gripped Fhiro's shoulder. 'Stop it.'

Fhiro froze.

'This place is filled with spies,' murmured his father. 'Do not draw attention to yourself. You've done enough of that already. If she is going to reveal anything important to you, she will find it impossible if you are both being scrutinised.'

Fhiro nodded, face towards the floor.

'And she is not your friend,' said Oljon. 'She is the enemy.'

Fhiro glanced across the expanse at Chenessa. He wondered if he could see her that way. Her pleasantness seemed genuine. Then he saw her grim-faced guard, Tubrin, staring at him from beside her. There was such fierce hate in those smouldering eyes, Fhiro feared his heart might be torn from his body without Tubrin even laying a finger on his chest.

He looked away.

CHAPTER 14

Later they had lessons under the trees of the palace gardens with Chenessa's tutor, Theon. He was an ancient priest, with a thin tangled beard. Fhiro wondered if he had earned the right to rejuvenation. If he had, Fhiro hoped it was scheduled soon; Theon did not look destined to remain among the living for long. With a voice that had seen clearer, better days before, the priest asked them to draw some advanced sorcery circuits. Imial found them tricky, but Fhiro had finished them all within a matter of minutes. He looked around to check on Chinda's progress, and was troubled to see she had almost finished too. Sadly Theon realised this, and gave them both more exercises. Then, after an hour, the subject changed to crystal studies.

'I wish we could be out enjoying the yala beast festival,' said Imial, drawing one of the animals on his exercise book.

'Don't worry,' said Chenessa, 'tomorrow's Saturday. I've spoken to Palis and organised us a trip into the city.'

'A trip into Riletta?' asked Chinda.

'Quiet, now, children,' croaked Theon. 'So if a fleet of ships bears crystals with an aura of one light-minute each, what is the smallest possible number you would need to fully envelop a haven?'

Imial groaned.

As they worked Theon chatted, almost to himself. 'Of course, you would never settle for the minimum protection. Crystals might fail and leave a gap for an enemy to sneak between them in hyperspace. One needs layers upon layers of crystal-auras to prevent invaders from teleporting too close.'

'Who protects the havens?' asked Chinda.

Fhiro shook his head. He was sure he'd known this at her age.

'A haven provides its own starships, but the pilots are from the nations it supports with resources and intelligence,' answered Theon. 'Does anyone know the most reliable protection for a haven?'

'Hide it,' said Fhiro without looking up.

'Very good, Fhiro. Yes, keep it secret, hidden and safe, or it won't be there much longer! Without a haven one will have to pay dearly for any space-worthy craft.'

'But you can make ships with planet-grown materials,' said Chenessa.

'Yes,' said Theon, nodding, 'but they are more likely to have faults in their surfaces and burn up during atmospheric entry.'

During the break Yogric came to pester them, intent on undoing whatever evils Theon might have wrought upon their minds. Without intending to, Fhiro and Chinda still got into an argument with him.

'If you can't learn, I can't help you,' muttered Yogric, turning his back to them as he continued his conversation with Imial.

Chinda shared a grin with Fhiro and shook her head.

When the final session began Fhiro sighed. A talk about local history was to be delivered by one of the palace tutors. Unfortunately this tutor had a voice lacking any intonation, and a face barely capable of expression. Fhiro hoped he could stay awake to the end, but within minutes he found himself fascinated. He already knew that Hithostun was the strongest nation in the vicinity, but now learned how the others constantly watched and negotiated with each other to protect the balance of power. Countless wars had been fought to prevent the establishment of a local hegemony.

After the sun had set and the gardens grew dark, they were

dismissed. Fhiro reminded himself of the training Ghorad and his father had given him before he, Chinda and Imial began discussing arrangements for the next day with Chenessa.

'Well I hope you can come,' said Chenessa. 'I'll see if I can persuade them to let us visit one of the markets.'

'I heard there'd been rioting in parts of the city,' said Fhiro.

'Palis will know where's safe,' said Chenessa, 'and Tubrin would be more than a match for any rioters.' She looked over her shoulder.

Fhiro saw that the scar-faced Creedate warrior was receiving a blessing from Theon. A respectful distance away from everyone was Ghorad, observing both Tubrin and the Children.

'What's Tubrin doing?' asked Chinda.

'I don't know,' said Chenessa. 'He's always seizing chances to ask for blessings from holy people.'

Fhiro looked at Imial, but the ambassador's son seemed lost in his own thoughts. He turned back to Chenessa. 'It was strange yesterday, watching your mother argue with Valachrad.'

At the mention of his father's name Imial snapped to attention. 'Yes,' he added, 'it's not nice to see them fighting.'

'You're nice,' said Chinda. 'I bet your mother is too, really.'

Chenessa laughed. 'My mother is my mother. I'm not sure what more I can say about that.'

Fhiro wondered how much he should say. He looked around, checking there were no Creedate priests within earshot. 'Do you think they pretend to be more aggressive than they want to be?'

Chenessa shrugged. 'All this deceptive behaviour. They say it's the essence of the art of war, but it doesn't half make life complicated.'

'Well it won't stop me talking to you,' said Chinda.

Chenessa smiled at the younger girl. 'Will you be coming to the dig site, Chinda?'

'I hope so,' said Chinda. 'Depends on whether my mother is going.'

'You'll put in a good word for her, won't you Imial?' asked Chenessa.

'Er, of course.' Imial nodded.

'And are you going, Fhiro?'

'If my master's going,' he replied.

'Excellent.' Chenessa turned. Tubrin was walking towards them.

Tubrin ignored the boys, shot a suspicious look at Chinda, and then grunted at Chenessa.

'Well, I must be off.' Chenessa smiled at them as she was led away.

Fhiro, Imial and Chinda followed Ghorad back towards the Kartnan Embassy.

'She didn't give us the name of anyone her mother trusted,' said Imial, letting out a sigh.

Fhiro checked their surroundings. They were walking across the grass that stretched between the keep and the walls bordering the palace enclosure. The embassy was visible, but there was no one close enough to hear them. 'Maybe Valachrad's got the wrong idea about this.'

'My father is never wrong,' said Imial.

'At least she knows that we three don't want to go to war with her people,' said Chinda.

'A month ago you *were* her people,' said Imial.

'No!' shouted Fhiro. 'We were Followers of The Calling, not members of the bloodthirsty Creedate. You're so ignorant.'

'Fhiro,' said Ghorad, 'please, not so loud.'

'Aren't we still Followers of The Calling?' asked Chinda.

'You might be,' said Fhiro. 'I don't know what I am any more.'

'Is that why you started that stupid conversation with that religious sage in front of everyone?' asked Imial.

'Shut up, Imial,' Fhiro growled.

'Promise you won't do that again, Fhiro,' said Chinda.

'I'm hardly going to run into Saflua now,' he replied.

'What was that noise?' asked Imial.

'What noise?' asked Fhiro.

'Quiet!' shouted Ghorad.

All four of them stood still.

A series of sharp cracks echoed off the keep wall, from the direction of the gates that led to the city.

'Sounds like rifle fire,' said Fhiro.

There was a loud, thunderous rumble.

'There's some mischief at the gates,' said Ghorad. 'Let's hurry back.'

They ran. Fhiro was glad that his father had included Imial in their training; the ambassador's son did not get out of breath until they reached a group of Kartnan soldiers patrolling the grounds outside the embassy.

'What's going on?' asked Ghorad.

'Trouble at the main gate,' said the officer in charge. 'We've sent scouts out to have a look, and Priest Veltir has gone to speak with our hosts.'

Ghorad marched them into the library and pushed them inside. 'Stay here,' he ordered.

Fhiro saw the Magellan archaeologists were gathered around a table, poring over books, documents and maps, while holding a fast-paced conversation in a language Fhiro could not understand. 'Where's Borlin?' he asked.

Cerilina glanced round. She looked a little flustered. 'We were just wondering the same thing. He went out this morning and hasn't yet come back.'

'I think he's had enough of us talking to each other in Magellan,' said the dark-haired woman sitting next to her.

'He'll be all right,' said Cerilina. 'Is your family all safe?'

Oljon burst in with Ghorad, at the head of a group of Kartnan soldiers. Safe within the embassy, he removed his mask. 'Chinda! Fhiro! Thank the heavens.'

'What's happening?' asked Chinda.

'Nothing too serious,' he answered. 'A riot has broken out by the gates. The Royal guards have it under control.'

'Borlin may be out there,' said Cerilina. 'He wanted to watch the evening festivities.'

'Hanu and some of the other advisers are out there, too,' said Oljon.

'Ma?' cried Fhiro and Chinda at once.

'Is she all right?' asked Chinda.

'I'm leading the extraction team,' said Oljon. 'Ghorad, want to come?'

'Why not,' said Ghorad. 'Will we scale the walls?'

'I suspect climbing the stairs will be simpler,' said Oljon, 'but we will descend by rope on the other side.' He turned back to Fhiro and Chinda, pulling them both into a tight hug. 'We'll be back after things have settled down.' He gave them a squeeze.

Fhiro found being squashed in his father's arms a comfort against his worries for his mother.

'Ready when you are,' said Ghorad.

Oljon released his children. 'Stay out of trouble. I'll tell Captain Jard he is responsible for you now.'

'Bring Ma back safe, please?' begged Fhiro.

'She's sensible,' said Oljon. 'The riots are between xenophobic Niquani extremist groups and she's been sticking to areas popular with the Followers of The Calling.' He patted Fhiro on the shoulder and left.

'So one minute we're staying away from the Followers of The Calling, and now we need to be closer to them?' Fhiro collapsed into one of the soft green chairs spread throughout the library. It moulded itself snug against him, and should have made him feel comforted and warm, but it was no substitute for an absent father and mother. It just made him miss them and his old home on Andelic.

'I'm sure she'll be fine,' said Cerilina.

'Thanks,' said Fhiro, but he did not believe it. Even if Oljon made it back with her, the entire family would not be safe until it was a long way away from Pelorn.

Cerilina smiled, then turned her attention back to her colleagues. Within an instant the table of the Magellan archaeologists was alive with conversation again.

'Probably best just to stay behind these walls,' said Imial, sitting down next to him.

Fhiro sensed Imial was frightened too, but the last thing he needed to do was share concerns with the ambassador's son. 'And bore ourselves to death?' he asked, trying to sound as assured as possible. He saw his sister was still standing, her arms folded. 'Why don't you sit, Chins?'

'Scared for Ma and Pa,' she answered.

'Where's your brother?' asked Imial.

'He's not due back today,' said Fhiro. 'They're off doing exercises north of the city.'

'Aren't there hegel Niquani extremists?' asked Imial. 'What if they glide over the walls?'

'Hegel flyers? They aren't that fast,' Fhiro replied, 'and crystal-fire weapons aren't affected by gravity or wind, so they get shot down easily.'

'What if they're wearing anti-crystal armour?'

'It's expensive and usually heavy,' said Fhiro. 'If they do have it they'll probably struggle to take flight. Commandeered

transport birds would be more trouble, but the palace keep is well prepared for an aerial assault.' They had all seen the surface of the keep. It was covered in surface-to-air cannons, with additional turrets clustered across the walls protecting the palace enclosure.

They sat in silence for a while. Eventually Chinda came and squeezed on to the seat with Fhiro. He put his arm round her, and she rested her head on his shoulder. They sat still for some time, listening to, but not comprehending, the words of the Magellan archaeologists. After a while, though, Fhiro's curiosity got the better of him. He adjusted Chinda so that she was resting against a pillow. She kept her eyes closed as he did this, but he knew she was awake. Then he stood up and took a few steps to where Cerilina was sitting at the head of the long table she shared with her colleagues. As he neared, he noticed some of the other archaeologists catch sight of him, and then glance at Cerilina. Cerilina turned to look up at him.

'Don't mind me,' said Fhiro. 'Just wondered what you were all talking about.' The silence, now that he had interrupted them, was deafening.

'Check it all again,' Cerilina ordered a group at the far end of the table. Then, looking back at Fhiro, she smiled and said, 'Don't worry. If we were talking Galactic you wouldn't have to ask.'

Fhiro saw notes, drawings and maps on the desk. Many of the archaeologists had sketches of a dark, sleek shape, with what looked like a hound's head at one end. Some of the images even included its clenched, bared teeth. But it was not like any canine species Fhiro had ever seen or read about, and he was sure he was not looking at depictions of a real living creature. Its body looked abstract or artificial, more so than he would expect any creature conjured by the sorcerers to.

Fhiro gasped. 'Is that the Sufferer ship?'

Cerilina's eyes widened. 'Yes,' she said.

'You've seen it?' asked Fhiro.

'This morning,' said Cerilina.

'What was it like?' asked Imial, getting up from his chair.

'What you'd expect from such a place,' said Cerilina. 'Rather unsettling, even if the Sufferers that were flying it are now long dead.'

'We're starting to look a bit stupid,' confessed Fhiro, gesturing towards Chinda and Imial, 'because unlike Chenessa, we don't know anything about them.'

'She knows about the Sufferers, does she?' asked Cerilina. She turned her chair to look at the children.

'You have to tell us about them,' said Imial. 'For Kartna's sake, it's important!'

Cerilina laughed. 'You really don't want to, or need to know about them. They're dead, remember!'

'So we've got nothing to be afraid of,' said Fhiro.

'Do you really want details about the religion that sought to bring as much pain and suffering to the galaxy as possible?' asked Cerilina. 'The people that made a precise science out of torture and mutilation? Do you really want to contemplate the reasoning they followed, and how they wound up inflicting horrid agonising injuries to themselves, their own children, and anyone they could get their hands on?'

Fhiro was taken aback. 'I knew they were bad,' he said, 'but I didn't know that.'

'They tortured their own children?' asked Chinda, pulling her legs closer to herself.

Cerilina's eyes widened. 'You didn't know that much?'

Fhiro shook his head.

Cerilina placed her head in her hands. 'I should never have spoken.' She gave them a pleading look. 'Please don't tell your parents about this!'

'You can't leave it at that,' said Imial. 'Tell us more!'

'I don't mind getting scared,' said Chinda, 'and I could use a good nightmare. They make sleep exciting.'

'Chinda's right,' said Imial. 'Nightmares can be fun, sometimes. Except when they're …' He fell silent, his brow furrowed as he stared at the floor, deep in thought.

'No,' said Cerilina. 'I shouldn't. Ask your parents, or your tutor.'

Imial and Chinda made glum faces. Fhiro was too lost in his own head, trying to imagine what beliefs would lead to such horrid practices.

'I'm sorry,' said Cerilina. 'If they give me permission to say more, and we can find the time, I'll do it. All right?'

'Our parents never have time,' moaned Chinda.

'And Yogric's an idiot,' said Fhiro.

'He is not,' said Imial. 'Yogric is very wise.'

Cerilina laughed. 'I've got to get back to working with this lot now. There's much to discuss if we're going to be as useful here as we hope to be. This Poshokan mountain sounds incredibly interesting. Apparently even explosives can't break into it.'

'Really?' Any mention of the Poshokans was enough to get Fhiro excited.

'The Poshokans were here all right,' said Cerilina. 'They've imprisoned something inside a mountain, and they've done it in typical Poshokan style.'

'What's that?' asked Fhiro.

'Perfectly,' said Cerilina. 'There seems absolutely no way in.' She smiled once more, then turned to be with her colleagues.

'I'll get my father to order her to tell us,' whispered Imial. 'Don't worry.'

'He won't do that,' said Fhiro. 'Maybe we should just ask Chenessa.'

'And look like fools?' asked Imial.

Fhiro sighed. 'What kind of a weird religion would make people want to torture their children?'

'And themselves?' said Chinda.

'Or anyone,' said Imial. 'Weirdos. The Calling isn't much better. They torture people. They kill children. They build mountains out of decapitated heads on ...'

'Again, you ignorant muppet, that's the Creedate,' said Fhiro. 'Stop blaming all of The Calling for what the Creedate are doing.'

'But most Followers of The Calling are in the Creedate,' said Imial. 'If The Calling was really a peaceful religion, they wouldn't be fighting for the Creedate.'

'It's not that simple,' said Fhiro. 'Just because most of them are being stupid, doesn't mean they all are.'

'And most of those fighting for the Creedate have no choice,' said Chinda. 'If they don't, they'll get tortured or killed.'

'Maybe the Sufferers were like that too,' said Imial.

'She said the Sufferer *religion* was evil,' said Fhiro, glancing over at Cerilina. 'There's an important difference.'

'Sounds the same to me,' said Imial.

'I guess if you're too stupid to know the difference,' said Fhiro, 'then it would sound the same.'

'I'm not stupid!' said Imial.

CHAPTER 15

'You got back!' Fhiro jumped on to his mother. He had been so excited to hear her voice he was out of his bedroom door, and into the dining area he shared with his family, before he had fully woken up.

Hanu grinned and hugged him back. 'I should do dangerous things more often if it gets me lovely hugs from you.'

'No,' said Fhiro. 'Don't do dangerous things. What happened?'

'I'd rather not talk about it,' said Hanu. 'But we made it back all right. That's what matters.'

'Don't scare me like that,' said Fhiro.

'Scare you?' Hanu chuckled. 'I'll promise to be safe if you promise too, little mister.'

Fhiro started squirming away. 'I will. I promise.' Then he noticed Chinda, sitting next to them, with a hateful look on her face. 'What's up with you?' he asked.

'I think she slept badly,' said Hanu.

'You know that's not it,' said Chinda.

'What then?' asked Fhiro, detaching himself from his mother. The look in his sister's eyes troubled him.

Hanu sighed. 'I'm not going to the excavation site, and therefore we can't justify bringing Chinda.'

Fhiro felt a trickle of fear down his spine.

'Tell them I've applied to be an Aculei apprentice,' said Chinda, 'or that I've been adopted by Valachrad. I might as well be; he decides what's happening in my life these days anyway.'

'Chinda!' cried Hanu.

There was a knock at the door. Fhiro pulled his dressing gown tight around him as he went to see who it was, leaving his sister and mother in silence.

Ghorad and Imial stood before him.

'Fhiro, get Chinda,' said Imial. 'Palis is calling for us. We're going to the market, remember?'

'We're still going?' asked Fhiro. 'I thought after yesterday …'

'Palis says not to worry,' said Ghorad.

'Yesterday's riot was crushed,' said Imial, 'and he won't allow terrorists like that to stifle our plans.'

'If he says so,' said Fhiro.

Hanu joined them. 'Honestly? Valachrad wants you all to go out again?'

'Yes, ma'am,' said Ghorad.

Hanu shook her head. 'I can't believe it. He doesn't even have the decency to tell me in advance.'

'It was the plan from yesterday,' said Imial, looking defensive.

'For Aten's sake!' said Hanu.

'Ma!' cried Fhiro and Chinda at once.

But she did not seem phased by her transgression.

'Can you be ready in half an hour?' asked Ghorad.

'We'll be fine, Ma,' said Fhiro, with more confidence than he felt.

She knelt down and clutched both of them close.

An hour later their transant dropped their group off close to a tall arch. Animal riders, wagons and the occasional transant circled the ring-road around it, flooding in and draining away through six, broad avenues.

'This area looks like it's full of Niquani,' said Fhiro. There were yala beast flags fluttering everywhere, from the wagons on the road, the hands of children and the poles on the

rooftops. 'After yesterday, aren't we safer in an area more populated by Followers of The Calling?'

'This is a tourist hot spot,' said Palis, 'and it's well policed. We're also a long way from the narco-tavern district.'

'Narco-taverns?' asked Chinda.

'Of course,' said Imial. 'Only in the Smugglers' Union.'

'Your societies have missed out on some very safe and enjoyable recreational substances,' said Palis. 'If your guard would allow it, I'd suggest you try some.'

'Palis,' said Ghorad, 'I shall protect my charges from such corrupting influences with terminal force, if necessary.'

Palis laughed. 'I apologise. We really don't see it that way around here, at all!'

'It's not really a Smugglers' Union when they've legalised everything they used to smuggle,' said Chenessa.

'When the Smuggler Lords became the rulers of these worlds they felt it their moral duty to smuggle their products into the possession of foreign people oppressed by misguided regimes and rulers,' said Palis, leading them forward as he spoke.

'Moral duty?' asked Chenessa. 'The profits had nothing to do with it, I'm sure.'

'But still,' said Fhiro, 'it must have been a bit of a change for them to start ruling people when all they'd done before was dope them.'

Palis sighed. 'Except that they had, in various ways, already taken over many roles traditionally the responsibility of the state. The main problem was that, while before they could blame the ruling government for the woes of the people, it soon became apparent that they would have to take better care of society if they wanted to remain in power. You'll find most narcotic substances are legal in these parts, but there's usually a catch. In Pelorn, for instance, there are very strict rules to deter over-indulgence.'

They started walking away from the towering arch, much

to Fhiro's disappointment. He had wanted to look at the pictures and symbols running up its walls. They weren't quite like anything he had seen in *Mythologies of the Galaxy.*

'Have to be careful of what you eat and drink out here,' said Chenessa. 'For now, take us to the bazaar, Palis!'

Dressed in inconspicuous clothes, and despite not having a troop of robed Creedate priests with them, the children and the guards still had trouble shaking the crowd that had noticed the transant; the hollow creatures were a luxury vehicle, reserved for the very rich. Palis failed to fend them off with polite conversation and explanations. In the end Tubrin and Ghorad were quite rough with a few people. With their disguise temporarily rumbled, Fhiro worried about how easy it must be for Creedate agents to track them.

They neared a row of stalls. Fhiro thought the shouting merchants would give him a headache long before they made him want to buy anything. Palis stopped them for a while at a lamp seller. Chenessa, Chinda and Imial were impressed by the detailed patterns fashioned into the shiny surfaces of the more expensive items on display. Theon, Chenessa's tutor, knelt down and explained how to discern the work of a master craftsman from a more amateur piece.

Fhiro thought the etched stone wall that made the side of the merchant's stall was much more interesting. Strange faces, attached to oddly angled limbs, gazed out at him with glee, menace and madness. The weathered look of the details suggested the design was ancient.

The neighbouring merchant, having no luck selling wooden tables for the moment, laughed. 'Do you want to buy the stone, rich boy?'

'How old is it?' asked Fhiro.

'As old as you want it to be,' said the merchant. 'It certainly looks old!'

'You idiot!' shouted the lamp seller. 'That piece of wall is an antique.'

'May your lamps catch fire and burn your stall to the ground!' said the carpenter.

'I curse your business!'

'I think we'll leave here now,' said Ghorad.

Chenessa soon dragged them into the main bazaar. Its interior, patterned with tile mosaics and hanging tapestries, was illuminated with oil lamps and hanging lumia-crystals, but also rays of sunlight from its high windows and its damaged, gap-ridden roof.

'I like the gold shop,' Chenessa said.

'Of course,' said Imial. 'Shiny metals have always been a good substitute to adore for those without real gods to believe in.'

'They make very nice things out of it actually,' said Chenessa. 'At least I accept gold is gold and don't go around pretending to myself an oversized lion, made by a bunch of sorcerers, has magical powers.'

'Blasphemy!' cried Imial.

'Please, all of you, we're trying to keep a low profile,' said Ghorad.

'Then put a lid on him!' said Chenessa, glaring at Imial. She glanced over her shoulder and then whispered to the Kartnan ambassador's son, but loud enough so Fhiro could hear, 'You'd best make sure Tubrin doesn't overhear you mocking The Calling. He's not as diplomatic as your bodyguard.'

Imial looked worried by this, and then confused. And then, as far as Fhiro could tell, he seemed to just forget about it and carry on as though nothing had happened.

They went deeper and deeper inside the bazaar. Crowds of people pressed on them from all directions. Fhiro saw someone reaching into Imial's bag while he was stuck,

squeezing between two earthmen who smelled like they had not washed in weeks. Fhiro slapped the thief's wrist. It recoiled and disappeared into the mass of bodies, like a snake darting under a rock.

'Let's see if they sell baby Hayemoths!' said Chenessa when they passed a shop full of noisy cages housing strange creatures.

'What are they?' asked Chinda.

But Fhiro had seen something much better. 'I'm going to the weapon shop.'

'No, you're not,' said Ghorad. 'We can go there after.'

'It's right opposite!' Fhiro protested.

'I don't want to look at weapons,' said Chinda.

'Fine,' said Ghorad, sighing. 'I can watch the entrances of both shops from here.' He planted himself in the space between the two shops.

Fhiro grinned. He walked inside and fell in love with the place immediately. It sold many close-quarter weapons. There were knives and bats, but also duelling swords and a variety of other unusual objects intended for cutting, piercing and smashing.

'We stock our firearms out the back,' said the owner, ''cos of regulations.'

'Can I see them?' begged Fhiro.

The owner turned to a half-open door. 'Oi! Man the store. I'm takin' this kid to see the firearms.'

'Yeah,' came the response.

Fhiro followed the owner through a set of doors to another room, the walls of which were lined with locked glass cabinets full of projectile and crystal-fire weapons of different shapes and sizes.

'Stinkin' regulations,' said the owner. 'Don't half hurt sales making everyone come out the back here.'

After demonstrating a thorough understanding of how crystal-fire rifles were constructed, and accurately declaring one item presented to him as an inferior model to the Mark 18 he used back home, the store keeper started trying to impress Fhiro by showing off increasingly superior hardware. 'And this is what the Pelorn Forces use as standard equipment. The V14. It's a projectile weapon with a good range and stopping power. Rate of fire is a little slow for some, the recoil is quite strong and many say it sacrifices too much accuracy for reliability. But it's stood us through many a tight spot. I was shouldering one of these twenty-four years ago.'

'You fought for Pelorn?' asked Fhiro as he looked down the sights.

'During the war of Vinaran succession,' said the shopkeeper as he gazed out of a window at the sun drenched streets outside. 'Took a round in the chest during the final battle with Norio. Didn't get to see them surrender.'

Fhiro thanked the shopkeeper, promising to return with his master. He walked past the overmuscled hegel, whose skin was plucked nude of feathers, who had been left in charge of the front part of the store on his way outside, but saw no sign of Ghorad or any of the others.

'Was it you they were lookin' for?' asked the hegel.

Fhiro felt light headed all of a sudden. 'Why didn't you tell me?'

'I didn't know the owner had a kid out there,' said the hegel, scratching his featherless head.

Fhiro ran off. He wondered if the agents Valachrad had spoken of had lost sight of him too. What if, by some stroke of bad luck, the Creedate spies knew where he was, but the Kartnan ones did not! He felt fear's fingers snake around his heart.

He looked into every stall he passed, but saw no sign of

them. Soon he found himself outside the bazaar itself. The midday sunlight splashed off the cloth roofs of the stalls and the pale parasols of sun-conscious pedestrians. He tried to shade his eyes with his hand, but even the glare from the stone surface of the public square bothered him. Looking this way and that, every few paces he had to dodge out the way of those preoccupied with carrying sacks of goods on their heads and shoulders. He noticed a crowd gathering around him, its attention on two men standing upon a stage in the middle of the square. One had long hair and cried out with a shrill voice, 'Come closer, all! Come to witness today's most vivid spectacle.'

The other man's head had a protruding mouth that was studded with long teeth. As Fhiro approached he saw it was the Lizardman mask of an executioner.

'Ladies and Gentlemen!' shouted the long-haired earthman. 'Today we bring before you five, sorry, lost fools. They enjoyed the freedoms of our society that were won by the sacrifices of our ancestors. The wondrous, life-enhancing substances we can experience here free from fear of persecution, are still denied throughout much of the galaxy by misguided and oppressive rulers. This is our heritage, a heritage we must protect.'

Fhiro tried to leave, but the press of the crowd behind him was too strong. As people struggled to get nearer the stage, they jostled and barged him, forcing him nearer to it.

'But these five sorry fools! Their selfishness got the better of them. They enjoyed more than they should have, and chose to harm others as a means to feed their appetites. If we allow such behaviour to continue unpunished, we would all be tempted by such selfishness! Society would crumble, and new rulers from afar would impose their closed-minded ignorance upon us.'

The press of close-packed bodies was getting tighter, and the hot weather beat a growing stench from it.

'There is no punishment for enjoyment here. There is not even a punishment for addiction. But those who break the law to serve their cravings will be used as a warning to the rest of us.' He turned towards the side of the stage. Fhiro could not see what he was looking at, for the crowd obscured his view. 'Bring them up!'

Five people, two earthmen, one earthwoman, a male yeal and a female hegel, were led on to the stage and lined up in a row. They were chained together. 'See our kindness!' said the long-haired earthman. 'Even now they have been given as much of whatever substance they desired! Witness them in the states they have chosen for themselves.'

Somewhere a strange instrument started playing, with low notes, to the beat of a drum. The executioner took out a knife. Fhiro turned away. He had to get out of here. There was a chorus of cries and gasps from the crowd. Shock and fear were audible all around him, but outbursts of excitement and glee were prevalent and unmistakable.

'Sorry, moving through,' said a tall, wide-shouldered hegel pushing his way past Fhiro. 'Get out the way you sick perverts.' He ploughed a path through the dense wall of bodies that had been obstructing Fhiro.

Seeing this, Fhiro snuck in behind the hegel, using the space created to get away from the stage. It was hard work, and those who had been displaced by the hegel were fast to slot back into their original positions under the pressure of the crowd around them. Fhiro endured the strong wafts of body odour, absent-minded elbows against his ribs and shoulders rubbing his face.

However, each step he took he lost ground, and after far longer than Fhiro imagined it would take to kill five, incapacitated people, the crowd had sealed in after the hegel

he had been following, and his progress was halted. Rendered idle by his circumstances, his curiosity overcame his resolve, and he turned around.

The executioner was only on his fourth victim. He had cut off three fingers and was now severing the left hand from the arm at the wrist. The criminal stared blankly as the hand dropped to the floor. A fountain of blood spurted over the executioner's apron as he worked, now cutting further up the arm, and then hacking at it. Fhiro saw the other three bodies, dismembered and crumpled up, on top of each other behind the executioner. The final victim waited, gazing off in other directions, sometimes looking at the crowd, oblivious.

Fhiro looked away, feeling tears well in his eyes and as though his stomach was turning itself inside out. He was sickened by the crowd, and ashamed of himself. He could do nothing, but worse than that, it was getting to him like the pathetic little boy he was. Dorrick was training with the Pelorn air force. Would he balk at such sights?

He stumbled, his vision blurred. Arms caught him. He wiped his eyes and smiled as he saw a friendly sight.

'Come this way, child,' said Master Saflua. 'This is no place for you.'

Master Saflua led him around a corner to a cafeteria and sat him down. The owner was about to ask them to leave, but another customer volunteered to buy the Master and his guest cups of Yellow-bean tea.

Fhiro hoped Ghorad and Palis would find him soon. Had they given up looking? Had they been captured or killed by Creedate agents? What would they say if they did find him with Saflua? His hands trembled as he brought the tea to his lips, his mind flashing images of the last victim's disinterested face, the pile of body parts gathering on the stage, and the excitement of the crowd.

'Why were you out there, young Fhiro?'

'Lost my friends.' He tried to stop the cup of tea from rattling against its saucer as he put it down. 'Caught up in the crowd …' He sniffed.

'There, there,' said Saflua, 'I am sure your guards will find you soon. Let us just stay here for now. Don't want to move from place to place in case they miss us!' He took a sip from his own cup.

Fhiro wiped his eyes again. He could no longer hear the cheers of the people watching the execution. He hoped it was all over. Nearby an earthman balanced a sword on his chin while a hegel played a box-shaped, stringed instrument that Fhiro did not recognise. Passers-by threw money to one or the other. Further away someone dressed up as a yala beast pranced about to the delight of a group of children.

'Why?' asked Fhiro, blinking back his tears. 'Why did they do that?'

'The executions?' asked Master Saflua.

'I thought this was the Smugglers' Union,' said Fhiro.

'This form of so-called justice snaked its way out of a murky, evil past,' said Saflua. 'If one lives according to the law then the use of narcotic substances is almost applauded. However, many a nation has been brought to its knees by the consequences of widespread addiction among its populace. The crude fix chosen here was what you just witnessed; crimes committed under the influence are awarded the death penalty.'

'That sounds harsher than the laws on Andelic,' said Fhiro.

Saflua's eyes widened for a moment, and then he smiled.

Fhiro froze for a moment, then felt a cold fear, worse than any he had ever known, turning the blood in his heart into ice, and spreading through every vessel of his body until even his skin went cold.

'It's all right,' said Saflua. 'I already knew.'

Fhiro tried to speak, but he barely moved his lips in silence.

'How is your mother?' asked Saflua.

Fhiro's mind was somersaulting in panicked terror.

'Is she all right?'

Fhiro managed to nod.

'That's good to hear,' said Saflua. 'I miss our conversations. She and I used to speak at length, you know.' He looked around at the tables near them before leaning closer to Fhiro. 'Sadly there weren't more like her back then. There still aren't now, though I do entertain hopes for Chenessa. Whether that's good for Chenessa or not, I don't know, but we need more inquisitive minds in the High Tower.'

Fhiro frowned.

'Your mother was one of the few that could stand up to both Avithen himself, and Thurgon,' said Saflua, chuckling, 'and survive. In fact, she seems to have outlived both of them!'

'How?' asked Fhiro.

'She had a very sharp mind and spoke it very very well,' said Saflua. 'She could disagree with the prophet in a way that did not make him look foolish, and yet he knew she had bettered him. She did so with Thurgon too. He, however, might not have stayed his hand were he not afraid how the prophet would react.'

'She said she tried to persuade him,' said Fhiro. 'She tried to persuade the prophet to change things.'

Saflua closed his eyes. 'I know. She sought to achieve the impossible. Perhaps she was brave, perhaps she was foolish. Perhaps she just had more hope than I did.' His crinkled lids parted again, and his irises shone bright and blue between them. 'I can't say I've achieved any more than she did by doing things differently. In fact she, at least, has produced you; a very fine young mind if I am any judge at all.'

'Er, thank you,' said Fhiro. 'Who are the Grafters and what are they going to do to my family?'

Saflua was taken aback, but then he laughed. 'Nothing, I should hope! Don't worry about them. Your secret is safe with me.'

Fhiro eyed the old man. He tried to pick up his tea again, but this time his hands trembled even more than before.

'Really, Fhiro,' said Saflua, 'you're all right. I have no interest in seeing people tortured and killed in Aten's name. It does not fit with my interpretation of the scriptures.'

They sat for a while in silence. Fhiro watched the shadows cast by the people in the square. 'Why were you out here, Master Saflua?'

'You saw what was happening,' answered the old sage. 'I go near terrible things to pray for those in need of it. Some need more help towards salvation than others.'

'You were praying for the addicts?'

'Not just them,' said Master Saflua, 'but also the crowd, the presenter and the executioner. All were engaging in acts that Aten would be most displeased to see. I pray they are shown to the path, and that they come to follow The Calling.'

Fhiro thought about this. Had he known he would bump into Master Saflua today he would have spent all night thinking of questions to ask him. 'How is it that some people need saving more than others, if anyone that is not saved goes to hell anyway?'

Master Saflua smiled. 'Some people are further from saving than others. They have the longest path, and need all the help they can get.'

'So prayer only helps the really bad people?'

'You are very quick,' said Saflua, chuckling again, 'but this is in the details of the scriptures. However, I suppose you aren't the Aculei adept I took you for. I shouldn't underestimate how much you know about The Calling.'

'If you understand it fully,' said Fhiro, 'can't you explain it without expecting me to go through the whole *SOP*?'

'Try not to use such an abbreviation,' said Saflua, now looking a little displeased.

'Sorry,' said Fhiro, regretting upsetting Saflua, who had just shown him such kindness. 'The *Scriptures of the Prophets*.'

Saflua exhaled. 'I shall try, Fhiro.'

'Because surely,' said Fhiro, 'if you did a little bit for a lot of people close to being saved you would end up with a lot more saved people than by doing a lot for, say, that executioner?'

Master Saflua's face held its smile, but his eyes did not.

Fhiro felt wrong pushing the extra part of his question forward so soon, but he sensed Saflua was trying to escape, rather than face his line of enquiry. It was unfair for a sage as distinguished as Saflua to tell him to go and read the *SOP*.

'Whether Aten hears our prayers or acts on them remains the subject of extensive research and study by the priests of The Calling across the galaxy,' said Saflua, 'but especially by the Church of Elders. However, Aten is more likely to hear the voices of those close to aligning their souls with him. For those who have turned to ways of evil, the chance of their plight being noticed is less. I spend much of my time begging that Aten looks for them, and offers their souls what help he can.'

Fhiro sensed his own mind moving. Somewhere, through the clouds of time that obscured the future, he sensed a target. He went for it. 'I know what you'll say to this, but the word "can" is wrong. If Aten is all powerful then "can" or "cannot" doesn't apply. It's meaningless.'

'You know I will point you towards having faith?' answered Master Saflua. 'You know rightly. Without faith you cannot understand.'

'So please explain faith,' said Fhiro. But was this the right question to ask? He was giving Saflua another chance to throw smoke in the air and dance out of sight. 'Wait – why don't I explain faith and you can correct me?' It bordered on being

hostile, but he had to make progress. He just *had* to. His mental inertia was breaking. Now was the time. 'Parts of The Calling are impossible to explain. The only way we can understand them is by having faith. Having faith means believing something … Believing in something when reason would have us not believe. Correct?'

'You're conflating matters,' said Saflua. 'True reason …'

'Except that is exactly what it means,' said Fhiro. 'What if I was born in a land where there are two different religions. Let's say there's The Calling and there's the religion of Kartna. They both try to persuade me to follow their beliefs. Neither can prove that they're definitely correct, though. Believers of each say they are committed to their religions. When I think about their religions I don't think one makes more sense than the other. So they each ask me to have faith in their religion because, they tell me, having faith will make me believe in their religion better. Which one do I believe in?'

'When you immerse yourself in The Calling,' said Saflua, 'its message will reach deep into your soul and bring you in to Aten's peace.'

'And a religious Kartnan would say the same thing,' said Fhiro. 'It would appear a part of my soul should recognise the correct religion. Do you think that those who hear of both the religion of Kartna and that of The Calling, but choose to follow Kartna are, in fact, missing a special religion-recognising ability?'

'What do you mean by a "recognising ability"?' asked Saflua.

'You're saying that some people are definitely going to hell because they were made differently, by Aten. They're unable to recognise the true religion when they hear about it,' said Fhiro. His words were tumbling out. He tried to slow himself down. 'That means Aten has damned them to hell before they

even embarked on life. Aten can't really care for these people!'

'Like I said before, Fhiro, you need to have faith to understand this,' pleaded Saflua.

'Faith?' Could Saflua come up with nothing but the circular faith argument? Was he, like everyone else, trying to get him stuck, and tangled in knots, to stop him from moving forward? 'Faith is the ignoring reason so you can believe something that doesn't make sense. So for the wise person, who is genuinely interested in finding the correct religion, or deciding which divine power to believe in, assuming there is one, The Calling has no interest.' Fhiro extended his arms in disbelief. 'People who blindly follow what their parents or friends tell them, or who make a lucky leap of faith, and happen to find themselves believing in The Calling, however, are welcomed into the heavens. Are those people who don't give their religion much thought the people Aten really cares for? Aten's approach to this makes a mockery of all thinking species in the galaxy. Sentient species, like us earthpeople, think we're special, and better than the animals we eat, because we think, ask questions and use reasoning to reach conclusions. When you ask me to have faith you're asking me not to think. You're asking me not to reach a real conclusion. You're asking me to blind myself and jump, but you offer me no good reason to jump in the right direction.'

Saflua frowned. 'Fhiro, you do not unders–'

'I may as well roll a dice to decide whether I go to heaven.' Fhiro spoke over him. 'Or wind up burning in the eternal fires of hell. And why would I want to go to your heaven anyway, if all I would find there is a load of idiots who don't even bother to ask themselves why they believe what they believe?'

'Young Fhiro!' cried Master Saflua.

'He insults the Master!'

Suddenly Fhiro became aware of the earthman who had

bought them the yellow-bean tea. Around them a crowd of people had been drawn near by the rising volume of Fhiro and Master Saflua's conversation.

The earthman gripped Fhiro by the collar and dragged him up out of his chair.

'No!' cried Master Saflua. 'Let him go!'

'Get off!' shouted Fhiro. With his legs off the floor he was unable to generate torque to his movements, or bring a powerful blow against the man holding him. Before he could think of a plan to defend himself he was dropped, and fell to the ground.

Another assailant stood above him. 'How dare you say such foul things about The Calling! You dishonour the Church of Elders!'

'Bring him to the Congress for Judgement!' cried someone else.

'Judgement!' screamed a female voice nearby.

Fhiro saw the mob was growing. What madness had possessed him to shout at Master Saflua in public? He was dragged and pushed out of the cafeteria. He managed to strike one of his attackers in the ribs with his knee, but as soon as he had done so someone picked up his foot and carried it. His other leg he flailed wildly and managed to kick someone, but another pair of hands grabbed that leg too. He bit a wrist that was reaching across his chest, but a retaliatory blow to his forehead disorientated him.

Facing upwards, he saw the upper floors of buildings on either side. The crowd shouted: 'Heretic!' 'Infidel!' 'Blasphemer!' The heat of the bodies about him grew, compacted by the press of numbers joining the marching mob. The smell of sweat and unwashed clothes filled his nostrils.

'Ghorad!' he shouted. 'Ghorad, help!' His mind raced, thinking of names to call for. Would Valachrad's other agents

not act now? 'Palis! Imial! Chenessa!' He felt the crowd taking him around a corner. 'Tubrin! Ma? Pa?' It was fruitless. 'Dorrick? Chinda?!' He wanted to pray. He wanted to pray but he did not know who or what to pray to. All of those around him, hauling him somewhere, were convinced they were doing the will of Aten, their God.

The buildings above appeared to be in shadow as they turned down a narrow alley. Would they kill him here, where they might not be seen? There were so many in the mob, surely one of them would report the culprits, but perhaps they did not even know each other. His murderers could flee and disappear with ease. He saw large sticks being carried in the arms of those around him, raised above the heads of the crowd.

He had contemplated death many times before, but now the thought of it wore down on him like a boulder on his chest. Would they beat him with blunt sticks? Would they cut him with knives? Would it be quick? Would they try to make it painful?

He tried to calm himself. He tried to slow his breathing. He tried his best …

He failed.

Above, the air brightened. He was in another square now. A tall building loomed overhead. It resembled the large worship congress hall in the city of Kadgel, back home. His captors brought him inside and Fhiro watched the gold plated chandeliers, hanging from the painted ceiling, float past as he neared the altar.

'We bring before you a blasphemer!' cried one of the mob. Others cheered.

'Get thee gone!' cried a voice from ahead. 'We will have no bloodshed here! Get out of this congress hall!'

The mob dithered. Fhiro felt himself start to move again,

but in the opposite direction. 'Help!' he cried, hopeful that the authoritative voice he had just heard might be that of a priest with enough courage to intervene on his behalf.

'You'll get all the help you want,' leered a toothy yeal above him, 'from the devils in hell!'

'They'll help you understand the error of your ways,' said another, 'with their hot knives, and barbed ropes! Oh, they'll help you all right!'

Fhiro felt a sharp blow to his scalp.

The cries of the mob were loud again. He was back out under the sun. He could see it above and to his right. It was bright. It was beautiful.

'Here is the blasphemer!' cried an earthman near him, rage in his eyes.

'Please!' cried Fhiro 'No! I–'

'Here is the blasphemer!' the earthman shouted again.

Please, God. Aten. Forgive me.

There was a loud crack of gunfire, followed by two further shots. The earthman hesitated and his face looked troubled as he peered above the heads of the mob. He looked at Fhiro, then back at where his eyes had been fixed before.

Fhiro was falling to the floor, having been released by all his captors almost at once. He expected, at any moment, a flash of steel to speed towards him, or the unexpected sting of metal piercing his flesh.

He saw Ghorad and Palis were running towards him.

The mob was gone.

CHAPTER 16

Fhiro watched reflections of the lumia-crystals in the ceiling sparkle on his redberry juice. He snuggled his back into the soft sofa, cautious not to rub his head too hard against the headrest because of the bruise on his scalp.

'Thank Aten you're all right!' said Dorrick, rushing in. He sat down next to Fhiro.

Fhiro forced a smile. 'Thanks. How are you?'

'Me?' Dorrick looked surprised by the question. 'I didn't just almost get murdered.'

Fhiro slumped deeper into the sofa.

'Ma says this Master Saflua is one of the few voices of reason that Marallel keeps close to his inner circle,' said Dorrick, taking a deep drink from Fhiro's mug. 'Sorry – this yours?'

'Don't worry,' mumbled Fhiro.

'Do you want me to fill up another one?' asked Dorrick. Fhiro did not answer, so Dorrick filled up another mug anyway. 'Ma thinks Saflua just feigns obedience to the Church. Were you trying to make a fool of him?'

'Sorry,' said Fhiro, recalling Saflua's perception of his true identity. This time he had no excuse – his selfishness had put his whole family in great danger. His parents would probably throw him off the twisting spiral roof of Kartna's Embassy when they found out, if Creedate agents did not abduct and murder them all first. 'I know he's supposed to be so wise, but it felt like he was trying to pull wool over my eyes as well.'

'As well as who?'

'Everyone,' said Fhiro. 'Whenever I argue it feels like people are trying to trick me.'

'Maybe it's not them, then, Fhiro. Maybe you've just got woolly eyes,' said Dorrick. 'I can't believe you had a chance to play spy, and ruined it so badly. You're not discreet; you're an assassin magnet!'

Dorrick was right. They'd probably throw him from Pelorn's palace keep, that towered over Riletta like a semi-spherical mountain.

Dorrick sat in silence. He reached out for a drink again, but just stopped himself when his fingers were an inch from Fhiro's redberry juice. 'Fhiro,' he said eventually, 'I'll always be there for you. You're my brother.'

Fhiro felt conflicting emotions collide. He was desperate for signs his family still cared for him now. He knew he did not deserve love from any of them.

'You're my brother,' said Dorrick, 'but you're a total idiot. Right now I hate you.'

Fhiro did not know what to make of this last statement, but the worse-than-fatal threat of possibly bursting into tears subsided. His current, pessimistic worldview remained in place. His mind had floundered for a moment, but was now back on stable, if demoralised, footing again.

Dorrick stood up and strode to the doorway. He paused before leaving, and said over his shoulder, 'Good luck.' Then he was gone.

'Look after yourself Dorrick!' Fhiro said after him, but got no response. He took a moment to breathe before attempting to drink the redberry juice. His hands were still unsteady. He struggled to remember when he last had them under control.

'Fhiro!' Imial scurried in and sat exactly where Dorrick had been a moment ago. 'How are you doing?'

'I'm all right.'

'I'm so ...' Imial looked at the floor, as though his mind was racing to find the right word, but in the end, evidently one word would not do, '... very very pleased and impressed!'

'What?'

'A Kartnan Aculei apprentice priest made a fool out of The Calling's most esteemed sage!'

'Where did "most esteemed" come from?' asked Fhiro.

'That's what Yogric says,' answered Imial.

His mother would be the one throwing him off the palace keep, regardless of what she had said the other day. 'I didn't mean to do that. I was hoping he would explain why my ideas were wrong.'

'And he didn't, so he looked foolish!' exclaimed Imial.

'He didn't get a chance,' said Fhiro. 'I got dragged away before he could answer me. Anyway, those arguments I used against him I could easily turn on your religion, Imial.'

Imial shrugged. 'Who cares. Yogric thinks you're fantastic!'

Fhiro sighed. 'My brother hates me, and Yogric likes me. Which is the stronger sign that I'm becoming a detestable waste of space that no one worthwhile wants to be around?'

'Don't get ahead of yourself,' said Imial, looking concerned. 'Yogric probably doesn't really like you.'

'Oh, all right,' said Fhiro. 'I hate the Creedate. They've ruined my life.'

'They'll ruin everyone's,' said Imial. 'Anyway, some good news: we're going to the excavation site tomorrow!'

'Fawast?' For a moment the idea of being surrounded by hundreds of miles of forest dispelled all of Fhiro's fear and self-loathing.

'Yes.' Imial winked at him. 'We weren't going to go for a few more days but, after today, the King wants negotiations to move faster. My father thinks he wants to reach a deal, and get our support, before there's a rebellion.'

'Because of me almost getting killed today?' asked Fhiro. 'That's why he's changing his plans? Our hosts must really regret my arrival here.'

'Maybe,' said Imial. 'But even if Pelorn doesn't like you, who else are they going to ally with? The Creedate have gone back on their word too many times and built too many skull mountains to be trusted by anybody. Kartna is the only power this side of the galactic core that can challenge them. We're the obvious choice.'

'But the Creedate are nearer,' said Fhiro.

Imial frowned. 'They'd be silly to let that influence them.'

'Chenessa will never talk to me again.'

'Probably not,' said Imial.

'And we made all this effort to get along with her.' Fhiro had liked making friends with Chenessa. 'I've ruined it.'

'You should probably stay here with your sister,' said Imial, 'all things considered.'

'Take that patronising look away with you!'

'It would only be sensible,' Imial replied. 'However, your Aculei father is coming, so apparently,' Imial frowned, 'we ought to pretend we're proud of what you said to that Master Saflua, and not act like we're worrying about it.'

Fhiro felt embarrassed, jealous and humiliated that Imial had heard a conversation concerning his actions and decisions regarding his fate. However, things had played out in his favour so far, and he was in no position to disagree with anyone about anything right now, so he held his tongue, took a deep breath, and pretended he had not realised this. 'So other Kartnans will be nice to me?'

'I'll try to,' said Imial. 'I can't wait to see the dig site. The forest is supposed to be very different. There will be strange alien trees that didn't evolve on Earth, or any of the homeworlds of the starfaring species.'

Imial kept talking long after Fhiro had stopped listening to his ambitious plans for the impending trip. Then Fhiro's mother was in the doorway.

'Fhiro,' she said, 'sorry I couldn't get here earlier. We've been, well, busy.'

'Hello Hanu,' said Imial.

'Hi Imial,' Hanu replied. 'Fhiro, can you please come with me?'

Fhiro, head bowed, walked straight to her. He dared not meet her eyes.

'Bye Fhiro,' Imial called after him.

As they passed through the corridors of the Kartnan Embassy a number of officials paused to pay Hanu their respects. It was like being back on Andelic again, Fhiro thought. Back home everyone had held her in high regard for her work on the Green River Council, yet she was probably a thousand times as influential now. He tried to imagine her when she had lived among the Creedate, and the power she must have wielded then. He knew his ma so well, and yet there was so much to her he had no idea about. It made him feel all the more ashamed of his recklessness.

She took him to a courtyard. It was dusk. An orange light filtered down from the sky above. She led him to a swing that overlooked the pond where geese cackled to each other as they padded in and out of the reeds.

'I'm sorry Ma,' he said as he sat beside her.

'Don't be sorry,' she said, not looking at him.

'I've ruined everything.' He watched the reeds sway as a trickle of wind, siphoned off by the walls above, sank into the courtyard. He wondered how angry she was, and how much more angry she might become if she found out he had revealed their identities to Master Saflua.

'You'll be going to the dig site tomorrow,' said Hanu.

'Imial told me,' said Fhiro.

'I'll miss you,' she said, taking his hand.

Though he knew he deserved it, Fhiro felt more troubled by the fact his mother was not shouting at him. 'You're sure you can't come?'

'No,' Hanu replied. 'There's a lot here to make sense of. Nobles and officials are holding meetings in secret, and some high-ranking individuals have vanished.'

'What?' asked Fhiro. 'Where are they going?'

'Difficult to tell,' said Hanu, 'but usually when people vanish during times like these, it's permanent. Maybe the King's hold on this planet isn't as strong as he'd like us to believe.'

'Do you think the Creedate are behind it?'

'It's a possibility,' said Hanu. 'I've advised Valachrad to act as though he's more than willing to go to war with them.'

'But we're trying to avoid that.'

'It's so that any offer of a peaceful solution is taken seriously,' said Hanu. 'If we look afraid, the Creedate will be sure to push us harder before they reach any compromise, or think we're bluffing. Marallel is always looking to expand. He may think he can invade these worlds and that Kartna will do nothing.'

Fhiro swung his legs and looked at the muddy earth beyond the grass. 'I'm sorry I argued with Master Saflua. I didn't want to upset him.'

She reached out and hugged him tight, tears streaming down her face. 'I almost lost you again today!'

Fhiro struggled to breathe, but managed to free one of his arms enough to partially return the embrace. 'So you don't hate me for being a blasphemer?'

'I don't think like those fools,' she said, squeezing him again. 'They would offend Aten with great evils rather than think about what they're doing.'

'Do you rethink your ways?' asked Fhiro.

'Always,' Hanu replied. 'As would Master Saflua.' She drew herself away from him and looked into his eyes. 'You know, he came by here an hour after you got back?'

Fhiro froze.

'He wanted to pass on a message,' Hanu continued.

'Did he speak to you?' asked Fhiro.

Hanu's eyes narrowed. 'No.'

Fhiro tried to look unsurprised. 'What was the message?'

'He said not to worry about what you discussed,' said Hanu.

Fhiro looked down.

'He insisted the message be repeated, and that you would know what he meant. He wanted you not to worry about it.'

'Oh,' said Fhiro, frowning as he considered this. 'All right.'

'Fhiro, what did he mean?' Hanu made no attempt to disguise her suspicion.

'Not sure,' said Fhiro. 'I suppose he doesn't want me to worry if I've offended him.'

'Master Saflua is one of the cleverest people I've ever met,' said Hanu. 'It was a strange message, Fhiro. It must mean something.'

'It means not to worry, then.' Fhiro shrugged. He did not have the strength to tell her the truth. He was committed to this lie now. 'That's what the message said, right?'

She seemed to relax a little. 'I hope you're right.'

'I'm glad he's not upset,' said Fhiro, 'or at least not so upset he couldn't bring himself to tell me not to worry. Do you think he's upset?'

'He's a difficult one to read.' She grinned. 'Like you.'

'Is that a good thing?'

'Depends.' She relaxed her embrace slightly.

A fight broke out between two of the geese by the pond, and Fhiro found his attention divided.

'The two of us often contended with Avithen on spiritual matters,' said Hanu. 'Master Saflua insisted that there were

themes to The Calling that were more important than the teachings of the prophets themselves.' She sighed. 'I worry about him. It's a miracle he's still alive.'

'How did you survive, then?' Fhiro watched his mother, imagining her arguing with the prophet. She had been the very sort of person the priests back home told them all to pray for. Someone close to the Church of Elders with the wisdom and courage to transform it back into an institution dedicated to peace.

'I don't know,' she answered. 'Perhaps Aten was with me, but then again, perhaps not. I didn't persuade the prophet.'

'Maybe he was convinced,' said Fhiro. 'Maybe that's why he went to a swamp cave, or whatever it was.'

She bowed her head. 'Perhaps.'

The wind whistled in the reeds. The geese had stopped fighting. One of them was flapping its wings and barking at the other birds. Fhiro wondered if geese enjoyed arguing with each other. Then he wondered if one of them was shouting because the others did not argue back.

'Be mindful of the Creedate girl,' said Hanu.

'What d'you mean? I was supposed to become her friend.'

'Valachrad wants you to do that,' said Hanu, 'but perhaps he's got it wrong. Perhaps their agenda is different. Perhaps she is trying to get you to slip her information.'

'What information?'

Hanu shrugged. 'If that's what she's up to, it's best you don't know what she's after.'

'I think she's a nice person,' said Fhiro. 'I think she is.' He imagined Chenessa laughing at his naivety from the roof of a tall, dark tower, surrounded by evil gargoyles with menacing grins. The image did not quite fit for him.

'Look after yourself, Fhiro,' said Hanu. 'Don't let your father forget where his true loyalties lie when you're out there, even when he's protecting Valachrad. You come first, remember?'

CHAPTER 17

'This is amazing,' said Chenessa, lying down on the grass next to Fhiro. 'I've seen forests, but I've never camped in one.'

Fhiro was not sure if the luxurious giant tents they would be sleeping in really counted as camping, but he was too glad Chenessa was still talking to him to argue. 'This journey is the best.' And it was. Despite the hostile looks from Creedate priests and Reshna's bodyguards, a constant fear he might accidentally call Priest Veltir 'father', and rumours of sinister monsters living in Fawast's forests, he was having a great time.

There was a loud rustling sound far to his left. He turned and saw the enormous emerald-feathered bird that had carried them here. It raised its head out of the giant basket it had been gorging from. Its eyes of glittering orange blinked, and its wide, serrated beak opened and closed as it swallowed huge volumes of food.

He felt the grass brushing against his skin as he turned back to the night sky again. 'The stars are so clear out here,' he said. 'We're so much further from the Galactic core than I'm used to.' In truth it was the closest he had ever been to the core, and it mesmerised him.

'You must have seen these stars on the way here,' said Chenessa. 'You must have seen all kinds of beautiful things in space.'

'This is better.' Perhaps it was the smell of the trees, the bushes and the grasses. Perhaps it was the planet air – so much fresher and more real than the recycled gases running through the Siwob and the Blind Vizier, or the air of the city. He

remembered that as an earthman he, like all starfaring species, had evolved on a similar world, surrounded by abundances of life, environments of immeasurable complexity, and the relentless, deadly threats that drove evolution. Fawast was known as the wild continent.

This thought made Fhiro sit up and check on the nearest sentry.

A collection of soldiers from Pelorn were entrenched where the hill sloped down into the forest. They had a wide range of vision, their view illuminated by the starlight.

'Are you all right?' asked Chenessa.

Fhiro lay down again. 'Yes.' He relaxed. The deadly monsters, lurking in the forests, shadowed the migrating herds. All journeys into the continent, including this one, were planned carefully to avoid unwanted encounters.

'How come they let you stay out here in the end?' Chenessa asked.

'I said it was no less safe than hiding in a tent,' Fhiro replied. 'If anything got past the sentries, at least I'd be able to run away.'

'Is that even true?'

'Ghorad gave up trying to stop me, and my master didn't mind.'

'Fair enough,' said Chenessa.

He noticed her breathing. It was louder than the rustling of the small creatures in the forest. The ones that were so small they did not fear drawing attention to themselves in the dark. 'How did you get out here?'

'I snuck out,' she said. 'Won't be long before they realise.'

Fhiro thought for a moment before uttering his next sentence. 'I'm really sorry about the whole Master Saflua thing.'

Chenessa laughed. 'Don't be sorry. I'm sure he feels terrible that you asked him a question, and some idiots tried to kill you for it.'

'He doesn't mind being asked questions?'

'Isn't that why you asked him?' asked Chenessa.

'Good point,' said Fhiro, though he doubted Saflua would want to finish the conversation.

'We're always arguing,' said Chenessa.

'Really?' asked Fhiro. 'You and him? What about?'

'The Calling,' said Chenessa. 'It doesn't make sense to me.'

'It doesn't make sense to me either,' said Fhiro, 'but I didn't want to upset him.'

'You won't have,' said Chenessa. 'Does your religion make sense, then?'

Fhiro sighed. 'Sort of. There's a lot I have to learn, though.'

'Perhaps that's both of us, then.'

The breeze strengthened, dampening the sound of the living forest, and making the trees sway.

'We can't both be right, though,' said Fhiro.

'What do you mean?' asked Chenessa.

'The religion of Kartna doesn't allow for The Calling to be correct, and The Calling doesn't allow for the Kartnan gods.'

'So do our cultures have to destroy each other?'

Fhiro imagined the war Valachrad had spoken of. The war that was almost inevitable. He imagined those he knew and loved suffering and dying. 'Hope not. Can't they learn to exist beside each other, and work out their differences peacefully?'

'If Aten is merciful,' said Chenessa, and then she whispered, 'assuming he exists.'

Fhiro laughed. 'Do you talk about these things with your mother?'

'I don't get much of a chance to talk to her at the moment,' said Chenessa. 'Not about things like that. She always has those priests around her.'

'That's annoying,' said Fhiro.

'There's always Theon,' said Chenessa. 'He's very wise. He doesn't have strange backward ideas either.'

'You trust him?' asked Fhiro.

'Chenessa!' cried a voice from the darkness.

'That's Hussuf,' said Chenessa. 'I guess I've been noticed.'

Fhiro felt his heart sink.

She sat up, then turned back to look at him. 'I trust Theon. My whole family does. My mother even holds her private prayers with him.'

'Then he really is trusted,' said Fhiro.

'Chenessa!'

The grass obscured all of Hussuf apart from the top of his feathered head, which bounced with every approaching stride.

'Bye Fhiro,' said Chenessa, and then she left.

'Bye,' he said after her, but he was unsure if she heard.

The chirping and croaking of the creatures grew louder. Fhiro imagined them, hobbling about in the darkness through the bushes. He knew some foreign insects had reached Pelorn and survived, so perhaps he might have recognised a few of the creatures contributing to the forest's song. The rest, he suspected, were insectoids of all kinds of shapes, colours and sizes that had evolved here. He wished to see them, but he had heard the trees hid predators, and smaller biting, stinging nuisances.

The galaxy drifted above him, silent and beautiful. He could drink up the view forever.

Fhiro knew he could not stay out all night.

* * *

'Did you see that?' cried Imial from across the carriage. He had found a space between the Creedate and the Hithostun delegations to peer out the window at the view below.

It was two hours since they had stopped for their midday meal, and eight since they had broken camp. The forest below was even more glorious than it had seemed the day before, but Fhiro did not find himself calling over every occupant of their carriage whenever he saw something of interest. He hesitated before running across, first glancing over to where Reshna, Tubrin and the Creedate priests were sitting. One of the priests was watching him, again, but the rest were reading, conversing or otherwise distracted. At least the sinister prelate elder had stayed in Riletta.

He made himself stand up and join Imial at the other side, avoiding paying any special attention to Theon; he had yet to talk to Valachrad about his conversation with Chenessa the night before. He looked out of the carriage window. The forests of Fawast sprawled across the hills all the way to the horizon. Waterfalls glistened as they burst over rocks, surrounded by the vines and trees that draped the mountainsides. 'What is it?' It was delightful, but Fhiro could not see what made this view different to the others he had seen.

'In that lake!' said Imial. 'At the bottom of the falls. Something huge in the water.'

A distorted shadow travelled beneath the waves where Imial had pointed. At first Fhiro thought its movement might just be a trick of the light, but then it changed direction. Limb-like projections stretched out and pulled back, two at a time, dragging it forwards.

'Is that a Snorel beast?' Chenessa asked Palis.

'How do you know about the local ecology?' asked Imial.

'I had a lesson on it before you arrived,' she said.

'Is it dangerous?' asked Fhiro.

'Yes,' said Palis as he finally reached the edge of the carriage. He was struggling with motion sickness. 'That is a Snorel

beast. No, they aren't usually dangerous.' He scouted out a few other directions, checking there was nothing else informative he could tell them. 'May I sit down again now?'

'A person riding an animal,' shouted Imial. 'It's carrying wood on its back, too!'

Fhiro could see a furred creature make its way along the shore of the lake. A mountain of material had been strapped to it. Close to its neck sat a figure carrying a thin stick.

'There are people out here?' asked Fhiro.

'Holy ecologists, some military personnel, and illegal foragers only,' said Palis.

'You're very lucky to live here, Palis,' said Chenessa. 'I didn't expect Fawast to be this magnificent.'

Fhiro could not see himself developing Chenessa's flair for buttering up officials this way. The thought of saying such things, with a smile like hers on his face, made him want to cringe.

'Thank you,' said Palis, looking almost too weak to stand.

She was right, though. Fawast was beautiful, but so was much of the rest of Pelorn. Fhiro's favourite place remained the last town they had stayed in; a remote, ancient settlement at the frontier of civilisation. Pillars decorated with effigies of long forgotten gods and demons supported asymmetrical winding-shaped roofs. The most bizarre examples had been converted into museums, while others now housed restaurants and drinking taverns. Fhiro had wondered how offended the earlier inhabitants might have felt to know the ultimate fate of their cherished temples.

The carriage jolted. Fhiro saw the great green wings either side of them stiffen, gliding through the turbulence.

'Do we really need to fly so low?' asked Chenessa.

'Lower is safer,' said Winle, the Hithostun ambassador.

Fhiro did not like Winle. She exuded hostility. Oljon sat

near her, but his expression was unreadable behind his mask. Being unable to see his father for so long was making Fhiro uneasy. It was bad enough being away from his mother and siblings.

'You children really should be strapped down for this.' Ambassador Reshna was not as cold as Winle, but he found her attention far more troubling. He hoped she considered him too lowly to ever raise the issue of his transgressions against her religion. He was sure, though, that she and her staff harboured ill thoughts towards him; right now four Creedate priests glared at him under their furrowed bushy brows. He wished he could pray his identity remained safe. That Saflua had kept his secret. But he suspected his was the last voice Aten would want to listen to right now.

'We're wearing helmets,' said Chenessa. 'Can't we stay and watch? The scenery is so lovely.'

'She's a heavy bird,' Imial said to Fhiro with a knowing expression. 'Only severe turbulence could rock her.'

'The kind of severe turbulence you get while flying near cliff-tops,' said Reshna.

Fhiro made a show of adjusting his helmet, hoping to undo some of his reputation as a troublemaker to the Creedate. Imial and Chenessa did the same.

'I don't feel sick up here,' said Imial, happily, watching Palis strap himself in with difficulty.

'Well done,' said Chenessa.

The pilot made some signals to Palis, who turned to them, mastered his stomach and called out, 'Secure your helmets. We are making our final descent.'

'We're already there?' piped Imial.

'It's about three o'clock,' said Chenessa, 'and it's supposed to take one and a half days from the last town.'

His helmet secured, Fhiro sat next to Imial and strapped

himself in. He watched the three vanguard birds ahead of the aircade accelerate away, scouting for danger on the approach to the dig site. One then flew up into the clouds to check for threats lurking above. The other two descended and circled around a large bluff that towered above to their left.

'Do you suppose the dig is on the other side of that mountain?' Imial asked him.

'I've not been here before either, Imial.'

As their own bird rounded the immense corner of rock, turning northwards, a large lake became visible. Sloping up from its banks was a mighty mountain, of which the rock face to their side was a mere limb. An extensive complex of scaffolding clung to the lower part of the mountain at the edge of the lake. Mounds of dirt and rock were gathering near the scaffolding at the end of a procession of walking shapes. Fhiro wondered what they were; some of them looked much bigger than earthmen.

At the lake's eastern edge a thin waterfall trickled over a sharp drop into the forest below. Near it a path snaked away from the scaffolding, wound its way down the steep drop, and then cut through the forest into a clearing at the bottom of the mountain. Within this open space was a white stone structure with three shining gun-turrets on its roof. Two other paths stretched away from the front gate of this building. One reached north, where it ascended a slope to run alongside a landing field runway. The other went east where it entered the forest and disappeared from view.

As they descended, the tiny figures Fhiro had noticed earlier became easier to see. He watched them hauling giant sacks and boulders away from the scaffold. 'What are they?' he asked.

'I don't know,' said Chenessa.

'Hockers,' said Oljon.

The children turned and looked at Fhiro's father. Chenessa, and also some of the ambassadors, looked a little unsure of how to react to the Aculei mask.

'Yes,' said Palis. 'Great for manual labour. Bigger and stronger than any starfaring person, though considerably less intelligent.'

Regarding the size of the starfaring species, Fhiro knew Palis's statement was inaccurate. Lizardmen had the potential to keep growing even in old age. There were legends of evil fugitive Lizardmen, existing on the fringes of the inhabited galaxy, and growing to immense sizes in secret.

For some reason this made Fhiro recall Yetco and the other Pichis back on Andelic. He had always thought it a bit insulting that they did not count as people, just because they had not yet reached the stars. It seemed especially wrong when the term people was used to describe the savage Lizardmen.

'These were imported from Hithostun,' said Winle. 'I offered them in good faith but Pelorn insisted on paying.'

'Keeping their options open,' said Ambassador Zakil. 'They don't want to be indebted to any of us.'

There was silence as the bird completed its descent. They arced around to approach the runway from the west, passing over the eastern edge of the lake as they did so. A tall fence surrounded the landing field, enclosing a number of huts and temporary structures arrayed in a haphazard fashion. Upon touching the ground, the steed that carried their carriage had to run a hundred metres before slowing to a gentle halt. Fhiro had to admit it was a far nicer landing than anything Siwular had provided him with in the past. He wondered what Siwular was up to now, and hoped she was safe.

The other birds in the aircade began to touch down around them. Palis stood and opened the door out of the carriage and commanded an attendant to prepare the exit staircase.

Ambassador Winle and her guards were the first group to leave, followed by Reshna, Chenessa and the Creedate guards and priests.

Oljon nodded to Valachrad and Captain Jard, Kartna's most senior military officer from the Blind Vizier, and the three of them stood up. Fhiro unstrapped himself and joined them. Ghorad and Imial also made their way to the staircase. Walking out of the carriage Fhiro felt the breeze on his face again. Unlike the previous landings, however, his ears were filled with chirping and harking of birds. Most of the noise, he realised, was from creatures unseen, hidden within the huts and pens around the runway. The beasts they had all arrived on were also in a frenzy of communication, singing to the rhythms and music that surrounded them. Fhiro was so distracted by the racket that he did not notice the large group of Pelorn soldiers ahead of them until he was down the stairs and standing on the grass.

The Kartnan soldiers that had accompanied Valachrad rallied close around the ambassador. Soon all of the delegations were in tight-knit groups, identifiable by the unique uniforms of their soldiers.

'Welcome to the Old Harvester Fort,' boomed a tall earthman at the head of the column of Pelorn soldiers. Flanking him were an earthman and a yeal. Fhiro observed all three were attired as military officers from their host nation. The foremost earthman gestured towards the white building Fhiro had seen during the descent. 'I am General Calthorn, and I hold authority here.'

Even from the landing field, which was at a higher elevation than the clearing in which the fort stood, the monstrous size of its three gun-turrets unsettled Fhiro; they had not been a fraction as terrifying when seen from above.

'I hope your journey was comfortable,' continued Calthorn.

'This fort was not, I must warn you, built with the entertainment of foreign ambassadors in mind, but it is the kindest lodging you will find for hundreds of miles. I recommend you make yourselves at home. My men will show you to your quarters. When you are ready, do join us for food. We have prepared a banquet in your honour.'

'May I ask,' said Ambassador Zakil, 'when we will be able to see the dig site? Much as I appreciate the offered hospitality, I do not wish to tarry here longer than I need to.'

Calthorn laughed. 'Tomorrow you may visit it yourself, ambassador. However, your security is my only real concern. If you would like detailed information before then, you might send one of your servants or other members of your staff to the rock face.' He smiled. 'It is not the safest of places, especially while it is being worked on.' Calthorn turned back to the rest of them. 'There is only so much room in the fort, and to provide what comfort we can we must insist the majority of your soldiers and assistants be housed outside of it. A small village has been erected for this purpose, and my men will assist you with these arrangements.' He looked down the slope that led from the landing field to the fort. 'Meanwhile, I hope you have not been airborne so long that you have forgotten how to walk.'

The Kartnan delegation stayed together as it followed Calthorn and the other delegations down the slope towards the building.

'One of the local tutors taught me about this place,' said Chenessa, as they walked through the giant gates of the Old Harvester Fort.

'What did they used to harvest here?' asked Fhiro.

'Ingredients from the forest,' she answered, 'for narcotic production, of course.'

'And then Gedrilla was overthrown,' said Palis, 'and the

activities of the fort became legal, so they no longer needed to be hidden so far into the wilderness.'

'My ancestors built this place,' said ambassador Winle. 'The Hitho clan controlled a large portion of this planet before the Day of Chokes.'

'The Day of Chokes?' asked Fhiro. He knew Imial was too proud to ask.

'The day when the Smuggler Lords assassinated the leaders of the nations they sought to control,' said Winle. 'Every senator, congressman, governor and lord was gathered in one place.'

'And for their protection,' added Reshna, 'each ruler had brought a troop of bodyguards and advisors, sourced from the very crime families that were plotting to kill them. It was supposed to be a peace conference.' Her face creased into a grim smile. 'Weapons were not allowed, but before the meeting was over, half of the attendees had been choked to death.'

'A dark part of our history,' said Winle, 'but who can name a successful power untarnished by a single, regrettable tale?'

When Winle and her guards were out of earshot, Fhiro turned to Palis. 'If Hithostun built this fort, why don't they rule this planet? They clearly want to.'

'The Hitho inherited plenty of worlds,' Palis whispered back. 'The agreement following the Day of Chokes denied them this one. I do not think they expected it to elude their clutches for this long, though.'

* * *

A few hours after informing Valachrad and his father about his conversation with Chenessa, Fhiro was with Imial, on their way to the room they shared, when he felt a tap on his shoulder. He turned around. 'Yogric?'

Imial's tutor's eyes narrowed as he peered at Fhiro. 'You had better not have betrayed me.'

'Betrayed?' Fhiro could not hide his puzzlement.

'Your information about Theon had better be accurate,' said Yogric. 'I don't like taking risks. I'm not that sort of man! Now you've got me playing cloak and dagger with the Creedate girl's tutor.'

'I – I just did what I was told,' said Fhiro.

'What you were told?' Yogric snarled, 'You're enjoying this aren't you! Well I'll make you sorry!' Yogric dashed away down the corridor.

'What's that about?' asked Imial.

Fhiro checked the corridor. It was empty, and they were in the quarters allocated to the Kartnan guests. 'Guess your pa thinks Chenessa really was giving us a message.'

Imial frowned. 'It's a shame it was you that brought the information. Yogric clearly doesn't trust it.'

'No, he doesn't,' said Fhiro, sighing.

'What is it between you and him?'

'Him,' said Fhiro.

An hour later, as Fhiro lay on his bed, unable to sleep, he asked, 'What do you reckon they're going to find?'

'Maybe they'll find a magic wand that makes people be quiet,' said Imial, yawning.

'I hope it's something amazing.' Fhiro took out and activated his Gravi-trap, watching it tremble and dance on his hand.

'And give our empires something to fight over?' Imial tucked himself deeper under his blanket. 'Sounds great.'

Fhiro deactivated the gravi-trap. 'Do you think some of Cerilina's clouder friends look weird?'

'Which ones?' groaned Imial.

'Just some of them,' said Fhiro. 'Who's that one Cerilina's always sitting with?'

'Some of them have strange faces.'

'Really?' asked Fhiro.

'Their expressions are a bit sluggish.' Imial yawned again.

'*You* paid attention to their facial expressions?'

'My father always taught me to be vigilant when studying a face,' said Imial. 'He often asks me to describe people's faces to him. He says that after years of practice, one grows better at reading the thoughts of the mind behind it.'

'So what does a "sluggish" expression mean then?'

'Nothing,' said Imial. 'I told my father that someone had sluggish expressions, years ago. He didn't think it was important.'

'Oh,' said Fhiro. 'Maybe it's a clouder thing.'

'They probably interbred with yeals,'

'Earthpeople *can't* interbreed with yeals.'

'Whatever,' said Imial.

CHAPTER 18

The next day Fhiro and Imial were up and out of their rooms long before anyone came to wake them. They were begging Cerilina and Borlin for details about the dig site when Ghorad found them.

'It's really interesting,' answered Cerilina, shouldering a sack of equipment. 'But don't ask me. You'll see it for yourself soon enough.'

'A word of warning, though,' said Borlin, on his way to the door, 'stay with your guards. No need to risk being trodden on by one of those hockers. Don't forget the falling mounds of rock either. And wear a helmet!'

The boys set off with Valachrad and Oljon a little later.

It was a steep, winding walk up the side of the mountain to the lake, and all the while the faint clinks of metal against stone from the excavation site grew louder and louder. Once the slope evened out Fhiro looked towards the misty horizon behind him. The sun was still rising in the east, but the forest below was dark. The tree canopy rose and fell with the hills, and jutted and dived with the ravines and the gullies. Here and there, in the wide spaces between the mountain peaks, it was penetrated by unstable-looking rock formations draped in hanging greenery.

'Stay close to me, apprentice,' said Oljon.

'Yes, master,' said Fhiro. 'It's really humid out here.'

'Welcome to your first rainforest,' said Oljon. 'Be glad it's the dry season.'

The lake by the mountain was clean and untroubled except for a waterfall to the northeast, a few streams entering it from

the southwest, and where it drained over the falls Fhiro had seen from the sky, earlier. He imagined the mountains further north also fed into the vast body of water, but he could not see the far bank very well.

'Hello!' Chenessa, who had been ahead of them, detached herself from Tubrin to greet him. The grim faced Creedate guard watched the boys, his hand drifting close to the gun at his belt as he did so.

'Hi Chenessa,' said Fhiro without looking at her. He and Imial were both too disconcerted by the look in Tubrin's eyes.

'It's a beautiful lake,' Chenessa said. 'It's a shame we can't swim here.'

'Why not?' asked Fhiro.

'The Chissids,' she replied. 'Didn't you hear?'

'Enlighten us.'

She grinned. 'Rows of poisoned yellow teeth. They'll eat you alive if you fall in the water. Can't say I've met one. Maybe we should come here after dark. They like to maraud along the shores at night.'

'I knew there would be exciting animals around here,' said Imial. 'I thought they were just with the herds. We *must* come back here after dark.'

'With guns,' added Fhiro.

'We're not coming back after dark,' said Ghorad.

Imial scowled.

A tall, cream-skinned, bipedal creature, lumbered past them, carrying a giant sack of gravel. Its beady eyes, close to its temples on the upper half of its head, stared one way and then the other.

'Is that a hocker?' asked Fhiro.

'Obviously.' Imial tutted.

'Yes,' Ghorad confirmed.

The Creedate ambassador, Reshna, led the group ahead of

them. Fhiro considered that either Chenessa had a knack for sneaking away from the priests and guards that accompanied her mother, or that they were less vigilant than Ghorad. 'How are your quarters?' he asked her.

'All right,' she replied. 'All the rooms with good views have been taken. My mother wanted one, and the guards needed to be able to watch the grounds outside it, so I'm stuck deeper in. At least I've got a skylight.'

'I think we're all boxed in,' said Fhiro. 'Imial and I don't even have a skylight. Just crystal lamps.'

As they rounded a bulge in the mountainside the clamour from the excavation site grew. Between crunches of metal against stone, explosions shook the air, making Fhiro wince. He found it impossible to accustom his ears to this noise because of the unpredictable timing of the detonations. When the rock face did come into view he saw hundreds of hockers at work. Some swung axes and hammers while others worked on the scaffold. Men climbed up and down ladders, and ran back and forth carrying loads and tools.

General Calthorn approached from ahead and had a few quick words with Reshna. Then he spied Oljon and came towards the Kartnan delegation. 'An Aculei priest,' he said, almost shouting to be heard over the noise. 'It's an honour to meet you.' They shook hands. 'Is your training as gruelling as they say?'

'Worse,' laughed Oljon. 'Priest Veltir, at your service.'

'I thought you served your God-Emperor,' said Calthorn.

'Serving the future allies of Kartna is a service to the God-Emperor,' said Oljon.

'Very well,' said Calthorn.

Fhiro noticed that Chenessa was listening in to his father's conversation. He considered his mother's warning, but smiled at her all the same. Chenessa smiled back.

'They do not seem to be making much progress,' said Oljon. 'When did you start digging here?'

'The mountain rock has been broken and blasted away with little difficulty,' said Calthorn. 'However, the barrier we have come up against is one only the Poshokans could have made.'

'I heard about this,' said Valachrad. The ambassador had only just caught up with the rest of them. 'Whatever is under this mountain was meant to be protected.'

Calthorn nodded. 'It can be damaged, but only with great difficulty. We might have to ask for special exclusion options from the SABAc council to make a good dent in it. However, if we level the mountain, that would defeat the point.' He laughed.

Valachrad forced a smile. 'Countess Jeberrel informed me of a possible entrance, somewhere deeper down.'

'Yes,' said Calthorn, 'if the documents aboard the Sufferer ship are to be believed, there may be a passage running all the way to the edge of this lake.'

'But the King, surely, would insist the lake is drained to expedite the excavation,' said Valachrad. 'I do not understand why he has to wait for this organisation to proceed.'

'You speak of the Guardians of the Environment and Culture of Pelorn,' said Calthorn. 'They are powerful. It is not so much the contents of this lake they are protecting; Chissids are loved by none. It is the consequences to the rivers fed by these waters, and their dependent ecosystems.'

Valachrad's disbelief was evident on his face.

Calthorn folded his arms. 'I am no politician, and I may regret speaking my mind with you, but the bitter taste of dishonesty does not sit well with me. There are tensions within our population. The Niquani are very sensitive to any attempt to erode their identity and religion. Ignoring the concerns of the Guardians of the Environment and Culture in the current

climate would be seen as an attack on Niquani culture, especially if it is perceived to be motivated by a desire to please certain foreign powers.' His face broke into a mischievous grin.

'We would do everything asked of us to allay such fears,' said Valachrad.

'I'm sure you would,' said Calthorn. 'The King knows what I think. If he had listened to me, this lake would no longer be here. I would not overrule the Guardians of Pelorn, as they're known, in an effort to curry your favour; I'm Niquani through and through. However, knowledge is power, as they say. Any head start we might have on all the other interested groups, desperate to get inside this mountain, is a welcome gift from the spirits.'

'I see,' said Oljon. 'The King tolerates your disagreeing with him?'

Calthorn laughed again. 'I am his nephew through marriage. He knows he has my loyalty. He is a good king who wants what is best for his people, at the end of the day.'

'That is all we want,' said Valachrad.

'This find is one of those historical moments,' said Calthorn, watching the activity around the scaffold. 'It could bring us glory, or prosperity. It could bring us nothing. And it could destroy us.'

'That is what we have come to talk about,' said Valachrad. 'How not to let it destroy you.'

'Good luck to you,' said Calthorn. 'You know what our leaders will say: Not good enough! Offer us more glory, riches and power! I am glad I do not currently sit upon any high councils. My job is far simpler.'

'Related or not,' said Valachrad, 'you must be accomplished to be in charge of this place.'

Calthorn smiled, but did not reply. 'Come, I will make them stop so that we can go nearer.'

Fhiro realised that Tubrin and one of the priests had ambled nearer to Chenessa and himself. He could tell that the priest, a female yeal who appeared to be fumbling with the strap of her helmet, was of an advanced age by the multitude of criss-cross creases in her skin. Fhiro made a mental note to watch what he said as he strapped on his helmet.

Once the work had stopped, he followed the trail of people, with the general ahead of them, towards the rock-face.

Some workers watched them as they approached. Earthmen, yeal and feathery hegel rested on their pickaxes, while others sat in the sun or drank from flasks. The hockers seemed oblivious. They sat or lay down to rest, placing their tools on the ground. One had even closed its eyes.

'Is it snoring?' asked Fhiro.

'Even hockers need to sleep,' said Ghorad.

The broken rock had been taken away in vast quantities, leaving a glistening, shiny white surface underneath. It reflected the light with a bright brilliance that made it difficult to look at in the sun. Fortunately the scaffold meant that most of it was in the shade. Calthorn led them to where the shadows were deeper. There were many people here; including one small recci. Groups of them were huddled together, studying the white material. Some looked at it under lamplight, and others with magnifying devices. There were shards of the material on tables, being chipped at or dipped into chemicals.

'Hello Fhiro,' said Cerilina, taking off her eye-protectors.

'Ah,' said Borlin, 'the Kartnan boys have joined us at last.'

'That rock looks very white,' said Imial.

'It does,' said Cerilina. 'Come take a closer look.'

'You see,' said Calthorn, as the children took it in turns to touch and scratch at the surface, 'it's impervious to almost everything.' He lifted up a pickaxe and swung it at the surface.

The point bounced back with a loud clang. 'No dents, no sparks,' he said, resting the tool on the floor.

'This is not rock,' said Cerilina.

'It's another mysterious Poshokan secret,' said Borlin. 'Makes you wonder what warranted its use. It can't have been cheap to make.' He looked at Fhiro. 'Remember what I told you? Sneaky Poshokans. Sneaky!'

'I gather these are the archaeologists you brought,' said Calthorn.

'We are,' said Borlin. 'All from the Greater Magellan, except me.'

'Yes,' agreed Ghorad. 'He rolled out of a wine bottle.'

Oljon laughed and Fhiro smiled.

'Well I'm sure you think you're very funny,' said Borlin, his eyebrows raised. 'You know this expedition might never have happened if I hadn't introduced our visitors to my contacts working for the Kartnan Senate.'

Cerilina rolled her eyes, and then turned to Calthorn. 'I'm Cerilina. Pleased to be at your service.'

'It feels like you're all saying that to me today,' said Calthorn, shaking her hand. 'So what useful information has your expertise brought us so far? Have you any idea how to speed this up?'

'Afraid not,' said Cerilina. 'We sent a message to the haven that received the samples that were gathered earlier. There are some important tests we wanted them to consider.'

'Ah yes,' said Calthorn. 'Havens are very useful for such things.'

'If I know the Poshokans,' said Cerilina, 'then knowing how this substance is made will only be a small part of the puzzle to getting inside.'

Fhiro tried to imagine the Ancients, and what great technological wonders they might have had at their disposal,

when they had created the mountain. 'Have you tried looking around the mountain? Or further up it, for a way in?'

'Nothing yet,' said Calthorn. 'I can't quite tell how these Poshokans intended to breathe.'

'I'm sure we'll get in somehow,' said Cerilina.

Fhiro saw Chenessa was watching the archaeologist with admiration. 'Do you want to talk to her?' he asked.

'I don't think she'd want to talk to me,' said Chenessa. 'I'll never be as amazing as she is.'

'What do you mean?'

'She's earned her importance,' said Chenessa. 'If I ever get anywhere, people will say it's because of who my mother is.'

'I don't know,' said Fhiro. 'How do you know her mother isn't the Queen of Irenzel?'

Chenessa frowned at him. 'What's Irenzel?'

'A clouder nation,' said Fhiro. Then he turned to Cerilina's friend working on a bench nearby. She was the one he had tried to describe to Imial, who he thought looked different. He tried to get a better look at her face, but she was wearing thick goggles and a face protector. He watched her submerge a fragment of the shiny, white material in a glass container full of dull yellow liquid. She then picked up a grey granule from the work surface, with a pair of tongs, and plunged it into the liquid. Bubbles erupted, and then a bright, green light blazed from the tips of the tongs.

Fhiro returned his attention to Chenessa. 'Cerilina's nice. She told us a bit about the Sufferers.'

'You didn't know about them already?'

Fhiro wanted to punch himself in the face.

'Of course we did,' blagged Imial. 'She just knew a bit more.'

Despite knowing he should be grateful, being rescued by Imial just made Fhiro's blood boil.

'I remember when Theon taught me about them,' said

Chenessa. 'I had nightmares for a while. He used to make up stories to cheer me up. I feel so sorry for that Poshokan they had on their ship.'

'The one they were interrogating?' asked Fhiro.

'Apparently she killed the Sufferers and herself to stop them finding this place,' said Chenessa. 'So brave.'

Fhiro dreaded to think how horrid the Sufferers must have been for suicide to become the goal of their captives.

The archaeologist had finished her experiment and was watching them. 'There's no need for children to learn or worry about the Sufferers. They're gone.'

Fhiro took the moment to study her face very carefully, but failed to detect the sluggishness of expression Imial had alluded to.

'There are more than enough perils today,' said the archaeologist, 'for us to have to live in fear of dangers past.'

'True,' said another voice.

They turned and saw that Theon, Chenessa's tutor, was with them.

'Throughout history many great evils have been overcome, and the future is better for it,' said the old Creedate priest. 'But we must always learn from history and strive to prevent tragedies from recurring. Whether we follow The Calling or not, all should feel united in our determination to defeat evil and build a better future.' He smiled at Chenessa, and then at the other children. 'Making progress, I hope?' he asked the archaeologist.

'Perhaps,' she replied. 'Not as much as I'd like. I hope the havens bring us answers.'

Theon laughed. 'The sorcerers do not think with our sense of time or urgency, so don't expect your answer soon. Good luck!'

CHAPTER 19

It was still dark when Fhiro woke. 'What's going on?'

Imial was already sitting up in his bed. 'Are people shouting?'

'Sounds like it,' said Fhiro.

They tried and failed to interpret the voices outside as they got dressed. When they exited their room, the corridor was empty.

Then Ghorad stormed around the corner into view, stopping when he saw the boys. 'You two, go back to bed.'

Fhiro rubbed his eyes. 'What's going on?'

Ghorad pointed in the direction from which he had come. 'General Calthorn is here, with twenty of his men, and he means to search our quarters.'

Three Pelorn soldiers marched up behind Ghorad. 'Hold still, Kartnan!' One of them levelled his rifle at the back of Ghorad's head.

Ghorad grimaced and turned to face them. 'Don't you dare talk to me, you dog. Before you walk in here uninvited, brandishing your weapons at us, you'll do well to remember that this nation of yours is but a shred of refuse in the Galactic cesspit that once was the Smugglers' Union. Next time you blink, it might be gone.'

'Is that so?' said the soldier. He was an earthman, and he grinned as he adjusted his grip on his weapon. Meanwhile other Pelorn soldiers continued ahead, passing Fhiro and Imial.

'Private Jammit,' shouted Calthorn, appearing with his

officers, 'I cannot demote you any further. Infuriate our guests without good cause again and you'll be dropped deep into the forest, unarmed and alone.'

'Yessir!' Jammit drew his weapon away from Ghorad.

'What is the meaning of this?' asked Ghorad. 'This is a diplomatic mission.'

'If this is a diplomatic mission, where is the ambassador?' Calthorn walked up to Ghorad, his palm resting on the pistol at his belt.

'My father will bring the wrath of the Senate upon you all!' cried Imial.

Ghorad exhaled.

'Valachrad's son?' Calthorn's eyes did not stray from Ghorad. 'The boy doesn't know, does he?'

'General Calthorn!' Captain Jard, with Oljon at his side, stormed past Fhiro. 'By what right do your men think they can search these premises?'

'This is Pelorn's territory,' said Calthorn, 'not your Embassy.'

'Valachrad will be furious,' said Jard.

'If he wanted to object,' said Calthorn, 'he should not have fled from here in the middle of the night, taking with him any chance of shielding you all from the stench of guilt he has brought to this place.'

'And what, exactly, is he supposed to be guilty of?' asked Jard.

'The ambassador paid fairly for the bird and its pilot,' said Oljon.

'The departure of any ambassador from this fort without my permission is illegal,' said Calthorn, 'because I say it is. Save your indignation. You will have an opportunity to explain his dreadful timing soon enough.'

'You wish to question us?' cried Jard. 'You would not dare!'

'I hope your shock is sincere, captain,' said Calthorn. 'If it is not, diplomatic immunity won't save you from me.' Calthorn

turned to the officers beside him. 'Escort these three men to my command room for …' He paused to think for a moment, then grinned. 'An interview.'

'May they keep their arms, sir?'

'No,' said Calthorn, without glancing at the weapons worn by Oljon, Jard and Ghorad.

'Where is my father?' Imial pleaded to Ghorad and Jard.

'Your father is safe,' said Oljon. 'He had to leave.'

'Why?' cried Imial.

'I promise we'll explain on our return,' said Ghorad.

'I must be allowed to brief my men,' said Jard, 'or this search may degenerate into chaos and violence.'

The Pelorn officer escorting them nodded.

'Boys,' said Oljon, 'go back to your rooms and cooperate with the search. Do not answer any questions without speaking to one of us three first.'

Fhiro just managed to stop himself from saying Pa. 'Master, will we be all right?'

'Don't be afraid.' Oljon rested a hand on his son's shoulder.

Fhiro wished he could see through the Aculei mask.

'But where's my father?' asked Imial again.

* * *

Valachrad's chief servant, Yelba, and two of her colleagues, waited with Fhiro and Imial while Pelorn soldiers searched their room, and then insisted on clearing up the resultant mess. Fhiro's half-hearted offers to help were ignored.

Fhiro looked at Imial and saw the worry on his face. He tried to imagine how he would feel if it was Oljon who had gone. He moved closer to the other boy. 'Are you all right?'

'Why would he leave without telling me?' Imial looked away.

'There must be a good reason,' said Fhiro. 'Yelba, any sign of my father and Ghorad?'

'Not yet,' she replied.

'Your pa will be fine,' said Fhiro. 'We would've been told if there was something to worry about.'

Imial's glum face suddenly snapped into a proud stare. 'I do not miss my father. I am fine. I am *not* afraid.'

'Er, all right,' said Fhiro.

'Imial,' said Oljon as he walked in, followed by Ghorad and Jard, 'forgive us. You deserve an explanation.'

Imial sat on his bed, frozen, his eyes fixed on Oljon.

'Wait a few moments for Ghorad to confirm that the search party has definitely left, and you'll have it,' said Oljon.

'Of course,' Imial stammered. 'I have no problem waiting, at all.'

Soon they were in the meeting room that Valachrad had favoured for his official business. The blinds over the window, which looked out at the forest, were drawn closed. Fhiro was beside Oljon, now without his mask, while Imial sat by himself, his gaze shifting every few seconds.

'Last night,' Oljon said, 'your father went to meet with Reshna and Theon. Ghorad and I accompanied him.'

'So what happened?' asked Imial.

'Reshna never appeared,' said Oljon. 'We spent an hour watching for signs of movement, fearful that those wretched lake creatures might descend the slope towards us in the darkness. We eventually gave up, returned, and held a meeting.'

'Why didn't she come?' asked Fhiro.

'We assumed she had never intended to,' said Oljon, 'and that the meeting was merely a ploy to test how willing we were to negotiate. We feared Reshna planned to report that Kartna was afraid of the Creedate. Therefore we decided that

Valachrad must fly back to Riletta as fast as possible, in order to refute any such accusations, and manage our response.'

'But she would have been lying,' said Imial. 'My father was never afraid of those monotheistic fools.'

Oljon sucked in a short breath. 'How things are may not be as important as how they look,' he said. 'And that's why we're in our current predicament. General Calthorn learned of Valachrad's departure and was most displeased. However, that alone did not cause the outrage you just witnessed. Three other developments have only just been brought to our attention.'

'Have they drained the lake then?' asked Fhiro.

A smile flashed across Oljon's face, but it was no sooner there than it was gone. 'No. The first thing to stir Calthorn's fears was the disappearance of Reshna. The Creedate reported to him that she was missing, and in light Valachrad's flight, this was suspicious.'

'How could he think such a thing?' Imial's eyes were hot with fury. 'My father would not harm an ambassador.'

'Further evil befell this place before the night was finished,' said Oljon. 'Not long after Valachrad had left, the birds on the landing field erupted into a frenzy of shouting and disorganised birdsong. They even started pecking and clawing at one another. No sooner had the Pelorn soldiers restrained them all, the creatures started to convulse and die.'

Fhiro immediately thought of the magnificent beast that had carried them all this way. 'The birds are dead? All of them?'

'All the birds have been poisoned to death,' said Oljon, 'including the messenger birds. Since then one other bird has flown in and landed here. This is the only flight-worthy bird we have access to, but it is not large and has already travelled a long way.'

'How will we get out of here?' asked Imial.

'We must wait for this one remaining bird to summon help, at the nearest relay beacon,' said Oljon. 'Hopefully we will be stranded here no more than six days.'

'Well it's lucky that it did arrive just now,' said Imial. 'Any earlier and it might have got poisoned too.'

'I'd agree,' said Oljon, 'though I wish it had never arrived at all, for the news it brought was the worst of all.'

* * *

'Thank you, all of you, for coming here,' Calthorn boomed from the recently erected stage in the Great Hall. Light poured in through the giant skylight above his audience, and streamed through the windows that lined the upper walls.

Fhiro stood with Ghorad and the clouder archaeologists behind the long table occupied by most of the Kartnan delegation. Some of the others sat, including Imial whose mood had only worsened since the morning.

Elsewhere, tables had been pushed aside to make more space. Calthorn had invited everyone, leaving only those required for perimeter defences outside.

From time to time Fhiro would catch a distrustful glance or snarl thrown in his direction. This was despite General Calthorn's earlier declaration that his initial suspicions about the Kartnan Empire had been put to rest. The risk of meeting eyes with these accusers, however, was not enough to deter Fhiro from searching the room for Chenessa. The poor girl had lost her mother. He was desperate to find her and tell her that Kartna had had nothing to do with Reshna's disappearance. The Creedate might be his enemy, but he would happily help them find her if only he knew how. However, among the lines of Creedate priests gathered at one

edge of the room, including Hussuf, her mother's guard, there was no sign of Chenessa or Tubrin, her grisly-faced guard.

'Some of you may already know this,' continued Calthorn, 'but it is important you understand the magnitude of the danger we are in, so that you might better accept the decisions I have made concerning all of you.' He looked around the room, eyeing each group, one at a time. 'Valachrad, the ambassador of Kartna, has left us. He bought and paid for a bird and a pilot, to fly him away from here last night. I have questioned his officers and advisors, and have even risked the wrath of the Kartnan Senate by searching the quarters his delegation was housed in. I do not believe Valachrad had a part in the evil that has befallen us. At least, I suspect him no more than I suspect anyone else here. That, for me, is enough reason to insist that the Kartnan delegation is treated with the same respect and dignity today that they received yesterday.'

Calthorn paused to watch those before him again, but when the crowd remained silent he carried on. 'At some point during the night Reshna, the Creedate ambassador, disappeared from her quarters, and has not returned. Also vanished is her advisor, friend, and tutor of her daughter, Priest Theon. The remaining Creedate delegation know of no reason why she would have left. Her disappearance alone would be troubling enough, but in the early hours of the morning we discovered a further, evil crime. Every bird on the landing field has been killed.'

There were murmurs and growls from about the hall. Fhiro felt the angry stares and hateful looks multiply, but he resisted the urge to look back at them.

'The Kartnans are lying to you!' shouted a voice.

Fhiro clenched his fists. The unfairness of the accusation infuriated him. He hoped Calthorn found the real perpetrators soon. He wanted them to be punished, though perhaps by a judicial system less gruesome than Pelorn's.

'I have spoken on this matter,' said Calthorn with a lowered voice, 'and that is the end of it. Only the Royal Courts or the Security Inquisition have the authority to overturn my decision, and they are far from here. Meanwhile we have a greater concern to deal with.'

'Greater than leaving these treacherous swine among us?' asked another voice.

'Another statement like that and I will enforce order,' said Calthorn, pointing to the row of his soldiers before the stage. 'That would be regrettable for all concerned.' He let the warning sink in for a moment. 'Before the sun came up this morning Dr Watchal, an ecologist working for the Guardians of the Environment and Culture of Pelorn, arrived here from the south. His team have observed an event that has not been witnessed in a thousand years.' He took a deep breath. 'The Fawast migration is heading this way.'

There were gasps from around the hall.

'Impossible!' cried Zakil, the Iap ambassador.

'The holy embodiment of the spirits?' called another.

'The spirits have risen to protect the mountain!' cried a local archaeologist. 'We are blessed!'

'In another three days,' Calthorn continued, 'they will arrive in this valley.'

'Can we not escape them?' cried Shali, the Vinaran ambassador.

Among the varied responses from about the hall, Fhiro sensed confusion was the strongest.

'Are these herds dangerous?' asked one of the Creedate priests. 'You Niquani worship the spirit creatures.'

'The gravelings are coming!' shouted Evix, the ambassador of Norio.

Fhiro turned to ask if Ghorad knew what gravelings were, but saw the guard was busy studying the reactions spreading across the hall.

'The spirits of Pelorn *have* risen to protect the mountain,' shouted another local work hand, 'and they have risen up to destroy us.'

'Everyone be silent!' shouted Calthorn. 'The herd, and its predators, are still far away, and we have time to prepare. Dr Watchal can attest that your danger is far less than you think.' Calthorn turned to his side where a short yeal stood, wearing a mud stained cloak and a slopingwide-brimmed hat.

The doctor stepped forward and cleared his throat. 'The migration shall bless this place,' he said.

Many voices in the crowd rose up and said, as one, 'Praise be to the spirits!'

Dr Watchal bowed. 'Remember, we are not part of their universe. The gravelings and the curuski occupy the spirit realm of the yala and the vicows. They do not recognise us as friends, foes or food. Stay within the fort. Stay inside and pray for forgiveness and salvation.'

'An ecologist,' muttered Ghorad to Fhiro. 'Here such a person is a holy man.'

'Those creatures will not respond to our prayers,' said Shali. 'If they have any awareness of what we are, and what we are doing here, then their objective will be to tear us limb from limb, and devour us, for we have defiled the sacred land.'

'They will not harm us,' said Watchal, 'if we do not harm them. We have gone to great lengths to minimise harm to the forest. They are testing us. Testing our resolve to stay true to our beliefs.'

'May the spirits be merciful!' called out another voice.

'We have firearms,' called out Hussuf, Chenessa and Reshna's hegel guard. 'What kind of threat could such creatures cause us?'

'We do not fight with the wild spirits,' said Watchal. 'Great lengths are taken to avoid contact between people and the

devils that destroy the physical manifestations of the beloved yala and vicow. What records we have of such conflicts are ancient and unverified.'

'They say gravelings stand eight metres tall,' said Shali, 'and have the strength to tear down a house. That even cannons cannot bring them down.'

Fhiro felt nauseous. Surely they would not have to face down such a terrifying creature.

'They are tall,' said Watchal, 'but their physical forms are mortal. If we have no other choice they may be slain. But only if there is no other choice at all.'

There was more murmuring across the hall.

'Those that devour the yala and the vicow earn no love from us,' Watchal continued. 'However, only when necessary do we risk upsetting the cycle of death and recreation that is the basis for the spiritual balance of Fawast.'

'If they are dangerous,' said Zakil, 'and difficult to kill, should we not make our way as far from here as possible?'

'The front of the migrating herd is too wide,' said Dr Watchal, 'and the beasts will spread out in this unfamiliar terrain. Escaping their path altogether will be impossible.'

'The creatures, surely, won't be climbing the mountain,' suggested Ambassador Shali.

'There are reports of both curuski and gravelings climbing uphill to forage for prey,' said Dr Watchal. 'This mountain, here, would deter them, but it would be no guarantee of safety.'

'Flight is not the solution,' said Calthorn. 'Logistically it is impossible. There are many of you; guarding and feeding you all, on the move, is not something we have the supplies and equipment for.'

'So you want us to sit here and do nothing?' asked Ambassador Shali.

Calthorn grinned. 'No. I will have all of my available staff

outside today, felling trees. Once we have cleared enough space we will start a forest fire to burn away any incentive for these creatures to linger here, and give our turret gunners a clear view of all that dares to approach us. The Guardians of the Environment and Culture of Pelorn will have to accept my apologies.'

Dr Watchal gasped. 'You would not *dare* to sabotage the sacred forest in this way! The spirits are already angered by what we have done here. You wish to be eternally damned as well? You will be tried in court!'

'I'm damned either way,' said Calthorn. 'My primary concern is the safety of our guests. Therefore work is to start immediately. All Pelorn citizens must remain in this room to be counted and equipped for their tasks. We should appreciate volunteers from our foreign visitors, if any are able to lend a hand.'

Dr Watchal's eyes could not have got any wider. He glared about at the audience before him. 'Are none of you true Niquani? You cannot stand here, or obey his orders! This man will bring ruin upon us all!'

'These people are under my authority,' said General Calthorn. 'Holy man or no, if you encourage them to disobey me I will have you shot.' He turned to his audience. 'Dr Watchal's bird can carry eight passengers. With a pilot and two soldiers, that allows room for all five ambassadors, whose whereabouts we still know, to fly to safety.'

'There are children here,' said one of the Creedate priests. 'Allow Reshna's daughter, Chenessa, to accept her place.'

'Valachrad's son is here also,' said Captain Jard.

'My husband has come,' said Ambassador Shali. 'Take him instead of me.'

'That's my bird you're talking about!' cried Dr Watchal. 'The yala spirits be merciful!'

'There is only so much room aboard this flight,' said Calthorn, 'and the five remaining ambassadors are my priority. I will permit no substitutions. If a place on this bird is rejected, it will be filled by another guard. The ambassadors must represent their sovereign nations to our King in Riletta as soon as possible. Whatever evil has plotted to place us in such terrible peril clearly seeks to stall the ongoing negotiations. I'll sooner die than let it have its way.'

'Well I never,' said Dr Watchal. 'I bring you valuable information in good faith, and you repay me by robbing me and destroying the continent?'

'Dr Watchal, you have my gratitude,' said Calthorn. 'Now get out of my sight.'

CHAPTER 20

Fhiro watched the bird carrying the ambassadors fly into the sky and race towards the horizon. He was with Imial. Behind them were Pral, the Kartnan soldier who had greeted Fhiro and his family when they abandoned the Siwob, and Ghorad. The presence of the two men reassured him. Other guests had also come outside to watch the departure and Fhiro studied them intently. That someone he was watching might have played a role in the recent, sinister developments troubled him down to his soul.

Dr Watchal had insisted the migrating herds would not arrive for three days, but Fhiro kept wondering if he was wrong. He imagined hordes of yala beasts, and other giant creatures, suddenly bursting out of the trees and charging towards him.

He blocked the thought from his mind and took in a deep breath, letting the scents and pollens of Fawast fill his lungs. They were rich alien smells that felt fresh and ancient all at once, very unlike the Earth-based flora he was familiar with.

Fhiro's gaze drifted towards the south. The trees loomed tall and their branches reached out towards him, casting long shadows. The leaves rustled as a gust of wind tore through the forest, crossed the clearing, and billowed Fhiro's cloak. 'The trees look so very old,' he said.

'They've stood here for centuries,' said Ghorad.

'They've been alive long enough, then,' said Imial. 'Better they burn than we get eaten.'

'What if the Niquani are right?' asked Fhiro. 'What if there

are spirits on this planet? Maybe the mountain *is* protected by magic.'

'Then the magical forces should have appeared and explained this to us in Interspecies Galactic,' said Imial. 'Otherwise they either want us to get hurt, or they're a bit rubbish. In either case the forest should burn.'

'I'd agree,' said Fhiro, 'but have you ever heard of a religion in which the gods always made that much sense?'

'Of course,' said Imial. 'Our Kartnan gods are pure and are always clear in their …'

'All right!' Fhiro stopped him. 'I walked straight into that. Save it.'

'What?' asked Imial.

The sounds of axes hitting wood reached them from the east. Fhiro watched the men heave their tools back and forth.

'Is that Chenessa?' asked Imial.

Fhiro looked back towards the fort. There was a group of Creedate priests, but he could not see Chenessa among them. 'Do you think Reshna disappeared deliberately?'

'If so, the next question is whether she knew about the approaching herds,' answered Ghorad. 'Valachrad would never have left his son behind to face such peril.'

'Reshna can't be that evil,' said Fhiro.

'Indeed,' said Ghorad. 'Perhaps Marallel suspected Reshna's disloyalty. Perhaps she has served her purpose, been eliminated, and this coming danger is merely the next act in his grand scheme.'

'I hate Marallel,' said Fhiro. But just then he caught a glimpse of the Creedate ambassador's daughter. Her face was downcast. The wizened old men and women around her moved in and out of his line of sight, obscuring her.

He made to walk towards her, but stopped when he felt Ghorad's hand on his shoulder. 'No. Not now. Your

conversation will be watched, and who knows what kind of dangerous interpretations, correct or not, might be made.'

'I want to tell her it wasn't us,' said Fhiro. 'I can't have her thinking we did something to her mother.'

'Telling her that would suggest it was reasonable to suspect us,' said Ghorad. 'It might alert our enemies to the truth, that she was communicating with you for her mother and Theon.'

'You think they still don't know?' asked Fhiro.

'We don't know what they know,' said Ghorad. 'If in doubt, keep the enemy in the dark as much as possible. If the priests, or that fearsome looking guard, suspect Reshna of conspiring against Marallel, Chenessa will be in danger.'

Tubrin came into view behind Chenessa. He stared back at Fhiro across the distance between them, his dreadful gaze even more intense in its fury than it had been in the Hall of Resolutions. This time, however, Fhiro stood still, braced himself, and stared back. His eyes stayed locked with Tubrin's for what felt like an eternity, until Ghorad stood in front of him.

'You play games with a wild beast!' said Ghorad. 'You have no idea how that feral man might react.'

Fhiro looked down at the ground. 'I don't see why I have to give in.'

'Because if he wanted to kill you, he might just go ahead and do so,' said Ghorad. 'Let's not provoke him, shall we?'

'Well can we talk to her at dinner?' asked Fhiro. 'We could go to the Great Hall.'

'Yes,' said Imial. 'They might even have some Snorel beast steak left.'

'Captain Jard approaches,' Pral interrupted them. 'It seems most of the delegation from Kartna is carrying an axe or a saw.'

'Ghorad, Pral,' said Jard, an axe resting over his shoulder, 'I've pledged our assistance to General Calthorn. May as well

lessen the hostility we've earned and save our own lives at the same time.' He threw the axe towards Pral, who caught it. 'Pral, join these fellows. Ghorad, come back to the fort. You, Veltir and I need to oversee our men and keep an eye on the boys.'

'Very well,' said Ghorad.

'Come on, men,' said Pral, nodding towards an untroubled part of the forest. 'Let's show these locals how it's done.'

'Can't we help?' asked Fhiro.

'We'll talk with Priest Veltir when we return,' said Jard. 'He's the one dishing out the tasks.'

Fhiro and Imial soon found themselves passing verbal messages between the different groups of Kartnan soldiers and civilians scattered about the fort and the surrounding area. Most were involved in clearing the forest.

'Young men,' General Calthorn said to them when they had delivered him a message from Captain Jard, 'I need a courier to take an order to the game keepers at the dig site. Could you assist me?'

'We have to return to Jard with your answer,' said Imial. 'Perhaps after that?'

'That will take too long,' said Calthorn.

'I could go,' said Fhiro. He saw Calthorn looking at him with suspicion. 'I can look after myself. I'll become an Aculei priest one day.'

Calthorn grinned. 'Excellent.'

Fhiro ran all the way to the dig site, catching his breath at the top of the slope behind the fort. As his lungs drank the air his eyes feasted on the greens and browns of the countryside around him. The lake was clear, and shone with the reflection of the sky, and the mountains to the north swelled beneath a blue haze. He hated the thought that it was all to be burned. He saw a gathering of hockers and elomules with some men near the excavation site and sprinted towards them.

'Elomules?' said the foreman, scratching his head as he read the message. 'What does he want to do with all these felled trees exactly? I thought he was just going to burn them all.'

'I don't know,' said Fhiro.

'I better send some men down with them,' said the foreman. He looked over his shoulder. 'Make sure they don't crush anyone, or get in the way of any falling trees.'

'Where will all the animals be kept when the herds arrive?' asked Fhiro.

The foreman's brow creased with worry. 'We'll cage them up here with a few guards and hope for the best. We normally stay too, to keep an eye on them, but we've been ordered to house ourselves in the fort with everyone else.' He turned to watch the hockers pounding at the rock face, each blow producing a deafening boom that obscured the fainter clangs from the earthmen, hegel and yeal at work. 'Poor things. The Chissids don't bother them. Perhaps these other animals won't either.'

'Will the guards be all right?' asked Fhiro.

'It's their job to get killed,' said the foreman. 'The hockers and elomules didn't volunteer for this. They're just being good, obedient workers.' He wiped his left eye.

Fhiro reflected on the foreman's sense of priorities as he hurried back to the fort. As he neared the crest of the slope, he saw Cerilina, Borlin and the other archaeologists. 'Haven't they put you lot to work on the trees?'

'We're the talent, you see,' said Borlin. 'Don't do unskilled work.'

'You're carrying a pickaxe,' said Fhiro.

Borlin grinned. 'I've better uses for it than trees.'

'Where are you all going?' Many of them were preparing their footwear and rucksacks by the side of the path.

Cerilina glanced about to check no one was near. 'Don't let the general know, but we're disobeying his last order.'

'Are you running away?' asked Fhiro. 'It's dangerous out there.'

'No, no,' she laughed. 'Those animals aren't arriving for a few days, but we've been told to stay within sight of the fort or the excavation site, at all times. The thing is, a lot of us left tools up on the mountain when we tried to find another entrance into it.'

'You're going to go fetch them?'

'It won't take long,' said Cerilina. 'We'll be back by tomorrow, latest, and then we'll hunker down with the rest of you.' She smiled. 'It's a nice walk. Difficult, but the views up there are amazing. To be honest, that's probably half the reason I'm going back up there. Maybe more than half! And to think the entire spectacle will be laid to waste by these beasts and a fire. It's such a tragedy.'

Fhiro looked out over the forest again and wished he could join her. 'What do you want me to tell people if they notice you're missing?'

'You can come too, if you want,' suggested Cerilina.

'Really?' asked Fhiro. Then he considered his duties. 'They'd probably look for me, and they'll probably look for you too.'

'I'm sure your master won't notice,' said Cerilina. 'He looks very busy.'

Fhiro smiled. 'Thanks, but I've got tasks to do. I'm running errands for General Calthorn now.'

'Going up in the world, then?' Borlin laughed. 'Next stop: the Kartnan Academies, then the Senate itself!'

'All right,' said Cerilina. 'If anyone asks about us, don't lie. Tell them we knew the risks, and they aren't to worry.'

'If you say so,' said Fhiro.

Cerilina smiled at him. 'Hopefully see you soon.'

Fhiro sincerely hoped he did see her again, as he made his way back down the slope. He went as quickly as the narrow

path would allow. His heart stopped when a group of Creedate soldiers came trudging up the hill. He moved aside to let them pass, conscious of their stares as they pushed by. After scrambling faster to get well away from them, he stopped to catch his breath and looked out over the forest ahead.

A tall, silver-leafed tree crashed to the ground to the south. The men at its trunk took a moment to breathe and wipe their foreheads before seeking out their next quarry. Fhiro wondered about the Chulop tree stone he had planted, by a stream, near Chimahess. Perhaps a hungry creature had found and eaten it. Perhaps it had taken root, but was destined to be nothing more than firewood when the wrong set of eyes fell upon it in the cold of winter.

He was snapped out of his daydreaming by the sight of Chenessa, striding towards the southeastern edge of the clearing. She was by herself. Her bodyguards and priests were nowhere in sight.

'Chenessa!'

She did not hear him, so he ran towards her.

'Chenessa!'

She walked on to a narrow path that passed into the forest. Soon she was underneath the trees.

'Chenessa!'

His voice was drowned out by the snapping of branches as another tower of living wood and rustling foliage struck the earth. He had lost sight of her and ran faster, passing under the trees himself, feeling the shadows envelope him. Ahead, further along the path, the darkness seemed less, and light filtered through the green above, giving the path a yellow glow.

'Chenessa!'

CHAPTER 21

'Chenessa!'

'Oh, Fhiro.' Chenessa froze.

He looked at her, his eyes as wide as hers. 'What are you doing here?'

'What are you doing here?'

'Following you.'

'Why?'

'Because,' said Fhiro, frowning. He was not entirely sure. 'Because you're walking into the forest, and they're planning to burn it down.'

She paused. Then her hands clenched into fists, and she started to tremble.

'What?'

'How *dare* you approach me!' she cried.

'I wanted to say,' gasped Fhiro, 'we all wanted to say that we had nothing to do with …'

'I should never have trusted you.' She looked away from him, her eyes watering.

'Chenessa–'

'Don't come near me!' She backed away, palm outstretched towards him.

'I'm not going to hurt you,' said Fhiro. 'You know me!'

'I was a fool,' she said. 'So was my mother. She said you looked honest.'

'I am!' Fhiro seized her mother's vote of confidence. 'I know Valachrad is an ambassador, and they probably lie all the time, but really, he had nothing to do with any of these

bad things. He went to talk to your mother and she wasn't there.'

Chenessa looked past Fhiro at the men working in the clearing. 'I should have listened to … Hussuf and … Tubrin.' Her words were broken up by her sniffling.

'When Valachrad didn't see your mother he thought he'd been tricked,' added Fhiro. 'He thought she might already be on her way to Riletta herself.' He wondered if he was disclosing too much, but he was desperate. Then he wondered if he was desperate for the sake of the Kartnan Empire, or desperate for himself. 'When we heard she'd disappeared, we thought it was a Creedate plot.'

'Don't dare accuse us,' she snarled. 'You're the ones with something to answer for.'

'But we didn't do anything! I don't know what this weird conspiracy is, with your mother, the poisoned birds, and the animals coming, but it's not from us. We only just got to this planet.'

'The Kartnan ambassador was the only one to have escaped before things got dangerous. That's suspicious.'

'He left his son here,' said Fhiro. 'He'd never have done that if he knew the danger. You don't know Valachrad, but he's not like that. Just as your mother wouldn't have left you.'

Her head jerked away from him, her eyes clenched shut. She wiped away a tear as it ran down her cheek.

'I'm so sorry, Chenessa.' Fhiro wished he could think of something else to say.

Chenessa started walking deeper into the forest, and then she started running.

Fhiro followed after her. The canopy above remained thin. The path was clear and bright beneath their feet.

After thirty paces she slowed down, burst into tears, and dropped on to her haunches.

'Chenessa,' said Fhiro again as he slowed, knelt and put his arm around her shoulders.

She shrugged his arm loose. 'Get off! If it hadn't been for you she'd still be here.'

'I had nothing to do with it. I thought I was helping to prevent a war.' He reflected on the gravity of the statement, and considered the absurdity of how far he had come since he wandered the paths, mountains and fields of the Green River Valley. He missed home. He missed his own mother.

At least he had one.

'I thought I was helping too,' she uttered between sobs. Her breathing settled a little and she shook her head.

'It's not your fault,' said Fhiro.

She buried her face in her arm.

Fhiro decided to stay silent. He felt terrible. He did not want to imagine what she was feeling. He glanced around. The trees had been pruned and tended to. This was not a simple path hewn out of the forest. For a moment he wondered if Chenessa's behaviour was an act, designed to trick him into following her where the Kartnan soldiers would not be able to see or help him. He peered between the trees but saw nothing in the shadows. He looked at Chenessa; if this was an act of deception then he was totally outclassed. His doubts about her intentions dissolved with one look at her face.

After a while she opened her eyes. Her makeup was smeared. Fhiro had not realised she had been wearing any. 'I'm going further in.'

'Why?' he asked.

She stood up and strode forward.

'Do you want to get away from someone?'

'Everyone,' said Chenessa. 'And I wanted to see these gardens before they got burnt down.'

'What gardens?'

The space between the trees widened. All manner of plants, many with winding, curving stalks, sprouted from beds of grass and moss-coated rocks. At their tips, and jutting from their stems, were flowers of pink, yellow, turquoise and blue.

'They made a garden here?' asked Fhiro.

'And they're going to destroy it,' said Chenessa. 'Didn't you wonder where the ambassadors went while we had tuition after seeing the dig site?'

'Aten's left knee,' breathed Fhiro.

'Where did you learn that blasphemous expression?' she asked.

'I used to follow The Calling, remember?' He was sticking to the official story. He was safe.

'Oh yes,' she said. 'You didn't say that when we first met.'

'I'd been told not to talk about those things,' said Fhiro, 'but I kind of had to after Master Saflua.'

'Exactly,' said Chenessa. 'You're not really my friend. You're just another nosy diplomat.'

'No,' said Fhiro, 'I am your friend.'

'Kartna and the Creedate are almost certain to go to war, now,' said Chenessa. 'We're enemies.'

'Do you really support what the Creedate are doing?'

'The Creedate have done terrible things,' she said, 'but Kartna is no beacon of kindness and mercy. They've done their fair share of foul crimes, including massacres. The difference is Kartna claimed its power ages ago, and most of the bad things they did have been forgotten. What Marallel does is not because he's a Follower of The Calling, it's the natural consequence of war and conquest.'

'Then don't conquer places,' said Fhiro.

'They're afraid,' said Chenessa. 'I'm afraid, too. Avithen said that if we didn't fight and expand, we'd be subjected to the same, or worse, by others. He was probably right.' She stepped further

into the garden, tears running down her cheeks again. One fell and splashed on her dress. 'It's beautiful,' she said, looking at the plants around them. 'I'm glad my mother got to see it.'

'Don't …' Fhiro stopped himself. 'She might come back.'

'You think she might have been kidnapped?' Her eyes dared him to challenge her. 'Only a highly trained group could have abducted her without leaving a trace for General Calthorn to find. If that's what happened, their demands will be huge, and Marallel will never pay them. He never does.'

'There could have been a political misunderstanding,' said Fhiro. He made a few nervous glances into the surrounding woods. 'Could kidnappers still be out here?'

'My mother's dead,' said Chenessa.

'Don't say that,' said Fhiro.

She did not respond.

Fhiro looked into the forest again. 'We might be in danger out here.'

She ignored him and carried on, skirting around foliage that had grown out into the path.

He followed her, almost failing to see a low branch as he turned a corner. 'Chenessa?'

'Look at those,' she said as she approached a cluster of bright colours bursting out of a crowded, thorny bush.

'I know Calthorn sent men to scour the area,' said Fhiro, 'but they probably aren't patrolling the forest south of here. This place isn't safe.'

Chenessa closed her eyes and took in a deep breath from a flower that was brimming with bright yellow petals.

'I think we should just go back,' said Fhiro. 'Your mother wouldn't want you to get kidnapped.' Then he wondered if, somewhere in Chenessa's mind, the chance of a reunion with her mother had become worth more to her than her freedom, or even her life.

She stayed silent.

Fhiro frowned. 'They might set fire to the forest soon.'

'I don't care.'

'What?'

Chenessa turned away. 'Anyway, Calthorn is overreacting.'

'Says who?'

'He's working everyone to death to get the forest cleared within twenty-four hours, but the herds aren't expected to reach here for three days. He's become paranoid because of this conspiracy, or whatever you call what you Kartnans are up to.'

'It's not us,' said Fhiro. 'Please believe me.'

She shrugged and set off. 'You don't have to come.'

Fhiro's imagination drifted to thoughts of what monsters might be accompanying the herds, and whether they liked eating children. He followed after Chenessa, hoping she decided to turn back soon. 'How long before your guards start looking for you?'

'I think Hussuf will take some time to realise I've gone,' said Chenessa. 'I sent him on an errand before I sneaked off.'

'Well as long as it's not Tubrin that finds us,' said Fhiro. He shuddered. 'I bet he'd use my blood to clean his boots, and chew on my eyeballs while he fashions my bones into cooking utensils.'

'His heart's in the right place.'

'If you say so,' said Fhiro, 'but it's probably covered in poisoned spikes, and pumps acid blood round his body.'

'Maybe,' she said, and a smile flashed across her face for an instant.

Could she be cooling down? Fhiro's heart leapt at the thought.

He heard the trickling of water ahead, where the path sloped downwards. At the bottom of the slope a stream crossed the path over a bed of rocks, pebbles and mud. Tiny

silver-green creatures swam with the water. They were small, fast, but had six fin-like limbs, and bore little resemblance to any fish, amphibians or insects Fhiro knew.

'Now, how do we get across?' she asked.

'Are those little things in there poisonous?' Fhiro was still peering into the stream. 'What about chissids?' He shuddered.

'Chissids won't be here,' she said. 'They're too big to hide in shallow water like this.'

'Let's just go back, please?' Fhiro tugged at her sleeve.

'And I thought you might have come down here to kill or torture me,' she said. 'You're more scared than I am!'

'You sound almost disappointed,' said Fhiro.

Chenessa started to take off her shoes and socks.

'Are you crossing barefoot?' Fhiro had no sooner asked her than she had got up and walked across the stream. She started drying her feet when she reached the other side, before putting her socks back on.

Fhiro took a moment to find his voice. 'Did anything bite you?'

'No.'

Fhiro studied the stream again, and then the path on the other side. He planted a tentative foot on to a rock that was submerged by a thin layer of running water.

'You'll get your shoes wet,' said Chenessa.

'I'll stick to these shallow parts.' He hopped across in a flash.

Chenessa rinsed her hands in the stream and stood up. 'I bet the stream goes to the lake.'

Fhiro shook his head and followed her. 'It had better be a good lake after all this.'

They continued down the path.

'Look.' Chenessa pointed to a bright yellow fruit hanging from a branch. 'Wonder if it tastes nice.'

'Please don't!' cried Fhiro.

Chenessa walked close to the dangling fruit, but then jumped back as a cluster of tiny brown creatures flew off the branch. 'Linids!'

'Linids?' Fhiro covered his eyes. 'We're definitely going to die out here.'

'They're a native insect-like life-form,' said Chenessa. 'I wasn't going to eat that fruit.'

Fhiro was glad she was starting to sound more like her old self again. 'Let's just find this lake and go home.'

'Home?' She looked at the ground. 'I'll never go home again. Not like it was.'

Fhiro thought about his old home. He never expected to see Andelic again, but at least his mother was not missing.

The path turned in the direction in which the stream had been flowing.

'Look,' said Fhiro, 'I've got to ask, but I probably shouldn't.'

She said nothing.

'If you don't believe in The Calling, what do you believe?'

'None of your business,' she said.

'I just want you to have hope, is all,' said Fhiro. 'Whatever happens.'

'What does that mean?' she asked, scowling at him.

'Well,' said Fhiro, 'if I was worried about death, mine or someone else's, I'd like to think that they went somewhere better. You know, afterwards.'

'Is that what the Kartnan gods tell you?' she asked. 'Are you trying to convert me?'

'No!' said Fhiro. He was a bit unsure about the Kartnan position on heaven anyway. 'Just that I don't want you to be any sadder than you have to be.'

'What kind of a stupid statement is that?!' she cried. 'My mother's missing. I'm sad. Why is that so hard for you? You're as bad as those stupid priests!'

He decided to drop the matter.

After a while the scowl melted away and she looked up again. 'There's light ahead.' She walked faster. As they neared a bend in the path the silver surface of a lake appeared beyond it.

'How big is it?' Fhiro hurried after her.

'Do you think that island is very far away?'

Fhiro reached the water and took in the lake. Along its northern edge, trees jutted from steep, muddy banks. Many bent over the still, glimmering surface like old men, reaching outwards with thick leafless branches that penetrated the lake like the legs of giant, wooden spiders. Beyond them, heavily laden branches rose in bushy bulbs and higher up, narrowed into winding points. The island rose up with rocky sharpness on one side and mellowed into a pebbled shore on the other. It was covered with a disordered canopy of long furrowed leaves atop spiny trunks. Near it a smaller brother of a stony mound sprouted a solitary sapling.

'It's so beautiful,' said Chenessa.

'It's very quiet,' Fhiro muttered. 'There was far more noise in the forest we were camped in a few days ago.'

'Those tree felling enthusiasts probably scared all the wildlife away.'

He nodded. Then he pointed to a collection of blue and orange, shelled creatures, a few feet away, climbing up a thick tree root on spindle-thin legs. 'Not everything's been scared away.'

Chenessa crouched for a better look. 'Linids are very creative.'

Fhiro watched the creatures and Chenessa for a while. 'Does Master Saflua know you don't follow The Calling?'

'Yes,' she answered.

'Did Theon or your mother know?'

'Theon should have,' said Chenessa. She stood up and stretched. 'It's his fault for teaching me so much about religion and philosophy. Wish I hadn't ever questioned my beliefs.'

'Well,' said Fhiro, 'if it's the right religion, then it should stand up to questioning, shouldn't it?'

'Clearly yours doesn't either.'

Fhiro made a face. 'I'm open to other ideas. I just haven't heard any good ones.'

'Remind me, why do you want to be an Aculei priest?'

'I thought it would be ... well ... exciting. They learn blind-sight and everything.'

'What's blind-sight?'

'You know, remembering targets even after you can't see them. Takes loads of practice.'

'What, to shoot them?'

'Of course.'

Chenessa shook her head and started walking again. 'I think all religions are stupid.'

Fhiro said nothing. She seemed to have reached the conclusion he felt he was heading towards.

'And if they're all so wrong about everything else, I can't see how they're right about there being an afterlife.'

'They might be right about that,' said Fhiro. He looked ahead. 'It looks like the path is going back into the woods again.'

'I wish we had time to swim.' She drifted back near the water and leaned over it.

'I wonder if there are Chissid in there too.'

'Oh!' She recoiled from the water. 'Horrid thought. You're obsessed with Chissids.'

'Sorry. You told me about them.'

Chenessa walked away from the lake's edge. 'Aren't you glad

you came? Surely this is much more fun than delivering messages or carrying wood or whatever you were doing earlier.'

'Are you having fun? If you are, it'll make me feel better.'

She smiled for almost an entire second. 'Nothing is fun now, but I'm glad I came here.' She led the way forwards again and started to ascend the path as it sloped back into the forest. 'You're hardly a zealot, and I got the impression the Aculei were quite rigid in their ideas. Do you really want to be like that scary man in the mask?'

Fhiro turned to hide his grin. 'I don't know.' The path was steep, and his concentration was consumed with the task of heaving himself up, step by step.

'This forest is so beautiful,' she said. 'The galaxy is so beautiful, and yet all we do is fight and murder each other. I just wanted to be happy. What a stupid idea that was.'

'It's not stupid,' said Fhiro. 'Happy sounds good.'

'Is that what you want?' she asked. 'I assume the Aculei don't seek wealth and riches.'

'Being wealthy makes you powerful, though,' said Fhiro. 'We need weapons and food.'

'So what do you– Wait. What was that?'

'Footsteps,' said Fhiro. They were coming from the direction of the clearing.

Carefully, they climbed to the top of the steep rise and peered over. Thorn-studded bushes and overhanging branches obscured the way forward.

The sound of running footsteps grew. Then a figure burst round the corner and skidded to a halt, staring up at Chenessa.

It was Hussuf, Chenessa's hegel guard. 'Chenessa! Where have you been?' Then he saw Fhiro and drew his pistol, his gaze scouring the trees around them.

'Hussuf,' cried Chenessa. 'Relax! It's not a trap. I led him

down here. I just wanted to see the scenery before they burned it all down.'

Hussuf looked at her over his short beak, and then at Fhiro. His eyes narrowed. 'What have you been talking about?'

'Nothing,' insisted Chenessa. 'Please don't point that gun at him! He hasn't tried to hurt me.'

As Hussuf approached him Fhiro backed away, turning to avoid being forced further into the forest. His heart was pounding. Chenessa was sincere, but he did not know Hussuf, and the Creedate guard had the means to interrogate him and, if necessary, disappear him.

'Were you planning to harm her, boy?'

'No,' said Fhiro. He tried to slow his breathing. This was not fair. Hussuf was bigger than him and armed too. If only his father were here. 'I followed her into the forest because I was worried about her.' He looked up at Hussuf, straight into the guard's eyes. He felt anger building inside. 'If you'd done your job properly I wouldn't have needed to come out here.'

'Chenessa,' said Hussuf, 'Marallel will not look kindly on your actions. Conversing with the likes of this foreign priest-boy will bring your allegiance into question.'

'Marallel will just have to put up with it!' said Chenessa. 'I'm sick of prancing about in whatever special way he wants me to. Now put that gun down.'

'Not while I need to protect you,' said Hussuf. 'Protect you, and all of us, from this Kartnan scum.'

'You will obey me!' shouted Chenessa. 'I'll report your cowardly interrogation if you do not stop this.'

'You are the one in trouble, little girl,' said Hussuf.

'My mother's disappeared!' said Chenessa. 'Trouble is nothing to me. You can all go to hell!'

'Chenessa,' Hussuf faced her and his stare intensified, 'you forget yourself! Do not dare speak in–'

At that moment an enormous taloned hand swept out of the forest and clasped Hussuf. The guard cried out in pain, but as the thick fingers around his torso closed in against each other his voice died, and blood frothed and spluttered from his beak. The huge claw lifted Hussuf through the air, and brought his broken form before a vast, horned head. Black eyes studied the Creedate guard, and below them rows of sharp, yellow-stained teeth emerged as the creature parted its lips. It opened its huge maw and packed the hegel inside it. Then its jaws crunched together as though there was nothing but dried leaves between them. The cracking of Hussuf's bones was audible above the snorting grunts that rumbled from the monster's ridged gills. As traces of blood trickled down its chin it stooped its head and gazed at Fhiro and Chenessa.

Were there any air in Fhiro's lungs he would have screamed.

CHAPTER 22

'Run!'

Fhiro grabbed Chenessa's arm and pulled her after him down the slope.

As they reached the lake a terrible roar blasted the air behind them. Fhiro felt his insides turn to jelly.

They scrambled along the water's edge. The mud was wet and slippery. Fhiro struggled not to fall. He was aware of Chenessa behind him, gasping as she fought to keep her feet.

He looked over his shoulder; nothing followed, but loud cracking sounds came from deeper in the forest. 'Keep going!' he whispered as loud as he dared.

'What if it's waiting ahead of us?' panted Chenessa.

'We have to get back to the clearing,' said Fhiro. 'Keep going and keep your voice down.'

All went quiet except for the smacking of their shoes against the earth. Fhiro felt his lungs burning and his muscles ache, but he forced himself on. He was not going to accept death, and he had been trained to exert himself under stress. But he had no idea about Chenessa's conditioning. He glimpsed only terror in her face. He hoped she could keep up.

The creaking of wood in the forest broke the silence.

'The path turns up there,' Chenessa pointed.

Fhiro tried to think. 'Is it a forest creature or something from the plains?'

'What do you mean?' There was panic in her voice.

'Did you learn about it?'

'I think it's a graveling,' said Chenessa, 'but no one knows much about them.'

'If it's from the forest, it'll move faster through the trees than us.'

'So we should take the path?' she asked, her eyes wide.

'Forget I spoke,' gasped Fhiro. 'It's a lot bigger than us. It'll outrun us in the open. We'll fit between the dense trees.'

'We're going through the trees then?' she asked. 'You're sure that's a good idea?'

'No.'

With that he left the path and dived straight through the underbrush of the forest. He could hear Chenessa's rapid breathing keeping pace behind him. He leapt over a thorn bush.

'Ouch,' she muttered a moment later.

'You all right?'

'Just get us out of here!'

He prayed to Aten he had not just doomed them. Scrambling between trees and bushes was not a fast way to travel.

A rhythmic thumping shook the ground. Cracks and crashes gathered in magnitude behind them.

Fhiro glanced back.

The towering creature was launching itself through the forest. Pouncing between the thicker trunks, and forcing smaller trees out of the way with its giant, taloned hands, it came faster and faster towards them.

Just looking at it, Fhiro felt his flesh being ripped from his body. He could feel his bones splintered by the monster's teeth. He forced energy into his legs, desperate to overcome the terror that threatened to paralyse them. 'Go, go, go!' he cried.

And to his relief Chenessa kept going. They splashed across the stream as it passed through the forest nearer the lake. His

shoes, now wet with water though, felt heavier. Another thing to slow them down. Another reason they were going to die.

He aimed for where the forest was thickest and darkest. They ducked under low branches that clawed their hair, and scrabbled through a cluster of thick trunks. As they broke through, Fhiro gasped. A solid wall of bushes barred their way. There was no option. He leapt at it. Clawing aside the thistles and brambles, he felt the burn of a dozen tiny knives slashing across his skin. Chenessa was behind him, battling to stay close enough to dodge the branches he had pushed aside as they swung back at her.

As they scrambled through to the far side, an alien shriek sounded from behind. Fhiro's heart raced. Trees spread out ahead. They were almost clear of the forest.

At a sudden crash of wood, Fhiro checked behind them. The beast was stopping to bend branches, to push trees aside, as it fought its way into the denser patch of forest.

They were gaining distance. There was hope.

Then the monster changed direction and tore its way towards the path. It seemed to look into his eyes in that instant. Its expression changed, and it seemed to Fhiro that it snarled at him.

Fhiro turned the way he was heading, but too late; his foot caught on a root. He crashed to the forest floor, his face and arms grazed and cut by the sturdy plants that broke his fall.

Chenessa pulled him upwards. He kicked himself off the turf, running the instant his soles made contact with it again. They sprinted as fast as they could, weaving between the hedges, trees, and the layers of unfamiliar, alien plants.

If they made it through this, he could thank her. If they made it through.

And then the pounding of heavy feet against the earth returned, and came louder and louder.

Fhiro did not look back this time. His fear drove him forward as fast as he could go. Warm sunlight hit his face. He looked up and saw the canopy was getting thin. The trees were coming to an end.

A man carrying an axe appeared and looked at them, bewildered. 'Were you two making that racket?'

'Run,' shouted Fhiro as he raced past.

An instant later came a shout, then a scream.

Ahead Fhiro saw men and women drop their axes and speed towards the fort. Soldiers in uniforms of different nations took aim with their rifles and fired a mixture of crystal-fire and projectile ammunition over him.

'Keep your head down!' he shouted to Chenessa.

'It's not working!' cried a Hithostun officer as the two of them darted through the wavering group.

'To the main door!'

The eruption of screams built in number and magnitude. Fhiro dared only to turn his head enough to glance at Chenessa, and saw tears streaming down her face.

There was shouting from everywhere. 'Back to the fort! Man the turrets!'

Those fleeing the beast stormed the large, open gate at the entrance chamber. Fhiro and Chenessa were jostled from every direction as panicked civilians and soldiers collided into one another as they converged on the gate. And then they slowed down.

'Keep moving!' Fhiro cried. They had to get inside. It was the only place that was safe, but people were cramming together, tighter and tighter ahead of them. The clamour of nervous, frightened voices, from all around him was continuous, and made it impossible to hear the thudding of giant footsteps, but further behind him the gunfire was getting louder, and increasing in frequency.

It was coming.

'Let us get in!' cried Fhiro, but his words were lost amid the shouts of everyone else.

A yeal woman in front looked over her shoulder. 'It's here!' she screamed.

Fhiro started to turn his head, but he had barely begun to do so when his eyes caught sight of a blurred shape racing across his field of vision. He followed it instinctively, until the form smashed against the outer wall of the fort. The mangled corpse of a uniformed soldier slid down towards the floor, limbs bent in unnatural ways, blood pouring from its head.

Fhiro felt sick. It could have been him. It still could be him.

The cries of shock and horror degenerated into chaotic screaming.

The weight of the crowd intensified. It lifted Fhiro and Chenessa off their feet as it gathered momentum.

'Chenessa!' Fhiro tried to reach out and catch her hand.

Chenessa screamed as she was pulled further and further away from him.

Every face he saw was stricken with terror. He was pushed inside the entrance of the fort, the shadows of the interior replacing the glare of the sun outside. He was inside, but the overwhelming urge to run still gripped him. He had to get further in. Deeper in.

The stampede of people crushed against him. He winced as elbows rubbed against his ribs, and arms bashed his ears. It became a struggle to breathe from the pressure against his chest.

Ahead he could see people of all species barging their way out of the entrance chamber into the hallways.

The beast roared again, but from much closer, and powerless to influence how fast or where he was moving, Fhiro turned to get a proper look. Between the heads of those

struggling to get past him he saw giant legs, kneeling down, and the monster's horned head, like a depiction of a devil from the mythology of The Calling, looking through the gate opening. Its huge arm reached into the entrance chamber and swiped at the crowd. It drifted away, clutching an earthman in mid-air. Its victim screamed as he was lifted and pulled toward the creature's open mouth, but went silent when his head thudded into the upper frame of the gate. An instant later the limp body was devoured in a flurry of its gnashing jaws.

A deep booming sound echoed through the ceiling and the walls. The beast jerked backwards. Dark liquid poured from a wound on its right shoulder. It howled and leapt on to the fort roof, disappearing from view. Three more booms followed. A waterfall of the dark liquid poured over the open gate entrance. The beast slid off the roof, landed in a crumpled heap, and lay still.

There was an outburst of further cries at the sight of this. Fhiro himself could not believe he was safe yet. Around him people were still scrambling over each other, trying to get further into the fort.

'It's dead!' someone shouted.

A group of troops surrounded the animal. One climbed up on to its head and fired several shots into its mouth.

'Stop running!'

The crowd slowed. Fhiro felt himself slide down until his feet made contact with the ground again.

He was alive.

Surely not. Surely he had not survived. He had been metres away from the thing. It had charged through trained, armed soldiers as though they were made of paper.

He felt his face, body and limbs. He checked his scratched, bloody and bruised legs.

He should be dead.

Soldiers shouted orders and began to disperse people, checking for injured among those that had fallen to the ground in the stampede. Groups, couples and individuals collapsed, exhausted, against walls or on to the floor, crying and wailing. Some screamed in pain.

Fhiro felt an urge to be sick. His heart still pounded. He looked at the dead creature, its clawed fingers still pointing into the air. They had been meant for him.

As he staggered between the shaking, cowering and embracing survivors he searched for Chenessa. He had lost her what felt like an eternity ago. She was not nearby. With dread he moved closer to the monster's corpse. He passed where an unconscious hegel woman was being resuscitated on the floor, battered by the stampede as it had trampled over her.

Please, Chenessa, please please appear.

His feet trod through pools of blood from where deadly wounds had been inflicted upon the crowd by the creature. To his right he saw a corpse. A civilian male earthman, a deep linear wound down his back, his torso twisted where the spine had been broken. Beyond him there was a group of bodies being tended to by soldiers. Fhiro braced himself, and walked over to study them.

He checked the first face. It was not Chenessa. His heart thumped louder. He checked the second. Also not her.

Then he heard her voice.

She was sitting on the floor by the wall, clutching her knees.

Relief flooded his veins. 'Are you … Are you all right?'

She shook her head. 'I killed him.'

He fell to his knees next to her. 'W– What?'

'Hussuf,' she sobbed. 'He'd be alive if I hadn't gone into the forest. All of those people would be alive.'

'No!' said Fhiro. 'Please, Chenessa, that's ridiculous!'

'He's dead because of me. She's dead because of me. He was … Ma …what …' Her words became indecipherable.

Fhiro tried to put his arm around her again, and this time she let him. He hoped she did not think he was strange for doing so, but the contact felt good. Good to connect with her. She who had survived this with him. 'It's not your fault. No one expected monsters now.'

Oljon appeared, wearing his pointed Aculei mask. 'Fhiro!' he cried. Then he saw Chenessa.

'It's not your fault!' Fhiro said to her. Then he removed his arm from behind Chenessa's neck and, shaking, stood up to look at his father.

'You have a lot of explaining to do, apprentice,' said Oljon.

Tubrin rushed into view. He planted his furious gaze on Oljon and then Fhiro. The priests that followed him surrounded Chenessa.

'Are you all right, young madam?' one asked her.

Tubrin took a step back, still watching Fhiro and Oljon, then spun his head to check the other groups of people nearby, his eyes burning with fury. Fhiro thought he looked ready to draw his weapon and kill everyone in the room.

'Whatever you were up to,' said Oljon, 'I hope it wasn't your idea.'

'Chenessa …' Fhiro stopped himself. 'I should've known better.' He thought about Hussuf. 'Her bodyguard got killed … by that thing.'

Oljon pulled his son to into an embrace. 'Forgive my anger, Fhiro,' he whispered, and then, getting closer to Fhiro's ear. 'It terrifies me to think of losing you.'

Fhiro collapsed into his father's arms. He had to bite his own lip to stop himself from weeping.

'Be strong, son,' Oljon whispered. 'Let's get out of here.'

* * *

Work resumed around the clearing within an hour. Now there were graves to be dug as well.

The turrets on top of the fort stayed on permanent alert, manned on short shifts to ensure vigilance and fast reactions. The civilians of each of the visiting nations were now sealed within their quarters, guarded by a troop of their own soldiers. Paranoia and fear had reached a new level throughout the fort.

Fhiro had asked about the archaeologists. Cerilina, Borlin and their friends had not returned from the mountain. There was nothing to be done for them now except hope they could get high enough to escape the fire and could find refuge from marauding beasts.

A low-pitched, crackling murmur from outside grumbled into a steady roar as the night drew on.

'We've got to see it,' said Fhiro.

Imial, lying in his bed, said nothing.

'Come on!' Fhiro got out from under his own covers and started changing.

'Haven't you been through enough today?' asked Imial.

Fhiro paused at the door. 'I have,' he said, but he still needed to see it. He pushed the door open and marched into the corridor.

Before it shut behind him Imial came through as well. 'We're supposed to be in bed, though.'

'So the worst they can do is send us back there,' said Fhiro, creeping along the corridor. He glanced over his shoulder. 'Try not to make such a racket.'

'I'm being quiet,' said Imial in a harsh whisper.

Fhiro followed the corridor to Valachrad's meeting room. He was almost at the door when it opened in front of him. Fhiro stopped fast, noticing his father's face before Imial

bumped into him, sending him sprawling. 'Hi Pa,' he said, his face an inch from the floor.

Oljon sighed. 'I can't say I'm surprised.' He took Fhiro's arm and pulled him up, then opened the door for them. 'Be quick, though. You should both be asleep.'

The Kartnan soldiers and officials, an orange glow across their faces as they stared out, made way for the boys at the window.

'It burns orange,' said Imial.

The forest was gone, replaced by black shadows, violent flames and clouds of smoke and ash. 'What were you expecting?' Fhiro asked. 'It's carbon based life out there.' He was sad to see it burning, but it was a beautiful sight to behold. The fire was everywhere, as far either side of the window as he could see.

When they returned to the same room in the morning all Fhiro could see was a charred wasteland. Black and grey spikes pierced the air everywhere he looked, and there was a powerful smell of burnt wood. 'How come it stopped?'

'It rained in the night,' said Oljon.

'As though the forest spirits willed it to,' said Fhiro.

'They aren't real, Fhiro,' said Oljon.

'Is anything?' When his father did not answer he asked, 'Any sign of Cerilina or Borlin?'

'No.'

After lunch, with still no word on the archaeologists, Fhiro decided he wanted to see Chenessa, and after much persuasion, Ghorad agreed to take the boys to the Creedate quarters. However, the elderly female yeal priest sent out to greet them turned them away: 'Sorry dears, she's resting.'

As the light outside dimmed, the lumia-crystals came alive with the energy that had been soaked up from the sun by their connected sister-crystals elsewhere on the fort surface. Then they too went out like stars hidden by unseen clouds.

Fhiro had trouble getting to sleep again that night. Looming forms, with sharp claws, chased him through dark corridors in his dreams. Sinister overweight men, who looked much like Valachrad and King Suloa, beat low-pitched drums above. The walls exploded, knocking him off his feet. Others, running with him, were crushed by tumbling masonry. The beasts in pursuit stumbled, rocked by erupting fires.

He awoke in darkness. 'You awake?' he asked Imial.

'Y-yes,' Imial stammered through chattering teeth.

The loud booming sound from his dream resonated through the room.

Fhiro got up and walked out into the corridor.

Imial scrambled out of bed and followed him.

Ghorad was talking with Pral. 'Go back to sleep,' he said.

'What's going on?' asked Fhiro.

'The turrets,' said Ghorad. 'They've been busy this night.'

'What are they firing at?' asked Fhiro.

'They are warding off beasts that come too close,' said Ghorad. 'They're trying not to kill any, but from what I hear a number of those fell creatures that attacked us before have been slain.'

'Do you think those monsters will get in here?' asked Imial.

'Not at this rate,' said Ghorad. 'Just try to sleep, Imial.'

Imial looked at the floor, then at Fhiro for a moment, and then at the floor again.

'Go to bed!' Ghorad ushered them into their room.

Fhiro tried to sleep, but between worrying about Cerilina and the other archaeologists trying to survive with all the creatures about, and the booming sounds above, he struggled.

'How did you manage to get away from … it?' asked Imial.

'I've been wondering about that too,' said Fhiro. 'Palis thinks the creature thought we were Chissids. That it assumed we must have disappeared into the water, or it would have chased us down to the lake.'

'How did you know what to do?' asked Imial. 'That monster was huge!'

'I didn't know what to do,' Fhiro admitted. 'I just made my best guess and hoped. I don't think I'd be here if I'd stayed still.'

Imial seemed to shift in his bed so that he was on the edge of it, and as close to Fhiro as he could possibly be. Fhiro wondered if this was some plan to reduce the risk of being eaten in case a monster got into the fort.

As the night rolled on, and Fhiro drifted in and out of consciousness, he saw that Imial was often awake and watching him, or just looking at the door.

'Imial,' Fhiro whispered as loud as he dared without disturbing his own, resting body, 'please go to sleep.'

Imial just looked back at him, silent.

Fhiro turned away. He knew, before he fell asleep this time, that his dreams would be cruel to him again. He tried not to imagine gleaming eyes, set above sharp teeth, watching the fort from not so far away. He tried to forget the graveling's roar.

* * *

'I would like to update you on our present situation,' Calthorn announced to the packed dining hall. The sleeping bags, used by those brought within the fort walls the day before, had been piled on top of each other at one edge of the great room. The skylight still filled the vast space with illumination, leaving little work for the crystal lamps in the walls.

'The ambassadors should have reached the capital by now,' continued Calthorn. 'The King should be sending aid, having received word of our misfortunes from the relay beacons. We expect it to arrive tomorrow evening or the day after. As many of you will have heard, we encountered trouble in the early hours of this morning. But have heart! Our brave gunners

were able to keep the beasts at bay. None came close to our gate. Thanks to the heroic efforts of you all with the forest clearing, our men have a clear view of all the creatures that approach. With the will of the spirits that watch over all of us, we will see through this peril.'

The soldiers of both Pelorn and the other nations cheered. Fhiro wondered how Calthorn had managed to remain in such good favour with these people, when they had endured such ill fortune under his watch.

'On a brighter note,' said Calthorn, 'we will be allowing people up on to the roof in small groups to watch the migrating herds for a while. If there is any consolation to be had from these unfortunate events, let us at least enjoy observing the spirits in their physical forms. Their magnificence is unparalleled, however terrible and dangerous they may be.'

After a few groups of adults had enjoyed the view from the turrets and returned safely, Imial and Fhiro were granted their request to go as well.

'What beast is what?' asked Imial.

The captain on the roof began to describe the animals as best he knew. There were countless yala beasts, usually in packs surrounding their young. They were huge and ate directly from the trees and the grass. Intermingled with them were the vicows. These were quite similar to the domesticated cattle of Andelic, but wild, thinner and stronger. The captain explained that, in general, both creatures were quite harmless unless induced into a stampede. That when their predators attacked from one direction a huge mass of animals might flee, levelling woodland in the process.

As they watched, a yala beast or a vicow would occasionally stray into the clearing. The turret gunners would fire close to them and the beasts would move away.

'Can I sit in the turret?' asked Imial.

The captain and the gunner shared a look with each other.

'Of course,' said the captain, forcing a smile.

'You're lucky,' muttered Ghorad.

They had a turn each. Fhiro was fortunate enough to be sitting there when a few vicows started walking towards the fort. The gunner checked his sights were aimed correctly and gave Fhiro permission to pull the trigger.

Dazzling bright light burst from the turret's muzzle, and scorched a path through the air to where the vicows were heading. Upon impact with the ground, mud sizzled, and the charred remains of burnt trees and foliage disintegrated into scattering, glowing embers. The vicows turned and sped towards the rest of their herd.

'So unfair!' said Imial.

'Can't you be happy for your friend?' asked the captain.

Fhiro grinned. His first time firing a crystal-fire weapon had been one he knew he would never forget.

Many other creatures passed by, including the much smaller collitails. When the captain explained they lived off the insects drawn by the dung of the yala beasts, Imial snarled. 'It shall be your name for a week if you lose again at *Sky Lord*.'

Fhiro ignored him.

There were also low-flying bird-like creatures. The captain called them pelorni vultures. They rarely troubled people but lived off the carcasses of the dead herd creatures.

Then he pointed out a group of predators. 'See those strange things walking over there? One might mistake them for men if they stood still.'

Imial borrowed the captain's telescope. 'They have black eyes,' he said.

'Yes,' said the captain. 'Featureless black eyes. One never quite knows which way they are looking. They are called

curuski. They usually feed off the young vicows, but sometimes they gather together and swarm up on much larger animals.'

'Can this turret kill them?' asked Imial.

'Oh, easily' said the captain, 'and so can most of our weapons. It is only the gravelings for which the turrets seem essential. They are troublingly resistant to our rifles.'

'Where are the gravelings?' asked Fhiro.

The captain hesitated, and Fhiro suspected he knew how close he had been to one. 'I assume they must be lurking deeper in the forest, setting ambushes for the other creatures. They are a little big to be sneaking up undetected during daylight.'

'And what are those great big things over there?' Fhiro pointed further out to where large shapes seemed to be bobbing under and then over the forest tree tops.

'I think they must be Rithuels,' said the captain. 'It has been a long time since I was in school and I have never been posted to this continent before. With the exception of the odd bandit group that sets up a base out here, this place rarely requires a soldier's attention.'

'Who, in the fort knows the most about the creatures?' asked Fhiro.

The captain thought for a moment. 'Presumably the ecologist that spoke to us.'

'Let's get him to talk to us,' said Fhiro. He looked at Ghorad.

'I'll ask Palis,' said Ghorad.

'I believe he has holed himself up in the Barons' quarters,' said the captain.

CHAPTER 23

'Do we really have to have teaching today?' asked Imial, the next day, as Ghorad led them from their quarters.

'Yes,' said Ghorad.

'But Yogric is so annoying,' said Fhiro.

'Well Yogric happens to be unwell,' said Ghorad.

'So teaching is cancelled!' declared Fhiro.

'Actually,' said Ghorad, as he led them into a wide corridor, 'someone else has volunteered to teach you instead.'

Fhiro saw Palis standing in the corridor.

'Welcome, boys, Ghorad,' said Palis.

'Are you going to teach us?' asked Imial.

'I was going to show you around this fort,' said Palis, 'and then Ghorad told me how keen you were to know more about the spirit-beasts, so we came up with another idea.'

'It'd better be a good idea,' said Imial.

'Dr Watchal, the ecologist, has kindly agreed to teach you today,' said Palis.

'That strange yeal who brought the bad news?' Imial whispered to Fhiro.

There were several booming sounds from outside.

'The turret doesn't normally sound that way,' said Imial.

'Perhaps it needs a repair,' said Ghorad, 'or perhaps they've made some modifications.'

'I'm sure we'll find out,' said Palis. 'If the others don't arrive soon I can send someone to ask for us.'

'Who else is coming?' asked Ghorad.

Just then Tubrin rounded the corner, and behind him were Chenessa and several more Creedate guards.

'Chenessa,' said Fhiro.

Chenessa saw them. She looked as though she was trying to smile, but her expression ended in a frown.

'This is a . . .' Ghorad hesitated. '. . . welcome surprise, though I would like to know why the Creedate must bring so many guards to this *teaching session.*'

Tubrin stood still and stared at Ghorad. Then he looked over his shoulder at Chenessa and the other guards. 'Go,' he said to the men, and they left. Tubrin turned back to Ghorad, but said nothing.

'Thank you,' said Ghorad.

'Excellent,' said Palis. 'Would you all like to accompany me, then?'

Fhiro dropped back to fall into step beside Chenessa as soon as they set off. 'Are you all right?'

She frowned and shrugged.

Fhiro smiled at her. 'I'm so glad you made it, for what it's worth.'

'Thanks.' She bit her lip.

Fhiro noticed Tubrin, walking a few feet behind, was glowering at him. The smouldering hatred in the Creedate guard's eyes was so intense Fhiro felt his skin start to burn.

'Where are we having this teaching?' asked Imial.

'The Barons' quarters,' said Palis, 'where Dr Watchal has taken up residence.'

'Quite a smuggler's maze, this place, isn't it,' said Fhiro after they had walked for some time.

'They were in the business of hiding things,' said Chenessa.

Palis smiled at them. 'Not much further.'

Ahead, Imial was explaining something to Ghorad with enthusiasm that Ghorad did not seem to share.

'He's an interesting one,' said Chenessa.

'Imial?' asked Fhiro. 'I'd agree with that.'

Chenessa and Fhiro caught up with Imial, leaving Tubrin behind. One at a time they ducked under Imial's flailing arm as he gesticulated about the size of a bird he had ridden with his father the previous year. 'What's your ambition, Imial?' Chenessa asked.

'I'll go to an academy,' he said. 'With father's help, and if I get the right grades, I should get in.' Then he went silent and looked down.

'Is that the ambition?' asked Fhiro. He could hear Tubrin, behind them, picking up his pace to catch up. 'You just want to get into the academy? What about after that?' Before Imial could answer, though, Fhiro was quick to add: 'We of the Aculei have little knowledge of these things.'

Imial frowned. 'Well, if you get through academy training you'll almost always do well.'

'What do they teach you there?' asked Chenessa.

'In addition to learning academic rigour and developing expertise in a science or an art, they teach you to be a leader,' said Imial. 'You have to learn about politics, military strategy, and also religion.'

'So no thoughts on what you'll do after?' asked Fhiro.

'Most serve in Kartna's armed forces for a while,' said Imial. 'With good enough grades you can get promoted straight to a commanding role. Some great generals won battles months after graduating.'

'That sounds like a terrible idea,' said Chenessa. 'Are they that short of older generals?'

'I think it was during the wars with the stupid Ruks,' said Imial.

'It was,' Ghorad interrupted, casting a glance over his shoulder at Tubrin. 'Many of our leaders had been killed or captured in an act of treachery, so promotion during that war was very fast.'

'And our freshly trained generals were magnificent,' said Imial, turning his nose up at no one in particular. 'We have the finest military.'

'Did you think so well of your military during your Martial Uprising?' asked Tubrin.

'You know our history well,' said Ghorad. 'Indeed, promotion was fast then, too.'

Fhiro longed to know more about the Martial Uprising, if only to know what exactly his father had done in it, but like the Sufferers, it was a subject none of the Kartnans, even Ghorad, wanted to speak about. Fhiro suspected it was something of a taboo subject. He should have asked Borlin.

Thinking of Borlin, he hoped the archaeologists were safe.

Palis had brought them towards the southern part of the fort. They turned down a long passageway in which there was a set of silver-plated double doors. Palis opened them, and ushered everyone in.

The walls were red, and the furniture of the room was made from red stained wood. Lumia-crystals rather than skylights provided the illumination. 'This is the entrance chamber to the Barons' quarters,' said Palis.

'So this is where the ruler of this drug–' Fhiro stopped himself. 'I mean, this *narcotic substance* factory, lived?'

'These were their living quarters, and also the command base,' said Palis. 'General Calthorn preferred to set himself up closer to the Great Hall so he could have easier access to the visiting delegations and the entrance to the fort. There was also the matter of the protected status of this part of the fort.'

'Protected status?' asked Ghorad.

'The contents of this area,' said Palis, 'cannot be changed. It's to preserve this historic example of how our ancestors lived.'

'So Calthorn could not alter the room to suit his needs,' said Ghorad.

'No,' said Palis, 'and when you see the inside of it, you'll see why it would not quite do for him.' He walked forwards and knocked on the tall wooden door at the other end of the entrance chamber. He knocked again twice more before opening it himself. 'It's a large suite. He probably cannot hear us. We shall find him.'

At the far end of the suite they found Dr Watchal kneeling on the floor, staring up at a fire rising out of a bowl. On the other side of the room a keen-faced earthman, carrying a rifle, stood up. 'Are you the doctor's expected guests?' he asked.

'We are,' said Palis.

The bowl rested on a lattice of red-stained wood, filled with low-intensity lumia-crystals, which stretched out around the doctor, forming a shrine. Abstract, multi-limbed statues surrounding it cast shadows on the tapestry-covered walls beyond.

Fhiro wondered if Palis was going to give the doctor a lecture on fire safety, but instead Palis spoke to the armed earthman. 'You are dressed as an officer from Hithostun.'

'I'm Andric,' said the earthman. 'I was guarding ambassador Winle, but she no longer needs my services. She ordered me to protect the doctor here, while he contemplated the beast spirits and prayed for our protection.'

Palis turned to those he had brought with him. 'You see. There may be much history between Pelorn and Hithostun, and much of it incites the mind to anger. However, Niquani of all nations are united in their beliefs.'

'Your guests are not Niquani?' asked Andric. 'They must know to respect this place.'

'They do,' said Palis. 'Is the doctor expected to finish his contemplations soon? I did tell him we would arrive at this time.'

Dr Watchal stood and smiled. 'Yes, I've been expecting you.'

'Excellent,' said Palis.

The ecologist strode over to them. 'Sit here, children. It is such a pleasure to host you in this marvellous place.'

Fhiro nodded. He liked the alternative, if somewhat weird, decor. He noticed, however, that neither Chenessa nor Imial reacted, except to sit down.

'You wish to know about the creatures that inhabit this continent, do you?' Dr Watchal sat before them. 'Or did you want to hear recitals of ancient Niquani poems?'

'The animals, please,' said Imial.

'Very well,' said Dr Watchal, smiling again.

Palis and Andric sat down where they were, while Ghorad and Tubrin rested against opposite walls from one another.

'Is there any particular creature you would first like to hear of in particular?' Dr Watchal stared at Fhiro.

'Tell us about ...' Fhiro started.

'Gravelings!' said Imial.

Tubrin spluttered.

'Dr Watchal, please,' said Ghorad. 'This subject is not appropriate at this time, for obvious reasons.'

'It's all right,' said Dr Watchal, looking at Fhiro and Chenessa in turn. 'I understand that these are not creatures we want to actively remember, though when the two of you have recovered from your experience I would dearly like to know more about it. I, myself, have never been a fraction as close to one as you have. They may be despised tormentors of the worshipful yala and vicow, but their spiritual significance is not to be underestimated.'

'That's very nice,' said Palis, 'but it's also more than enough on the subject. Why don't we talk about–?'

'I don't want to remember that experience,' said Chenessa, 'but I would like to know more about that monster.'

'Gravelings?' asked Imial, hopeful.

'Yes,' she said.

'Me too,' said Fhiro.

Dr Watchal nodded, and glanced at Ghorad and Tubrin. Neither guard verbally protested, though both looked uncomfortable. 'Very well.' The Doctor adjusted his position and stared out into space. 'The thing is that to understand the gravelings, you must understand them in the spiritual context, as well as their physical sense. You see, the yala beasts and vicows, and other herbivores of Fawast, are sacred, for they sustained us Niquani through our early years, and have watched over our evolution as a culture, just as Pelorn watched over their evolution. However, would they exist without their predators? They are a symbiont twin. One cannot exist without the other. Their energies are lost when their physical forms die, and are then harnessed into new forms for the housing of the same spirits in their next incarnations. Only through perceiving this–'

'No,' said Fhiro.

'... can the deeper comprehension–' Dr Watchal looked at Fhiro. 'Sorry?'

'They don't need each other to exist,' said Fhiro. 'They *would* not have come into existence without each other, because the evolution of each influenced the evolution of the other. But right now, if you killed all the predators, then there would be a massive expansion in the herbivores. Loads of them would then die when they used up all the food, but others would still survive and there would be more herbivores overall. The predators need the prey, not the other way around.'

Dr Watchal closed his eyes and let out a long, lingering sigh. 'You are seeing this too simplistically. Viewing these creatures as mere animals prevents you from seeing what existence really means for them. They are temples that house the spirits

that we attune ourselves to. If you allowed them to expand in such a fashion there would be a crisis of communion between spirits and their physical forms.'

'So there are only so many spirits,' said Fhiro, 'and if you allow them to breed too much you might have spirit-less herbivores running around?'

'I'd prefer it if it were not put so crudely,' said Dr Watchal.

'Didn't the animals from this planet populate the wildlife of the surrounding systems?' asked Fhiro.

'Yes,' said Dr Watchal.

'So how come there were enough spirits for all those entire planets, then? You can't really be worried about a yala beast population boom on Pelorn.'

'The spirits were merciful in their expansions, or possibly divisions, to encompass our sister nations,' said Dr Watchal. 'Their ways are mysterious, though magnificent.'

Fhiro wanted to say more. He was fed up with all these religious authorities spouting nonsense all day long. However, he controlled himself. He could see Ghorad glaring at him. He had to stop causing trouble.

Dr Watchal smiled again. 'Only when–'

'Can I make a suggestion?' said Chenessa. 'Maybe it would seem less mysterious if you considered the yala beasts as animals, and not as spirits?'

'This attitude does shock me!' said Dr Watchal. 'I offer to teach you the mysteries of our culture, our way of life, and you insult my statements without the slightest shred of care or compassion.'

Palis's jaw dropped open. He glanced at Chenessa and then Tubrin.

'You can't pretend that critical thinking doesn't apply where Niquani philosophy is concerned,' said Chenessa. 'It's too important. People are dying and killing each other every day

over these beliefs. You should think more carefully about your statements.'

Andric stood up. 'And no doubt you feel your Calling and all its contradictory teachings is more carefully thought through?'

Tubrin stood, hand on his pistol, and glowered at Andric. 'Do *not* speak so of The Calling.'

Tubrin's reaction startled Chenessa. 'I didn't mean to cause offence,' she said, speaking fast. 'Forget I spoke so.'

'You cannot go about insulting entire cultures when it pleases you,' said Andric, taking a step towards Chenessa, 'then walk away from your mess so easily.' His lips formed a cold smile, while his eyes flashed with anger. 'Why, little girl, perhaps you should think more carefully about your statements!'

'I apologise!' said Chenessa quickly. 'I was wrong. Please accept my apology.'

'There is no need for you to apologise to this fool,' said Tubrin, still glaring at Andric. 'Show respect to the daughter of our ambassador.'

'All right!' Palis raised his hands to restore order. 'Andric, she has apologised. Please accept and apologise yourself. We need to end this conversation now.' He glanced at Fhiro. 'An apology from you, young man, wouldn't hurt either.'

'Sorry!' blurted Fhiro.

Andric grunted in annoyance, but then he stood tall. 'I apologise for causing any offence. I said what I said because I had been offended myself. However, I should have considered that these two are only young and have yet to learn to not go about criticising the faiths of others. No belief exists that cannot be shaken to its foundations by questions put forward out of context and understanding.'

Palis smiled. 'Very wise, Andric.'

'Clearly, then, you have ignored the message of The Calling, if you have even heard it at all,' said Tubrin, 'because no sound mind can dispute the compelling arguments that guide the soul towards Aten's embrace.'

'Any argument is compelling if disputing it amounts to suicide,' retorted Andric.

Tubrin's eyes glowered. 'I have had enough of playing diplomat here. You Niquani are as bad as these snake lovers.' He gestured towards Imial, Fhiro and Ghorad.

'Tubrin!' cried Palis. 'Please calm down.'

'You insult our gods?' asked Ghorad. 'Tread carefully now, Creedate dog.'

'Why?' asked Tubrin, now turning to Ghorad. He pointed at Fhiro. 'You Kartnans make no effort to restrain yourselves. This boy mocks this ecologist priest here and now. Earlier he ridiculed Master Saflua in public. If he knew the punishment he deserves according to our laws, he would quake in dread. We have dungeons where the blasphemers go, locked away to be enlightened through excruciating pain. Better to experience a year of hell, here in this galaxy, than an eternity of it in the afterlife.'

Fhiro felt fear like an ice-cold knife cutting his heart into tiny slivers, as his mind conjured images of the cruelty and torture he might yet be subjected to, if he were ever to fall into Creedate hands.

'Just you even try it,' said Ghorad, his hand now resting on the butt of his own pistol.

'Think you could stop me?' Tubrin snarled. 'I know your type. You'd slither away rather than stand and fight.'

'Only cowards waste words when the time is nigh,' said Ghorad.

Tubrin swept back his cloak and draped a hand across one of several knives fastened to his belt. 'Call me a coward? Dare

to think that *I* am afraid?' He grinned. 'Perhaps I should teach you a thing or two about fear.'

Ghorad's arm twitched. The next instant both he and Tubrin were aiming their pistols at each other's faces.

Palis put himself between the two of them. 'Enough!' he cried. 'There will be no violence here. You are on our planet and are subject to our laws. You also stand in the presence of a holy shrine and his reverence, Dr Watchal.'

'Small fish should know when to get out of the way,' said Tubrin. 'Against the will of Aten, your laws are nothing.'

'You Creedate will churn up the galaxy and turn it into the stench ridden waste your heartworlds have become,' said Ghorad. 'You forget yourselves. Imperial boots will crush your hordes underfoot, and our glorious fleet will turn your armadas into ash.'

'You see!' said Andric, pointing it at Tubrin and Ghorad. 'We are just little people in their eyes. To be swept aside in their contest for galactic domination. No wonder they think nothing of mocking our ways.'

A booming sound shook the room.

Fhiro glanced at both bodyguards, terrified that either of them, but especially Ghorad, might now fall to the ground.

There was another deep, thunderous boom.

'That's the southern turret,' said Ghorad, his hands unflinching.

Similar but fainter sounds echoed through the walls.

'They're all firing,' said Palis, 'and far more frequently than before. Will you two put aside these petty differences and do your jobs? Something is amiss out there and you want to fight each other?'

'Petty differences?' asked Tubrin. 'These petty differences hold the fate of your planet at their mercy.'

Palis gasped. Andric chambered a bullet in his rifle and aimed it at Tubrin.

The booming continued.

Fhiro did not want anyone to die. His big stupid mouth would finally draw blood, and if it was not his own, it might be poor Ghorad's.

'Can you all stop?' cried Chenessa, tears falling from her eyes.

'You two foreign powers,' said Dr Watchal, 'have no idea what you are doing here, do you? You might laugh at our ways, but the forests of Fawast will soon correct your misunderstandings. Sadly I doubt either of you will live long enough for the spirits to forgive you.'

Ghorad holstered his weapon, but remained where he stood, his eyes fixed on Tubrin. 'Chenessa's right. We need to find out what's happening.'

Tubrin lowered his weapon too, and then holstered it. 'I will not forget this, Kartnan.'

Fhiro almost fainted, so overwhelmed with relief on seeing Tubrin put his gun away.

Palis turned to Andric. 'Please check the corridor. We'll see you in the entrance chamber to the Barons' quarters in a moment.' After Andric left Palis addressed the others, 'All of you, we may be in danger. I implore you to forget about this senseless arguing. We must hold it together, despite our frayed nerves and the foul cloud of conspiracy and paranoia that hangs over us.'

'Agreed,' said Ghorad.

Tubrin pulled his cloak closer about himself.

'Please follow Andric as far as the entrance chamber and remain there,' said Palis. 'I'll follow you all.'

'A nice little chain of babysitters we are now,' murmured Tubrin as he marched Chenessa to the front, ahead of Ghorad, Imial and Fhiro. 'We look after these children, and you're looking after us?'

'Something like that,' said Palis.

Fhiro resented Tubrin taking the lead position, but he felt better knowing the Creedate guard could not just shoot Ghorad in the back whenever he wanted to.

Palis walked into the hallway, casting a glance back into the entrance chamber from time to time to check on Ghorad and Tubrin. 'Andric!' he called towards the east.

Whenever Palis's attention was not with them, though, Fhiro's fear of Tubrin rose again. The Creedate guard looked determined to avenge his honour, and his stare had no focus other than Ghorad. Ghorad, though, seemed oblivious to this, and Fhiro wondered where he found the confidence to act so calm.

After a minute the Hithostun guard returned.

'What news?' asked Palis, as Ghorad and Tubrin left the entrance chamber to hear what Andric had to say.

'I've passed many soldiers,' replied Andric. 'They've all been ordered to return to their posts, but they don't know why. Some haven't even stopped to talk.'

'What new devilry is at work now?' asked Ghorad.

A crash ripped through the air, startling Fhiro, accompanied by the screeching of tearing metal. The floor and walls shook.

'That was to the north,' said Andric.

'The main gate?' Ghorad hesitated. 'We should stay here until someone speaks to us.'

Fhiro ventured out after the guards. At the far end of the corridor he could see soldiers running. The crack of projectile weapons echoed in the distance.

'Rifle fire,' muttered Tubrin.

A shrill scream pierced the air.

'This does not bode well,' said Ghorad.

Fhiro retreated into the entrance chamber. He stared at

Imial, and then at Chenessa, as images of the graveling attack came to his mind. Could another of those creatures have made it to the fort wall?

'I was among our troops only yesterday,' said Andric. 'Why is it that I'm left looking after this man when there is finally some action?'

'Do not get ahead of yourself,' said Ghorad. 'All our skills may be called upon soon.'

'Your charge is safer here I suspect,' said Palis.

'Please, Andric,' said Dr Watchal, 'you are under no obligation from me to remain.'

'Ambassador Winle made me pledge to protect you,' said Andric. 'And yet, nothing is happening here. We need more information. One of us should venture north to find out.'

There was more booming from the turrets, and each time Fhiro flinched. Further cracks and rattles of rifle fire followed.

'I think you are right,' said Palis, 'and I think you are best placed among us to go. I will protect Dr Watchal until you return.'

'I cannot leave my charge,' said Tubrin, 'or I would willingly go with you.'

Ghorad nodded at Andric, who then sped off.

'Children,' said Ghorad, 'stay in the entrance room. Dr Watchal, I suggest you do the same.'

'What's going on?' asked Imial.

'You know as much as we do.' Ghorad showed the boys through the doors. 'We'll hear something soon enough.' Once they were in the entrance chamber of the Barons' quarters, Ghorad returned to the corridor.

Imial sat down and twiddled his thumbs. Chenessa was gazing at the floor in silence. Fhiro tried to catch her eye, but she did not look up. Despite being with them, he felt alone and afraid. It felt like death, foiled in its attempts to take him

several times now, was rolling the dice once more. It was not a game Fhiro wanted to play.

He saw that Dr Watchal was praying. 'What are you praying for?' he asked, hoping for an answer that might lift his mood.

'That the will of the spirits be done,' said Dr Watchal, without opening his eyes. 'There is little point in praying for anything else.'

'Because the spirits will do what they want anyway?' asked Fhiro. 'Why pray, then?'

'Fhiro!' Imial glared at him.

'Sorry,' muttered Fhiro. He saw, however, that Chenessa had turned away from Dr Watchal, and that there was a hint of a smile on her lips. This made him feel better.

'I'm sure we'll be fine, everyone,' said Imial, nodding to himself. 'Don't worry. Ghorad is very good.'

Fhiro frowned. He looked at Chenessa again, but she still faced a different direction. Perhaps she feared talking to him now Tubrin's temper was up. Fhiro studied the Creedate guard through the doors to the corridor. Tubrin's outward calmness was little disguise for the hostile energy ablaze within.

A while later Ghorad called out, 'Andric is returning, and with help.'

Fhiro and Imial crept closer to the doors to hear what was said.

'A swarm of curuski have attacked the fort,' said Andric, his breathing heavy. A group of soldiers had come with him. 'There was a stampede of yala and vicows that stormed straight into our walls.'

'How come they came towards us?' asked Ghorad. 'Dr Watchal, what is happening?'

The doctor walked past Fhiro and Imial to speak to the guards from the doorway. 'Such stampedes may happen of their own accord, but they may also be triggered by predators.

Why they came towards the fort, though, does not make sense. It is an obvious obstacle.'

'General Calthorn suspects they took the path of least resistance,' said Andric. 'The clearing is far easier going than the forest.'

'The damned clearing!' cried Tubrin. 'First the birds are slain and now this!'

'You see,' said Dr Watchal, 'the spirits avenge the great savagery General Calthorn has unleashed upon our world.'

Fhiro peered round the doors into the corridor. He recognised Yelba, Valachrad's chief servant, and a few other civilians standing with the Hithostun and Pelorn soldiers Andric had brought.

'We cannot blame Calthorn,' said Ghorad. 'The decision was sound. I have never known a general so willing to take responsibility for so many mishaps.'

'It is the sign of a general who has made too many mistakes to try to hide them,' said Tubrin.

'Let's not have another disagreement, shall we?' asked Palis.

Some of the soldiers Andric had brought looked startled by the tone of Palis's voice.

Andric raised his hand to calm them. 'Trust me; our Kartnan and Creedate guests seem in need of such gentle reminders from time to time.'

'Calthorn's intentions have always been noble,' said Palis, glaring at Tubrin. 'He could not have predicted this.' He looked at Dr Watchal. 'Really, I hold you in high regard, but I have no wish to hear further, misguided statements against the general.'

'Soldier as you will, soldier,' said Dr Watchal, 'and close your ears at your own peril. I shall wait within the Barons' quarters and pray for our survival.' He disappeared into the rooms beyond the entrance chamber.

'We have no idea how smart these gravelings are,' said Ghorad. 'Are they territorial? Or have they got wind of the fresh meat behind these walls?'

'It is a costly meal, if so,' said Andric. 'Many curuski and gravelings have already been felled attempting to enter here. I consider this ill fortune for all concerned.'

'Tell us, Andric,' said Palis, 'how do our defences now stand?'

Fhiro scowled as Imial tried to squeeze past him to hear better.

'The troops have withdrawn from the front rooms and are fighting the curuski in the corridors,' Andric replied. 'Their task is complicated by vicows that have accidentally found their way inside, and civilians that must be escorted to the main hall. However, being far down the southern end of the fort, it is Calthorn's wish that we remain here. This place should be easy to defend, and it is dangerous to make the journey to the main hall with so many foul beasts lurking in the corridors in between.'

Tubrin snarled. 'This news is grim.'

'How many breaches have there been?' asked Ghorad.

'Many, it seems,' said Andric. 'We encountered a group of curuski ourselves on our way down here.'

'They want us to hold here until when, exactly?' asked Ghorad.

'We have carried enough supplies to last until tomorrow,' said Andric, 'by which time we expect to be extracted. If, at any point, Calthorn feels the corridors have been successfully cleared, then he will send us word.'

'I see you have chosen an old friend of mine to bring with you,' Ghorad remarked.

'Who?' asked Andric.

Ghorad pointed to one of the Pelorn soldiers who had

accompanied Andric. ‘This one and I had a little misunderstanding recently.’

Fhiro recognised the Pelorn soldier who had pointed a weapon at Ghorad’s head the other day.

‘Private Jammit?’ asked Palis. ‘We can send him back if you wish.’

Jammit hung his head.

Ghorad sighed. ‘No. Just keep him under a close watch. Meanwhile, I am pleased to see you, Yelba.’

‘I’m here to provide for Imial,’ she said, raising her eyebrows.

Imial squealed in delight from the entrance.

‘But keep us alive and we’ll keep you fed,’ she added.

* * *

The soldiers that Andric had brought stayed on guard in the corridor while the rest remained in the entrance chamber. The tension between Ghorad and Tubrin was so fierce Fhiro feared he would be cut in half every time he passed them. Watchal, meanwhile, emerged and disappeared according to his own desires, to either pray at the shrine or be closer to the spirits that were roaming so close by. Yelba and her colleagues found the kitchen within the Barons’ quarters and prepared them all some lunch. All the while the sounds of gunfire varied in frequency and intensity, with periods of silence between. Fhiro was glad he had brought some playing cards. They were a welcome distraction to occupy his mind, and anyone else who cared to play with him. At first it was just him and Imial, but soon Chenessa joined them, and after a while all the soldiers and servants were dealing themselves into games when on breaks from their duties.

But every time Fhiro started to feel himself relax, a sound

from somewhere in the fort would remind him how much danger he was in. Nearby people were fighting for their lives.

When the lumia-crystals had adjusted their hue to signify that the sun outside was gone, and the smells of Yelba's cooking had returned telling all of them that dinner was on its way, the guards in the hallway shouted that someone was coming. The boys followed Ghorad, Tubrin and Palis into the corridor.

Oljon had appeared, still wearing his mask, with a heavy rifle strapped to his back. With him were two Kartnan soldiers, one of which was Pral, the soldier who had greeted them aboard the Siwob.

'Why have you come, priest?' asked Tubrin.

'It is fitting I am with my apprentice in this dark hour,' said Oljon. 'If he is to become one of our number I must know how he processes his fear. Come, Fhiro! Let us hold our conversation.' Then he turned to the two men who had escorted him. 'I release you from the task of accompanying me, as instructed by Captain Jard. You may stay or leave.'

Pral and the other soldier looked at one another. 'With your permission, Priest Veltir, I think we would do better to stay,' said Pral. 'There are few fighters here and the night holds unknown dangers. Returning in the dark would not be wise.'

'Is there any word on when it will be safe again?' asked Ghorad.

'Not yet,' said Oljon. 'There are areas of the fort we still need to clear. These curuski appear in unexpected places. They have even climbed upon our roof and slain our turret gunners so that a graveling was able to inflict great damage to the entrance. It is now a precarious network of fortifications that protect the main hall and the civilians within.'

'What a nightmare,' said Yelba.

'There has also been another development,' said Oljon,

'though it seems of little importance now. The explosives Calthorn had prepared to drain the lake were detonated somehow.'

'What?' asked Palis. 'How?'

'Presumably from some tampering by the animals.'

'So has the lake drained?' asked Andric.

'Yes,' said Oljon. 'More than that, it has penetrated the repaired sealing in the lower chambers of this building where the narcotics factory used to operate. Those floors are filling with lake water as we speak.'

'There are floors underneath us?' asked Fhiro.

'I had hoped to show you, to be honest,' said Palis.

'Very strange,' said Ghorad, 'but if the lake hides an entrance to the mountain, at least we might finally get some answers.'

'Dr Watchal will be furious,' muttered Andric. 'I had best tell him.'

Oljon took Fhiro to a corner and brought their heads close together. 'Tell me of your fears, apprentice.'

Fhiro wanted to hug his father. 'I'm so glad you're alive!'

'The spirits of Pelorn will have to try harder than this if they want to kill me,' said Oljon through the mask.

Fhiro imagined his father was grinning.

'So, how are you?'

Fhiro thought for a moment. 'Afraid, I suppose.' He was so glad his father had come. 'I can't tell how much danger we're in.'

'I think it's fair to say it is significant,' said Oljon, 'but you're right. It's a very unusual situation, and these Niquani know surprisingly little about the predators that inhabit their planet, so careful have they been to avoid interfering with the ecology of this continent.'

'What if they attack us here?' Fhiro looked around, and wondered if he would hold it together if he saw hordes of monsters coming towards him.

'Whatever happens, try to stay calm,' said Oljon, as though he had read Fhiro's mind. 'You did fine on Calagan. Just make sure you stay close to me.'

Fhiro nodded. 'Is there a spare rifle I can have?'

'The last thing I want is for you to be in harm's way,' said Oljon. 'Just stay behind me or the others.'

'All right.' Fhiro nodded. 'What if there's a graveling?'

'They cannot fit through these corridors,' Oljon replied. 'The turrets are manned again, and are taking care of those fiends for now.'

After the evening meal the representatives from each nation took rooms to settle down in overnight. Makeshift beds were prepared from antique linen, cushions and blankets. Meanwhile, beyond the entrance of the Barons' quarters, the fort at large was silent.

At the end of the first three-hour shift, Fhiro leaned close to their door to hear Andric talking to Palis.

'Three hours without gunfire,' Andric whispered. 'If they have cleared the corridors they should send for us.'

'I would not,' said Oljon. 'It is dark now. They'd best wait until the lighter hours.'

The second watch, however, was not quiet. Gunfire erupted again. Only two shots were from the turrets. The rest was small arms fire.

Imial sat up in his bed. Fhiro could tell Ghorad, Pral, Yelba and the other soldier were awake, even though they were supposed to be resting. After a while Fhiro sat up as well, but said nothing. He tried not to imagine what might be happening elsewhere in the building, but failed to block images of gravelings flashing through his head. Some minutes later he heard Andric's voice shouting.

'Who goes there? Answer or we will fire!'

Then there were shots from nearby.

'Stay here, Pral,' said Ghorad as he got up and left.

Pral pulled his rifle across his chest, and followed Ghorad to the open door, keeping a watch out of it. Fhiro could see Tubrin marching out and heading towards the corridor.

'It's all right,' Ghorad said when he returned. 'Something came our way. Not human, but alone. It's gone now.'

'The fighting is still happening,' said Imial, as rattles of weapon fire could be heard in the distance.

'I don't like leaving others to fight on my behalf,' said Ghorad as he sat down. 'All we can do is sit tight and wait.' He lay down. 'Wait, and rest if we can.'

But Fhiro knew he would not rest well tonight. Much as he felt safer for his father's presence, the dangers lurking the corridors that night strained his frayed nerves.

Unaware he had fallen asleep, a hideous roar dragged him awake. The ground shook. He was sitting bolt upright in bed staring at the shocked face of Imial, who had sat up at the same time.

'What happened?'

Pral's voice answered him. 'Not sure.' The soldier stood by the door, calm and alert, rifle at the ready.

Fhiro felt his heart rate slow a little.

'The gunfight from around the main hall ended a while ago,' Pral went on. 'Much crashing and screeching, as though the fort was coming down around us. Then nothing until now.'

As he spoke, the gunfire started up again, louder than before, and intensified until all Fhiro wanted to do was jam his hands over his ears and dive back under the covers. There was no let up for what felt like hours, but then the barrage subsided, dying away to nothing.

After a moment, Pral asked no one in particular, 'Did we win the day?'

No one answered him.

CHAPTER 24

The lumia-crystals came alive at sunrise, channelling light into the Barons' quarters.

Fhiro was so tired. He had to rub his eyes longer than usual to convince himself they were working normally. He looked to his right; two of the sleeping spaces were occupied by Pral and the other Kartnan soldier. His father and Ghorad were absent. He looked in the other direction and saw Imial, his lower eyelids a much darker shade than normal, sitting up again. 'Breakfast?'

Imial nodded. He glanced at the bed next to him. 'Yelba's gone.'

'Let's hope she's making something.'

They made their way to the kitchen where they found Yelba had put out a plate for each of them. Fhiro had already begun tucking in when Yelba came to join them.

'Didn't sleep much,' Imial whispered.

'I know.' Fhiro recalled Imial's occasional whimpering throughout the hours of darkness, even after the gunfire and the screeching sounds had ended.

'You don't look too troubled, Yelba,' said Imial.

'Would it make you feel better if I looked worried?'

Imial paused for a moment, but then tucked into his porridge again. 'No.'

Oljon, Ghorad, Tubrin, Andric and Palis came to sit with them, and soon after Pral joined them as well. 'Sleep well, apprentice?' asked Oljon.

'Er, yes, master,' said Fhiro.

Ghorad raised his eyebrows.

'Well not really,' Fhiro admitted. He noticed that Tubrin was not looking at him. He wondered if the Creedate guard was still as angry as he had been the day before.

Chenessa walked in with the Creedate servant and paused in the doorway. She glanced at Fhiro, Imial, and then Tubrin, but remained silent.

Tubrin half nodded to her.

Chenessa took the seat opposite Tubrin, next to Imial.

'What's happening out there?' asked Imial.

'We don't know,' said Oljon. 'We should consider ourselves fortunate to have only encountered one of these creatures.'

'A creature that seems to have disappeared,' said Andric. 'I saw it fall, but it's no longer where I shot it.'

'What if our would-be rescuers arrive but are too preoccupied saving our comrades in the Great Hall to remember us?' asked Palis.

'I'm sure they won't allow that to happen,' said Ghorad.

'What if Calthorn and the senior officers who know of our whereabouts are slain?' asked Andric. 'The rescue mission may leave with only the survivors they can see. Who would want to stay in this place?'

'I expect a comprehensive rescue with a large force,' said Oljon, 'though I could be mistaken.'

'Staying here is risky,' said Pral, 'but then so is travelling.'

'There is another matter we should attend to,' said Oljon, 'sooner rather than later.'

'And what matter is that?' asked Palis.

'The matter of command,' said Oljon.

Andric's eyes narrowed. 'I had thought that Palis, being appointed to watch over Pelorn's guests, was already acting in this capacity.'

'We do well to look to Palis for leadership when we are

together as a group, with time to discuss our decisions,' said Oljon. 'However, just because he is from Pelorn does not make him best suited to lead us if we are faced with an immediate threat.'

The expression on Palis's face began to darken.

'I mean no offence, Palis,' said Oljon. 'I hold you in the highest respect.'

Palis was about to speak, when Tubrin spoke before him.

'I am loath to say this,' said the Creedate guard, 'but the priest is right. We are all free. Palis has authority because he is our host, but what keeps us together is not our fear of Pelorn's laws, but the safety of numbers.'

'You are our guests,' said Palis, 'and our laws do apply.'

'Yet if I tried to leave here, you would not stop me,' said Tubrin. 'I stay here because this land is crawling with fell creatures that have killed an unknown number of our comrades over the last twenty-four hours.'

'Something tells me you would rather not be sharing living space with us,' muttered Pral.

Tubrin shot Pral a distasteful look, but then continued. 'Staying together increases our chances. Together we are far more effective as a fighting unit.'

'I suppose I have to agree with that,' said Andric.

'And if we have to fight,' said Tubrin, 'we will be far better off if we have already appointed a leader, rather than deciding who to follow in the heat of battle.'

Fhiro watched Ghorad look from Palis to Tubrin.

'I wish to remain in charge of the other Hithostun soldiers,' said Andric. 'One of them will surely second me.'

'Is that really how we are to decide this?' asked Palis.

Fhiro looked at his father, wondering if the others realised he had been a general, and a veteran of the second legion of Kartna, even if Fhiro was not entirely sure what the second

legion was.

'On second thoughts,' said Andric, 'would you, Palis, suffer to follow my orders if I was in charge?'

'Would you suffer mine?' Palis sighed. 'And I am to be assured that the Kartnan fighters here, and Tubrin, have extensive combat experience?'

'I would be happy to lead you all,' said Tubrin, 'but something tells me this masked one has seen more of war than I have.'

There was a stillness in the room as all eyes turned to Oljon.

Fhiro realised he was biting his lip.

'I have commanded fireteams, platoons, battalions and armies,' said Oljon, 'and I have seen through all manner of threats, up close and from afar.'

Palis exhaled and then said, 'The priest, then.'

'The priest,' said Tubrin, leaning back a little against his chair. 'The idea of following your orders repels and intrigues me. It will be both an honour and a great displeasure to serve under your command.'

'You're welcome,' said Oljon.

Ghorad had been glancing between the two of them. When nothing untoward happened he seemed to relax.

'Let us pray,' said Oljon, 'that we can work out together what we can ahead of time. Let us pray that the need for me to take command is never upon us.'

'Amen to that,' said Andric. 'So, given that we still have the luxury of being able to discuss our problems, who thinks we should wait it out here?'

'I think we should stay here a little longer,' said Palis.

'I agree,' said Oljon, 'though not for too long. If we don't hear anything for a while we will need to investigate. There should be the sound of fighting soon enough if the corridors are being cleared.'

They sat down to wait. Fhiro tried to catch up on sleep, his

appetite for playing cards having been lost overnight.

Every hour Imial would ask Yelba for another snack, and Fhiro was usually awake enough to request a portion for himself. The Creedate and the Pelorn servants, with nothing better to do, helped her with each of these tasks, and they always made enough for everyone. On the third occasion, as all of them shared plates of buttery pancakes, Andric spoke up, 'The servants might run out of ingredients for cakes if we wait much longer than this.'

'I'm fine waiting here,' mumbled private Jammit between mouthfuls.

Fhiro was not comfortable with private Jammit remaining among them. However, he did agree; they were safe here.

'We have heard no message, no shouts, no shots and no screams,' said Palis. 'It is too strange.'

'I cannot bear the thought of having abandoned my men like this,' said Andric. 'I vote we move north.'

'But if it is so unsafe that Calthorn has sent no word to us,' said Oljon, 'then it would be unwise to go looking for him.'

'We could send some of us ahead to check,' suggested Andric.

'We are not in the thick of battle right now,' said Palis. 'We could vote, but then none of us would be bound to the outcome. I for one feel we need to make some contact with our friends in the north.'

'If some of us are leaving anyway,' said Oljon, rising to his feet, 'we should all go. But these curuski wait in ambush. An advance team should march a little ahead of the rest of us to check for unwanted guests lurking in the corridors.'

'I will lead this advance team,' Andric volunteered.

What calmness he had managed to achieve drained away from Fhiro as they prepared to set off. He could tell Imial and Chenessa were at least as miserable as he was about this.

Four soldiers, led by Andric, set off ahead. Fhiro, and the other civilians, left afterwards, with the remaining bodyguards and soldiers around them, filling the wide corridor. Fhiro knew there was a good distance to cover between the southern end of the fort where they were based, and the Great Hall to the north of the main gate.

'Tread quietly,' said Oljon. 'The curuski don't need their strange, black eyes to hear us. Don't make things easy for them.'

'What if we knock something over?' whispered Imial. 'Will we all die?'

'Oh, just be quiet,' said Chenessa.

'We shall live if the spirits wish it,' said Dr Watchal.

Fhiro tried to smile at Dr Watchal, but fearing he looked as insincere as he felt, he turned away, and found himself watching his father directing the men. The fighters were doing a good job of keeping their formation. Oljon exuded the authoritative air he used during training exercises. It seemed to compel obedience and determination in trained adults, just as it had always done in Fhiro and his siblings back home.

But back home had been just exercises. This was real.

After a few minutes Andric's group returned to report. 'Ahead the corridor becomes dark,' he said. 'It appears the lighting cables have been damaged. We have crystal-torches to light the path, but we could go around it by heading west at the next junction.'

'Afraid of the dark?' Tubrin asked.

'Always,' said Ghorad. 'Our foe may see better in it than we do.'

'Let us stick to well lit corridors if we can,' said Oljon.

Andric went to scout the west passage. When the rest of the group caught up with him he looked grim. 'I think I know why the night held particular peril for our men.' He showed them

the entrance to the lower chambers. Shining his torch down it he revealed the water level was almost at the top of the ramp, with trails of blood leading into it.

'The lower chambers have been completely filled with water from the drained lake,' said Ghorad.

'Chissids must have found a way to enter the lower floors with the water,' said Andric. 'They would have stayed in the depths during daylight, but I fear that during the night they either overpowered the men left to guard this section, or found it unattended when those men had been called elsewhere.'

'And from these stains upon the floor,' said Ghorad, 'it seems that they inflicted some losses.'

'A cursed way to die,' said Palis. 'They have many terrible claws and venomous yellow teeth. Chissids are the stuff of nightmares.'

Chenessa recoiled at this.

Fhiro felt his blood curdle at the thought of yellow teeth biting his flesh, and sharp claws dragging him underwater.

'Let us hope it was not many that met this end,' said Oljon. 'I will pray for them.'

'We all will,' said Tubrin.

They made their way north again. The walls became studded with scratches and bullet holes. Splatterings of black and red blood darkened every surface, but Fhiro saw no bodies.

'A rifle,' said one of the men at the front of the group, 'and a pack.'

'Give it here,' said Oljon. He examined the rifle for a while longer than Fhiro suspected he needed to. Then Oljon looked at Fhiro. 'I know what I said yesterday, but I think it best if you take this,' he said. 'My orders are unchanged, in that you should remain safe and under our protection at all times.

However, if you are unfortunate enough to have a clear shot at something that threatens us …' He stopped and looked around. 'I assume no one here minds if I arm my apprentice? He is already well schooled in the arts of war, and will not engage except on my command.'

No one said anything. Some of the soldiers gave Oljon strange looks when he could not see them, but settled a little when they saw the trust in him exuded by Ghorad and the Kartnan soldiers.

Fhiro slung the rifle strap over his shoulder. He knew his father had spoken the truth about his knowing how to use the weapon, but he did not feel comfortable having it. Some of the soldiers shot him uncertain glances. Did they fear he might kill them by mistake?

Fhiro felt a pat on is shoulder.

'Come on,' said Ghorad.

Fhiro looked up and saw the Kartnan guard was smiling at him. It reassured him, and he smiled back.

'Your master trusts you with that?' asked Chenessa, when he had caught up with her.

'Why can't I have one?' asked Imial.

Fhiro said nothing, because he was not sure how to answer either of them.

Soon Andric returned to them, his face ashen.

'What is it?' asked Oljon.

'The corridors surrounding the great hall, they are unguarded,' said the Hithostun guard. 'There is evidence of fierce fighting, and terrible damage to the structure of the building. I fear … I fear what could have done this. I don't know what's become of the turrets. Should I investigate them, or make for the Great Hall?'

'Find out what you can of the Great Hall before we arrive,' said Oljon. 'Do not enter unless you're sure it is safe.'

The corridors surrounding the hall were as Andric had described. Along with discarded excavation tools, helmets and spent projectile magazines littered the floor. There was even a single, bloodied boot. As they made for the doors to the hall they saw Andric there, shaking his head. 'It does not look good from out here,' he said.

'Is there anything moving?' asked Oljon.

'It looks empty,' said Andric.

They gathered together before passing through.

As Andric pushed the doors to either side the contents of the hall became visible. Fhiro was shocked by the broken, crushed, and upturned tables and furniture. The makeshift canteen was in ruins. The sleeping materials were torn and scattered.

'There was a terrible fight here,' said Tubrin, stepping forward and picking up a spent bullet casing in his hand.

'And where has everyone gone?' asked Andric. 'This is most unlike battles I have seen. There was fighting, but there are no dead.'

'Our foes were not people,' said Oljon. 'Our friends are gone. Taken away to be devoured. I only hope they were slain sooner, not later, and before they had endured much torment. One cannot guess the habits of these alien creatures.'

Glass crunched under Fhiro's feet. He looked up at the huge overhead skylight and saw that most of it was shattered. The morning light shone upon the west wall with uneven brightness, passing through the few portions of glass still held in position by the supporting metal framework.

'So what do we do now?' Imial whispered in Fhiro's ear. 'Are we going to be eaten too?'

Many of the soldiers knelt among the broken furniture and scattered ornaments. Some clutched remains of clothing, or searched in great anxiety for familiar items.

'And what of Calthorn?' asked Andric.

'I know the general,' said Palis. 'He would not have fled. He would have died doing his duty.'

'Then let us grieve the loss of a great man.' Oljon bowed his head.

'What about Captain Jard?' Fhiro asked Oljon.

'He will have served his country well,' said Pral.

Tubrin knelt, basked his face in the sunlight and placed his palms over his eyes. Fhiro recognised the gesture from the formal mourning prayer of The Calling.

'Come,' said Andric, 'we cannot spend too long lamenting in sorrow. We may befall the same fate soon enough.'

'Could it be that a graveling was involved here?' asked Ghorad. 'The level of damage to the structures in this room is beyond my expectations.'

'The window above?' suggested Fhiro.

'Perhaps such a creature could have made it through these wide halls if it was determined to,' said Oljon, 'or as Fhiro said, the large skylight.'

'If gravelings can get in here,' said Pral, 'then we are all dead men.'

'Yet if we hide in the southernmost part of the fort,' said Andric, 'the rescue mission may miss us. What if they leave us? Or flee back to gather more men?'

'We should learn of our surroundings,' said Ghorad.

'Agreed,' said Palis.

'You two,' said Oljon to a Kartnan and a Pelorn soldier, 'check the turret we passed on the way here.'

'I will take these two men of Hithostun to explore the immediate area,' said Andric.

'Do not go outside,' said Oljon. 'The rest of us must prepare to withdraw to the south.'

They gathered themselves while five of their number disappeared to investigate. No sooner were they ready to leave

when shots were heard. Then hasty footsteps approached the great hall.

One of the Hithostun soldiers appeared. 'Andric is slain!' He ran inside. 'They came from the north. They are still in this building!'

'Who? What?' asked Oljon.

'The black-eyed ones!'

'Curuski,' said Palis.

'Where is your other man?' asked Oljon.

'Fallen also,' said the soldier. 'I slew three of the creatures but more appeared.' He paused for breath.

'What of the men we sent to inspect the turrets?' asked Tubrin.

'We'll pass them on the way south,' said Ghorad. 'We can look for them then. Let's get out of here.'

'What was that sound?' asked Chenessa.

A soft hissing came from the corridor. It stopped, then started again, but a little louder.

'That is the sound of the curuski,' said Oljon. 'Let us assess their number, diminish them, and move on. Ready, men! Pray to your gods. We will need their strength.' Oljon knelt down, thirty metres from the door, and steadied his rifle. The others bearing arms readied themselves in similar positions.

Fhiro hesitated. He saw a space next to his father and knew he could take it.

A clawed hand appeared on what remained of the door and pulled it away. The curuski peered its head around and faced the inside of the room, its featureless black eyes searching from side to side. Its jaw, similar to that of the graveling, was shut tight, but its sharp teeth were visible beneath its out-turned lips.

Fhiro forced himself forward, knelt down next to his father, and shouldered his rifle. His heart beat like a machine gun in

his chest. He forced his arms to stay steady, and aimed down the sites at the curuski's head. Without thinking he adjusted his handling of the unfamiliar weapon as though it were one he had practised with before. In all the training his father had given him, had Oljon imagined a day like this one?

'Give the order to fire, priest,' said Tubrin, 'and I'll send this demon back to hell.'

'Watch him for a moment,' whispered Oljon.

The creature crept into the room, glancing in all directions. It hissed, and three more entered after it.

Oljon looked behind them. 'There is no way out of this room, apart from the door before us. If those things come within a metre of you, consider yourself dead.' He returned his attention to the curuski. 'Take aim and fire on my mark.' He paused for a second, and then said, 'Engage!'

Fhiro did not fire. He watched the four curuski break apart under a mix of projectile and crystal-fire.

'Right flank, advance. Weapons free,' commanded Oljon.

Pral and two other soldiers made some tentative steps. Ghorad headed over to lead them. He pulled further away toward the south-western wall to get a better view through the open door. 'Corridor looks clear from here.'

'Left flank, check the western corridor,' barked Oljon.

Tubrin took charge of the left-most men, and did the equivalent manoeuvre to Ghorad. 'Aten is merciful,' he said.

Oljon nodded to Ghorad who approached the door. Quickly he darted out of it, followed by one of the men behind him. They looked up and down the corridor. 'Clear!'

'Let's move!' said Oljon. 'Right flank take point. Left take up the rear. Children and civilians in the middle. Fast!'

They rushed into the corridor. Ghorad's men led the way. There was nothing ahead. Fhiro made himself keep moving. He would not let himself be afraid. He could not afford to be.

Ghorad reached a junction in the corridors. One of his men sprang forward to check the way was clear to the south. He then advanced a short way. Ghorad followed, but drew back firing into the corridor. Soon all of the men that had gone with Ghorad as part of the vanguard were occupied shooting in different directions at the corridor junction.

Fhiro's froze.

Oljon went up to join Ghorad, taking one of Tubrin's men with him.

'Reloading!' shouted Ghorad.

Oljon stood beside Ghorad and covered for him. 'They seem to have stopped. Advance down the south passage, now.'

Fhiro went up to the front with Imial and Chenessa. There they hesitated.

'Come on!' Jammit grabbed Imial and Fhiro and dragged them towards where Oljon and Ghorad were advancing.

They staggered around a corner with Jammit, but then the Kartnan soldier went ahead.

'The roof is opened here,' said Ghorad. 'Watch above.'

'More coming from the north!' cried one of the men behind them.

'We're too exposed here,' said Pral.

'Get out of that junction,' said Oljon. 'Get into the corridor where there are fewer approaches to cover.'

As Fhiro followed his father he heard screams from behind him, and then the shoving and pushing of bodies against each other. He looked back and saw Tubrin unleashing great savagery upon the neck of a curuski with his knife. Black liquid spurted all over the Creedate guard. Another soldier grabbed Tubrin and pulled him away.

A claw lashed out in front of Fhiro. He stumbled, lost his balance and fell to the floor as he dodged out of its way. The thin arm, swiping from above, then caught Dr Watchal by his

neck, its nails biting into his flesh. Fhiro saw the curuski reaching through a tear in the ceiling, lifting the ecologist up toward its opening jaws. Without thinking Fhiro raised his rifle and fired into the creature, and its arm went lax. Dr Watchal fell, profuse quantities of blood pouring from his mouth.

Yelba ran to him, her eyes full of fright. 'Close your mouth. Can you press on where the blood is coming from?'

Another curuski dropped down behind Fhiro, staggering as it landed. As Fhiro scrambled with the rifle, trying to turn about and aim, he saw Tubrin rushing towards them. The curuski had now righted itself, its prominent black eyes gazing at him. Fhiro fumbled with his rifle, struggling with the handle and the barrel in the confined space.

The monster stalked towards him, each step coming faster than the last.

Resting against the wall was idle excavation gear. Tubrin sprinted, grasped a pickaxe by its handle, closed the distance between himself and the curuski in an instant, and swung the tool at its head. The sharp end embedded itself into the creature, distorting the shape of its face. The guard's momentum crashed the two of them into the side of the corridor, though Tubrin kept his footing while the limp curuski crumpled, dark blood drenching Tubrin's already soiled garments. Tubrin released the pickaxe, and his rough hands hauled Fhiro on to his feet. 'Keep moving.'

Fhiro was too dazed to respond.

'There are doors on either side ahead,' shouted Ghorad.

'Clear the rooms quickly!' said Oljon.

Ghorad dived into one while Pral raced into another. But Ghorad immediately withdrew. 'Not clear. Not clear at all!' he cried. He pulled his comrade out with him, throwing grenades into the rooms as they made their way back. 'There's an opening in that room to the outside!' he cried, an instant

before the grenades detonated, pounding Fhiro's ears with the force of their blast waves.

'Ahead!' said Oljon whirling his weapon to his shoulder and firing over them.

The way forward was too difficult. Fhiro watched, in horror at the creatures clamouring through the corridor. When one fell, another leapt over it. They appeared to be in a crazed frenzy, whether driven by the scent of food, or rage at the loss of their brethren, Fhiro could not guess, but there were so many of them. Too many.

As Palis knelt to reload his rifle, a curuski burst from one of the rooms Ghorad had tried to clear earlier. It moved towards Palis faster than Fhiro could have imagined a two-legged creature could travel. Palis went for his sidearm, but had it barely out of its holster when the monster pierced the Royal guard's shoulder with one claw, and buried another into his chest. Oljon shot it dead a second later, but now the advancing horde of curuski were too close.

'Fall back!' shouted Oljon.

'But Palis!' cried Fhiro.

'Palis is dead,' said Ghorad, 'and we will be too if we stay here.'

Fhiro faltered and teetered backwards, his feet slippery on the blood of dead curuski.

They retreated to the junction, but every direction they tried was blocked, until they found themselves withdrawing into the main hall. Tubrin threw a grenade into the corridor as he leapt inside, diving under the firing line of his comrades that were already through. He counted the men. 'We are down to a fighting strength of two soldiers, two guards, an Aculei priest and a young boy!' He looked at Yelba cradling the lifeless body of Dr Watchal. 'We seem to have lost our ecologist.'

'There are plenty of rifles scattered about in here,' said

Oljon. 'Arm the civilians.'

Fhiro knelt next to his father again, his rifle aimed at the door. He could hear the curuski flooding down the corridor towards the hall. He saw shapes pass by outside, too fast to take a clear shot at, and then like the bursting of a dam, a score of the monsters charged through the door towards them.

It happened so fast. Fhiro aimed, fired, aimed, fired, aimed and fired. Creature after creature fell, collapsing, or sometimes splitting apart. The fear of missing his next target was so overwhelming there was no chance to feel any relief when he hit his mark. Fortunately the others with him were at least as effective, and the first wave of curuski was destroyed.

Fhiro could hear Tubrin try to convince one of the servants to help, shoving a loaded weapon into his hands. 'Flick that down, and fire with this trigger. Stay in front of us. If you aren't shooting at things, keep the gun pointed down! And if in doubt, do nothing.'

'I can't see very well,' Fhiro heard the man shout back.

Fhiro turned to see Tubrin wrench the rifle off the man and offer it to Yelba, who had laid Dr Watchal upon the floor.

'I heard your instructions,' Yelba said, taking the weapon and walking to join the others facing the door.

'How are we going to get out of here?' asked Fhiro, as Yelba knelt down next to him.

'Stay calm,' shouted Oljon, firing off a burst of rounds at another curuski as it pounced through the door. It collapsed, black blood pumping out in all directions. 'They cannot come forever.'

And then, as though Oljon's words predicted it, the onslaught slowed.

Ghorad stood up. 'They seem to have stopped.' He took tentative steps towards the door, looking through it as he had done earlier.

Fhiro saw a shadow flicker across the room. He looked up, but could see nothing through the shattered skylight. He looked ahead again, wiped his forehead, and adjusting the grip on his weapon.

A shard of glass fell from above and landed in Ghorad's shoulder.

Fhiro felt his heart sink right through his chest.

'Ghorad!' cried Imial.

Ghorad's left arm went limp and his rifle fell. He clasped his shoulder, looked through the corridor one last time, and then up.

The shadow reappeared for a moment, and then a graveling, larger than the beast that had chased Fhiro through the forest, crashed through the skylight opening. Its many-taloned foot landed square upon Ghorad, crushing him.

Imial wailed. Fhiro felt himself jump back in alarm.

The graveling paused to survey the people in the room. Its outstretched claws flexed, and its teeth gleamed. Its mouth widened and its face contorted into what could only be, to Fhiro's mind, a grin of pure menace. This foe was invincible, and this time there was nowhere to run.

CHAPTER 25

Fhiro felt his fragility with a force he had never experienced before. His tiny insignificance. His weak uselessness. He was to blink out of existence, nothing more than a spark in the course of eternity. No mortal could survive the merciless gaze of the universe for long, and his time was now up.

The graveling's jaws opened and unleashed an awful roar that made Fhiro's guts twist. Gods, Aten, or an empty void of nothingness awaited him, and this hideous monster, purposefully appointed or assigned by accident, would send him there.

It bent its neck and bellowed again.

A servant and private Jammit panicked and ran towards the far side of the Great Hall. The others fell back, leaving Fhiro the furthest forward. He felt someone grab the collar of his shirt and drag him away, the material of his clothes biting into his neck and choking him. He could hear Imial's voice from close by.

The graveling stepped forward and lowered its head.

From his left Fhiro saw a blur of motion. A man in dark clothes ran straight towards the creature, shouting. Those about Fhiro started to fire at the monster's face. It recoiled, hurt, and staggered back. Then it forced its head forth, as though struggling to overcome the pain of the projectiles and crystal-fire. The blurring man was close to it now. The graveling swung an arm, but the man had already moved beyond the arc of its sweep. The creature hammered its fist into the floor, yet now the man had dived and begun climbing

up its left leg. The graveling tried to shake off its assailant, but to no avail. The figure was climbing up the spikes upon the monster's back, and then he was at the back of its head, holding on to one of its horns. No longer moving so fast, Fhiro could make out the pointed top of his father's mask. Fhiro called out in fright.

Oljon threw what looked like a strap, or a belt, around the graveling's neck, and fastened it. Then he released himself, springing from the monster, falling a great height. The instant his feet touched the ground, though, he was running towards the shattered furniture lining the edges of the room.

The soldiers resumed their firing.

Fhiro shouldered his weapon, aimed down the sights at the creature's eyes and opened fire. The beast flinched under the onslaught, but then steadied itself and made a swipe with its claw, catching Oljon's leg, flinging him across the room.

Fhiro lowered his weapon and sprinted to where Oljon's body collided with the wall.

Oljon pushed himself up and saw Fhiro. 'Get to cover!'

'Pa!' Fhiro heard himself shout beneath the thunder of gunfire.

'Get down!' Oljon hobbled to his feet and dragged Fhiro behind an upturned table. Fhiro glanced over it to see the beast turning towards them. It started to walk, and then run, oblivious to the damage being inflicted upon it by the others, its movements and face burning with determination and power.

Oljon knelt behind the table and pulled Fhiro down with him.

'Pa!' cried Fhiro.

Oljon held Fhiro tight and flattened him against the floor.

Fhiro was squashed. He struggled to breathe under his father's weight.

A deafening explosion shook Fhiro's body, and blasted the table they were using for cover into them. The two of them rolled over twice. Fhiro's ears stung. Dazed, he tried to push his father away and orientate himself.

Oljon stood up, rifle ready, leaning to one side. The moment he was up, however, he relaxed and lowered his weapon.

Fhiro's wits were about him now. He stumbled to his feet, in time to see all three parts of the graveling's head make contact with the floor. Its body staggered and fell, jets of dark liquid pumping through the stump of its neck, up as high as the skylight through which it had entered.

The others pulled away the tables they had been hiding behind, crying with joy and delight. Tubrin ran across to them.

'Think I've sprained an ankle,' said Oljon, limping towards him. 'I am no longer what I was in my youth.'

Tubrin laughed and held out his hand to support Oljon. 'I must say, I have seen many valiant acts in my time, but what you did just then …' He trailed off. Then he looked at Fhiro. 'No wonder you have such skill with a rifle, if you are training up to be like this!' He hauled Oljon over to where the others were catching their breath.

'There were explosives in the belt?' asked Fhiro.

Oljon nodded.

'The Aculei!' cried Jammit, having rejoined the rest of his comrades now that his nerve had returned.

'Stop, everyone!' said Oljon. 'We are far from safe. We need to search for heavier weapons and more explosives immediate–'

More shadows flickered across the room.

'May the gods have mercy on us!' said Yelba.

The sky beyond the broken glass of the skylight was tranquil. Clouds drifted across it high above. Then a dark shape appeared, claws gripping the window's edge. Glass

splintered and fell in tiny pieces, shattering and scattering as they hit the floor below. Another graveling's head appeared. Not as large as the last, but its black featureless eyes showed no fear of the small band of people below it.

'Fire!' shouted Oljon.

As Fhiro fumbled with his rifle, he saw Tubrin looking up in despair. Then a fearsome resolve swept over the Creedate guard's face. Tubrin removed his belt, and began attaching grenades and explosives from his pack.

Beyond him Imial and Chenessa had picked up a rifle each. Yelba was discharging her weapon in the same direction as the soldiers.

But the creature was fast. It had fallen to the floor, breaking its fall on the body of the fallen beast, and had started running towards them, oblivious to the bullets and crystal-fire smattering into it.

And then there was a familiar noise. A brilliant beam of fiery energy descended upon the graveling from above, cutting short its roar. The beast stopped, a smouldering hole smoking from within its torso, pouring blood down its chest and abdomen. It did not look up at them, or turn around. It crashed to the floor in a heap, its head landing only a foot away from Fhiro's toes.

The survivors looked up again. A man stood upon the edge of the skylight carrying a huge, shoulder mounted weapon. Behind him multitudes of birds flew across the sky.

* * *

After a three-day, hard ride back to the palace compound they were returned to the Kartnan embassy.

'Thank the gods for your return.' Valachrad clutched Imial to his chest.

The troop of Pelorn soldiers that had been guarding the Kartnan survivors withdrew. Beyond them many of their comrades had already formed a wide perimeter around the Embassy.

'Here to protect us?' asked Oljon.

'And keep an eye on us,' said Valachrad. 'Thank you, Ishthen, for returning my son.'

Oljon acknowledged this with a short nod. 'How're my wife and children?'

'Come inside,' said Valachrad, smiling, 'and you can meet them!'

The moment they passed through the second set of doors Chinda was trying to jump on top of her father, while Hanu did her best to grab all of them into a single embrace at once, while simultaneously pulling off Oljon's mask.

'It's so good to see you!' said Hanu. 'Thank Aten you're all right!' She kissed Oljon's lips.

Oljon grinned. 'It's good to be back.'

'You're all right Chins?' asked Fhiro when he had struggled his head free.

Chinda paused, then hugged him. 'Maybe it's a good thing I couldn't go.'

'Couldn't agree more,' said Fhiro.

'Where's Dorrick?' asked Oljon.

'Training,' said Hanu. 'I think he prefers flying to piloting.'

'So much that he won't even greet us on our safe return?' asked Oljon.

'The unit he's been attached to have asked him to go with them for all their exercises,' said Hanu. 'They've stepped things up around here.'

'I suppose he's helping rebuild our bridges with Pelorn,' said Oljon.

'All of your family have done much to that end,' said

Valachrad. 'I will be sure to pass on my highest commendations to the Senate on our return.'

'Does that mean we've got a home to go to after all?' Hanu whispered to Oljon.

'I think so,' said Oljon, 'if we can get off this planet alive. How have things been here?'

'More of the same,' she said. 'Fewer disappearances, but still lots of secretive behaviour. It's not just us the soldiers are watching. Every entrance to the keep is being checked at all times, and the King's secret police are everywhere. Creedate spies have been sighted too, but what they're up to we can't guess.'

'I suppose with the disappearance of Reshna, the King is especially suspicious of all his guests,' said Oljon, 'and even his friends.'

'Except that this was starting to happen even before news of her disappearance arrived,' said Hanu.

They followed Valachrad and Imial through the corridors of the Embassy. Hanu held Fhiro close to her on one side and Oljon on the other. Chinda attached herself to her father's free hand.

Valachrad turned to Fhiro. 'A special thanks to you, young Fhiro,' he said. 'I heard you displayed great courage. You will make a fine Aculei priest one day, I am sure!' He winked.

Fhiro smiled. 'Imial was brave too,' he said.

'I'm very proud to hear it.' Valachrad looked down at his son. 'Incidentally, how is your Creedate friend faring after all she's been through?'

'Chenessa?' asked Fhiro.

'Is she all right?' asked Chinda.

'She's been quiet ever since her mother disappeared,' said Imial.

Valachrad cast his eyes to the floor. 'Don't we all wish that hadn't happened.'

Fhiro watched Valachrad, wondering if the round and smiling ambassador could have been responsible for the bizarre occurrence that started off all the bad luck at the Old Harvester Fort.

'Ghorad was so brave,' said Imial. 'He fought alongside Ishthen, and was leading soldiers into battle when he died.'

'He was a great man,' said Valachrad. 'The finest bodyguard I could have found for you.'

'He was the best,' said Imial. 'He deserves a monument. There should be a statue of him.'

Valachrad nodded. 'Would you like to design it?'

When they settled down into one of the audience halls Imial plunged himself into this task, drawing sketches. Beside it he included dimensions – but he kept crossing these out in order to increase them.

Fhiro noticed the number of officials and officers seemed fewer now that Jard and many others had passed on at the Old Harvester Fort. It sank home that all these people were now dead, and this took a heavy toll on his heart.

One face he did recognise was Vawal, the lieutenant who had, with Pral, greeted them on the Siwob. Pral, meanwhile, was also sitting with them, having been promoted twice with immediate effect for his bravery over the preceding days.

'I won't keep you long,' said Valachrad, 'for I know you have travelled far and need to bathe and rest. Ishthen must be desperate to catch up with his family! I do, however, want to enlighten you all on some developments, at least in brief. We can discuss how we will tackle them in due course, but it will be good to have your minds stewing in the meantime. But before I go on, are there any extra pieces of information I should know about that might make further sense of these mysterious times? Anything else you learned after I left?'

'Beyond the contents of the report I sent on ahead,' said

Oljon, 'very little. Tubrin and Ghorad almost came to blows after another argument was started by … someone.'

Fhiro looked at the floor.

'But the Creedate guard had plenty of chances to kill us all if he had wanted to,' said Oljon.

'If the Creedate were the architects of this horror,' said Valachrad, 'I suspect that none of their representatives that stayed at the fort were privy to its design or execution.'

'Poor Chenessa,' Chinda whispered.

Hanu, her arm already draped over her daughter's shoulder, pulled Chinda closer. 'Shall we send the children ahead?' she asked. 'They don't need to be part of this conversation.'

'They don't,' said Valachrad, 'and if you wish it, then we will send them away. But I feel the children have earned the right to listen if they wish to.'

Fhiro and Chinda nodded with enthusiasm. Imial was still absorbed in his drawings.

'Another report arrived just before you did,' said Valachrad. 'The excavation site under the mountain has been entered.'

'Entered?' cried Oljon.

'I understand the lake was drained,' said Valachrad.

'Yes,' said Oljon, 'and it filled up the lower levels of the Old Harvester Fort. I did not know anything further, though.'

'It is huge inside, apparently,' said Hanu. 'At the centre, and reaching right to the top of the mountain, is a tall structure that can only be entered through a protected door.'

'Well the environmentalists can't stop us there, surely,' said Oljon. 'Why don't we just blast through it?'

'Because,' said Hanu, 'the on-site experts suspect this tall structure may be the very device the Sufferers referred to in their documents.'

Fhiro gasped.

'Not only that,' said Valachrad. 'The significance goes

further. Its position, shape, and inscriptions about this hidden facility imply that this object can do that which no one has managed in recorded history. It can defy gravity itself.'

'The Poshokans defeated gravity,' said Oljon, 'and only built one such craft capable of doing so? That sounds bizarre to the point of lunacy.'

'Does it work?' asked Fhiro.

'Who knows,' Valachrad replied. 'The King's men are trying to break in gently, as it were, and acquire the device, or whatever one calls it, intact.'

'Is it like a ship?' asked Fhiro.

'Sort of,' said Valachrad, 'though it is tall, rather than long, and not shaped like a ship that might glide to a safe landing after atmospheric entry. It does appear to have a name, however.'

'What's the name,' asked Imial, distracted from his drawing.

'*Gravity's Arrow*,' said Valachrad. 'At least that's how the Jashpuri ambassador has translated the engravings on its side.'

'Jashpur are here?' Oljon's eyes narrowed. 'And they are at the excavation site?'

Fhiro knew of Jashpur. Another great galactic power, but one located further from the near quadrant than Kartna.

Valachrad shook his head. 'Halbat is his name, and indeed he will be going there soon. He interpreted a copy of the inscription that was sent here with the report.'

'Jashpur?' said Imial. 'Did they kill the birds?'

'I am surprised by their presence,' said Oljon, 'but would not suspect them of such a treacherous plot, especially so far from home.'

'These are not normal times,' said Valachrad. 'However, they can justify their presence. Their interest in ancient times exceeds our own, so they might have taken rumours of this discovery more seriously than the rest of us. Even so, I happen

to have some other, more likely theories, to explain this run of misfortune.'

'You do?' asked Oljon.

Valachrad smiled at Hanu. 'Thank your wife. I am indebted to her. She has a good head for conspiracy theories.'

'Blame it on a misspent youth ducking and weaving my way through life on Indin,' said Hanu.

Valachrad laughed his booming laugh.

'So what are we considering?' asked Oljon.

'Everything, of course,' said Hanu. 'Importantly, we're failing to see a likely scenario in which Reshna is found alive and well.'

Oljon nodded. 'I had little hope for her.'

'Even if the Creedate have disappeared her,' said Hanu, 'they will probably have done so permanently. Now that Valachrad has partially implicated himself in her disappearance, her reappearance in death is expected.'

'And with some solid evidence to convince the King of my guilt, we could see some very troubled times ahead,' said Valachrad, 'both in the immediate term, but also with Kartna's reputation and her relationship with Pelorn and these neighbouring powers.'

'What solid evidence do you speak of?' asked Oljon.

'There is none,' said Valachrad, 'at least not yet.'

'You think the Creedate will create something to implicate you?' asked Oljon. 'If they have her body, then they certainly have the means to. However, I cannot imagine a clear-cut case, what with a crime scene that has been trampled over by millions of animals, and given the possible motivation to frame you, there should be enough uncertainty for us to keep you out of Pelorn's dungeons.'

'I agree that any evidence found upon Reshna's body will seem suspicious,' said Valachrad. 'Do not limit your concerns

to the Creedate, however, Ishthen.'

'You have already implied that you do not suspect Jashpur,' said Oljon. 'The only other power present, that's capable of wrestling with us, are the Creedate.'

'I think what you might not have considered, dear Ishthen,' said Valachrad, 'is not so much who should have done this, but who would have.'

Oljon rested back in his chair and took in a breath.

'What are you talking about?' asked Fhiro.

Oljon sighed. He looked at Valachrad. 'Then they are fools.'

Valachrad nodded. 'But such actions are no surprise to we who have lived so long. When destined to lose, hope tempts out the most outlandish delusions.'

Fhiro glanced from one parent, to the other, and to Valachrad.

'If this spirals into war,' said Oljon, 'then they have, essentially, all committed suicide. Is there anyone we can reach? Persuade to do what's in the interest of the Niquani?'

'We've done what we can already,' said Hanu. 'Whether we were heard or not, we don't know. We're new here. It's been difficult to get an audience with Countess Jeberrel, let alone the King, and the neighbouring powers only ever entertain us with their lowest officials. In the end we had to risk involving people we are far from sure of.'

'But on the bright side,' said Oljon, 'there is no hard evidence to link us with Reshna's death.'

'No,' said Valachrad.

'How long must we wait to see this played out?' asked Oljon. 'This perimeter around the Embassy, I assume, has taken away our chances to disappear to Kartna.'

'Not that such a move would be viewed kindly by the Senate.' The ambassador leaned back in his chair. 'Tomorrow,' he said, 'the second rescue party will return from their search for Reshna, but we can already guess their report. The

Creedate captain, who just arrived on a cruiser in orbit above us, will want blood for blood. This will be the perfect time for the true culprits to play their hand, if they ever will, for King Suloa will be desperate to snatch up anything that shifts the blame for a dead Creedate ambassador away from Pelorn.'

* * *

The next morning Dorrick returned and joined Fhiro, Chinda and Imial for breakfast. Fhiro gave his older brother a long-lasting hug.

'I didn't think I'd be missed by you,' said Dorrick. 'Can't believe you're the Aculei apprentice you've been cracked up to be all along.'

Fhiro let go. 'Training going well?'

'Yes,' said Dorrick. 'You'd love flying. Bet you'd be good at it too.'

Fhiro scowled. 'Have I really got to wait two years?'

'Only a year and a half now, surely?'

Oljon and Hanu marched into the room.

'What is it?' asked Chinda.

'As we predicted,' said Oljon.

'What did you predict?' asked Fhiro.

'Reshna's body has been found,' said Hanu.

Chinda started to sob.

'Poor Chenessa,' said Fhiro, while his parents went to put their arms around Chinda.

Even Imial looked cowed by the news. 'She might have been the enemy, but her daughter was nice.'

'Any sign of the archaeologists?' asked Fhiro.

Oljon nodded. 'There are remains scattered all over the area, and it will take detailed analysis to establish which person fell where. Plenty of corpses wore the garments of our clouder

friends, however.'

Fhiro felt distraught. He had held out hope they would be alive. The news crushed him. He had not known Reshna, but he had become friends with Cerilina and Borlin. Strange but likeable Borlin.

Chinda cried a little louder.

'I should have been nicer to Borlin,' said Fhiro.

Oljon patted Fhiro's back. 'Borlin was a good-humoured man, and Cerilina lived her life to the full. Didn't she say she wanted to experience the mountain view again before it was too late?'

'Some people are born to live bright and die young,' said Hanu. 'Hopefully you children of mine will find a way to do one without the other.'

'The King has invited all the foreign delegations for a Grief Prayer in memory of the dead,' said Oljon.

'What's a Grief Prayer?' asked Imial.

'I think we can guess,' said Fhiro. 'Can we visit Chenessa?'

'That won't be possible,' said Hanu.

Fhiro nodded. 'I just want her to know it wasn't us.'

'I hope one day she will,' said Oljon, 'but there's nothing you can do about that now.'

CHAPTER 26

The only words Fhiro understood during the Grief Prayer were those uttered by Countess Jeberrel at the beginning. Niquani chanting, in a language he did not recognise, followed for two hours, but he was too busy remembering those who had passed to notice the time.

The visiting delegations were escorted from the prayer room by a troop of Pelorn guards.

'Where are we going?' Pral asked the Pelorn officer leading them. 'The exit from the keep is not this way.'

'You're to be taken to the King's audience chamber,' said the officer.

'Can we at least know why?' asked Valachrad.

The officer said nothing.

'What's going on?' Fhiro whispered to Oljon as they approached the huge elevator shaft at the centre of the vast keep. Large hockers, with bright silver armour-plates strapped to their arms and scalps, heaved on thick cables beside it, dragging boxes full of people towards the keep roof.

'Apparently our host does not trust us,' said Oljon. 'Stay calm and look confident.' He placed a hand on his son's back. 'Exude trustworthiness.'

Fhiro did his best.

They ascended high into the air, the tugs of the hockers mitigated through the system of pulleys that moved the elevators. After transferring elevators four times, they were directed to a series of rooms where everyone, from Valachrad to the most junior servant, was searched.

'What do they think they're playing at?' cried Imial when he joined Fhiro, Valachrad and Oljon on the other side. The Kartnan delegation had been allocated its own cordoned-off part of a large chamber.

Seats were there for those who needed them, but even Valachrad had chosen to stand now, watching from afar the members of other delegations talking to one another in their own groups. 'Stay calm, son,' he said. 'I had expected something like this.'

'This rudeness is unbearable,' said Imial. 'We should invade this stupid planet and teach them a lesson.'

'Now, now, my boy, let's not start a war with the very nation we're trying to forge an alliance with.'

They were held in this chamber for a while longer, even after the last delegation to arrive had been searched. Then Pelorn soldiers in ceremonial masks and armour appeared through hidden doorways in the walls.

'Come with us,' said one who had appeared close to where Valachrad was standing. 'Behind these walls are stairs that lead to the King's audience chamber.'

Valachrad nodded. Oljon and Fhiro stayed closed to him as they passed more guards lining the staircase.

The walls of the audience chamber were crystal clear. Fhiro saw the city stretching out into the rolling hills and mountains that lined the horizon. He realised in alarm that he was high above the enormous, hemispherical roof of the keep. What he had assumed was its tall spire was, in fact, a tower.

Then he noticed the king, sitting on a golden throne, in front of which was an uneven mound covered in a thick cloth.

The guards guided Fhiro, along with the rest of the Kartnan delegation, to an area between the thick, marble pillars spaced through the chamber. The other delegations were organised in a similar fashion. There were, however, no seats for any of them.

Valachrad spoke to the masked guard nearest him. 'May we pay our respects to his Majesty?'

The guard turned his head by a fraction. 'The King already acknowledges your respect and support.'

Valachrad turned to Oljon, Hanu, and his other advisers, and frowned.

Fhiro's lack of understanding at what was going on did nothing to calm his nerves.

Once everyone had arrived and settled there was an uneasy stillness. Fhiro found his attention drawn to the cloth-covered mound again. At the front of the Kartnan group he had a good view of the other delegations. Many people, such as Shali of Vinara, whose husband had perished at the fort, looked miserable and exhausted. He was amazed she had composed herself enough to be present here. Others stood upright, eyes unflinching. Fhiro wondered if they were as anxious as he was. Near the King's dais was a delegation wearing uniforms and patterns he did not recognise. A tall man stood at their head. Opposite them were the Creedate, in the place of honour at the King's right-hand side. Neither Chenessa nor Tubrin were with them, but in front of the robed priests was the cruel-eyed prelate elder Fhiro recognised from before, and a man in military dress with a derisive look on his face.

An earthwoman whispered something to the King. He nodded. She then turned to face them. 'King Suloa welcomes you to his audience chamber.'

'Finally,' whispered Imial.

'Be quiet,' Chinda nudged Imial.

'I am sorry to have brought you here in this manner,' announced Suloa without even looking at his audience.

'King Suloa,' said Zakil, one of the few ambassadors who had not brought and lost someone dear to them during the

disaster at the excavation site, 'I must protest at this treatment. We are ambassadors, entitled to …'

'Silence!' Suloa's voice rumbled. 'The welcome I have extended to you, ambassador, is to be short-lived.'

Zakil froze.

'There is a reason for your treatment,' Suloa continued, 'just as there was a reason that Reshna, the Creedate ambassador, was cruelly put to death near the Old Harvester Fort not long ago.'

Fhiro double-checked that Chenessa was not among the Creedate.

'She was not merely killed,' continued Suloa, 'but tormented in her last moments, and found rotting where she had been left by her captors to die in agony.' He peered into the eyes of those around him. 'Glorthig,' Suloa indicated the grim-faced, Creedate man near to him, 'is a Creedate captain who arrived yesterday to hear this news. I have promised him justice for Reshna's murder, and today he will have it.'

Fhiro felt his heart start to pound. He became aware of a deep rumbling noise. Gasps from behind him caught his attention. He turned. Members of the delegations from Kartna, Iap and Baworl were looking outwards at the city. Fhiro moved towards the transparent walls, his mother allowing him and Chinda through to get a better view, just as three thunderclaps resonated through the chamber.

Over Riletta a swarm of attack birds and dragons swooped through the clouds and darted between the towers. Several scattered plumes of smoke rose skywards beneath them. A bright burst of light erupted from the base of a building as Fhiro watched, and then the structure was gone, replaced by a rising cloud of dust.

'As most of you are aware,' the King continued, 'there has been trouble on Pelorn.'

Fhiro slid and squeezed back to his original place. He was afraid. Something very bad was happening. He felt his father's hand upon his shoulder again, but it did not carry the same assuredness as before.

'The situation here has become venomous,' said Suloa. 'Venomous and evil. The approach of the gentle benevolent ruler is not suited to these times. Suffering must be accepted if it is to be endured.' He nodded to a guard standing at the other end of the cloth-covered mound. 'It is at times like these that the burden of leadership lays most heavily on a King.'

The guard stepped towards the cloth and gripped it with one hand. He paused, his mouth flinching for a moment, before he grimaced and pulled the cloth away. Beneath it, piled on top of one another in a disordered, bloodied mess, were over a hundred severed heads.

There were cries, some more stifled than others, from across the chamber.

Fhiro was too afraid to make a sound. At the top of the mound, lying on its side, was the head of Countess Jeberrel who had greeted them upon their arrival on Pelorn.

Oljon's grip tightened on Fhiro's shoulder.

'The Creedate and Kartna have come from far to win our favour,' continued King Suloa. 'With either of them behind us, I would have become the most powerful ruler in this region. I deny that I might ever have compromised the interests of our people, for I am, and always will be, Niquani. Yet these fools were swept up in paranoia and lies, convincing one another that I might permit the mark of the Niquani to be erased from the galaxy altogether for my own gain.' The King sighed. 'No matter how well intentioned, yet misinformed, they may have been, their actions would have brought us all to ruin.'

Fhiro noticed Winle, the Hithostun ambassador, twitch.

King Suloa looked back around the chamber. 'I have

identified, interrogated and delivered justice to those over whom my authority would not be disputed, but you before me now pose another problem. I know that this great mischief, only brought to an end this very morning, was supported, and in part orchestrated by many of you, and yet you represent entire nations I have no wish to anger. Alas, something must give, and I will see that justice and retribution prevail.' Suloa gestured towards the mound of heads. 'My sacrifice is not the only one that is due today.'

Winle cleared her throat. 'King Suloa,' she said, 'that you have uncovered a conspiracy at home is not in any way confirmation that any other nation had anything to do with it. As Zakil said before, we are ambassadors. We all mourn Reshna's death and those others who perished under your protection at the Old Fort.'

'Under my protection indeed,' said the King, 'and it is because of this that I will spare no effort, nor hesitate at any obstacle, to secure justice for these terrible crimes. Therefore, while you have all been here my soldiers have searched every one of your embassies, hunting for clues that would implicate those responsible.'

'You would not–' Winle began.

'A physical belonging of Reshna's, that was missing from her person, has been found during the searches,' King Suloa interrupted her.

This King could turn violent on them at any moment, Fhiro thought. He assessed the number of guards. There were at least twenty from Pelorn but many more among the delegations of the ambassadors. However, the Pelorn guards were all armed, and there would be many more between this chamber and any safe exit from the keep, let alone the planet. They were entirely at Suloa's mercy. He felt his own neck, glad it was whole and not cut in two, unlike poor Countess Jeberrel.

'A locket has been found,' said Suloa, 'one which her priests have verified as the one Reshna wore around her neck at all times. One in which she kept her encoded instructions and orders. It seems as though the acquisition of this locket would link well with both the motivation and the act of murder of the Creedate ambassador. No doubt she was tortured to provide her captors with the means of deciphering the code. Whether she did yield or not, and how much value the information might have been to these enemies, we do not yet know. Still, those who took it have much to answer for.'

Fhiro felt his father's hand slip away.

'The locket was found within the Embassy of Kartna.'

Fhiro felt his spine freeze as the King seemed to stare straight at him. He looked away, only to meet with the burning eyes of the Creedate captain.

'But there is more,' continued Suloa. 'Though it was found in the Kartnan embassy, it was in the possession of a person not of the Kartnan staff, but of one of my staff who, under questioning, has been revealed to be a Hithostuni spy.'

'Lies!' cried Winle. 'What proof have you of this?'

King Suloa appeared to take no notice of her. 'Disaffected nobles and officials would not dare attempt to depose me without support from our neighbours, and such support was willingly offered. Hithostun and her partners knew that an alliance between Pelorn and the Creedate, or Pelorn and Kartna, would upset the order of power in this region. With Reshna's death, and the guilt pinned on Valachrad, they could expect this to be impossible, and expected the Creedate and Kartna to become too busy killing each other to bother us, the Niquani, for years to come. They no doubt hoped further that, if this discovery under the mountain did have value, the Niquani might benefit exclusively from it.'

'We are not responsible for Reshna's death!' cried Winle.

'Your guilt is already proven to my satisfaction,' said King Suloa. 'Our captives have been interrogated for much of the day that has gone by already. Your spy, who still lives for now, said his orders to place Reshna's locket in the Kartnan Embassy had come from you, yourself.' He looked at all the Niquani ambassadors. 'You wish to be treated with respect, so I will offer you this: Confess all and you shall be spared the forge.'

'What?' asked Winle. 'You think we would confess to that we have had no part in? We at least deserve a trial!'

'Except, Winle,' said Suloa, 'I already know you are guilty.'

'And you refuse to show us the evidence!' she cried. 'You search for a scapegoat as you squirm under the wrathful gaze of the Creedate.'

Suloa glowered at her. 'The Creedate may be powerful, but I must do what is right for all our people. You have committed a great crime, Winle, and now you shall pay the price.'

Winle's breathing became heavy, her eyes bulging from her head.

The Pelorn guards were moving in now and began placing chains on to the wrists of the ambassadors.

'You cannot accuse me of causing the death of my husband!' cried Shali. 'I was not part of this.'

'Yes you were,' said Suloa. 'I believe you took a risk, and that you underestimated the danger you placed him in. I am sorry for your loss.'

'No!' Shali shouted, her voice lingering in the air as she broke down, her aides rushing to help her.

Zakil had to be forced to the floor before he could be secured, and one of his aides was beaten unconscious in the scuffle.

'There is no need to bind me in chains,' shouted Evix, the ambassador from Norio. 'I shall answer your questions, but

know this.' He turned to the Creedate captain. 'We did not harm the Creedate ambassador. We may have schemed, but it was only against one another, and as we Niquani have done for time immemorial. The only difference between before and now is this mountain, and the powerful empires it has drawn here.'

'Do not give in to his intimidations!' cried Winle.

'Do not interrupt him again, Winle,' said the King.

Evix shifted his prosthetic arm and cleared his throat. 'I have nothing more to say at this time. Interrogate me if you will. I will tell you what was done, and what was not done. If you need your forge to convince you of my honesty, so be it, but my answer will remain the same. We did not kill Ambassador Reshna.'

'Honesty will be rewarded with kinder treatment,' said Suloa. 'Take them away.'

Evix bowed his head.

The guards continued arresting members of each delegation. Shali fought with them, and initially they were gentle with her, but after a few moments they held her down to apply the chains to her wrists.

A low-pitched laugh grew in strength. Heads turned to identify its source, and soon all were watching Glorthig, the Creedate captain.

'King Suloa,' said Glorthig, 'this is quite a circus of lies you have uncovered. I cannot decide what I find more amusing: the pathetic bickering and self importance of these pitiful nations, or the belief that this little demonstration might be enough to save you from my master's wrath.'

The guards placing chains around the wrists of the ambassadors paused and glanced towards the King.

'I am sorry for the tragedy that has befallen your ambassador,' said Suloa, 'but as you can see neither I nor the legitimate ruling body of this nation, were responsible.'

'Forgive my behaviour,' said Glorthig. 'There would be an ambassador standing before you, courting your favour with honey-coated words, were she not slain, but days ago, *upon this planet!* These are my terms: Hand over to me these wretched fools you accuse of murdering her, along with all of their staff members and suspected associates, and sign over the rights to this unknown treasure that hides within your mountain, and over which her blood was spilled. When we have learned what we will from it we shall duly make it available for your nation to study.'

'Never!' Winle, as yet unchained, leapt at the Creedate captain, a thin blade suddenly in her hand. Glorthig was swift to respond, though, and in the next moment her arm was pinned behind her neck and the knife prised from her fingers.

'There will be no blood shed in this chamber!' shouted the King. 'Glorthig, though I understand your grief, and though I wish to appease Marallel in his anger, might I suggest that you report to him all that I have done to avenge his fallen ambassador, and I will look forward to welcoming her replacement to continue our negotiations.'

'You suggestion has been noted,' said Glorthig, standing up, kicking Winle's blade behind him.

'You are only a captain,' said King Suloa. 'I must wait for a response from your master.'

'You have until I can return here from the Nubro region with an army of Followers at my back, to agree to my demands.' Glorthig pointed at the pile of heads on the dais. 'If this small mound frightens you, know that upon my return I would leave a pile of dead so high that even this very palace would cower in its shadow. Your unblinking, lifeless eyes, King, will have the honour of staring out over all you once ruled, and all you have lost, like countless other fallen, foolish rulers that resisted the will of Aten before you.' He swept his

arm across the room. 'And it will be the same for all of your wretched nations. You who pride yourselves on your pathetic, Niquani culture. You will know of your own insignificance when I wipe you out of existence!'

'King Suloa,' said Valachrad, 'ally with us and we will commit our forces here to defend you. The Creedate will not attack you if Kartna is your friend.'

Glorthig's breath hissed as he turned to glare at Valachrad. 'I dare not guess Marallel's mind when I tell him of your actions, ambassador of Kartna. The galaxy is not infinite!'

'It is not, in space or in time,' said Valachrad, 'and it is best you consider that when you threaten us.'

Glorthig's eyes blazed. 'So you have the measure of us, do you? I think you're a little far from home to be waving sticks when you cannot reach us with them.'

'I will ally myself with neither of you!' said King Suloa. 'The Niquani will stand together to protect what is rightfully ours against *all* aggressors.'

Valachrad and Glorthig stared at the King.

'These ambassadors betrayed us all,' said King Suloa, 'but this was an opportunistic, though foolish act of people working in secret. They were not ordered to do so by their superiors, who had no time to hatch such a plan after it was known that a delegation from Kartna was coming here. My wish, and that of my people, and all our neighbours, is that the Niquani become united under one banner and grasp the destiny that fate has given us. This discovery is a message, and we cannot afford to ignore it.'

'We did not kill her!' cried Winle.

The guard who was now holding the Hithostun ambassador tightened his grip on her clothes, choking her for a second, while his comrade checked the chains on her arms.

'With the greatest respect, King,' said Valachrad, 'and I

would say this in private if Glorthig were not about to leave this room with his decision made, please realise the danger your people face. Even if this Creedate captain fails to overcome the combined forces of the Niquani, Marallel may choose to make an example of this place, and then you will have no hope, and you should expect no mercy.'

'Fail to overcome the combined forces of what?' asked Glorthig. 'These fools bicker over scraps in the path of a hurricane of fire. There are none among them capable of leading their disorganised militias against me, assuming they could agree to be led by one another at all!'

There were murmurs throughout the room.

'You underestimate our resolve,' said King Suloa. 'But we will enjoy seeing your hopes turned to despair.'

Glorthig strode off between the groups of chained, sullen-faced ambassadors.

Valachrad spoke as he passed. 'There is a commander I can lend them. King Suloa may not accept an alliance at this time, but perhaps he will accept a gesture of goodwill. I will lend the skills of a general more accomplished than any other in this sector of the galaxy.'

Glorthig stopped, whirled and stared straight at Valachrad. 'And where is this general?' He laughed. 'Is he you? I know your reputation. There are no tales of military victory worthy of record to your name. As for the rest of your staff,' he laughed, 'all of your senior officers were killed in the fort but days ago.'

'He is here,' said Valachrad, 'in this room.' He looked at Oljon and nodded.

Oljon stepped on to the carpet that separated the two sides of the room.

Glorthig turned to him and some of his guards, seeing the strange Aculei mask, readied themselves.

Slowly Oljon removed his mask. 'It has been a long time, Glorthig.'

Glorthig's eyes narrowed and his brow furrowed. 'I know your face.'

'You do,' said Oljon. 'Why, I recall rehearsing self-defence drills with you, such as the one you used on Winle just now.'

'The Creedate army? I only practiced with officers ...' And then Glorthig's eyes were wide, and there was horror in his face. 'You! You!' He stepped back, trembling, then stumbled and fell. Quick to right himself he stood again, but now his stance was stooped, his finger pointing at Oljon's chest. 'No! It cannot be!'

'Who are you?' asked King Suloa.

'Ishthen! Devil's child! Damned above all others! Doomed to rot in the pits of hell forever among the most wretched and evil beings that were ever conceived! Curses upon you! I spit upon you! Die a thousand deaths!'

'My name is Ishthen,' said Oljon.

'I have heard that name,' said King Suloa.

'Burn and suffer in anguish! Slayer of the prophet!' cried Glorthig.

'I slew no prophet,' said Oljon. 'I killed Thurgon, the high general of the Church of Elders who led the Creedate forces before Marallel.' Oljon nodded. 'I killed that man, but the blood of Avithen stains the hands of traitors from within the High Tower.'

'Do not poison our ears,' said Glorthig. 'You walk with the Kartnan Empire?'

'He was sent by the Kartnan Empire,' said Valachrad.

'Then war it will be!' cried Glorthig. 'A rain of fire will extinguish your foolish gods. The wrath of Avithen be upon you all!'

'Avithen had not Thurgon's depraved appetite for death,' said

Oljon. 'He wished for the Followers of The Calling to defend themselves, not to exterminate and subjugate entire planets and star-systems. He was martyred by the High Priests when he stood between them and their lust for power.'

'Lies!' said Glorthig. Straightening his back and rising up to his full height, he shook his pointing finger. 'Marallel will hear of this! He will hear that you are here!'

'I will wait for him,' said Oljon. 'Send him my regards.'

PART 2

CHAPTER 27

Fhiro could hear footsteps outside his cell. He closed his eyes, shutting out the sight of its bare walls, rolled over on the hard bed and tried to cover his ears. The screaming from two cells down the corridor had kept him up most of the night. He was not sure how much more he could endure; three days so far and he craved sleep, good food, and his family more than he had ever thought possible. He almost wished he had something of interest to tell the strangers that questioned him; the conversations were becoming so repetitive.

The truth was what his father had told him to say. His father. He hoped Pelorn's cruel sense of justice would exercise some control in its dealing with his family and the other members of the Kartnan delegation, but the way King Suloa had dealt with his local ambassadors gave Fhiro little hope.

The screaming prisoner paused. To take a breath? Why was he screaming? Had his torturer needed a break? Fhiro had been fed and watered and no one had physically hurt him, but he was sure they could change their approach any day now. The thought of the forge had him wincing in anticipation of hot metal weapons pressing against his skin.

Then the screaming resumed, far louder and more violent than before.

Clicks from the handle of Fhiro's cell door told him it was being unlocked. It was too early for questioning. He had not even been fed yet. He dreaded the thought that his questioners had decided on a new approach. Fhiro sat up. He was afraid, but he had done nothing wrong. He would meet whatever

cruel fate was planned for him with as much defiance as he could muster.

Light poured in from the door as it opened. Fhiro had to cover his eyes.

'Fhiro!'

'Dorrick?' Fhiro jumped out of bed, squinting in disbelief. He rubbed his eyes.

'You're released.'

'What?' He ran forward and embraced his brother.

Dorrick burst out laughing. 'What's the big surprise? Thought you'd finally been convicted of antisocial troublemaking?'

'Quit messing around.' Fhiro scowled.

Dorrick ruffled Fhiro's hair, still grinning. He felt a lot older to Fhiro, all of a sudden. Dorrick was in his air force uniform. There was something more tangible and grounded about him now.

'So I'm not going to be tortured?'

'Not by these guys,' said Dorrick. 'I'm sure when the Creedate get here, though, you can expect a bit of that.'

'Great,' mumbled Fhiro.

'Anyway, you're all free,' said Dorrick. 'The others are in a different prison, but they'll be at the embassy soon.'

'Thanks Dorrick.' Fhiro released his grip. Then he realised he had been weeping, leaving wet marks on his brother's coat. He turned away, covered his face, and wanted more than anything to die if it would spare him the shame.

'Hey Fhiro.' Dorrick put his arm around Fhiro's shoulders, and spoke softly. 'Hey, bro, it's all right.' He pulled Fhiro's head to his chest. 'You're safe now.'

Fhiro felt himself being guided out of the cell. He pulled his head free from his brother's arm and looked to see where they were going. He was still squinting, as the sunlight in the

corridor was strong. Guards made way for them to pass. Two cells down, on the right, the screaming was at its loudest. Fhiro saw its source; a man, his ankle chained to the post of his bed, spat at his cell walls while he shook and writhed on the floor. The image troubled Fhiro, but the absence of torturers made him feel relived, and also foolish.

Outside the tower where Fhiro had been held, they walked across the grass towards the gate of the prison complex.

'Were you in here too?' Fhiro asked.

'I was on duty when everything happened, nowhere near the excavation site,' said Dorrick, 'and my wing commander vouched for me.'

'So you weren't?'

'No.'

Fhiro frowned. Dorrick seemed to have had a very lucky streak of late. 'Why'd they release us?'

'Halbat, the Jashpuri ambassador, helped negotiate a deal between Valachrad and the King.'

'Pelorn is going to ally with Kartna?'

Dorrick sighed. 'I don't think so.'

The guards by the gate saluted Dorrick, who saluted back.

'Did they lock up Chins?' asked Fhiro.

'No, thank Aten,' said Dorrick. 'She was allowed back to the embassy, but she's not there now.'

The guards opened a door in the gate, and Dorrick led Fhiro through.

'What d'you mean?'

'While you were here they allowed the remaining Kartnans to leave,' said Dorrick. 'Most of us stayed, but we let Chinda go.'

'What?!' Fhiro turned and glared at his brother.

'There's a war coming, Fhiro,' said Dorrick. 'We'll be lucky to survive it. She's a million times safer anywhere else but here.'

'Where are they taking her?'

'Kartna,' said Dorrick.

Fhiro was stunned. He said nothing as they walked from the prison complex towards a collection of transants on the road nearby. They were still inside the palace compound. The palace keep rose up into the sky on one side, and the walls bordering the palace enclosure hid the horizon on the other.

They neared the first set of transants, but went around them.

Fhiro looked at Dorrick. 'Are we walking the whole way around the keep?'

'No.' Dorrick frowned. 'This is much faster.' He pointed to a group of blue-winged birds surrounded by other men in the same uniform as Dorrick.

The brothers boarded one of the creatures, while the other air force fighters climbed on to their own birds. Dorrick ordered his bird into the air, and then they were all away. Air blasted Fhiro's face, and the city came into view over the walls. The morning sun danced off the pale stone buildings and the horizontal branch-like structures that connected them to each other. The damage from the King's bombardment was hard to notice at this distance. It was beautiful to behold. He remembered his trips to the lab upon Siwular, and his face creased into the biggest smile it had known in days.

After a minute they had made their way around the keep and begun to descend towards the Kartnan embassy. Dorrick landed the bird with expert precision.

'You're a pro at this now, Dorrick.' Fhiro could not hide how impressed he was.

'Come on.' Dorrick helped him off the saddle.

'Later, Dorrick,' said the other air force men, and then the group of them took off into the air and left.

Dorrick and Fhiro alone entered the Kartnan embassy, and

went to the same courtyard Fhiro had visited with his mother. The geese were quieter than before, but the engravings on the walls were easier to see in the daylight.

They sat on the bench and servants brought Fhiro a warm goblet of tea.

'The food's not quite as good as it was when Yelba was with us,' said Dorrick, as the servants left, 'but it's got to be better than what you've been getting used to the last few days.'

'Definitely,' said Fhiro, taking a deep sniff, and then drinking heavily. 'So Yelba went too?'

Dorrick nodded.

Fhiro heard a commotion, and then his parents burst into the courtyard.

'Boys!' they both cried.

Fhiro managed a smile as the four of them embraced.

'Where's Chins?' asked Hanu, confused.

Dorrick told her.

'What? Whose idea was that?' She broke down in tears. 'My baby! Where is she?'

Fhiro tried to comfort his mother, all the while wondering what his poor sister must be feeling, isolated from the rest of them.

Dorrick and his father put their arms around Hanu, as though they might physically protect her from this awful news.

'She'll be safe,' said Valachrad, walking into the courtyard with Imial. 'I would have done the same for Fhiro and Imial, but they were being questioned too.'

'Then let's all leave,' said Hanu. 'Let me join my daughter.'

'It is not so simple,' said Valachrad. 'Ishthen must stay and carry out his duties of leadership as has been promised.'

'I'm happy to lay my life down in the service of the Empire,' said Oljon, 'but I can't work while my family is in peril!'

'They are hostages,' said Valachrad. 'Chinda was lucky. They would have kept her too had we hesitated a moment longer.'

'Are you a hostage Imial?' Fhiro asked.

Imial puffed out his chest, but stared wide-eyed at the far wall, his fear at the prospect poorly hidden.

'He is,' said Valachrad, 'but I have agreed for you four to be placed somewhere safe, or as safe as I can find for you at a time like this.'

'Where?' asked Oljon.

'The one place where the Creedate will be most careful when they attack,' said Valachrad. 'Gravity's Arrow.'

'Are you mad?' cried Hanu.

'They are *certain* to attack there,' said Dorrick, horror on his face.

Fhiro's mind reeled at the thought of being thrown into danger's path again.

'They will roll back the defences across this entire planet in time,' said Valachrad, 'and then the populace will be put to the sword. At the excavation site, you have a legitimate reason to be attached to Ambassador Halbat from Jashpur. His associates have the greatest chance of being spared.'

'Nothing is for certain where the Creedate are concerned,' said Oljon. 'They might butcher the Jashpuris and claim a case of mistaken identity.'

'Perhaps,' said Valachrad, 'but they don't need more fronts to fight. At least the officers of their elite forces should know to seek instruction from higher up in the command structure before executing Jashpuri diplomats.'

Fhiro did not feel inspired with hope.

'You took my baby from me,' said Hanu, crying. 'My baby! My child! My daughter! Where is she?'

'She is safe with Yelba,' said Valachrad. 'Do not worry about Chinda.'

Fhiro watched his mother collapse into his father's arms. Oljon lowered her down and comforted her, himself half-kneeling on the floor, as she sobbed into his shoulder. 'I'm so sorry,' he said. 'I've let you all down.'

'It's all right, Ma,' said Fhiro. 'Yelba's a great cook.'

'I'll never see her again,' mumbled Hanu.

'You will, Ma!' cried Fhiro.

'And at least she's safe,' said Dorrick.

'Preparations are underway for you to depart within the hour,' said Valachrad, turning to leave. 'I am so sorry for what distress you have endured among us. Know that your contributions will never be forgotten, and the Empire is forever indebted to you.' With that he left, taking Imial with him.

Fhiro turned to his father. 'Was this a mistake?'

Oljon sighed. 'I made the right choices given what I knew at the time, but had I known what we were walking into here ...'

'My baby,' said Hanu. 'My poor baby is gone.'

'I'm so sorry,' Oljon said again.

'It's not your fault,' said Fhiro. 'It's Glorthig's and Marallel's.'

Dorrick had drifted a few paces away, and was toying with a thin reed of grass. He threw it to the ground. 'Well that's it then. We're committed.'

Hanu wiped her eyes and stared at her oldest son. 'What do you mean, committed?'

'I'm not going to the excavation site,' said Dorrick. 'I'm staying with my unit.'

'You will *not!*' said Hanu.

'Dorrick,' said Oljon, 'if I'm to lead an alliance, defending this planet, I need to know you're as safe as you can be.'

'I've come of age,' said Dorrick. 'I've dodged standing up against them this long, with one excuse or another. I'll fight them here, whether it makes a difference or not. I'm one

opponent that won't hide away from them and their shock dragons.'

'You have never seen a shock dragon,' said Oljon. 'Light weaponry like you will be carrying barely scratches them. Heavy weaponry is a challenge to aim mid-flight. Go with your mother and brother, please.'

'You cannot stay,' said Hanu.

Dorrick looked back at his parents, his expression unflinching. 'I know it grieves you, but I … I've made my decision. I'm sorry.'

Hanu wept again. She leant over and clasped Dorrick's hand. 'Please, Dor', for me! For us!'

Dorrick looked back into her eyes, but he said nothing.

Hanu bowed her head and cried.

'Do you have to, Dorrick?' asked Fhiro.

'I'll see you when you get back,' said Dorrick, and he smiled, but it was a forced effort, and Fhiro sensed his brother did not believe it.

Fhiro walked over and hugged him. 'I've known you my whole life,' he said. 'You can't go. You can't die.'

'We all die some day,' said Dorrick.

Pral, the soldier who had been with them at the fort, and had greeted them on the Siwob, appeared at the doorway. 'Ishthen, they must leave now. The Jashpuri ambassador is waiting.'

Fhiro felt Dorrick slowly let him go. He turned to his father. 'Can't we change the deal? If you aren't leading them, can we all go to Kartna?'

'It's not an option,' said Oljon, placing a hand on Fhiro's shoulder. 'I just wish it was.'

Fhiro saw tears in his father's eyes. 'Will you be all right, Pa?'

Oljon smiled, and stroked Fhiro's hair. 'I've commanded all

kinds of alliances, and combinations of forces, against all manner of dangers, but I've never felt fear like this before.'

Fhiro hugged his father.

'It's not the Creedate,' said Oljon, 'though their hordes may block out the sky, and though they may find me, torment me and slay me. Until now, until I met your mother, and until we had the three of you, I've never had so much to lose.'

Fhiro realised he was crying into his father's chest.

Pral coughed. 'Ishthen, I'm so sorry to intrude.'

Fhiro felt his mother pull him away from his father.

'Goodbye Fhiro,' said his father. 'Go now and prepare your things. I need to have a few words with your mother before she joins you.'

Fhiro retreated towards the door. He wiped his eyes. He did not care what Dorrick or Pral might think.

Dorrick waited at the door as Fhiro left, giving him a farewell nod, a sad, half-smile on his face. His father made him one final wave, and then was deep in conversation with his mother.

Pral took Fhiro to where Imial was waiting.

'Come on, Fhiro,' Imial said. 'At least one of your parents will be with you.' He humphed.

Fhiro sniffed. 'I never asked you about your ma before,' said Fhiro.

'I … I miss her … often,' said Imial.

* * *

After Hanu embraced him on her way out of the courtyard, Oljon's oldest son approached him.

'You're ready for this?' asked Oljon.

Dorrick nodded.

'You're younger than I was when I first saw combat,' said

Oljon.

'I'm ready,' said Dorrick. 'Send me back to my unit.'

Oljon shook his head. 'You'll be part of Valachrad's escort. We'll both need bird riders with us, but I can't have you protecting me.'

'Why?'

'Because I'm essential to this,' said Oljon. 'I might need to sacrifice my entire troop of bodyguards without the slightest hesitation to survive. I've done it before.'

Dorrick said nothing.

'They will try not to kill Valachrad if they can,' said Oljon. 'I'm to be tortured to death if they catch me. I don't want to think what I'd have to put up with if they capture you as well. For the duration of this battle you are not my son, understood? I am your commanding officer.'

'Yes sir,' said Dorrick, standing to attention.

Oljon nodded. 'I'm Ishthen. General Ishthen Niraltia.'

'Yes, general,' said Dorrick.

'Good,' said Oljon. 'Follow along for now until we find Valachrad.'

Pral returned.

'You didn't want to go with them, then, Pral?' asked Oljon.

Pral grinned. 'And miss another chance to serve alongside you? Against hordes of the Creedate?'

'Marallel may be coming,' said Oljon as he walked through the door into the Embassy interior. Pral and Dorrick followed him.

'All the sweeter shall the taste of victory be if he does,' said Pral.

'Indeed.'

CHAPTER 28

'Did Pa really kill Thurgon?' Fhiro asked his mother.

They had stepped outside the Old Harvester Fort. The forest air smelt good, though it did not feel the same as before. Much of the surrounding countryside was now a desolate, burned-out waste.

'It's a lot to take in,' she replied, 'I know. It was bad enough telling you as much as we did when we left Andelic.'

'But this is crazy,' said Fhiro. 'And the Creedate think Pa murdered Avithen.'

Hanu put her arm around him and pulled him against her. 'We tried to spare you lives of threat and danger. Foolish idea, though. Running away from trouble just delayed it. At best we would have been leaving it for your children to endure. I'm so sorry.'

'Don't be sorry Ma,' said Fhiro. 'We'll always remember back home.'

'What we're doing here may save Andelic,' said Hanu. 'If Kartna goes to war with the Creedate, Marallel will be too busy to expand his empire.'

Fhiro looked around. He felt a lot more comfortable knowing the fort had been invested with a large garrison of troops, and that numerous turrets had been installed on its roof to defend against the Creedate, and any wandering creatures should they come this way. Giant beasts supporting heavy guns on their backs patrolled the area, and in every squad of soldiers at least two were armed with shoulder mounted crystal-weapons, powerful enough to knock out a Creedate shock dragon at range, or blast a graveling off its feet.

'Fhiro! Wait for me,' Imial called to them as he ran out of the fort.

'Ma, you coming to training?' asked Fhiro.

'Not this time,' said Hanu. 'I've got letters from your father to interpret.'

'Can't I read them?' he asked.

'Sorry.' The sound of her laughter gladdened Fhiro. She seemed so low now that Chinda was gone. 'Too much detailed information about preparations and negotiations. But he sends his love.' She kept smiling, but her face looked sorrowful again.

'Don't worry Ma. Chinda's the safest of all of us now.'

His mother grinned. 'Stop trying to read my mind. I worry about you, Dorrick and your father too, you know.'

'Let's go,' said Imial, having now reached them.

They waved Hanu goodbye and went to the training ground. Halbat, the Jashpuri ambassador, was there early, as always. He was tall, with a thin beard and dark hair. Behind him the transparent-screen enclosure, in which individuals could practice targeting in all directions, was already prepared.

'Not blind-sight training again,' moaned Imial.

'Don't be so bothered by it,' said Fhiro. 'You'll get better.'

'You will improve, Imial,' said Halbat, passing him the blindfold and pistol. 'Fhiro had already been taught the fundamentals by his father. You'll catch up.'

As usual Imial missed all the targets by a long way, though Halbat assured him he was improving.

Fhiro entered next. He gave himself a moment to put all his cares and concerns out of his mind, just as Halbat had advised him to, but it was difficult.

He heard the door close behind him.

Relax, he told himself. Muscle memory. Confidence.

He stood in the assigned position, studied the ten targets around him one last time, loaded his weapon, and placed the

blindfold over his eyes. He aimed where he thought the first target was, then fired ten times, once for each target, as Imial had done, and then removed the blindfold.

Two.

Not his best at all, he thought.

'Good,' said Halbat. 'We'll have another go at the end of the session.'

As usual, their scores after training were somehow worse than the ones from the beginning.

'I hate blind-sight training,' muttered Imial. 'It's almost as bad as knife throwing.'

Fhiro said nothing. He was very good at throwing knives.

'Not everyone masters blind-sight,' said Halbat, 'but knives are easily come across. People don't always expect them to be deployed at distance effectively. Never underestimate the power of deception.'

'Can you overestimate the power of deception?' asked Fhiro.

'Well,' said Halbat, 'of course, I suppose. I'm just trying to emphasise a point.'

* * *

'This is costing a fortune!' cried the Iap ambassador. 'The Creedate attack shows no sign of materialising. Pirate activity has escalated within our borders. We cannot maintain this level of readiness much longer.'

'The city around us is engulfed in rioting and looting,' said King Suloa. 'Niquani and Followers of The Calling are murdering each other in the streets every day all over this planet. You do not shoulder burdens alone. We must trust in Ishthen.'

'Your waiting may soon be over.' Oljon walked into the war-chamber, and crossed the bridge to the suspended platform

where the ambassadors and their officers stood with King Suloa. 'There has been another flurry of Washlight activity at Pelorn's borders, stronger than the others.'

'Supreme Commander,' said the new Baworl ambassador, 'I hear the mutinous troops have been dealt with.'

Oljon nodded. 'And I would like to thank Admiral Kyusec for her help with this. It cannot have been easy to turn her guns on her own ships.'

'The Calling is tolerated, like all religions in Hithostun,' said Admiral Kyusec, 'but treason is not.'

'Do you think this Washlight represents the Creedate?' asked King Suloa. 'Have they arrived?'

'I had begun to hope they might never come,' said the Baworl ambassador.

'They will come,' said Oljon.

'I commend your acceptance of Ishthen as your commander,' said Valachrad, addressing all of them, 'but you would be wiser still to ally yourselves with Kartna. If Marallel sends larger forces here from the Creedate heartworlds, nothing you can do will stop him taking everything that you have.'

'Ishthen's leadership, though we are grateful for it, is a necessary evil,' said King Suloa. 'Such an alliance, though, would be to sacrifice mastery of our own destiny.'

'Your expectations are incorrect,' said Valachrad. 'We would bring you greatness, not harm.'

'And the fury of the Creedate will differ little whether we are allied or not,' said Oljon. 'If anything, an alliance might limit their wrath.'

'We have made our choice,' said King Suloa.

'Indeed,' said the Hithostun ambassador. 'Perhaps if, in times of peace, you had come to know our people better, you might understand us.'

A man raced across the further bridge, from the crystal-telegraph, and presented a message to one of the Hithostun officers. The officer was very still as he read it, and then looked up. 'It is confirmed. Creedate scout ships have entered Pelorn's local volume.'

There was silence for a moment, and then all of them followed the officer to the map where he began plotting the positions of the Creedate ships and the movements of the alliance's skirmishers that had been ordered, in advance, to react to such an intrusion.

'It has taken him two weeks,' said Admiral Kyusec. 'What sort of host could he have gathered in this time?'

'He has been most active in Nubro,' said the Hithostun ambassador.

'The Nubro region provided a force more than a match for this alliance to Marallel, years ago, when Thurgon sent him to subjugate the Yefellic peoples,' said Oljon. 'They remember fondly, the riches they acquired through plundering and sacking. Nubro isn't quite the power it once was, but Glorthig will have found no shortage of volunteers there.'

'So we are to contend with volunteers?' Kyusec laughed. 'Our trained forces will deal them heavy losses at every turn.'

'Volunteers yes,' said Valachrad, 'but almost all citizens in those parts undergo military training.'

'They are like us,' smirked the new Vinaran ambassador. 'Culturally similar, but always fighting each other.'

'They are also far more numerous,' said Oljon, 'but Glorthig is not Marallel. Pulling off this feat will not have been easy. On the other hand, if he had delayed another week, a more definitive force could have been sent from the Creedate heartworlds. Let us hope his ambition conquered his reasoning, and that he has arrived underpowered, and ill prepared.'

'Could he have at his disposal forces sent here from the Creedate heartworlds?' asked King Suloa.

'Only if those forces were sent this way in advance of Reshna's death,' said Oljon.

'May the gods forever curse them if so,' said the new Hithostun ambassador, 'though I would not put it past Marallel.'

'Nor would I,' said Oljon as he studied the map, while the crystal-telegrapher's assistants arrived, one by one, to mark out the positions of the arriving Creedate vessels.

'How long until our defences make contact with the enemy?' asked Admiral Kyusec, scratching her chin.

'Another twenty minutes,' said Oljon.

Admiral Kyusec stepped back from the map. 'I must return to my place at the helm of our fleet.'

Oljon nodded. 'May your spirits watch over you.' He looked at the other officers nearby. 'Any questions from the rest of you?'

'No sir,' they replied.

'Then you remember the plan,' said Oljon. 'Now execute it.'

Some of the admirals and captains uttered prayers and promises to the spirits as they left.

'Is the underground command centre prepared?' Oljon asked the King's Vizier.

'We expect to confirm its safety in twenty hours,' she replied.

'We will be going there in ten,' said Oljon. 'Send word.'

'Very well.' She departed from the table.

Information continued to feed through, with assistants placing markers across the map. When units were too close to each other to be distinguished, the location in question would be tagged, and another, smaller, three-dimensional map would be used to provide further details.

After two hours they received word of larger ships

appearing at the aura boundary.

'Three flotillas of Creedate dreadnaughts have appeared here,' said the map assistant as he placed the units on the large map. 'The Baworl skirmishers have turned back.'

'And they will die,' said the Baworl ambassador, 'because you made them overreach themselves. The triangulated fire will destroy all of them.'

'Probably,' said Oljon.

'A waste of Baworl's precious trained forces,' said the Baworl ambassador, scowling.

'A necessary sacrifice in order to lure the enemy deeper,' said Oljon. 'Make them think you all rejected my offer to lead you.'

Another map assistant jogged towards the large map from the crystal-telegrapher. 'Two full Nubro fleets have appeared just here.'

'That is a large force to be inserting into the battle so early,' said Valachrad. 'Do you still think Glorthig is in command?'

'Glorthig might have done this out of arrogance,' said Oljon, 'and a Nubro commander might have done this to surprise us.'

'How can you understand this?' asked Dorrick.

Oljon looked around and saw his son. 'Nice of you to join us.'

'We've inspected the layout of your command centre under the city,' said Pral. Both he and Dorrick wore their bird-riding gear, with thick gloves, light-weight mail, and helmets under their arms. 'The hockers are being worked harder than some of them can endure, and the defences will not be ready for another sixteen hours. I understand you plan to go there in eight?'

'Yes,' said Oljon, 'if only to settle in. The defences will be ready before they are needed.' He looked at the Vizier. 'Warn them of the risk to their King if they do not hurry up.'

'It is the ground defences that are delayed,' said the Vizier,

'and the city is a mess of clashing hostile groups. Half the soldiers we stationed here have been diverted to control unrest in the streets. A coordinated attack by enough civilians might breach the perimeter of the new command centre and put the King in danger.'

'Send us more men, then,' said Oljon, 'if you have doubts.'

'We have no men to spare,' said the Vizier.

'We will need more men,' said Oljon. 'If necessary some areas of the city may have to go undefended.'

The Vizier took a step back, glanced at King Suloa, and then nodded to Oljon. She whispered some words into the ear of her assistant.

Dorrick walked closer to the large map. 'How are we doing?'

'First blood to the enemy,' muttered the Baworl ambassador.

At that moment a map assistant arrived from the crystal-telegrapher and with slow reluctance removed the Baworl skirmishers from where they had been pursued by the dreadnaughts. 'The Baworl skirmishers have been eliminated,' he said. 'Only a few ships survived.' He then moved the dreadnaughts a slight distance further towards the planet.

The Baworl ambassador walked away from the map.

'Come on, Dorrick,' said Pral, 'let us leave them for now. You'll have plenty of time to learn how such maps work at the academies in Kartna.' He slapped Dorrick's shoulder.

Dorrick looked back at his father as he left the war-chamber. Oljon's attention was so consumed by his work he did not see his son leave.

'Trust your father,' said Pral. 'He knows what he's doing.'

Over the next twenty-four hours the divided, factional and highly suspicious alliance Oljon led carried out his orders to the letter, much to his relief.

The Nubro and Creedate fleets that had chased the Niquani skirmishers fell straight into a trap. They retaliated by sending

enough ships to undo the ambushing forces, but by then the Niquani ships had disappeared, leaving mines and explosive-rigged debris where they had been, inflicting further heavy losses. Oljon gave the impression that the majority of the forces were from Pelorn, and had many of these jump into the battle as though they were being called in by panicking commanders. It was then that Admiral Kyusec's armada arrived, having been hiding a short jump away. Some hours after the battle in the space around Pelorn itself had begun, the Nubro and Creedate forces started to retreat. Using the methods that Oljon had encouraged Admiral Kyusec to implement, the retreat soon became a rout, and the Niquani fighters started to deploy jump-disrupter-crystals to prevent their opponents from escaping, and thus destroyed more ships.

Oljon knew that the surprises and tricks he had delivered were nothing new, and that they had been used numerous times before in wars across the galaxy over the ages. The true mark of his success was knitting his forces together so well that they could implement such a plan. The command structure, the communication and supply network, and persuasion of influential Niquani generals, admirals, officials and rulers, many of whom were rivals of one another, was a feat he knew few could have pulled off. He felt reassured that his abilities had not dimmed with age, and allowed himself a glimmer of pride as the adjustments to the map confirmed that his forces had won. Then he looked towards the crystal-telegrapher in anticipation of the message he knew was coming.

'We have won!' cried King Suloa.

Oljon still said nothing, glancing between the large map of Pelorn's local volume and the crystal-telegrapher base on the far side of the underground war-chamber.

The Niquani ambassadors congratulated one another. The

Iap ambassador looked particularly relieved.

'We may have won,' said Oljon, 'and all of your fleets performed admirably, but stand down none of your units. There may be more to come.'

Two hours passed. Food was brought in to the war-chamber, but Oljon forbade them to drink wine or consume any narcotic they routinely forbid troops and commanders in battle.

'I should never have doubted you,' said the Baworl ambassador, his head bowed. 'Accept my apologies. My men fought and died well. They will be remembered as heroes.'

One of the crystal-telegrapher messengers came running towards them. Oljon raised his finger to silence the Baworl ambassador. The messenger's face was marked by shock and dread.

'It's all right,' said Oljon. 'Tell me.'

The assistant approached him. 'Four giant …' He was lost for words.

Oljon nodded. 'Four Creedate fleet carriers have arrived in Pelorn's local volume.'

The messenger nodded.

'How are they configured?' asked Oljon. 'Have they arrived at the same spot?'

'No,' said the messenger, 'and small fleets have arrived at other sites as well. They are surrounding the planet.'

'Demonstrate on the map,' said Oljon.

The crystal-telegrapher did so.

'What's going on?' asked the Hithostun ambassador. Around them many of the other admirals and generals had started to gather, the conversations on their lips dying fast.

Oljon watched until the messenger had finished his work. He studied the map for thirty seconds.

'Marallel is here,' he said.

King Suloa's mouth fell open. 'It cannot be.'

'Even if our entire alliance committed itself to this local volume,' said Oljon, 'we could not defeat him.' He looked back at the King, 'Your only hope is to ally with Kartna.'

King Suloa looked at him blankly.

The King's Vizier came to stand by her master's side. 'Your majesty, if we form an alliance there will be bloodshed across the city. We could not even prevent it erupting within the keep, or here.'

'If you do not ally with Kartna,' said Oljon, 'then your planet and all of your people are lost. Fighting in your streets will be the least of your concerns.'

'You don't understand,' said Suloa. 'It is not as simple as just making an alliance.'

'Stop him!'

Oljon turned and saw some of the King's guards and the Hithostun vice-admiral tackle a man to the ground. The Hithostun vice-admiral stood up. 'This man's blade was meant for the King. How is it your deepest lair is so full of traitors and spies?'

The King turned away from Oljon and faced Valachrad. 'I must consult what members of my government remain, and the nobles that have not fled, before accepting your offer.'

'Then do it quickly,' said Valachrad. 'The enemy will wipe the Niquani forces from the map soon enough. Then they will be invading this planet. The more you delay the less we can help.'

The King turned and left, taking his bodyguard and priests with him.

'What of our forces in space?' asked the Hithostun vice-admiral. He was nursing a small laceration to his arm. 'Admiral Kyusec will need direction if all is truly lost.'

'They should prepare to defend the planet as planned,' said Oljon. 'It may delay long enough for the King to agree to an

alliance. Then at the right time, Kyusec needs to escape.'

They all watched the map over the following two hours. The Niquani alliance configured itself into a defensive posture, and as the battle turned against them, its component ships began to jump off the map.

'The planet is lost,' said the Hithostun vice-admiral.

'This planet is not lost.' General Halari, leader of the Pelorn ground and air forces, had returned. 'The fight here has just begun. If you want safety, flee with your ship back to Hithostun to await news of our deaths.'

'I will stay,' said the Hithostun vice-admiral. 'I shall die with you.'

CHAPTER 29

Tokun was a captain of the Pelorn air force. Across the skies he led his squadrons of high-altitude bird riders towards the Creedate craft entering Pelorn's atmosphere over the ocean, six hundred miles west of Riletta. Ishthen had insisted their targets would be vulnerable this far out from the city.

'These craft carry the assault and shock dragons of the Creedate air force,' Ishthen had told him. 'They mean to decelerate over the ocean, and cruise on towards the city to deploy their loads. They will want to conserve the forces they have inside, so there is a high chance they will remain unguarded by the time you reach them.'

'How do you know they will not anticipate such a strike?' Admiral Kyusec had questioned much of Ishthen's advice in the beginning.

'They expect us not to anticipate where they will enter our atmosphere,' Ishthen had replied, 'and it is unlikely they are aware of how well trained and bred Pelorn's high altitude atmospheric squadrons are. Of course, they might take precautions, but it is still an opportune moment to strike and make much gain at relatively low cost. If they invade, they will expect our resolve to have been shaken, and that your adherence to my advice will have ended. They will assume you are hiding behind your city's defences, and refusing to take risks.'

'We will never cower away,' General Halari had said.

'I know,' said Ishthen. 'I believe in you.'

Tokun was closing in on the Creedate atmospheric craft.

Having just passed through the planet's atmosphere, he knew the ships were scorching hot, and travelling faster towards the city behind him than he was moving away from it. He had been warned that there would be too many enemy ships to count, but his wildest imaginations had not prepared him for what his eyes now saw. The sky ahead was filled with an expanding swarm of insects. He knew that each small black dot above the horizon was an enormous flying fortress, as large as one of Riletta's outer-city castles. As they neared he turned to check the resolve of the thousands of air-warriors under his command.

His men soared through the high winds, their birds beating the rhythms of the air with confidence and grace. He knew fear gripped them, as it gripped him, but he believed in them, and he had their trust.

He signalled to turn around and fly back toward the city, so that they would be moving slower, relative to their intended targets. He checked over his shoulder. The insects were insects no longer, but hulking shadows. He had seen battle before, but only once had he contended with an invasion from space, and his enemy then had been far fewer, and their craft tiny by comparison.

Then the ships passed beneath them. Tokun could feel heat radiating up to him. His bird, Lurica, shuddered. He patted her neck to sooth her and then gave the signal to begin the attack. Thousands of bolts of crystal-fire descended upon the ships about them. Their weapons were huge, shoulder-mounted cannons, but the high-altitude squadrons had been trained for accuracy at a distance, and their aim was true.

Explosions rocked the Creedate fleet. Some of the craft splintered into pieces, the heat from their surfaces incinerating their contents, leaving only charred remains to fall into the ocean below. But for every ship destroyed at least as many

passed through, unscathed. Behind them more continued to pour in from space.

Tokun wondered if the mission had been in vain.

'You will inflict as much damage as you can,' Ishthen had told him. 'The number that survive your attack will depend as much upon how many they send as it will upon the skill of your men.'

He had not failed. He had done his duty.

He saw steam and clouds form around some of the approaching ships. Dust billowed from the back of one of them, and then another.

'But surely the landing craft will release their dragons when they realise they are in danger?' Tokun had asked Ishthen this himself.

'When that happens, you will be outnumbered,' Ishthen had said solemnly. 'You will not be able to defeat them.'

'Where is the value in this sacrifice?' General Halari had asked.

'Every ship you destroy will vastly diminish the burden upon Riletta,' said Ishthen, 'and for every ship that releases its dragons to do battle with you, their cargo must rest after they have won their victory, keeping them away from the city and the forces defending it. You will have done Pelorn a great service, and if she survives this invasion, she will forever be indebted to you.'

So this was it, thought Tokun. His life was to end. He saw the form of his death emerge as the particles of dust came nearer. Knowing that there was little value in exercising discrimination in who they wished to eliminate, the Creedate had unleashed swarms of shock dragons into the sky. They raced towards him, brandishing their gnashing jaws in their armoured heads, their scale-coated limbs and wide, shining wings glinting in the sunlight.

Tokun steadied his resolve. He had not chosen to serve his nation so that he could hide and be eclipsed by the glory of others. He had chosen the difficult path: to train, to suffer, and then to die a violent death for his people. For the greatness of Pelorn, his King, Suloa, and the Niquani.

He cried his battle cry, though it was swallowed up by the wind so that none could hear it, and charged Lurica forward.

* * *

Fhiro stared out across the wasted forest and charred hillsides from the mountain's summit. The blackened greyness extended for miles east of the Old Harvester Fort below, but beyond it lush greens and silver streams burst forth, thriving as they had done for hundreds of thousands of years.

'What a mess,' said Imial.

'It's beautiful beyond the burnt area,' said Hanu.

'You should have seen it before,' said Fhiro. 'Poor Cerilina. She came up here just for this.'

'It wouldn't have made a difference,' said Imial. 'If the archaeologists hadn't gone up here they would have been in the Great Hall like everyone else.'

'Time we carried on, boys,' said Hanu. 'We need to get to the beacon.'

'How much further is it?' asked Imial.

'Another half an hour.' She looked to the two soldiers who had been sent to guide them, and one of them nodded.

'I wish they'd let us inside the mountain,' said Fhiro. 'I want to see Poshokan architecture.'

'You should see Kartnan architecture,' said Imial. 'Many magnificent structures of ours have stood for centuries. Every cornerstone in our heartworlds is priceless.'

'Sounds impressive,' said Fhiro. 'What if I offered eighty

trillion Kartnan Minas for a cornerstone? Surely they'd sell it then.'

'Not even the Merchant-Lords have that sort of wealth at their disposal,' said Imial.

'So they probably would sell it,' said Fhiro, 'so it isn't priceless then.'

'Come on boys.' Hanu was starting to sound impatient.

They followed her westwards towards the dip in the mountain's crest where the station was based. Fhiro enjoyed the view of the lake, now bordered by a rim of grey-brown silt and sand following its draining. In the distance beyond, he could see the mountains that towered over its northern edge. 'There must be a lot less water to live in, now,' he said. 'The Chissids must be scrambling over each other to eat.'

As they descended the final ridge to the relay beacon Fhiro looked to the south. Large clouds were gathering and moving nearer, and some of the forest was shielded by a grey haze. 'It just goes on and on out there.'

The box-like shape of the relay beacon became clear as they neared it. The two guards went ahead and knocked on the door of the station. It opened and a soldier peered out.

'Jammit?' said Fhiro.

'I remember you,' said Imial.

'Fhiro! Imial!' Jammit smiled. 'I couldn't have asked for better luck charms! Then again,' he said, sighing, 'it seems we're out of luck.'

A hegel officer burst out of the door. 'Hanu? Lieutenant? Thank the spirits. We've been trying to reach you!'

'You have?' asked Hanu.

'We've heard nothing,' said the lieutenant who had accompanied them.

'Our fortunes have turned!' cried the hegel. 'An unstoppable armada of Creedate fleet carriers have overwhelmed the alliance.'

Fhiro felt light-headed. The last news they had heard had been entirely positive.

'Did you not hear the sirens?' asked the hegel officer. 'We repeated them several times, as did the fort.'

'We heard nothing,' said Hanu. 'We must have been sheltered from the sounds during our passage through the narrow passes.'

'We must get you back down the mountain immediately,' said the lieutenant.

'Jammit can go with you,' said the hegel officer.

'Another message coming through, sir,' said a voice from within the station. The hegel ran back inside.

Fhiro noticed flashing lights, far away to west, obscured from the fort by the mountain. He saw that Jammit was staring at them too.

'May the spirits be merciful,' whispered Jammit.

'You can read the code?' asked Fhiro.

Jammit nodded. 'I'd dread to think where they would've posted me if I couldn't. I got an award and a punishment at the same time after coming back from this fort. First time that's happened in three hundred years, apparently.'

'Well done,' said Fhiro, 'I think.'

'No,' said Jammit. 'Not really.'

'Jammit,' said Hanu, 'what does the message say?'

'The Creedate are swarming the planet's atmosphere,' said Jammit. 'Our forces in space are in retreat.'

'They've reached here that fast?' cried Hanu. 'We were routing the enemy when we set off up here. I came to deliver a special message for the supreme commander.'

'Their progress was still faster than expected,' said the hegel, who had now rejoined them. 'You haven't a moment to lose. I hope you're not too tired.'

CHAPTER 30

'Ishthen,' said General Halari as he approached Oljon, 'the Creedate invasion forces have breached our atmosphere with a large force just here!' He indicated a point on the map of Pelorn's surface.

Oljon studied it. 'This is Fawast. They have arrived above the land of the continent itself!'

Halari nodded. 'Technically not in breach of the Supra-Atmospheric Bombardment Laws, as they know this part of the planet is only occupied by natural fauna and military units.'

'Even so,' said Oljon, 'the law is still broken if they crash any of their craft upon the surface.'

'Would the SABAc council be strong enough to do anything about Marallel if they did?' asked the Iap ambassador.

'Kartna and Jashpur are just two of the galactic powers more than willing to enforce the council's decrees,' said Oljon. 'Alert those at the excavation site. Authorise Halbat's plan.'

'Halbat's plan?' asked the Hithostun vice-admiral.

General Halari nodded. 'So be it.' He spoke with his assistant who ran to the crystal-telegraphers.

'Halbat the Jashpuri ambassador?' asked the Hithostun vice-admiral.

'Why is this not something we are aware of?' asked the Hithostun ambassador.

'Because it concerns the defence of property belonging to Pelorn,' said Oljon. 'It is unlikely to have an impact on how any of our allied units conduct themselves, especially since it was only to be implemented if things got this far.'

'So what is Halbat's plan?'

'It will soon become clear,' said Oljon.

The Histhostun ambassador shot Oljon a stern look, but said nothing.

'Shall we inform the King?' asked General Halari.

'Valachrad is with him now advising him to do the only thing that can save all our lives,' said Oljon. 'I suggest you lend your efforts to the same end.'

'If the King allies with Kartna,' said General Halari, 'he may die even sooner than if he does not. This is the spiritual heartworld of the Niquani. You don't understand how much of a betrayal against our people it would be.'

'Betraying his people would be allowing them all to die,' said Oljon.

'In your mind,' said Halari. 'You are not Niquani. If we are extinguished, at least we perished faithful to who we are. If we allow ourselves to be absorbed into your empire, our ways will be eroded, diminished and forgotten.'

'I would ask how many of your citizens feel the same way,' said Oljon, 'but I know this line of argument is fruitless. Take death, then, if that is what you want. Kartna will contest these lands with Marallel, whatever you choose, but at this rate it will be over a carcass of a planet, littered with all our corpses, if King Suloa's stubbornness holds out against good sense.'

* * *

'Is that the siren?' asked Hanu when they were halfway to the bottom.

The lieutenant stopped, took out a device and pointed it towards the fort. It emitted a sequence of flashes of light, and after a while the fort responded in kind. 'An invasion force approaches,' he said.

'How far away?' asked Hanu.

'Closing in fast,' said the lieutenant. 'They are estimated to reach the fort within half an hour.'

'But it took us an hour to get here from the fort,' said Fhiro.

'How could they have got here this fast?' cried Hanu. 'They must have dropped ships directly over the land. They're defying the Supra-Atmospheric Bombardment Accord.'

'They must be confident in their pilots,' said the lieutenant, putting the device away, 'and desperate to secure this place. We must run. Go!'

He sped down the path.

Fhiro was quick to follow after, his fear swelling inside him. Hanu and Imial chased after him.

'It's Marallel,' panted Hanu.

'Marallel?' asked Fhiro. 'Here?'

'Concentrate on your footing,' yelled Jammit.

'Certain of it.' His mother's voice came from behind him, as Fhiro leapt down the steep path. 'Only best ships … best pilots … dare enter over land.'

'Marallel himself? You sure?' Jammit's voice.

'He wouldn't trust anyone else … to do that,' said Hanu.

'But where?' asked Fhiro, risking a glimpse at the sky.

'West-by-northwest,' said Jammit. 'When we round this ridge.'

The blare of the siren grew louder as they passed around the eastern slopes of the mountain, descending as fast as they dared.

'Look!' cried Jammit.

Emerging from the clouds above, far to the west, were thousands of tiny shadows, racing towards them.

'They're coming!' shouted the lieutenant.

Fhiro looked up every chance he had, and the black particles in the distance were larger each time. He felt sickly.

The knowledge that the bloodthirsty Creedate were approaching threatened to eat away his strength. He started to feel nauseous and wraithlike, as though he was draining away into another realm in advance of his impending death.

The surface-to-air defences erupted into a rattling barrage, and waves of fiery bolts sped upwards into the sky.

'By all that's holy,' said Hanu, 'they're upon us!'

Dragons, birds, and their riders sped towards the fort, but almost all of them were struck down by the wall of gunfire from the forest. Of the two dragon riders that broke through, one veered over the fort before being shot out of the sky. The other flew across the north face of the mountain, firing shots at the guards stationed there. Then the beast's wings stiffened, and it glided onwards to where they huddled in a group. Fhiro could see the dragon's eyes through its helmet, and the visor of its rider. The man on its back turned in his saddle, and shifted the barrel of his weapon.

'Get down!' cried the lieutenant.

Hanu leapt on the boys and brought them all to the ground just as the rattle of gunfire, and the whistling of projectiles tearing through the air, surrounded them.

The lieutenant raised his assault rifle, but jolted backwards and collapsed, a spray of blood blasting from his back.

Hanu leapt over her children amid the chips of rock and bursts of mud being cut out of the mountain by the hail of bullets. She snatched the rifle out of the dying lieutenant's hands, whirled around and knelt on one knee in a single movement. She followed the path of the departing dragon rider with the weapon's muzzle and fired once. She slung the weapon over her shoulder. 'Get up, all of you. Run!'

The dragon rider fell from his mount.

'And I thought your husband was dangerous,' whispered Jammit.

Hanu grasped Jammit's collar. 'If the Creedate realise who we are they'll kill us. Do you understand?'

'I think they're going to kill us all anyway,' said Jammit.

'We are with the Jashpuri ambassador,' said Hanu. 'Remember that.'

Jammit gulped.

'I need to know you understand this, or I swear to Aten I'll kill you right here.'

'Understood, ma'am,' said Jammit.

Fhiro was stunned. He had seen his mother angry before, but not like this. She had more than demonstrated her willingness to kill, and Fhiro had no doubt she would have extended this to Jammit if the troublesome soldier had answered incorrectly.

Hanu released Jammit and turned to check the lieutenant.

'Is he dead?' asked Imial.

Hanu nodded and took the lieutenant's side arm. 'We'll hold a funeral for him later, if we ever have the chance. Now go!' She ushered them all ahead.

Fhiro set off as fast as he could, but within moments his mother had leapt past him. Fhiro was aware of Imial's rapid breathing right behind him. He risked a glance. Imial's face was contorted with the effort, but he showed no sign of slowing.

'Advance scout party.' Hanu waved one hand towards the sky as she shouted. 'True attack to come from high above … with more devastation.'

Her words shot ice through Fhiro's veins. 'But … so many of them …' he panted.

'First wave were fanatics … died to show our gun placements.'

'But …' Imial barely had the breath to manage the single word.

'Don't slow down … Keep running … Faster.' Jammit again.

'Wet rocks!' said Hanu.

Fhiro focussed on the slippery rocks where a stream crossed the path.

'First wave all dead,' said Hanu. 'They'll send another before the real bombardment.'

'Good work,' said Jammit.

Fhiro felt his heart pound as he sprinted down the mountain, watching his feet all the way.

Imial gasped as he lost his footing. Fhiro instinctively shot out his hand to grab his friend, but Imial managed to right himself.

They rounded a turn in the path. The road leading from the dig site to the fort was visible a hundred metres ahead of them. Waiting there was Halbat and a group of soldiers.

Hanu stopped and waved them all to go past her. 'Keep going. Don't tire yet.'

Fhiro glanced at the sky. Dark shapes dropped out of the clouds above, and expanded, growing wings, heads and claws as they neared.

'More are coming!' he cried.

The rattle of gunfire almost responded to his cry, filling the air again with fire and carnage. Some of the beasts slowed and flew back, out of sight into the foggy canopy.

Fhiro sprinted for all he was worth, skidding to a halt in front of Halbat. Imial, a few seconds behind him, sunk to his knees struggling for breath. Hanu and Jammit caught up.

'Come with us,' said Halbat.

'We aren't going to the fort?' Hanu's question went unanswered as they raced in the opposite direction.

'Our squadrons have arrived,' cried one of the Pelorn soldiers.

Fhiro looked to the east and saw waves of birds and dragons rising into the air and firing at the invading forces.

An ear-shattering blast tore Fhiro's attention back. Debris flew into the air and dust gathered into a smoky mist ahead of them.

'They are bombarding us already,' cried Jammit.

Explosions came from behind them. As Fhiro looked back, the grounds around the fort erupted. Tongues of flame leapt high through clouds of debris. Fires burst forth from the charred remains of the forest. Blackened, skeletal trees stood out in sharp relief against the flames.

'They're targeting the guns,' said Halbat, steering the group down towards the lake. Soon they were running along a rough path that had been carved into the edge of its dried bed.

'We're going into the mountain?' panted Fhiro.

Halbat turned into a dug-out ravine. As they followed him, Fhiro felt a sudden upsurge in the bombardment. His ears rang. The push of the air almost knocked him off his feet. His last glance of the forest showed nothing but billowing flames and smoke.

'Keep going,' Jammit shouted. 'If they keep this up there'll be no air left to breathe!'

They all ran down the narrow hemmed-in path. At the end they were faced with a white wall. Fhiro recognised the Poshokan material. Cerilina and her team had had no luck breaking through, so what chance did they have now?

Halbat strode towards it, pulling a crystal activator from his sleeve.

'Look.' Imial was pointing at the white wall.

Fhiro could see lines in its otherwise flawless surface; lines that seemed to delineate a door.

Halbat activated it and it slid open. Fhiro heard his own gasp echoed by several others. A loud explosion jolted them all. Imial stumbled and almost fell. Fhiro cringed as his ears sang with the echoing blast.

'Come on,' said Halbat.

Beyond the open door lay a tunnel, illuminated along its walls with tiny lumia-crystals.

They all hurried inside as the ground shook beneath them again. Halbat impatiently pulled them all through the entrance and then moved his activator across the door in a multi-stage pattern. The moment it was sealed, sounds from outside were muffled. The air was still. In the sudden silence all Fhiro could hear was the ringing in his ears from the bombardment they had just escaped.

His mother was the first to speak. 'These crystal systems are still energised after all this time?' Her voice held wonderment. Then she seemed to shake herself back to reality. 'Where are we going?' she asked. 'They'll get through that door soon enough.'

Halbat didn't answer her question. 'Come on. We need to hurry.' They all began to run again. Mud from the entrance made Fhiro's shoes slip on the smooth floor. Imial's hand grasped his upper arm and kept him upright.

A change in the light signalled the end of the tunnel. They found themselves at the edge of a vast chamber. Fhiro stared out, taking in the vast pillars, the giant buildings, the suspended floors. It was the size of the port-city of Calagan, but he could feel the emptiness of aeons pressing down on them.

They reached a group of soldiers in Jashpuri uniforms. With them was a young dark-haired woman, with the Jashpuri insignia across her robes. 'Ah, my Lord,' she said.

'Ecrishia,' said Halbat, 'any progress at the entrance?'

Ecrishia shook her head. 'Everything we think of we enter, in every possible way. Still no luck.'

'Well we're out of time.' Halbat ran past Ecrishia.

'How's the battle outside?' asked Ecrishia, chasing after him.

'Before long the Creedate will have obliterated our defences,'

said Halbat. 'The sky above the clouds is swarming with their warriors.'

'You haven't said where we're going,' said Hanu.

'There has been an agreement between myself, King Suloa, Valachrad and Ishthen,' said Halbat. 'In the event of a Creedate attack here I have permission to board the device housed in this mountain and escape with it.'

'You think it can fly?' asked Fhiro. 'Can you fly it?'

'I had hoped to have at least tried to do so before the invasion began,' said Halbat, grimacing, 'but we've yet to even get inside. I guess there's no time like the present.'

'Why can't you get in?' asked Imial. 'Can't you just blast open the door and fix it later?'

'Unlike the walls of this structure,' said Halbat, 'the doors should be susceptible to explosives but we'd need so much we'd risk destroying the very technology we aim to discover.'

'If the Creedate do take this place,' said Hanu, 'then perhaps destroying it would be for the best.'

Halbat nodded. 'I do not have permission for this, though.'

'Sometimes the rules need bending for the greater good,' said Hanu. 'If Marallel gets his hands on such a technology then the future of the galaxy is bleak.'

Halbat said nothing as he led them onwards in silence.

They passed under a large arch into a corridor. A group of Pelorn soldiers, their faces fixed with hard, grim expressions, ran past them in the opposite direction. Other soldiers garrisoned the path ahead. At the end of the corridor were further guards, a few of whom were crouched behind mounted guns, either side of a smaller arch. Fhiro followed Halbat and Ecrishia through this arch, and then around a corner.

A muffled boom resonated from the direction of the mountain's entrance and the ground shook.

'They are trying to break in!' cried a voice.

Halbat led them through into a giant room. Fhiro gaped at the massive cylinder that reached up through the ceiling, dominating the space. Arrays of buttons and levers covered its surface.

Soldiers stood aside as Halbat approach.

'They will get through that door eventually,' said Halbat. 'Ecrishia, get to the terminal and continue what you were doing before, or just try something. Anything!'

'What is it?' asked Fhiro.

'We believe the artefact we seek is beyond that wall,' said Halbat, 'but the door is controlled by this locking system. We also have reason to believe the artefact will be destroyed if the lock is tampered with.'

'So you need a key?' asked Fhiro.

'Far more frustrating,' said Halbat. 'We need to crack their password. They've left a helpful reminder in case it got forgotten, but we can't make sense of it. It's aimed at Poshokan minds and we don't think like them.'

'What's the riddle?' asked Fhiro.

Another powerful vibration shook the walls and floor.

'Are they inside?' asked Jammit.

'It concerns their most fundamental rule, or approach, to determining their laws and philosophies,' said Halbat.

'Poshokan laws and philosophies?' asked Imial.

'Don't we know what that is?' asked Fhiro. 'I thought they were obsessed with reason.'

'They were,' said Halbat, 'but everything we've entered along the lines of adhering to reason has failed to unlock the door.'

Further, thunder-like sounds penetrated the silence.

Fhiro studied the machine that Ecrishia was working on. There were a great many buttons, each inscribed with archaic runes he did not recognise. Above them runes were inscribed on the wall.

'Can't you pick the lock?' asked Imial.

'We've tried,' said Halbat, 'and failed. We've now resorted to trying to find a way to tell when we are hitting the correct keys by listening carefully to the sound they make when depressed.'

'That sounds desperate,' said Imial.

'If you can crack this for us, boy, that would save us a lot of bother,' said Halbat.

'Well if it's this late in the day maybe we really should just blast our way through,' said Hanu.

Fhiro wondered if the assault rifle his mother was still carrying was making her prone to more destructive, violent thoughts. He pointed to the runes above the machine. 'Does this state the riddle?'

Halbat nodded. 'It reads "The future is filled with uncertainty, and there will ever be challenges that threaten us with oblivion. What law best guides us towards our goal?" Below is an alphabet. The correct sequence of letters and spaces must be entered to unlock the door.'

'Presumably this is a law they didn't follow,' said Hanu, 'or it didn't work, because the Poshokans were wiped out.'

'And we'll be joining them in oblivion if we don't figure it out, however useful it was,' said Halbat.

Hanu gave a mirthless laugh.

'Perhaps you're using it wrong?' asked Imial, cautiously.

'We have seen these devices before,' said Ecrishia. 'In the Jashpuri Republic such systems are antiques that carry great worth.'

'But none of us here have ever heard of this law regarding oblivion,' said Halbat.

'Perhaps you do know what to enter and you don't wish to do so,' said Hanu, 'for some reason that only Jashpur would understand?'

'Trust me,' said Halbat. 'I don't want to be stuck out here

when those fanatical murderers reach us.' As Halbat finished speaking there was another trembling through the floor. He turned to one of the Pelorn officers near him. 'Commander, we're either going to get very lucky very soon, or we'll have to abandon this place for a more defensible position.'

The commander nodded, and turned to one of his junior officers. 'Gather all the civilians.'

The officer nodded and departed.

Then Halbat turned to Ecrishia. 'How are you doing?'

'First three characters,' she replied. 'Probably.'

'Is that all?'

Ecrishia glared at him. 'I'm doing what I can. I know military passwords and protocols, but this is something I've never heard of. Just get me inside and I'll fly this thing for you.'

'Must be their main law, right?' asked Fhiro. 'One that governs the rest.'

'Yes, yes,' said Halbat, watching Ecrishia's fingers fly across the controls.

Fhiro wondered if Halbat had heard him.

'Probably,' said Hanu. 'Any ideas from that book of yours?'

'No,' said Fhiro.

By now more civilians were filtering into the room. Every time the ground shook or the walls trembled half of them startled or jumped.

'The Poshokans weren't like the Harmonisers, were they?' Fhiro called out to Halbat.

'No,' came the curt reply. 'Try …' and Halbat muttered something else to Ecrishia.

'Who were the harmonisers?' asked Imial.

'They thought everyone was right,' said Fhiro, 'even if they contradicted each other.'

'That sounds nice,' said Hanu, 'but not reasonable.'

Halbat was deep in conversation with Ecrishia now,

scribbling on paper and gesticulating with his hands. He gave her some new instructions, and Fhiro could feel everyone in the room tense in anticipation, then sink a little as each attempt was met with failure.

'Have you tried answers to stop people being unreasonable?' Imial called to Halbat.

'Worth giving it a go,' said Halbat.

'Don't be unreasonable?' Ecrishia's voice was sceptical, but she began typing all the same.

The room rocked again. Another explosion had hit the mountain.

'If we can't hear gunfire, they've not broken in,' said someone in the crowd. There was a murmur of assent.

They've got to solve this riddle, thought Fhiro, staring at the two Jashpuri agents working at the terminal. 'When you stray from reason, where do you go?'

'Emotion?' suggested Imial.

'Irrationality,' said his mother.

Halbat perked up at this. 'The Poshokans weren't against emotion. They celebrated it. They just insisted decisions be based on reasoning.'

'No room for gut feeling?' asked Hanu.

'If there was,' said Halbat, 'they must have found a way to justify it.'

'I'm pretty sure the answer won't be "Go with your gut",' said Ecrishia.

'Can I have a go?' asked an elderly, female hegel civilian from nearby.

'They're taking any ideas if they're good,' said Hanu.

'How about …' and at once all the civilians were throwing suggestions to the Jashpuri agents.

'Isn't reason intrinsic to thinking?' asked Fhiro.

'Is it?' asked Hanu.

'I don't mean if you're thinking about a picture, or a noise,' said Fhiro, 'but if you're coming to an opinion, you need a reason, don't you?'

'I suppose you ought to,' said Hanu.

'I wish my husband thought more about his opinions,' muttered the hegel.

The gathering crowd of civilians were losing steam. Halbat dismissed three of their suggestions in a row. Ecrishia pursued another line of thinking, but after her fingers made their way across the keys there was still no success.

A collective shiver went through the crowd as the floor vibrated again.

If only the Creedate would give up, thought Fhiro. He would probably think much clearer then. 'You should have a reason to reach an opinion or to make a decision.'

'What about a prophet?' Imial's eyes glinted. 'They're confident in their conclusions, but where are their reasons?'

'Even for a prophet,' said Fhiro, 'they would preach because they had reason to believe Aten, or the gods, had spoken to them.'

'Is it, "Don't listen to prophets"?' Imial called out.

Halbat frowned. 'I doubt it, but we aren't having much luck with anything else.'

But Ecrishia's entries remained unsuccessful.

Fhiro felt despair growing inside him. The civilians around him looked increasingly despondent. Even Imial looked deflated.

Fhiro closed his eyes. 'Maybe the Poshokans just assumed everyone agreed about using reason.'

'But what will it say then?' asked another member of the crowd.

'Something to encourage good reasoning,' answered Fhiro.

A huge vibration reverberated through the chamber.

'I can hear gunfire,' someone said.

Halbat straightened up.

Panicked murmurs filled the room.

'Please get us in!' cried a male Yeal standing near Halbat. 'Please!'

'It's far off,' Halbat reassured the man, but Fhiro knew they were done for now. If the defences outside were defeated, and the unbreakable door had been blown off its hinges, the hundreds of soldiers Fhiro had passed on his way through the mountain would not be enough to hold back the Creedate.

Hanu put her arm around him. 'Fhiro, you've got a good head.' As she said it she stroked his hair. 'You're thinking sounds a lot better than everyone else's I've heard out here. Don't give up.'

Fhiro looked at her. 'Don't you have any ideas?'

She smiled, but he could see her eyes were watering. 'I'll keep trying too. We have to keep trying, don't we?'

Fhiro nodded.

There was more gunfire, a fraction louder than before.

Fhiro steeled himself. 'To reach better conclusions … is sort of about avoiding bad ones.'

More gunfire, and explosions with a different quality to before. Traces of the blasts far away rippled through the air where they stood.

'Revisit your conclusions?' Fhiro suggested.

Halbat had been listening. 'Go for it,' he said to Ecrishia.

As Ecrishia typed away Fhiro kept thinking. 'But what law would make us keep revisiting our conclusions?'

'Go on Fhiro,' said Jammit, still standing near them.

Fhiro suddenly became aware of civilians and soldiers looking at him. He turned to see Halbat was watching him intently. So was Imial.

His mother smiled at him again, but said nothing.

'I guess you have to question your conclusions,' said Fhiro. 'You've got to question your laws. All of them. Probably all the time.'

'Have we tried that?' Halbat asked Ecrishia.

'No.' Ecrishia's fingers flew again as she keyed in his words.

Nothing.

She tried again with a slightly different version … and again … and again.

Fhiro counted. There were only so many ways to say the same thing.

The crack of gunfire was now continuous, and getting louder.

Ecrishia seemed to hesitate.

Fhiro clenched his fists. 'Always question the laws,' he blurted.

Ecrishia glanced round at him, then turned back to the keyboard.

There was a loud click.

For a moment, everyone froze. Ecrishia stared at the door. Hanu sucked in a breath.

Halbat rushed to Ecrishia's side and then pulled the door. It opened.

CHAPTER 31

There were cheers from the soldiers and civilians around them.

Hanu dropped her rifle and picked Fhiro up at the waist. 'Well done!' she cried.

'Good work,' said Imial.

'Er, thanks,' said Fhiro. He felt warm all over. Almost too warm, like his cheeks might set fire at any moment. When his mother set him down, he moved closer to Halbat to see through the door. Beyond it was a short bridge leading to an airlock in the wall of a tall, cylindrical structure, the top and bottom of which were shrouded in shadow. If Fhiro's eyes did not deceive him, it appeared to widen both higher up and down below them.

Halbat walked to the airlock and opened it. 'Thank goodness that part was straightforward.'

The rumble of explosions shook the air once more.

'Can we keep the civilians out until we've run a few investigations?' asked Halbat.

'Certainly,' said the commander, 'but be quick. I'll have them ready to board the moment you're ready.'

Officially part of Halbat's team, the soldiers allowed Fhiro, Imial and Hanu through, along with Ecrishia. They were followed by soldiers and the commander himself.

Fhiro sensed an unpleasant aroma test his nostrils for a brief moment as he went inside, but he forgot about it when glowing lights came to life in the walls around him.

'Where, oh where, are you getting your energy from?'

Halbat asked no one in particular. Fhiro followed him to a wide chamber with a circular platform at the far end.

'There are no stairs here,' complained Jammit. 'Didn't you say it was tall?'

'Judging from the amount of space it occupies, I suspect so,' said Halbat. 'We passed doors on the way here. Perhaps they lead to a way up.'

'I didn't see any doors,' said Imial.

'Poshokan doors are hard to spot if you aren't looking for them,' said Halbat.

'Perhaps this strange platform is operated by a pulley?' asked Ecrishia.

Fhiro saw there was no ceiling above the platform, just an endless shaft leading upwards.

'But then where are the hockers to lift it?' asked Imial.

'It's thousands of years old,' whispered Fhiro. 'The hockers are dead.'

Three thundering booms came in quick succession.

Halbat approached an array of buttons at the side of the platform. 'Reminds me of a simple sorcery terminal,' he said. 'I wonder if …' His eyes narrowed as he focussed on one of the keys. He pressed it.

There was a loud humming noise from the platform. Separations in the panels of the walls glimmered alive with light. The platform started to tremble, and then rose a few centimetres off the floor and hovered before them.

'Is this sorcery?' asked Jammit.

'It cannot be,' said Halbat, 'for there are crystals active everywhere. Sorcery fails when crystals are near.'

'So what is this?' asked Hanu.

'The legends are true. And not only did the Ancients defeat gravity,' said Halbat, pointing at the platform as it floated in the air, 'but they created some kind of a pseudo-magic using crystal-energy. How, I cannot imagine.'

'The spirits be merciful,' said one of the Pelorn soldiers. 'Our planet has been blessed!'

'I was beginning to wonder if this entire war was started for nothing,' said Hanu.

The rattle of gunfire, followed by another series of explosions, seized Fhiro's attention.

'Marallel may win this war,' said Halbat, 'but he must not claim this prize. There's more at stake here than the fate of this one planet.'

'Could Marallel have known about this?' asked Fhiro. 'Could he have known for sure that there was something important here?'

'No more than you or I,' said Halbat, still studying the terminal. 'The only people who ever seemed certain of there being something magnificent down here were the Sufferers.'

'The fighting is getting close,' said Ecrishia after the background sounds of battle were overlaid with a series of nearby shouts and bursts of rifle fire.

Halbat stepped on to the lift. 'Indeed. Would anyone like to join me?'

'Of course,' said Fhiro.

'No, Fhiro.' Hanu dragged him off the platform. 'Let others try first.'

'I shall join you,' said the Pelorn commander, stepping aboard, along with many other soldiers, including Jammit.

'According to the runes,' said Ecrishia, 'this key seems to indicate an important floor high above.'

'Take us there,' said Halbat.

There was a moment before the humming sound intensified. Then the lift accelerated upwards and out of view.

Fhiro tried to look up the lift shaft but Hanu pulled him back again. 'It might come back down and take off your head.' She tapped his forehead. 'That's a precious head you've got there. Very precious to me, anyway.'

'We're probably all going to die anyway,' said Fhiro.

'Don't be such a pessimist!' said Imial.

'You just bought us our greatest chance at surviving this,' said Hanu, gripping Fhiro's shoulder and pulling him close. 'You can't give up!'

He looked up at her, and saw her smiling at him. He had to try to be brave, he knew, but the thought of the Creedate, and Halbat's uncertainty as to how they might actually fly the device, left him feeling anything but confident.

They waited, listening to the sounds of fighting behind them getting closer and closer.

There was a humming sound from above. A second later the lift returned. The commander, private Jammit, and a few other soldiers were on it. The commander leapt off the lift. 'All of you are to board this and join the others already inside.'

The commander disappeared outside with a small escort, barking orders as he travelled further and further away.

'All right, boys,' said Hanu as she ushered them on to the hovering platform. 'This has to be safer than staying put.'

They all stepped aboard. Fhiro heard the sounds of shouting and fighting getting louder outside. He looked down through the hovering, transparent platform. A dozen rectangular-shaped crystals were embedded within the white Poshokan material under it. Between them a maze-like pattern of dark lines covered the rest of the floor.

'Ready, all?' asked Jammit.

Fhiro looked at him, and then up the shaft above them. He heard the click of Jammit depressing the button, and then he was rushing upwards, his feet heavy as the force of the floor against them threatened to burst the soles of his shoes. He felt relief at being taken further from the Creedate, but he did not feel safe. His mother put her arm around his shoulders, and this did make him feel better. Imial, next to him, stared

upwards, fear in his eyes. Fhiro put his other arm around Imial. They would make it. They had to. They would see Dorrick, Chinda, Oljon and Valachrad again.

The lift slowed and settled in front of an open archway. As they stepped out into the wide chamber ahead Fhiro noticed the far wall had a strange irregular surface.

'Is the outer wall broken?' Imial sounded alarmed.

'That's a transparent screen,' said Hanu. 'We're looking at the inner surface of the mountain rock.'

Some of Halbat's expert assistants, such as Ecrishia, were examining various items and panels in room. Fhiro noticed that the walls on either side of him did not reach the ceiling above, but were very tall partitions. At the near and far end they stopped short, allowing access to the other areas on the same floor.

As Jammit marched ahead to speak with Halbat and another Pelorn officer, Fhiro, Hanu and Imial walked to the far end and studied the rock of the mountain. Fhiro tried to peer down below them, but all he could see was darkness. Then he looked at the wall panels. They were etched with tiny lines that turned and crossed one another in a pattern he could make no sense of. 'I don't know how they wiped out the people here in the Great Dying,' he said. 'Shouldn't there be skeletons?'

'Maybe this place was empty when the Great Dying struck,' said Hanu.

'They left the animals alive too,' said Fhiro.

'Wish they hadn't done that,' said Imial, scowling. 'Ghorad would still be alive.'

Fhiro patted Imial's shoulder. He could have really used Ghorad's presence right now.

He turned and saw Halbat, hands moving furiously across the main terminal. The Jashpuri ambassador was close enough for Fhiro to see an auburn strand of hair get brushed from the terminal's surface.

The elevator arrived again. This time it was full of soldiers and civilians. The Pelorn commander stepped off with an escort of other officers and approached Halbat. Meanwhile Jammit manipulated the terminal, and he and the lift vanished down the shaft out of sight again.

'Are you making progress, ambassador?' Fhiro heard the commander ask.

'Yes,' Halbat replied. 'I have an understanding of these runes. These keys control levitation and translational movement.'

'So it really can fly?' asked the commander.

'It thinks it can,' said Halbat.

'It's two thousand years old,' said Ecrishia. 'Its thinking might be a little off.'

'You'd better hope it isn't,' said the commander, 'or the Creedate will be using our heads to redecorate this planet.'

'Like the other guys we left out there,' muttered a soldier.

Fhiro felt a deep pang of sadness as he realised how true this was. Most of the soldiers he had seen today were doomed, if not already dead.

'We will be sealing the door imminently,' said the commander. 'Do not expect more than a few more elevators to arrive before I give the order to take off.'

'An exit from the mountain must be opened first, though,' said Halbat, 'but that's the least of our troubles. The craft requires an activation process to be undertaken. Ecrishia is an expert at Poshokan military protocols. I hope she can unlock this soon.'

'I wish you could offer me more than hope,' said the commander.

'Send word to all your troops to be ready to brace themselves,' said Halbat. 'I have no idea if there's a delay between me giving this thing an instruction, and it actually moving.'

The commander nodded. He then turned to one of his subordinates. 'Seek out defensive positions.'

'There are turrets that should be manned,' said Halbat. 'If I am reading this correctly, the roof needs special attention. There is both an entrance to the interior there, and powerful gun placements.'

'So long as you don't plan on taking us into space with my men out there.' The commander looked around, pausing for a moment as he studied Hanu, Fhiro, and Imial, and the large crowd of unarmed civilians that had been brought aboard. 'We will also have to find a place for these non-combatants.'

'I work for Halbat,' said Hanu, stepping forward and allowing her assault rifle to swing a little more across her body, 'and do not wish to abandon my post as his advisor.'

'Perhaps,' said the commander, 'but this will be no place for children.'

Hanu nodded. 'I understand.' She returned to Fhiro and Imial and placed her hands on their shoulders.

Moments later Jammit was with them. 'The colonel will be sealing the door shut within three minutes, and has ordered that you depart then. He formally hands over command and responsibility for all units within this vessel.'

'He isn't coming with us?' asked the commander.

Jammit shook his head.

'If that is his wish, so be it.' The commander sighed. 'Halbat, make your preparations.' He checked his watch. 'Jammit, head back down and help ferry as many people up as you can. Tell me the moment the door is sealed.'

Jammit saluted and departed.

'Protocol executed,' called Ecrishia. 'The system's unlocked.'

'Excellent work,' said Halbat.

'Thank the spirits,' said the commander.

Fhiro felt a wave of relief.

'If I'm reading this correctly,' said Halbat, looking at the display before him, 'I can attempt to move this now.'

The commander turned to another of his officers. 'Tell everyone that they are to brace themselves in three minutes.'

The next group of soldiers arrived on the lift. Fhiro suspected most of the crates they were carrying held weapons and ammunition. Once these were brought aboard the elevator disappeared out of sight again.

The commander checked his watch. 'That's it. Three minutes has passed.'

'You want me to leave now?' asked Halbat.

The commander turned back to the elevator. A few seconds later it returned, full of soldiers. Jammit ran out from among them. 'The door is sealed. The Creedate are almost outside it!'

'Get us out of here!' ordered the commander.

'Everybody hold on,' called Halbat.

'What can we hold on to?' asked Imial.

'Can that really be the pilot's position if there isn't a railing or chair near it?' asked Hanu.

'I think we're out of time to find one,' said Halbat. He pressed a few keys on the terminal, and it lit up in front of him.

Fhiro saw that the terminals manned by Ecrishia, and some of Halbat's other Jashpuri experts, had also begun to glow.

'What are your displays telling you?' Halbat asked the others.

'This seems to be a readout of the ship's circuitry,' said Ecrishia. 'All seems to be in order, if a two-thousand-year-old diagnostic tool can be trusted.'

'When the alternative is being butchered by the Creedate,' said Halbat, 'I'll accept it.' He started working on the terminal again.

Through the transparent screen, Fhiro saw the interior mountain rock face moving downwards. Unlike the elevator, there was no sound or feeling.

'The mountain is collapsing!' said Imial.

'No,' said Halbat. 'Gravity's Arrow is flying.'

Fhiro gasped.

The walls vanished below them, and bits of stone and grass tumbled from above. Fhiro looked out over the mountain and at the horizon. The forests expanded forever into the distant mists, and the clouds fell upon them from above.

'We're flying!' cried Imial.

'By the spirits,' said the Pelorn commander.

'Check the other screens!' cried Halbat.

'Creedate dragon riders!' A Pelorn soldier came running into the room. 'They're approaching from the north!'

'Do our defences work?' asked Halbat.

Fhiro saw the clouds obscure the view in thick fog. Greyness shrouded the forest, and then replaced it completely. A moment later the visibility started to improve again. Flickering specks cluttered the sky like dark stars above the cloud canopy. Fhiro raced to the screen and looked to left and right. Angular, flapping shapes were everywhere.

'Dragons,' whispered Halbat.

Fhiro felt his mother's fingers grip his arms tight as she tried to pull him away. Before he could move, a thick-limbed creature descended towards him. As it neared, its jaws opened to reveal razor-sharp fangs, and its arms spread out, claws glinting in the sun.

Fhiro froze in horror.

The armoured head collided with the screen. Fhiro fell backwards with such momentum he thought he had taken the full impact of the creature.

But he would have been dead if that had happened.

His mother caught him as he stared at the armoured, riderless beast baring its teeth at him. Its tongue lolled and whipped as it snarled. He knew no book, story or drawing could have prepared him for the fright of coming face to face

with the horrific monstrosity that was a Creedate shock dragon.

'Let's get away from here!' Hanu dragged Fhiro back.

'I did not think they would be employing those things here,' cried the commander. 'Can we escape them? I don't see any sign of our defences reacting.'

Halbat studied the terminal. His hands glided across it, and lights flickered up in his face as he tapped it with his fingers. The clouds started moving underneath them, and the shock dragon bounced off the screen's surface and clattered away around the side of the craft.

Fhiro saw that none of its attacks had left a scratch on the screen. Now other dark specks in the air were converging on them, and growing in size. Most were manned, but some were riderless monsters like the first.

'Go faster!' begged Jammit.

'Silence, private Jammit,' barked one of the officers.

'Ecrishia,' Halbat shouted, 'go and check on our gunners and ensure they understand how to operate the weapons.'

The hum of crystal-fire blared through the corridors.

'I've unlocked the defences,' said Ecrishia.

Glowing rays of fire spread out from around, above and below them. Dragons and their riders disintegrated as rays of energy collided with them, their remains plummeting towards the ground. Meanwhile, the speed of the craft increased and the Creedate air squadrons struggled to keep up.

Hanu's grip on Fhiro's shoulders tightened, and he felt himself being squashed against Imial, who she also had in her grasp.

Projectile and crystal-fire was returned from the invaders, and here and there scratches were etched into the screen, but this seemed to have no effect on the output of firepower from the defences.

'We're losing them,' said the commander. 'Keep going.'

'How are our systems?' Halbat asked Ecrishia.

'All in order,' she replied. 'We have plenty of energy left to continue this for some time.'

'What kind of crystal is powering this craft?' asked Fhiro.

'Aten only knows what strange things the Poshokans must have thought of,' Hanu whispered back to him.

The fighting continued. The Creedate drifted further and further away.

And then the turrets went quiet.

'Take that you Creedate dogs!' cried Jammit.

Cheers erupted all around the room. Soldiers hugged one another. The commander patted Halbat on the back

Fhiro laughed aloud. He grabbed Imial and his mother and held them both. 'We did it!'

'Really?' asked Imial.

'We might be safe for now,' said Hanu, 'but we should take the commander's advice. You and the other civilians should get yourselves out of the way.'

'Oh, come on,' said Fhiro. 'We're safe! The Creedate got beaten!'

'I think it would still be wise,' said Halbat.

Fhiro scowled, but he felt elated. He paced about in excitement. With every step he took he thought his feet might rise up off the ground.

Imial stood up. 'I can't quite believe it.'

'Believe it!' said Fhiro. 'I can't believe I've managed to not get killed again.'

'Most people don't almost get killed as much as you do,' said Imial.

'Tortured and killed, in fact,' said Fhiro, 'but they're gone now. And we're in the most amazing discovery in a thousand years. Maybe two thousand years. We can't just go hiding away now!'

'Safety and security first, young man,' said the commander. 'Jammit, see to this. The rest of us will secure the roof.'

'Yessir,' said Jammit. 'Come on.' He gestured to Hanu and the boys to follow him.

By the time they had started to ascend the stairs they were part of a large crowd. Almost a hundred civilians, evacuated from the fort, were aboard Gravity's Arrow.

Fhiro pulled Imial's arm, bringing his head low.

'What are you doing?' asked Imial.

'Come on, let's get away from here.'

'Your ma will kill us if we run away,' said Imial.

'It's worth dying for,' said Fhiro. 'We could be the first people to explore some of this place since the Great Dying!'

CHAPTER 32

'How are our allies?' asked Oljon.

'The Baworl captain charged with holding the northern perimeter has fled and escaped our atmosphere,' said Halari.

'Send someone good to replace him.'

'Already done,' Halari replied.

Oljon watched the approaching horde of shock dragons through his binoculars. The turrets in the fields around the palace erupted the moment their targets were within range. Many beasts fell from the sky, torn into pieces by flak and showers of bullets. Higher in the sky glided atmospheric craft; troops and war beasts spilling out of their sides, parachutes unfurling as they fell. One large Creedate ship slowed and descended towards a patch of undefended land, but fire from the guns nearby concentrated on to it, and before it could touch down it cracked open and burst into flames. The debris that tumbled out of it included thousands of soldiers, some still writhing as they plunged towards the ground.

'Any additional instructions, Ishthen?' asked General Hilari.

'Reinforcements are needed at the palace,' said Oljon. 'Marallel has sent a large force with the sole objective of taking it, regardless of the surrounding city.'

'He cannot hope to hold the palace in isolation,' said Halari, 'and it is well defended. Such a costly operation makes no sense.'

'Soon the artillery barrage will commence, and by morning it will have reduced most of Riletta to rubble,' said Oljon. 'Tomorrow armoured transants will arrive with soldiers in

their millions and Marallel will seize what is left. Tonight's objective is different. Tonight he will murder your King.'

'What?' cried General Halari. 'King Suloa must agree to surrender for the populace to accept the terms.'

'I was mistaken when I assumed that would matter,' said Oljon. 'King Suloa must also approve an alliance with Kartna if the populace and the neighbouring states are to accept that. His life is a greater threat than his martyrdom.'

'Marallel would not stoop to such dishonour,' said Halari. 'There will be rebellion against his rule for as long as he–'

'There will be no rebellion when every inhabitant of this planet has been put to death,' said Oljon. 'The Creedate have done that before, and they will do it again. There is no resistance once they have won.'

General Halari took a moment consider this. He turned to his immediate subordinate. 'Send the ninth and twelfth to support the palace. Warn the Royal guard that the King himself is the target of this attack, and have him retrieved to safety.'

Balls of light burst out of the wall of the palace keep. Dragons and birds of the Creedate and Pelorn air forces spiralled around one another in battle across the sky.

'Your ambassador is with the King now,' said Halari. 'Would you like to recall him to the under-city base?'

'He will hear of these developments when the King does,' said Oljon, 'and he will stay by the King's side as long as the monarch still breathes, for his task is the most essential of all. If he fails to persuade Suloa to ally with Kartna then all is lost.'

* * *

King Suloa knelt again, and prayed.

Valachrad waited ten paces behind him, just outside the

paper-covered floor that was reserved for worshipping the Elements. The metal cube, that was the temple of the Life and Creation Element, was suspended and accessed by one of the many internal, interlinking bridges, high up inside the palace keep. It had taken them an hour to reach here after leaving the underground fortifications. Flying by bird or dragon had been deemed unsafe because of the unrest in the city. Now the Creedate Airforce was bombarding the keep itself, and shock dragons swarmed about its surface, waiting for a breach though which they might infest the interior.

The floor trembled, and from outside came the roar of explosions, the cries of anguished souls, and the crashing of tumbling masonry. Then there was another sound; a breathy curdling growl. It was not the noise of any bird or dragon Valachrad had ever encountered before, and he had travelled far and wide across the galaxy.

King Suloa bowed his head in humility, and offered tributes of water and fire to the temple altar.

'Your majesty,' spoke Valachrad, rising to his feet and walking on to the paper-covered holy ground.

'Silence!' cried the King's priest, standing up and blocking Valachrad's way.

'Do not let your religion guide itself to its own extermination!' Valachrad shouted at the priest, his booming voice deafening inside the temple. 'King Suloa, death has come to claim you and all of your people. Praying here does not ward it off, it invites it! You cannot tarry any longer.'

'They will not attack this temple,' shouted the King. 'They will not!'

The priest mustered himself to appear as tall as possible, and stared down at the Kartnan ambassador.

'Even if they recognised it as a holy place,' said Valachrad, 'the Creedate have no respect for faiths other than their own.

They have unleashed their shock dragons upon your beloved city. That is the regard in which they hold you, and all you care about.'

'Untrue!' said the priest. 'The Elemental tides will protect us here. Only they can guide the King to the truth.'

'If the Niquani knew their fate was to be decided by the gods of this *Element* religion,' said Valachrad, 'would they be any less angered than if you allied yourself with Kartna?'

'Do not lecture me!' shouted the King, turning to face Valachrad.

An inhuman shriek scorched their ears. The cries of people outside, struck mindless with fear and pain, came after it. All but a few of the priests and worshippers within the temple paused to look around, watching the entrance and the walls, and glancing at one another, not saying a word.

'They would not ...' the King's voice trailed off.

The screech of twisting, tearing metal drew all eyes to a section of the temple wall that had suddenly bulged inwards. Two great clawed fingers pierced their way inside, and then stretched and scratched out an opening. The shock dragon forced its vast shiny and toothy head inside, and its eyes gleamed as it spied the living things scattering before it. It turned towards the altar and released a burst of fire from its mouth, incinerating those worshippers too slow to escape.

'Come!' shouted Valachrad, pushing the priest out of the way and hauling the King towards the entrance.

The priest stood and watched them flee, then turned towards the creature that had destroyed his temple. Another wave of flames leapt from its mouth and engulfed him.

Valachrad barged through the outer temple door and ran down the ramp to the suspended bridge, pushing aside fleeing worshippers as they panicked and scrambled amongst each other. He led the King towards the hocker lifts, his mind filling

with doubt as to whether they might reach them alive. Peering over the low wall that lined the bridge he could see down into the abyss that was the long drop to the bottom of the keep. Through the vast indoor space flew dragons and birds wearing the insignias of Pelorn and Hithostun, locked in combat with the assault dragons of the Creedate, and the cruel-featured, unmanned shock dragons. Crystal-fire and smouldering projectiles lit up the battle, to the accompaniment of explosive blasts and screams.

Shrill cries came from the worshippers ahead. Valachrad saw that some of them had stumbled and fallen off the bridge, tumbling and accelerating through the air below him. To his right three birds swooped down and clasped the short wall that lined the bridge. From one of them a man leapt, carrying a heavy assault rifle in one hand.

It was Pral. 'Come King! Ambassador! Upon my steed!' he cried.

The ambassador led the way, but the shock dragon had now removed itself from the temple, and rushed towards them. It was upon Pral's bird within a second, tearing flesh from its neck and biting its wings. The other two birds detached themselves from the wall, their feathers blurring with movement as they hovered beside it, their riders shooting at the shock dragon. Pral knelt on one knee to steady himself, and aimed at the eyes of the monster before firing.

The shock dragon recoiled, one of its taloned hands swiping across the side of its face, before it turned and leapt upon its new assailant. Pral collapsed under the weight of its foot, and its outstretched claws glinted in the firelight as they tore at him.

'Get on!' cried Dorrick from the nearest of the two remaining birds. He landed his beast upon the wall again. His comrade flew behind the shock dragon and continued firing at it.

The King and the ambassador climbed up behind Dorrick. Once they had grasped the chains and linked themselves into the harnesses Dorrick beckoned his bird off the side of the wall and commanded it to drop, nose first. They descended through the raging, aerial fire-fight, gliding either side of the many bridges and interlinking structures inside the keep, only slowing when they neared its lowest floor. Above them the suspended corridor on which they had been moments ago, collapsed and fell after them. Dorrick pulled on the reins and guided them toward the gateway that the Pelorn troops still held, and out of the path of the falling stone and metal.

'Take us outside and over the city.' Valachrad turned to the King. 'You must say now, and I will call my fleet to assist us. Do you agree to the terms of the treaty we discussed?'

The King nodded, tears streaming down his face. 'I agree.'

They flew out over the main gate, hugging close to the palace wall to avoid being taken down by friendly fire. When Dorrick saw a clear path with no turrets firing he chanced his luck and sped towards the city centre. As they flew, Valachrad removed a device from his robes and aimed it at a nearby building. A bright green light shone out and illuminated a large part of its wall, reflecting off windows and casting shadows beyond its balconies and statues. He repeated this a few times and only stopped when he saw a similar, but far brighter, green light shining from the very same building, up through the sky and into space.

A shock dragon was drawn to this, and sped towards the source of the light, but it was gunned down by weapons concealed on the building's roof.

'We are all doomed!' cried the King.

'Take us to your father,' Valachrad said to Dorrick.

* * *

'You are insane,' whispered Imial harshly when they reached the top floor.

Fhiro turned around, finger to his mouth to silence his friend. 'Stop being a wimp. We can't pass this up. It's something we can talk about forever!'

'We are in the middle of a battle with the Creedate,' said Imial.

'They're miles behind us already,' said Fhiro. 'We've won thanks to the Poshokans. The Poshokans! The Ancients made this. Isn't that amazing?'

'The Creedate might come back.'

'They made this at least two thousand years ago,' said Fhiro, 'and it still works!'

'This thing might run out of charge and leave us stranded somewhere in Fawast.'

'Now you need to stop being such a pessimist,' said Fhiro. 'You're just worried about getting told off. Get your priorities straight.'

'I maintain you're insane,' said Imial, 'like I said before.'

'There's no time like the present,' said Fhiro. 'We've got to see all this before we're locked up in some containment room.' He started ascending the last flight of stairs.

'It might be dangerous *inside* here,' said Imial.

'Inside?' asked Fhiro. 'This place has been undisturbed for two thousand years. There's nothing in here.'

'What if we walk through a door and fall into a pit or something?'

'Look,' said Fhiro, trying a different tack, 'if you want to do what those soldiers tell you to do, or what Halbat and the Jashpuri Republic think you should be doing, then I guess we'll have to hand ourselves in.'

Imial looked at Fhiro with suspicion. 'You're ... all right then.' He looked up at the door to the top floor. 'But we know there are soldiers up there. They'll send us back downstairs.'

Fhiro ignored him and opened the door.

A collection of Jashpuri and Pelorn soldiers whirled round and stared at them.

'What are you doing here?' asked the Jashpuri captain.

'Is this a weapons cache?' asked Fhiro, studying the crates and racks of rifles about the room.

'It's no place for you two,' said the Jashpuri captain.

A man dropped down from the ceiling. Fhiro saw there was an open hatch above him. 'It's clear, sir. No Creedate aboard, or in sight.'

'Excellent,' said the Jashpuri captain. He turned back to the boys. 'I don't know how you got here. Wait there for one of my men to take you back down.' He turned away to continue a discussion with some of his troops.

'Right,' muttered Imial, 'so we're finally going back down, now.'

Fhiro grabbed him and hauled him out the door. 'No we're not!'

'What?'

'Let's get out of here before they realise we've disappeared,' said Fhiro.

'How much trouble did you want to be in exactly?'

'I'm not scared of these guys,' said Fhiro. 'My ma's going to kill us whatever we do, so we can't actually make things any worse.'

'Is that really the right way to be thinking about this?' Imial shook his head. 'I'm blaming you, whatever happens.'

They scuttled down the stairs for several flights, pausing whenever they thought they heard someone approach. The first area they found to investigate appeared to be a floor full of basic living quarters. 'Boring,' said Fhiro, leaving and closing the door.

'We should come back with some adults,' said Imial. 'They

might be able to explain more of what this place is. Like those Jashpuri experts.'

'We'll carry on.' Fhiro went down another flight of steps and opened another door. Inside was a deep darkness.

'Let's not go in there,' said Imial, walking down the stairs.

Fhiro closed it and followed. 'How will we ever know what's in them if we don't enter?'

'If we are going to fall down a pit,' said Imial, 'it will be after stumbling into one in pitch blackness. And anyway, that place smelt bad.'

'Smelt bad?' said Fhiro. Then he wondered if the Poshokans might have used poisonous gases to deter intruders, but then surely those gases would have dissipated over two thousand years – unless they were only released if someone opened a door or stepped on a switch. He decided to keep these thoughts to himself.

'Why didn't we take the lift again?' asked Imial.

'Because we'd definitely get found then,' said Fhiro. 'Look, another door!' He opened it.

The chamber beyond was enormous. They walked inside and found themselves standing on a balcony overlooking a large space where frames, hooks, and articulated contraptions hung from beams that crossed from one end of the room to the other. Doors, etched with Poshokan runes, were spaced evenly along the wall opposite the space. The balcony itself was wide and fenestrated, through which Fhiro could see further, similar floors below. 'What's this?' he asked. 'I didn't realise this place was so big.'

'It's a hangar,' said Imial. 'Have you never seen a hangar before? Those things are for birds and dragons to roost on.'

'Does old dragon dung smell this bad, even after two thousand years?' asked Fhiro.

'I wouldn't have thought so.' Imial looked down through the

balcony floor. 'There's a floor below us. It looks like something's down there.'

They descended a staircase to the floor below.

'This ship seems bigger nearer the top and bottom than in the middle.' Fhiro turned around and around as he took in its size. 'How totally weird. Look, there's a floor below this one too. Imial?'

Imial's eyes were transfixed on the far end of the balcony. A group of objects hung from the floor above. 'What are they?'

Fhiro hesitated for a moment. There was something wrong about what Imial was pointing to. Something very wrong.

No, he had beaten death today. He had survived. This new feeling of dread was not going to win over him. He steeled himself and marched forward. Imial followed.

'The further one looks a bit like a body,' said Imial tentatively, as they neared it.

Fhiro stopped. 'If it is, then it's missing an arm and one and a half of its legs.' He sniffed the air. The smell was worse here.

Imial took a few more steps forward and then stopped sharply, so that Fhiro bumped into him. 'That is a body. They're both bodies.'

The nearer object was a torso, part of a neck and fragments of jaw still connected to it. Blood and crust coated the chains that pierced its flesh and suspended it above the floor. The second body was that of a male earthman. Held up in a similar fashion, the head, the left arm and the right leg from just below the knee remained connected.

The feeling of dread returned, this time in force. There was nothing Fhiro could do to resist it.

'What …?' Imial mouthed something Fhiro could not hear. 'Why?'

'These can't … can't have been here for two thousand years,' said Fhiro.

'There are no animals to devour them if they'd been sealed inside,' said Imial.

'Animals and insects, no,' said Fhiro, 'but bodies carry bacteria. They'd still have decomposed. What is that?' He pointed at what appeared to be a clump of strange-coloured logs.

Imial approached and then recoiled in horror. 'Arms! Legs!' He bit on his own hand.

Fhiro went to take a closer look, and in doing so he came close to the second body. At the same moment he heard someone climbing the stairs outside the hangar.

The eyes of the drooping head in the second body opened, and shifted a little to stare at Fhiro. Its remaining left arm reached out and gripped Fhiro's shirt.

Fhiro scrambled at the fingers locked tight around his clothing.

The mouth opened. 'Run. They are coming.'

Imial screamed and ran away from Fhiro, passing the pile of limbs, and fumbled his way through a door at the end of the hangar balcony, slamming it shut behind him.

Fhiro finally tore himself free from the fingers holding on to him and stared at the scarred, bruised face that had just spoken. He recognised it. A face he had seen many times. At the palace keep. With Chenessa. 'You … you're …'

'Run!' said Theon.

Terrified out of his mind, Fhiro ran from Chenessa's missing tutor. He entered the nearest door. Turning as he closed it, he peered through a slit. He could see Theon's body, or what was left of it, relax. The arm flopped down and the eyes fell closed.

Fhiro's mind reeled.

The door from the staircase opened. It was far to Fhiro's right. Footsteps grew nearer, and into his sight walked someone else he recognised. Someone else he had never expected to see again.

'I heard the voice of a child,' Cerilina, the archaeologist, addressed Theon. Her white and grey clothes were unlike anything she had worn before. They reminded Fhiro of the combat-ready, but worthy-of-ceremony attire used by Ghorad, Palis, Hussuf and the other the secret service guards he had met.

Theon did not move or respond.

'Where are they?' she asked, tilting her head as she looked into Theon's eyes.

Theon's torso rose and swelled, then shrunk and sank with each breath, there being so little of him left attached below his waist to hold him still.

'How many children are there?' asked Cerilina.

Theon's eyes opened and he looked back at her. 'Your madness has finally eroded the last of your intelligence.' It took him a while to utter all the words, but they were clear enough for Fhiro to hear. 'There are no children here.'

'Quite resilient, aren't you,' said Cerilina, her voice becoming cold. 'You would be doing yourself a favour if you gave them up.'

'A favour?' Theon muttered. 'You and I have a different understanding of this word.'

'Theon, dear,' she said, caressing his cheek, 'do you resent me for the favours I have already shown you? We have shown you such kindness.'

Theon closed his eyes.

'Resist understanding if you will.' Cerilina stepped away from Theon and started walking towards where Fhiro was hidden. 'Perhaps it shall not be yours in this life, despite my best efforts. But do not fear. Where I have failed, the Devine Evil shall succeed.' She veered towards the entrance from the corridor.

Fhiro heard doors being opened and closed to his right, growing nearer and nearer.

'I shall find the children,' said Cerilina, her voice getting nearer with the click of each door being shut. 'You merely delay the inevitable by not telling me their whereabouts.

Fhiro struggled to think with any clarity at all. He wanted to walk out and talk to Cerilina, ask her to explain herself, and justify why she was not helping Theon. This was not Cerilina the archaeologist. She might be the same woman, but she was something else as well.

And she was about to find him hiding behind this door.

* * *

'Halbat?'

Halbat turned to see Hanu. 'Is everything all right?'

'Fhiro and Imial have run off somewhere.'

Halbat sighed. 'I should have ordered someone to keep a special eye on them.'

'I thought that's what I was doing,' said Hanu, adjusting the grip on the assault rifle she was still carrying. 'Unfortunately they've been taught how to creep around, undetected.'

Halbat eyed the weapon in her hands. 'You can probably put the weapons down, now. We should have plenty of warning if the Creedate try to intercept us again.' He turned around. 'You two, accompany Hanu here and help find her missing boys.'

Two Jashpuri soldiers nodded and walked over to her.

'It might be faster if we split up,' said Hanu, 'but if I know Fhiro, I suspect they went upwards.'

'Well you go up with these men,' said Halbat, 'and I'll send some others to search these lower floors for them.'

'All right,' said Hanu. 'Could they have used the lift?'

'I've been keeping an eye on it,' said Ecrishia. 'It's only ever done trips to and from this level, so I doubt it.'

'Thank you,' said Hanu, and she walked over to the staircase.

* * *

Upon closing the door behind him, Imial had initially done much the same as Fhiro, and looked through a spy hole across the balcony. He saw the woman approaching from the distance, but her face was obscured by the hanging body.

He could not believe those bodies had actually been alive; they had looked so dead. The one that had not grabbed Fhiro truly was a corpse, as there was surely no way it could still be alive with most of its head missing. Imial tried to shake the memory from his mind.

The body that *had* grabbed Fhiro was now speaking, and Imial realised the woman's voice sounded familiar, though he could not place where he knew her from.

He activated his pocket illuminator and flashed it around the room. Seated on a chair, but slumped over a desk, was a humanoid figure. The face was covered by a hood. Imial choked on his breath as he forced himself not to make a sound. He dared not touch the body for fear of finding another rotting carcass ready to poison the air with foul smells. Tools were scattered about, along with some crystals, and a gun. Imial's heart pounded. He wondered what Fhiro would do; he might be little better than a street urchin when it came to dignity and taste, but the son of Ishthen did seem to have fortune's favour whenever he was in danger.

There was a clanging noise from outside. Imial peered back through the spy hole and watched the woman begin opening each door and searching the rooms inside. He had to do something. She would find Fhiro before long, and then him. There was a weapon in the room. He had just seen it. Could

he bring himself to use it? He turned on his illuminator again and turned around.

The figure that had been slumped over the desk was now standing over him. His tall stooped frame allowed his face to be partially visible from within the dark cowled robe. Where his nose had been, two openings remained, each fitted with a filtering device. Sections of the lips were missing revealing exposed gums and teeth. Here and there a tooth had been removed, or broken into a craggy shard. Over large areas the skin had been thinned, so that the muscles were visible, rippling beneath the surface. The eyes were shot red, as though they had been sprayed with noxious chemicals, but despite this they remained wide open and stared down at Imial. Imial could hold in his breath no longer. He screamed.

* * *

'The Creedate are gone from sight, my Lord,' reported one of the Jashpuri soldiers.

Halbat sighed with relief. 'That is excellent.'

'Indeed,' said the commander.

Halbat started to nod, but then stopped himself. 'There was something I meant to check.' He returned to the command terminal where Ecrishia was controlling the ship. 'Could you just move aside for a moment?' Ecrishia did so, and Halbat explored the floor beneath the terminal. He picked up a single, auburn-coloured strand of hair. 'This yours?'

'Do I look like I'm sprouting random hairs of that colour?'

'I didn't think so,' said Halbat. 'When I came to this terminal, had anyone else come near it?'

'When we first arrived?' she asked. 'Besides myself, no.'

'But this hair was on this terminal when I got here. I brushed it off without thinking of it. Yet everywhere inside

this – this thing, is clean. There isn't even any dust.' He looked around. 'Commander, how are you remaining in contact with your troops?'

'I'm sending my lieutenant upstairs in a moment to check on their positions,' replied the commander.

'Check on them now,' said Halbat, 'and tell all of your men to stay on alert for possible threats within this craft.'

* * *

Fhiro watched in horror as Cerilina walked to the door where Imial had hidden himself. It opened before she could reach it. A figure in dark robes marched out, carrying Imial by his neck.

'Ah,' said Cerilina. 'Thank you, friend.' She pointed to the hanging instruments and railings beside Theon. 'Put him up here, beside the old priest.'

Imial screamed as he resisted. Cerilina's fist lashed out, connecting with Imial's jaw, knocking him unconscious. Fhiro saw blood oozing from Imial's mouth as Cerilina's friend carried him to where Theon was hanging. Fhiro could not see what they were doing, but he did not need to wait for Imial to start screaming to know it was something despicably evil. When Cerilina stepped aside, Imial was hanging in the air, his hands chained above his head. Blood trickled down his clothes and dripped on to the floor below.

'Welcome, little boy,' she said.

Tears flowed down Imial's face. He stared at her, but failed to utter anything coherent that Fhiro could understand.

'You never thought you'd see me again, did you?' asked Cerilina. 'What a lovely reunion. Us two, and the Creedate priest.'

Imial slowly turned his head and looked at Theon's face.

Whether he recognised the priest or not Fhiro could not tell. Imial's breathing did not look like it could be any more laboured.

'Don't worry little boy,' said Cerilina. 'I'm here to help, like I helped Theon.'

'Who – are – you?' gasped Imial.

Cerilina turned away.

Imial seemed unable to cry out any more. Fhiro could tell from his friend's expression that he was in great pain.

Cerilina was now facing Fhiro, though she could not have seen him watching her through the door. Her hands reached above her ears and she began to peel away her own skin – yet it was not her skin, but a mask. Beneath it Fhiro saw scars, wounds, cuts, and areas where there was but a thin layer of tissue covering bone, muscle or tendon. Much of her nose and ears were missing. There were also piercings of short, metal spikes jutting from her face. She turned to show herself to Imial, and once again Imial found the strength in his lungs to cry out. 'You wanted to know about the Sufferers, didn't you?' She stroked Imial's hair. 'Why just learn about us, when you can join us!' After Imial had screamed his lungs hoarse Cerilina turned to the man who had brought Imial to her. 'Bring the burners.'

Imial gazed at Theon's missing legs and arm and screamed. 'No! Get away from me!'

Cerilina's friend departed.

Fhiro felt sick. The sense of horror dragged his spirits into the abyss of his nightmares. He knew he had to do something. He searched his pockets for his illuminator and activated it. Careful to move as quietly as possible, he looked about. There was a large workbench, and there were hooks attached along much of the far wall and ceiling. He suspected this was where animals were killed and prepared for feeding to the creatures

roosting in the hangar. There were a few knives, but no firearms of any sort.

He took a deep breath to calm himself. This was not the time to panic. His father was not going to rescue him now. He had got himself isolated from his mother. He could not expect her to get to them soon. Even if she did, Cerilina and her friend would not have come here ill prepared. They were Sufferers, the most hated and feared people ever to have existed.

His enemies were a distance away, and no doubt skilled in combat and well armed if they expected to survive encounters with the soldiers inside the craft. He might be lucky with the first knife he threw, but he could not throw more than one at once, and any opponent standing after his first attack would then be aware of him. Knife throwing, he decided, was too risky. His only chance lay in surprise and getting close, but they would have a clear line of sight if he approached them, and could easily either shoot him or anticipate his attack. His chances of defeating them both in such a manner seemed very slim.

He looked through the space in the door again. Imial gazed upon Cerilina's face in terror. Behind him Cerilina's friend returned with a metal instrument, the tip of which glowed a hot bright orange.

'You see this fellow, here?' Cerilina gestured towards the torso with most of its head missing. 'He was one of the archaeologists from Pelorn who happened to tag along with us for a while. Unlike many of his friends we hoped he might see things our way, eventually.' She placed a hand on the ruined jaw that marked the highest point of the rotting corpse, as though she was brushing the image of a long lost friend. 'It wasn't to be so, sadly. He is with the Divine Evil, now, who will do with him what he does to all of us mortals in our next life.'

Imial appeared to frown a little, before being taken over by uncontrollable sobbing again.

'With Theon we didn't have such expectations,' said Cerilina, 'and have merely kept him alive as a tribute to the ruler of the Universe, so that we may be shown less disfavour upon our descent into hell. You, though, Imial,' she said, and Fhiro could not see her face, but he sensed she was smiling, 'your potential is beautiful to behold. I say, I'd much like to spend some time with your friend, Fhiro. He's quite a thinker, isn't he? Think he'd be able to see things our way too?' She looked around the room again, as though she was guessing which door Fhiro was hiding behind. 'You don't strike me as the type to venture in here alone.' She turned back to Imial. 'Where is your friend?'

Imial was still breathing very fast.

'Let's play a game, now shall we?' Cerilina took something out of her robes and moved it towards Imial.

Imial screamed.

'Leave him alone,' Theon uttered, and this time his eyes remained open.

'Why?' asked Cerilina. 'Are you going to save him?' She grasped Imial's hair and twisted his head so that he was looking straight at Theon. 'Look at this man. See what we do to those that wish to spare you from suffering.' She nodded to her friend.

The man who had brought Imial to Cerilina thrust the burning metal device through the back of Theon's head. It came out through the upper part of the priest's face. Blood spurted outwards, much of it vaporising and congealing immediately.

Imial screamed.

Some of the tissue had stuck to the burner and ignited. Cerilina's friend had to shake it at arms-length to discard these fiery pieces of flesh.

Fhiro's heart pounded in his chest and ears. He wished he

could calm it. Calm himself and think clearly. He was in immediate danger of vomiting. In fact he was about to vomit.

He stepped away from the door and swallowed the contents of his stomach that had attempted to escape. Now his throat and mouth burned, but he could hardly hear the sounds he had just made over Imial's screams. He looked through the door again; there was no sign that they had heard him. He felt tears running down his cheeks and blurring his vision. He was useless. He could do nothing, and they were torturing his friend.

He hated everyone for not telling him more about the Sufferers. It had been Cerilina herself who had told him the most he had ever learned.

Then he remembered what he had learned: death was a better fate than falling into their hands.

He considered this. They had Imial. They were hurting Imial, but he, Fhiro, was safe. If he tried anything he would, probably, end up like Imial, and be made to suffer unbearable pain by a people who had made an art form of torture. And then he would die, and then what? He would have suffered for nothing. No Aten was going to save his soul. There was no heaven. No afterlife.

Or was there?

There were knives in the room; he could end it all now on his own terms.

Imial's screams became louder and louder, and Fhiro covered his ears to block out the sound and the thought of it. The smell of burning flesh crept into his room, replacing the scent of decay that had fouled it earlier.

There was a knife. He might not kill Cerilina and her horrid, foul-faced friend, but he could kill himself. Thinking about it all logically, that was absolutely the sensible thing to do.

Could he bring himself to do it?

CHAPTER 33

Hanu climbed to the stop of the staircase. The soldiers Halbat had sent with her flanked her a second later.

One opened the door to their left. The light within lit up his face. 'This chamber is strange,' he said.

The walls of the passage beyond the door were full of glowing crystals, and its path looked circuitous.

'The heavens know what the Poshokans were up to,' muttered the other.

'We should investigate it,' Hanu said. 'Could you stay out here in case the boys come by?'

One of them nodded, walked a few paces back into the staircase and looked up it. 'Who goes there?' he called, smiling. Then his head jolted backwards as a gunshot broke the momentary silence. Red matter detonated out of the back of his helmet, and poured down the sides of it. His body collapsed and tumbled down the stairs.

The other Jashpuri soldier leapt out and aimed his rifle up the staircase.

Hanu raised her weapon and inched closer to the door. 'Are the Creedate aboard?' she whispered.

The Jashpuri did not answer her, but moved to get a better look at where the shot had come from. 'Run back downstairs,' he said, 'and tell Halbat and the Pelorn soldiers what's happening.'

'I can't leave you here,' said Hanu. The moment she finished uttering these words the soldier was exchanging gunfire. Something struck him in the shoulder. He collapsed on to one

knee. Hanu lunged forward to grab him, but before she could reach his arm to pull him out of the way he was knocked back several times by further shots, blood spraying out of his chest. He toppled backwards, falling head first down the stairs to join his comrade. Hanu kicked against the floor and flung herself into the passage they had just discovered. She crouched and turned to face the entrance, ready to fire at whoever came down after her. She was trapped, with no way of getting word to those downstairs.

Dorrick was at war. Chinda was safe on her way to Kartna – there was nothing she could do for either of them. But Fhiro was aboard Gravity's Arrow, and he was in immediate danger.

The need to find her son focussed her thoughts. Whoever had attacked was a very good shot, and showed no sign of wanting prisoners.

She heard them. The footsteps were so quiet. Her assailants were nearer than she would have hoped. She caught the start and end of a few whispered exchanges, but the words she did not understand. There were more soft footsteps.

She glanced behind herself. The corridor continued into a dark passageway. She realised she had already allowed her rifle to fall by her side, and was aiming her pistol the way she had come. She silently thanked her husband for all the training he had given her, knowing it had all been for a day such as this, which they both had hoped would never come.

A shadow darted into her line of sight, peering round the door. Hanu discharged a shot. A spray of blood on the far wall told her she had hit her mark. By the time she had heard the body hit the floor she was already retreating into the corridor behind her.

The corridor turned a corner and opened into a large, cylindrical chamber. Within it was the most enormous, smooth-surfaced crystal she had ever seen. She fought down

the urge to marvel at the sight. There could not be another crystal like it in the galaxy. It had to be powering the entire craft, she concluded. If a stray bullet hit it there was a chance it could malfunction, break, or discharge its energy. Any of these consequences could kill her child and everyone on board. The device would crash on to the surface for Marallel's forces to scavenge.

Lining the wall beside her, opposite the huge crystal were others, not much smaller than herself, glowing white and blue. She tore off her outer robe and pushed it down under one of these. Running back nearer the entrance she lay flat and readied her rifle.

Quiet shuffling footsteps approached. Her enemies were taking their time. Hanu wiped her brow.

There was a quick blur of movement. Shots were fired at her discarded outer robe. Two figures crept out. They were not close, but she felt both faces looked familiar. One of them was already turning his submachine gun in her direction, squinting.

Hanu shot him in the chest and he fell.

His female accomplice, however, had crossed in front of the large, suspended energy-crystal and started to spray bullets in Hanu's direction.

Hanu fired back and the woman stumbled, still firing shots until her magazine emptied.

A piercing pain shot through Hanu's shoulder.

She cried out, then steeled herself; her enemies were down but they might not be out. Her wound was superficial. She got up, watching the bodies down the sights of her rifle as she moved. The woman twitched, and Hanu fired twice more at her. The man remained motionless.

Hanu approached both bodies and checked neither was breathing, and then she ran towards the staircase, back the way she had come.

* * *

'Where is your lieutenant?' Halbat asked the Pelorn commander.

The commander looked away from the view, and then turned to one of his men. 'Find the lieutenant.'

The man ran off, but froze as he reached the divide in the chamber. 'What was that sound?'

'What sound?' asked the commander.

The soldier took a few steps forward and shouldered his rifle. 'Shots fired, sir.'

'Shots fired? You five, on me!' He barked orders at the group by the elevator. 'You three stay here. Watch the entrances.' With that he left.

Halbat nodded to Ecrishia, then followed the commander. The chamber on the other side offered a good vantage of the forest beneath. He made his way to the staircase, and caught a glimpse of the commander's men disappearing up it.

There was gunfire and screaming immediately.

Halbat picked up his pace, but then paused; behind him was the whirr of the elevator arriving, and further gunfire. He sprinted back, slowing to a creep as he neared the opening in the divider once more, and drew his weapon.

Now there was silence. A shadow flitted across his line of sight ahead, but when he checked again there was nothing. He readied himself, and hoped he could tell the difference from friend and foe when he moved into the open area. As he inched around the wall the elevator came into his field of vision. There was a man standing close to it. A man he did not recognise, carrying a weapon.

Halbat braced himself, then leapt out and fired at the stranger. He spun round and fired again, felling two others he did not recognise. A fourth figure fired back from the main terminal.

Pain screamed through his shoulder, his fingers went limp and his gun clattered to the ground.

On his knees, his good hand scrabbling for another weapon, he saw a booted foot close in before it collided with his face. Then he was on the floor with the muzzle of a gun jammed against his cheek. Only now he saw there were two others, one holding Ecrishia, and an earthwoman standing over a prone soldier.

'Well, well, well,' said a chill voice. 'And I thought we had outlived your kind!' Borlin placed his foot on Halbat's good shoulder. 'Don't try anything foolish.'

Halbat looked back at him, and his eyes widened. 'It cannot be. You were eradicated. Exterminated. You cannot be!'

'But I am,' said Borlin, 'and so are you!' He laughed. 'And I thought I'd never have the pleasure of trying to bring one of you round to our way of seeing things! We aren't that different, you know. Not that different at all.'

'You shall not break me,' cried Halbat.

'Perhaps,' said Borlin. 'You!' He called to Ecrishia. 'What is this one's name?'

'Die in hell!' came Ecrishia's muffled response.

'I wish I could,' said Borlin, 'for that would cut short the eternity of suffering I expect to endure. I shall work towards achieving blessings such as the one you have described by doing my duty in this life, which involves putting an early end to yours.' He nodded to the Sufferer holding Ecrishia, who then took out a dagger and cut across Ecrishia's back. She screamed. 'But there is no rush. We have time, still, for us to assist in preparing you for the next phase of your existence. I suspect soon you will want us to stop, and at that time you will tell me this man's name.'

* * *

Moments after Valachrad's agents in Riletta had shone the beacon into space, its light reached a messenger ship lurking in the shadow of a gas giant's moon in Pelorn's solar system. The Kartnan captain called to his navigator, 'Make the jump.'

The navigator, who had been preparing his crystals to be at a heightened state of readiness, activated them. A moment later these reached equilibrium with the overlapping complex crystal-aura network they were immersed in.

The jump was instant, as always. They found themselves facing the greatest armada the captain had ever seen. He communicated that Valachrad had secured the alliance.

* * *

Aboard the Kartnan Eradicator class Imperial Battleship, the Gift of Acrimony, of the Nearward Fleet Group, Admiral Castan interpreted the signal. 'We have an alliance. We are to proceed to Pelorn immediately. Execute order H41-Ebenezer. Tell Admiral Shulla to conduct a Counter flank on our signal.'

'Yes admiral!'

* * *

Imial screamed again.

Fhiro was paralysed with fear. Was he ready? He could not wait. He had to be ready. They would discover him soon. Possibly any moment now.

He threw the strange serrated hook away from himself, and it clattered on the floor.

He was committed to his plan now.

Imial's screams stopped.

Fhiro could hear the muttering and whispering outside. His frayed nerves were stretched to the point of snapping.

Footsteps approached, softened to hide their distance, but Fhiro had been taught many things by his father, and he could tell exactly how far away they were.

He was committed to a plan which would almost certainly bring forward the moment his life became an unending experience of pain at the hands of Cerilina and her Sufferer friends.

Someone was outside the door.

He could cut his own neck and end it now. Could he do that?

Imial made muffled sounds. Fhiro imagined that Cerilina was holding her hand against his mouth. 'Don't worry,' he heard her say. 'Your friend will be joining us soon.'

Cerilina was not coming towards him. It was the tall man Fhiro had seen carrying Imial.

One person. One opponent.

The door burst open and the man entered, bringing a vile stench with him.

Fhiro watched for signs that he had been noticed, but so far there were none. The door started to close behind his opponent and the man began searching the room. He knelt to peer into the shadows beneath the bench along the wall.

The door was almost closed now.

Fhiro leapt from his position above the door. He lashed out with his knife as his other hand grasped the man's head. The knife curled round and bit into his enemy's neck. Fhiro pulled it through to cut as many vessels as possible.

Blood sprayed, covering Fhiro's hands and face. The Sufferer writhed and spun, trying to shake Fhiro off. Fhiro lost his grip, and slid off his opponent, stumbling to his feet a short distance away.

The Sufferer grappled with his neck wound, and then floundered for something at his waist. Fhiro lunged forward

and kicked his enemy in the chin, grabbed the man's hair, and stabbed him repeatedly in his throat. When his foul-smelling adversary went limp Fhiro let go him.

'Be a good sport and keep him alive!' shouted Cerilina.

Fhiro felt at the dead man's waist and found a projectile firearm. His gaze raked it in the dim light. He hoped it was ready to fire. He ripped the cloak from the Sufferer's body.

'Fhiro!' cried Imial.

Cerilina was no longer holding his friend's mouth. She was coming too. Fhiro pulled on the malodorous, stained and bloody cloak. He raised the gun and aimed it at the door just as it swung open. Cerilina's mutilated face appeared, staring at him through unblinking, watering eyes.

Fhiro fired three times into her chest. She fell. Fhiro froze, his mind ringing with a thousand bells, as though the noise of the gunshots still screamed against his ears. He squatted down on the floor, glancing between Cerilina's twitching body and the view beyond her. He could see Imial's form, connected to the rack against which Theon's corpse was still attached.

'Fhiro!' cried Imial.

Fhiro stood up. Cerilina had stopped moving. He knew what his father would do. He fired once more at her face, and watched the foul, disfigured features break apart between the eyes.

'Fhiro!'

'Coming!' Fhiro stepped around the body and ran over to Imial. 'How do I get you down?' He peered behind Imial, and saw a number of dark spikes were sticking into his back from the rack behind him. Blood stained Imial's robe where they pierced it.

'Just lift me up,' said Imial, 'and I'll take my hands over this hook.'

'It might make you bleed more,' said Fhiro.

'Just get me down!' shouted Imial, who then stopped to gasp for air.

Fhiro grasped Imial's waist and hoisted him up. Imial cried out, but then moved his bound hands forwards and off the hook. Fhiro lowered him to the floor and Imial collapsed, sobbing. Fhiro sat next to him, and then used a knife to cut through the cords that bound Imial's wrists together. 'I need to see your wounds,' he said.

Imial whimpered as Fhiro examined him.

'The cuts are deep, but they aren't bleeding that much.'

'The things that went into my back,' said Imial, 'they weren't normal. They burned.'

'Some kind of haemostasis coating,' said Fhiro. He put pressure on two of them with his hands, and then tried to move himself so he could use his elbows on the others.

'Ow,' said Imial. 'Halbat must have dressings.'

'Actually,' said Fhiro, standing up and looking at Theon's corpse; it was covered in various medical dressings, 'I reckon there are some nearby.'

'I should check you,' said Imial. 'You're covered in blood!'

'It's not mine.' He took off the foul robes and wiped some of the blood off with them. The smell was bad enough to make Fhiro want to vomit, but then so was the smell of the corpse next to Theon, and the rotting limbs a few metres away.

'You put his clothes on?' asked Imial.

'Thought it might confuse her when she saw me,' said Fhiro.

Imial shook his head. 'Thanks Fhiro.'

Fhiro had just killed two people, and had been a hair away from winding up a torture victim like his friend, and poor Theon. But somehow Imial's words reached a part of him that made him start to cry. 'Don't worry,' he said, turning away to hide his tears. He jogged over to the room Imial had been in and searched it, wiping his eyes. There was a metal box with a

demonic face carved into the front of it. Inside were dark pouches, none of which reminded him of how medical dressings typically looked. He wondered if evil traps might lurk within them, but his friend needed dressings and was losing blood. Fhiro opened one up and found absorbent, and what might pass for procoagulant dressing materials, and scissors and other instruments. He ran back to Imial, cleaned his wounds and dressed them.

'That cleaning fluid stings!' said Imial.

Fhiro wondered if the Sufferers had intended this, and then feared that the dressing materials might have been impregnated with pain inducing substances. However, Imial stood up very soon, looking stronger than he had only moments before.

'Feel a bit better now.' Imial flexed his arms.

'I guess they're impregnated with something helpful, then,' said Fhiro.

'What?' asked Imial.

'Never mind.'

'We have to go,' said Imial, wincing as he took a step forward. 'We have to tell Halbat.'

'My ma's out there,' said Fhiro.

'And maybe a load more of these bad archaeologists,' said Imial.

'They were Sufferers,' said Fhiro. 'She taught us about them, and she was one.'

'Come on,' said Imial.

'I just killed Cerilina,' said Fhiro.

'She would have tortured you to death!'

Fhiro shook his head, trying to turn off the undying crack of the gunshots that had accompanied her demise.

His mother was in danger. He and Imial were still in danger. 'Let's go find my ma, or Halbat, or any soldier.'

'Anyone friendly,' said Imial. He picked up some of the cleaning solution Fhiro had left behind. 'You're still covered in blood, but then so am I.' He winced again.

Fhiro tried to wipe his face with one sleeve while he put his other arm around Imial's back and helped him forward.

'For a street urchin,' said Imial, when they had almost reached the door, 'you're not bad.'

This time Fhiro laughed.

'Fhiro,' said Imial, 'if you think I'm going to get caught by them again, or if you have to leave me behind, kill me.'

Fhiro stopped. 'You don't mean that.'

Imial stared back at him.

'I'm not leaving you,' said Fhiro.

'Promise me,' said Imial.

Fhiro did not know what to say, so ended the conversation by handing Imial a pistol. 'I found this in that room with the dressings. Safety's already off. You all right?'

Imial hesitated, then took it. 'Guess so.'

'Have it ready,' said Fhiro. 'Keep quiet now. I'll open this door.' He crept forward, put his hand on the handle, his other hand ready with his own weapon, and then glanced at Imial to check his friend was ready to shoot anything unfamiliar that might greet them in the hallway.

Imial nodded.

Fhiro pulled the door open. The corridor was empty.

He glanced up and down the staircase. He signed to Imial that it was clear.

They moved into the corridor, checking up and down the staircase again and again. They descended as quietly as they could, weapons ready, but for seven flights they heard no sound.

Then they stopped and listened. Fhiro felt a sense of dread overcoming him, and he started down the stairs without even waiting to explain himself to Imial.

Imial rushed after him, as fast as his injured back would let him.

At the bottom of the next flight were several bodies. Most of them were unmoving, but one was breathing.

'Ma!' Fhiro cried, all care to be silent suddenly lost.

Imial glanced down the next flight of stairs and saw the bodies of two Jashpuri soldiers.

Hanu opened her eyes. 'Fhiro,' she said between laboured breaths. She reached up and stroked his cheek.

'Ma!' Tears poured from Fhiro's eyes.

Hanu took in the blood on Fhiro's clothes, and her hands started groping him, searching for injuries.

'It's all right,' said Fhiro, catching her hands. 'I'm all right. It's not my blood.'

She looked at him, her eyes getting wetter until thin rivulets flowed back across her cheeks and on to her neck.

'Where are you hurt?' Fhiro asked.

Hanu pulled her shirt to the side. There was a wound in her waist, still seeping blood.

'Take this,' said Imial, passing Fhiro one of his spare dressings.

Fhiro pushed it into Hanu's wound.

'The archaeologists, they're here!' said Hanu.

Fhiro nodded. 'They're Sufferers, Ma.'

Hanu's eyes widened.

'We brought twelve,' said Imial, 'including Borlin.'

Hanu waved her arm at the bodies. The movement looked tired and feeble. 'I've taken … six of …'

'We've got rid of two,' said Fhiro.

'You?' asked Hanu.

Fhiro nodded.

'There may be more,' said Hanu, looking more alert now. She tried to sit up, but then she cried out and collapsed.

'Stay here,' said Fhiro. 'There must be a doctor aboard.'

'The–' Hanu nodded, then winced.

'Where is the doctor?' asked Fhiro.

Hanu lifted her head and clasped Fhiro's sleeve. 'Not yet. Tell Halb–' Her head rolled back again and she closed her eyes.

'Ma!' cried Fhiro.

Hanu did not reply.

'Don't leave me!'

CHAPTER 34

Borlin walked towards another of Halbat's Jashpuri assistants, whose head was being pushed against a terminal by a female Magellan archaeologist. 'If you do not tell us, soon enough we will tire of you and start to work on this fellow here. You wouldn't want that would you? Or perhaps you would like to watch us torment him?' He reached the assistant and stroked his hair. 'Save us all some trouble and tell me how to take this thing into space!'

The assistant wailed as the female archaeologist leaned forward, crushing his face against the terminal surface.

'Resilient,' said Borlin, nodding. 'No doubt you chose them yourself, ambassador, and now, because of you, they endure great suffering. Unfortunate, they must now feel, that they came here, no doubt drawn by the excitement of being part of the greatest discovery in the last two millennia.' Borlin smiled again.

'Only I know how to use it,' said Halbat.

'This woman over here seemed pretty capable but a moment ago,' said Borlin, turning back to Ecrishia.

'It is our knowledge. Not yours,' said Halbat.

'True. True. Well I had better keep you all alive just in case. I hope no one outside of this room was essential to this operation. We're having to dispose of everyone else we come across.'

Halbat said nothing.

'But there are a lot of civilians hidden away upstairs,' said Borlin. 'That's a lot of people to watch, ambassador. A lot of

people to witness going through far worse than we are doing to you, or your friends here. I wonder if any of them are young. We have ways of making people see the universe our way. We don't always succeed, but our methods are especially effective on children.'

'No!' cried Halbat.

Borlin laughed. 'Our commander is an expert in turning minds to our ways. Why, it was she that helped me to see the universe more clearly. See the hatred and suffering that permeated it, and that lives with us to our end, and after.'

'The children will not be yours,' said Halbat. 'None of us will. You're wasting your time.'

'Why, torturing has never been a waste of time,' said Borlin. 'All think as you do in the beginning. Why, I recall thinking it myself, once.' He looked at the terminal.

His movement was hampered by his position, lying on the floor, and by his paralysed arm, but Halbat was determined to reach his gun. It was inches from his fingers. As he reached for it, a shot was fired, sending the gun skidding across the floor. A second shot rang out and pain exploded in his ankle. He cried out, drawing his knees up to his chest and clasping the injured limb.

'Brave,' said Borlin, returning the gun to his belt, 'but foolish.' Then he paused, and looked at Halbat with mock seriousness in his eyes. 'Perhaps you're waiting for your friends on the roof to help you? I'm afraid it's quite hard to get back inside a ship when you've already been locked out. Harder still when the ship turns upside down. Let's see now.' He studied the terminal again. 'Yes, I think this is the control. Done. Do you see?' He indicated the view outside.

Halbat watched through the screen. The horizon was rising.

'We are rotating forward, and yet my feet feel firmly planted on the floor,' said Borlin. 'The gravity system here is truly

remarkable. I must declare my admiration for your people, for I cannot feel anything! Can you?'

Halbat said nothing. Bleeding from agonising wounds in his shoulder and ankle, he watched as the ship rotated forward, defeated.

The horizon rose further. More and more forest became visible. In front of the screen a man in uniform tumbled down from the roof, scrambling at the air as he fell, shortly followed by another.

'It shall not be long now,' said Borlin. 'For those who can hang on after we are upside down, they will then need to learn how to breathe in a vacuum. Our next destination must be space.' Borlin seemed to think about this. 'I must be careful not to enjoy all of this too much, for it might cost me in the next life.' He took a tablet from his clothing and swallowed it. He lowered his gaze, waiting, and then he shuddered.

Halbat glanced around the room while Borlin was distracted in his contortions and convulsions, but saw that one of the other Sufferers was watching him, the muzzle of her gun aimed in his direction.

'To think,' said Borlin as he gradually regained control of himself, and his breathing slowed back to normal, 'that the armies of Kartna and the Creedate are going to war for this? After you disappear with it, Jashpur might be thrown in too. I cannot think of anything more perfect and pleasing to the Divine Evil. Perhaps I should end my life soon afterwards to make sure he remembers what favours I have done in his service.'

Gun shots blasted the air from behind Halbat. Borlin rocked forward and fell on to the terminal. The woman who had been crushing the male assistant jerked to her left as she was struck in the shoulder, and then fell down as she was struck again in the chest. The man tormenting Ecrishia let her go and

dropped his tools, the contents of his head splattered across the screen beyond him. Borlin turned to face his attacker and froze.

Slowly Halbat turned around as well.

'Impossible,' said Borlin.

Fhiro walked into the room, not taking his eyes off Borlin. Imial staggered into view from the divider near the transparent screen.

'Is it clear?' asked Fhiro.

'Think so,' said Imial.

Borlin looked up at Fhiro. 'You …'

Fhiro felt his arm tremble as he aimed at Borlin. His rage was starting to get the better of him. He steadied himself.

'Don't take your eyes off him, Fhiro,' warned Halbat, struggling to his one good foot. 'If he moves, kill him.'

'You two have survived a lot, haven't you?' said Borlin, starting to chuckle. 'You might have won this battle, but it will cost you, child. You have killed, and that is no small thi–' Borlin's head juddered backwards and thudded into the base of the terminal, blood pouring from it, front and back.

Fhiro turned and saw the Jashpuri ambassador had fired the shot.

Halbat limped to the terminal and made some adjustments. The horizon started to descend in front of them as the ship righted itself.

'My mother's been shot!' Fhiro shouted to Halbat.

Halbat, however, was walking towards his assistant. He paused and shot the archaeologist lying motionless beside him, twice, before going to Ecrishia to examine the body near her.

'My ma's hurt!' Fhiro shouted again.

* * *

Dorrick weaved through the cluster of tall buildings that surrounded the entrance to the underground base. Creedate dragons dropped from the sky, their riders opening fire with light machine guns and crystal-fire weapons, until the network of defence turrets and patrolling Pelorn air squadrons shot them down. Soon there was a guard of twenty birds and dragons of Pelorn and Hithostun around Dorrick, King Suloa and Ambassador Valachrad. All of them descended into the pit and entered the underground complex, from where they flew under the city until they were beneath one of the hills on its outskirts. They disembarked and headed to the control room where Oljon stood with General Halari, poring over the maps and talking to the telegraphers.

'Thank all that's holy for your return,' said Oljon, clasping his son to his chest.

'We've summoned the fleet,' said Valachrad.

'How long before they can reach us here?' asked a Hithostun general.

'My nation is in ruins,' said King Suloa, shaking his head.

'We may yet survive, at least,' said General Halari.

'They will kill me,' said King Suloa. 'The Barons will see me executed.'

'Not if we execute them first,' said General Halari.

Hearing this, Dorrick glanced at his father.

'It's best we don't interfere,' said Oljon. He turned to Valachrad. 'How far out are they?'

'One jump,' said Valachrad.

King Suloa gasped. 'They are that close?'

'I apologise if I hinted otherwise,' said Valachrad.

'General Ishthen,' said a telegrapher as he approached Oljon, 'a vast number of craft have appeared at the aura boundary.'

'They are Kartnan,' said Oljon. 'Track them.'

‘Your fleet was here all this time?’ asked King Suloa. ‘How many are they?’

‘Enough for those forces of Marallel’s which we know of,’ said Valachrad. ‘He may have more hidden, though, for precisely the purpose of besting us in battle here.’

King Suloa took a moment to think about this, and then he snarled. ‘We have been your puppet throughout this entire course of events! You merely used this as an excuse to bring Marallel to battle!’

‘We did not make any of this happen,’ said Valachrad. ‘We have done what had to be done. And we came prepared.’

‘And I hope our preparations were enough,’ said Oljon, ‘for Marallel will have come with the same thing in mind.’

* * *

Admiral Castan’s fleet were fully engaged. The Creedate forces were spread out around Pelorn’s local volume, while Castan’s were concentrated. He was gaining the upper hand.

He witnessed beacons firing off from the Creedate fleet carrier that had remained aloof from the battle. The carrier that he suspected housed his enemy’s commander. He wondered if he was truly staring at the ship from which Marallel, infamous and brilliant ruler of the Creedate, commanded his hordes. Was his enemy pacing in frustration, or watching with a calmness of one who still has winning cards to be played?

‘Creedate fleet carriers,’ reported a crystal-telegrapher. ‘Five. All just appeared right behind us.’

‘By the gods,’ said Castan. ‘Marallel is not one for small gestures. He sends enough ships here to black out a sun and create a black hole! Prepare a rearguard action.’

‘Shall we summon Admiral Shulla?’

'Send word to her, now,' said Castan. 'Send false distress signals as well. She will know what to do.'

* * *

'The Creedate and the Kartnan forces are fully engaged,' reported a telegrapher.

'Excellent,' said Oljon. 'Wait half an hour for that information to filter through to the enemy forces around the city, then hit them with all of your reserves.'

The generals and admirals about them murmured agreement, and began messaging their own commanders who were scattered about Pelorn's local volume conducting its defences.

'What of me, father?' asked Dorrick.

'You may continue your duty guarding the King,' said Oljon.

'I don't need Kartnan guards,' said King Suloa, bitterness in his voice.

'Guard Valachrad, then,' said Oljon, and he leaned a little closer to Dorrick's ear, 'and watch my back while you're at it.'

Dorrick nodded.

* * *

The counter attack by the alliance's reserves overwhelmed the shaken Creedate forces about Riletta, driving them out of the city. Some of the commanding officers took the initiative to give chase and bombard the Creedate land forces that were still approaching, but were quick to turn and flee before their enemies could regroup and respond effectively.

The Creedate resumed bombarding the city soon, but now air superiority belonged to the alliance, and most of the

remaining citizens of Riletta were safely evacuated. By the time the Creedate land forces had reached the city the next day, Kartnan ships were dropping through the atmosphere over Pelorn-held territory and shoring up its defences.

The air war was renewed afresh, as Marallel now held large swathes of Pelorn territory into which he poured atmospheric ships. Fire filled the skies and space of Pelorn for three whole days until supremacy of the nearby space and air fell to Kartna. The Creedate land forces continued fighting for two more days, holding the ground they still had with every tooth and nail, hoping the circumstances in space might change, but they did not.

A stalled truce became an unconditional surrender. There were so many prisoners to be organised that the Kartnan military machine took over their organisation and deportation.

Among the high value ships captured by the Kartnan forces, none of the senior officers could be sure which vessel Marallel had commanded from. The fleet carrier that Castan had identified during the battle had jumped out of the local volume two days earlier, a day before the Kartnan forces had been certain they were going to win.

CHAPTER 35

The field surrounding the temple of the Matter Element grew dark. Fhiro recalled this was where he had first met Chenessa, and where he had first seen King Suloa and Reshna. The thought of the Creedate ambassador dying at the hands of Cerilina and the Sufferers made him shudder. He hoped, despite his all his doubts, that she was in a better place now.

'There's really a door here?' asked Dorrick, searching the temple wall.

'It was virtually invisible,' said Fhiro. He tried to spot it in the darkness, but knew his efforts were futile.

'You're not to go inside,' one of the guards reminded him.

'We know,' said Imial.

Fhiro turned back to where the Kartnan generals, admirals, diplomats and senators continued their merrymaking across the banqueting area. The three of them had asked to leave once they were full, but they had not been allowed to do so without an escort.

'Do you play any sports on this plain?' asked Fhiro.

'Not allowed, young sir,' came the reply.

'Do you stand in front of a mirror, practising annoying questions?' Imial asked Fhiro.

Fhiro laughed.

'So it's a Matter temple,' said Dorrick. 'Do you think they have a ball of something heavy inside it?'

'Maybe they've got a black hole in it,' said Fhiro, 'trapped in some strange crystal device.'

'That's impossible,' said Imial. 'It would destroy the planet.'

'Can't anyone tell when I'm joking?' asked Fhiro.

'Let's just walk around it,' said Dorrick.

Afterwards, on their way back towards the banquet, they skirted the pastures where the transants were grazing on the edge of the mountain. Some attendees were already leaving, and a few of them looked unsteady on their feet.

Walking a little ahead of the others Fhiro heard familiar voices from an outcrop of rock. 'Pa?' he called. He could make out a collection of large boulders on the grass with figures seated upon them.

'Fhiro! Dorrick!'

They walked on to the outcrop. Fhiro smiled when he recognised the four faces before him.

'You've stumbled upon our secret group,' said Hanu.

Since witnessing her inches from death a week before, Fhiro was overwhelmed with something bordering on ecstatic gladness every time he saw his mother alive. Her every movement was beset with pain now, but she still managed warm smiles whenever she saw her children.

Valachrad laughed.

'It won't stay secret if my pa keeps that up,' muttered Imial.

Valachrad laughed even louder, stepped towards them and lifted Imial into the air. 'Good! Good!'

Fhiro could see his friend grimace – his wounds were healed but Fhiro was sure they were still tender. However, Imial pretended to be unconcerned.

'It's not that secret, really,' said Valachrad. 'Only sort of.' He saw the three guards that were behind Dorrick. 'You may leave now.'

'Yes Lord Valachrad,' said one, and they left.

'I would say that everything I've said is to go no further than this group,' said Halbat. His arm was still in a sling, and his injured foot in a special boot.

'That is hardly worth mentioning,' said Hanu, 'when you're not saying anything at all!'

Halbat grinned.

Fhiro eyed the Jashpuri ambassador. 'Excellent. Now you're cornered. Tell us the truth! Who are you?'

'I'm the Jashpuri ambassador,' said Halbat.

'That's all he's willing to say.' Oljon shook his head.

'They say Borlin was asking you strange questions,' said Fhiro. 'The survivors from the bridge thought you two knew each other.'

'We certainly didn't know each other,' said Halbat. 'If I'd known there were any Sufferers alive today I would have pursued them with all my energies and seen them captured or killed as fast as the gods would allow.'

'Are you a Poshokan?' asked Fhiro.

'If Fhiro kicks off a dangerous argument will we be able to backtrack out of it?' asked Dorrick.

'There are no lynch mobs here,' said Hanu.

'So you are Poshokan,' said Fhiro.

'The Poshokan Empire does not exist,' said Halbat, 'and it has not done for over two thousand years. I do not belong to something that does not exist – that's impossible.'

'But you would if you could,' said Fhiro.

Halbat hesitated. 'I believe there were many good things about that empire. If I thought it had returned, in some form, I would seriously look into the possibility.'

'How many ways can you avoid answering a question?' asked Dorrick.

Halbat laughed.

'Maybe we should report your behaviour to the Jashpuri intelligence services,' said Oljon.

'Jashpur has my loyalty,' said Halbat. 'Like anywhere, it is far from perfect, but the culture is quite open to exploring and incorporating new ideas.'

'Do you have to leave now, Halbat?' asked Valachrad.

'Yes. I've told your engineers everything they need to know. This craft will be a powerful asset to Kartna if you can replicate it, but producing and assembling the right components will be a challenge.'

'A crystal that size won't be easy to come by,' said Valachrad, 'and we may never be able to reproduce Gravity's Arrow. But if we can understand how it works, a simpler, cruder alternative will still be of great value.'

'Quite,' said Halbat.

'Where are you going?' asked Fhiro.

'The Sufferers are alive. After I am healed I must go to Irenzel in the Greater Magellan and investigate further.'

'That's so dangerous!' cried Fhiro.

'It has to be done,' said Halbat. 'I know what to do if I think I'll be caught, but I won't stand by and allow the Sufferers to take strength again.'

'Don't get caught,' said Imial. 'Please.'

'Maybe we should be avoiding this subject,' said Oljon.

Fhiro looked at Imial, and then back at his father. 'No. We need to know about it. May as well be now.'

Imial nodded. 'Cerilina told us something. I don't know whether to believe what she said.'

'They believe in God,' said Halbat, 'but not a loving God that wishes them happiness. Their God is more like the Devil and the Shiatan from The Calling.'

'I was getting that impression,' said Fhiro.

'They believe that causing suffering in this life will appease the Divine Evil, who will repay them by lessening their own suffering in the afterlife.'

'That's totally messed up,' said Dorrick.

'Why would they think that?' asked Imial.

'It's about perspective,' said Halbat. 'It's very much like the

Poshokan belief system in some ways, but flipped around so it becomes twisted into something vile. Where it flips is on the question of what sort of a God made this universe. If you think the universe is a bad place, you are more inclined to see their viewpoint. If you see the universe as a wonderful place, filled with peril and suffering though it is, you would be protected from their extreme and horrid interpretation of why we exist.'

'Please find them,' said Imial. 'Find and kill them all.'

'I promise to do everything in my power to stop them,' said Halbat.

'I will pray for them,' said Hanu. 'If Aten can show them compassion and deliver them away from evil, then I will pray for his mercy in spite of their wicked deeds.'

'We all will,' said Halbat. He stood up, taking a moment to steady himself on his good leg. 'It has been a great honour befriending you all.'

'Thank you for looking after my family,' said Oljon.

Halbat laughed. 'They looked after me!' He ruffled Fhiro and Imial's heads. He paused at Dorrick, who was staring back at him, his eyes full of warning. Halbat burst out laughing and shook Dorrick's hand. 'When I have finished with my task I will come and find you all in Kartna,' he called over his shoulder as he limped away.

'You're welcome any time, friend!' Valachrad shouted back.

Fhiro watched Halbat disappear into the darkness.

Valachrad sighed. 'I must say that the outcome of our journey here, though we were never sure it would come to pass, has been most positive. I am so proud of all of you, but especially so of my son.' He put his arm around Imial. 'You have done very very well, my boy, to come through this so strong.'

Imial smiled and buried his head in his father's chest.

'Do you need some rest, now?' Valachrad asked.

Imial nodded. 'My back still hurts.'

'Let's go then.' Valachrad stood and smiled at the others. 'I'm sure we'll see you all tomorrow.

'See you tomorrow, then, Valachrad.' Oljon and the Kartnan ambassador embraced.

Valachrad gave Hanu a kiss on the cheek. Imial waved to Fhiro and Dorrick, and then he and his father were gone too.

'If only Chins was with us,' said Hanu, 'then we'd be complete.'

'She'll be waiting for us at the Empire's borders,' said Oljon. 'We'll catch up with her soon enough.'

Fhiro marched further on to the outcrop. 'Let's name this jutting piece of rock, then, and let's not call it the Siwob.'

'Still bitter about that?' asked Dorrick. 'Maybe we *should* call it the Siwob. Would make Chins happy when she finds out.' He leapt up and sat on the tallest boulder. Fhiro wanted to kick himself for not thinking of this sooner, and took the shorter one where Valachrad had been.

'Maybe the Siwob isn't such a bad idea,' said Hanu. 'It was our home, and we'll never go back there.'

'We'll never come back *here*, either,' Dorrick said.

'Probably not,' said Fhiro. 'I bet this would be a nice place, though. Maybe if there wasn't a war going on I'd come here for a holiday.'

'Speaking of the war,' said Dorrick, frowning, 'how could Valachrad see this journey as having had a positive outcome? War between Kartna and the Creedate is going to be terrible.'

'Because,' said Oljon, 'that is exactly what Kartna wanted all along.'

'Really?' cried Fhiro and Dorrick.

'We did all those games with Chenessa,' said Fhiro, 'trying to avert a war, and Kartna wanted one anyway?'

'Keep your voices down,' said Hanu. 'You aren't to mention this to anyone.'

'When did you find out this was their plan?' asked Dorrick.

'I was never told it was so, though I did suspect it from the beginning,' said Oljon. 'I only became sure that this was their original objective when our forces overwhelmed the vast armada Marallel had brought here.'

'He did say war was almost certain,' said Fhiro. 'I feel angry, now, though. Like I put myself in danger for no reason. Do you have any idea how bad I felt about almost blowing our cover so many times?'

'As your mother said,' said Oljon, 'do not repeat this, but you deserve to know. The Kartnan Senate wisely predicted that they would go to war with the Creedate sooner or later. Marallel must have been thinking the same thing. When news of this discovery reached the Senate it was considered an opportunity to go to war while appearing not to be the aggressor, and yet with an expected battle-zone into which their forces could be concentrated ahead of time.'

'If they wanted the fight,' said Fhiro, 'why was Kartna so bothered about not looking like they started it?'

'Because for all the future alliances they make, and treaties they sign,' said Oljon, 'their reputation is everything. You see how none trust the Creedate because of their misdeeds in the past. You see how Halbat supported Kartna's ambitions even though he is from a rival empire. Even if you're up to no good, it pays dividends to look like you're in the right.'

'Are Kartna up to no good?' asked Dorrick.

'What's a dividend?' asked Fhiro.

Oljon laughed.

'Kartna are only up to no good in the same ways as most nations,' said Hanu. 'They seek to control the galaxy one day. However, Kartna is willing to bide its time.'

'And rightly so,' said Oljon. 'That would be their dream, but they are realistic. They wish not to fall into the traps that other

empires have blundered into in the past. Their growth is slow and steady, as is Jashpur's for that matter. The Creedate have a different approach, an approach historically associated with destruction, death and short-lived power.'

'So Kartna wanted a fight with the Creedate,' said Fhiro, 'and they wanted it on terms they could better control, rather than waiting around for the Creedate to attack them whenever it suited Marallel.'

'Exactly,' said Oljon. 'This first battle was intended to set the stage for the war to come. A decisive victory here with heavy losses to the losing side would have a powerful impact on both resources and, most importantly, morale.'

'You generals are obsessed by morale,' muttered Dorrick.

'Never underestimate its power,' said Oljon. 'When the stakes are as high as they are in war, fear swings victories faster than numbers.'

'So they sent a delegation here,' said Dorrick, 'and hoped when Pelorn sided with Kartna, Marallel would attack.'

'Or that Marallel would just attack anyway,' said Fhiro, 'and Kartna could move in and save the day.'

'Yes,' said Oljon, 'either of those. Though Marallel might not have cared if this prize under the mountain turned out to be nothing at all.'

'What would they have done then?' asked Fhiro.

'I think that's where we came in,' said Hanu.

'Indeed.' Oljon's smile was grim, and he shook his head.

'They sent the wregg,' said Hanu, 'and through it ordered Oljon to meet with Valachrad. Being under Valachrad's command, your father would have had to reveal his true identity whenever, or if ever, Valachrad wished him to do so.'

'And trigger the war,' said Fhiro. 'That makes Kartna look a bit more like the aggressor, though.'

'I am innocent of killing the prophet Avithen,' said Oljon,

'and Kartna will back up this claim. Ambiguity smells a lot better than obvious guilt.'

'So you, or we, were plan B,' said Dorrick.

'Correct,' said Oljon, 'and if King Suloa had not been trapped in this over-complicated Niquani-pride political landscape, he would probably have done the intelligent thing and allied with us long ago, and my unmasking would have been unnecessary. However, my revelation also delayed Glorthig's attack. Had he launched an offensive faster, and against a divided Niquani alliance, he might have conquered Pelorn before Kartna was ready to intervene.'

'Really?' asked Fhiro.

'According to the information I have been fed,' said Oljon.

'But that might be a lie to make you feel better about having a huge price over your head forever,' said Dorrick.

'The price hasn't changed,' said Oljon, 'but my head is more obvious.'

They sat in silence for a while. The songs and merrymaking drifted across the cold mountain air. Fhiro pulled his coat tighter about him. He had not thought he would need it when he had departed during the summer sunshine that afternoon.

'So why were we trying to get to Reshna, then?' asked Fhiro.

'She was a potential ally,' said Hanu. 'Any inside information we could have got from her could have greatly helped us, and if she knew of a resistance movement that hoped to overthrow Marallel, that would be even more valuable. When one governs through fear, as Marallel does, there will always be those hoping to shake themselves free of it.'

'It is Kartna's hope,' said Oljon, 'that this loss will damage Marallel's invincible reputation enough that those who wish to topple him will have the confidence to do so.'

'Poor Reshna,' said Fhiro, 'and poor Chenessa.'

'And that tutor,' said Dorrick, 'though I never knew any of them.'

'Are we any closer to working out what they were up to?' asked Fhiro.

'The Sufferers?' asked Hanu. 'I read the report. The movements of the second group have been mapped out.'

'You mean the group that were not the archaeologists?' asked Fhiro.

'Yes,' said Hanu. 'They had arrived as traders around the same time, but there were only two of them. They stole a bird and flew it out to Fawast once they knew when you,' she looked at Fhiro and Oljon, 'were going there, and therefore when Cerilina and her vile friends would arrive. They had learned enough about the local fauna to direct the herds towards the fort for the appointed time, and that's what they did.'

'How come that wasn't predicted?' asked Dorrick.

'No Niquani would dream of doing it,' said Hanu. 'Hence, so much suspicion fell on Kartna and the Creedate when it happened.'

'And more so on Kartna when Reshna disappeared,' said Oljon.

There was another moment of silence.

'We should think of something more cheerful to talk about,' said Oljon.

'Though now is the time to get everything off your chests,' said Hanu. 'Any other questions?'

Fhiro thought for a moment. 'It's getting cold.'

Hanu laughed. 'It probably is time we turned in.'

'One last thing,' said Fhiro. 'How did Kartna win?'

'I think it helped that the alliance defeated the superior forces in the early stage of the battle,' said Oljon. 'That may have shaken a few of their commanders. However, the most

deciding factor in the end, regardless of what I said earlier about morale, is that we fielded a larger, more effective force.'

'We did?' asked Dorrick. 'The reports I get are so sketchy.'

'We did,' said Oljon, 'but I never said that, all right? As far as the Kartnan propaganda campaign is concerned, it was a victory against the odds. We are all to promote this view, understand?'

'I hate this game,' said Dorrick. 'Can't we just speak honestly?'

'You should have been with me and Chinda,' said Fhiro, 'having to talk nonsense to Chenessa all the time, and not let her know we were related.'

'You'll be entering high society in Kartna very soon,' said Oljon. 'You had all better get used to this.'

EPILOGUE

Fhiro, Imial, Dorrick and Chinda watched the planet from the viewing room.

'It's beautiful,' said Fhiro.

'It's going to be your home,' said Imial.

Fhiro marvelled at the clouds unfurling across the oceans, and the greens, browns and greys merge and disperse across the continents.

'When do you get to enrol in your academy?' asked Dorrick.

'Applications will be this year for all of us,' said Imial.

'Not for me,' said Chinda. 'I knew you'd forget me, just because I didn't come with you the whole way.'

Fhiro laughed and hugged her against him. 'Who are you again?'

Chinda pushed herself away, but left his arm draped across her shoulders.

'Guess we'll have our work cut out, then,' said Fhiro. 'Can't imagine they're easy to get into.'

'And I've got to break into one two years too late,' said Dorrick.

'I'm sure I'll get into one of the finest institutes,' said Imial, puffing out his chest.

Fhiro knew Imial well enough now to sense his friend's uncertainty. 'We could study together.'

Imial's eyes widened, then he looked back at Fhiro. 'You … ' He sighed. 'You put me to shame,' he whispered.

Fhiro let go of Chinda and moved nearer to Imial. 'You've nothing to be ashamed of.'

'You saved my life,' said Imial.

'What?' Fhiro frowned. 'I needed you too. We saved Halbat together.'

Imial shook his head, his gaze dropping to the floor.

'You would have done the same for me,' said Fhiro. 'You would have saved me if it had been the other way around,'

Imial stared back into his eyes. 'Believe that if you want. We'll never know if I could or not.'

Fhiro put a hand on Imial's shoulder. 'This academy we're going to.'

'There are hundreds of them,' said Imial.

'The best one then,' said Fhiro. 'The one we're both going to. They've got no idea what's about to hit them, have they.'

Imial gaped at him. 'The best and brightest of the entire Kartnan Empire,' said Imial. 'Even you might struggle for the best places.'

Fhiro grinned. 'Well if we don't try, we'll never know, right?'

'See you in the fall room,' shouted Oljon through the door, throwing a cylinder through the air towards them.

Fhiro reached out to catch the flying item, but Imial got there first, his fingers sealing around it as he snatched it out of the air.

All four of them stared at the cylindrical container in Imial's hand. None of them uttered a word.

Imial tilted it, and the pills rattled against each other as they moved from one end of the container to the other.

Chinda looked at her brothers.

Dorrick's eyes narrowed.

Fhiro grinned.

'Anyone feeling brave?' asked Imial.

The end

ABOUT THE AUTHOR

Jack Mann is an experienced academic writer having contributed to the medical scientific literature in his specialist areas. He is a Medical Doctor working in the UK. However, he has nursed an ambition to write science fiction since he was in primary school. His short story, The Sufferers, published in our 666 horror anthology is a taster for the world of Gravity's Arrow, which is his debut novel. He is already working on a sequel.

If you have enjoyed this book, please consider leaving a review for Jack to let him know what you thought of his work.

You can read about Jack on his author page on the Fantastic Books Store. While you're there, why not browse our other delightful tales and wonderfully woven prose?

www.fantasticbooksstore.com